ANTHROPOLOGY AND INSTITUTIONAL ECONOMICS

Monographs in Economic Anthropology, No. 12

Edited by

James M. Acheson

UNIVERSITY PRESS OF AMERICA

Lanham • New York • London

SEA

University Press of America,® Inc.
4720 Boston Way
Lanham, Maryland 20706

3 Henrietta Street
London WC2E 8LU England

Printed in the United States of America
British Cataloging in Publication Information Available

Co-published by arrangement with the
Society for Economic Anthropology

Library of Congress Cataloging-in-Publication Data

Anthropology and institutional economics / James M. Acheson, ed.
p. cm. — (Monographs in economic anthropology ; no. 12)
Includes bibliographical references.
1. Institutional economics. 2. Economic anthropology.
I. Acheson, James M. II. Series.
HB99.5.A58 1994 330.1—dc20 94–21983 CIP

ISBN 0–8191–9595–2 (cloth : alk. paper)
ISBN 0–8191–9596–0 (pbk. : alk. paper)

∞™ The paper used in this publication meets the minimum requirements of American National Standard for Information Sciences—Permanence of Paper for Printed Library Materials, ANSI Z39.48–1984.

Editor's Preface

The "new" institutional economics refers to a body of literature--primarily in economics--linking institutions and the behavior of individuals. The generation of institutions is traced to decisions and strategies of individuals, which, in turn are guided by those institutions. Institutional economists are also interested in the effects of those choices and institutions on economic performance. Two of the most essential concepts are those of *property rights* and *transaction costs*. Those unfamiliar with the basic concepts of the "new" institutional economics might wish to read the next chapter *Welcome to Nobel Country: A Review of Institutional Economics* before continuing with this book.

Twenty five years ago, the "new" institutional economics did not exist as a coherent discipline. There were a few economists who were writing about property rights, transaction costs, market failure, the development of rule structures and the ways these factors influenced economic performance, but they were considered marginal at best. In the past ten years, interest in institutional economics has blossomed, and the contribution of some of its most important practitioners has been recognized through the awarding of several Nobel Prizes.

In the past few years, a small group of anthropologists has become interested in institutional economics. Many of them have contributed essays to this volume. It is clear that they have taken on an enormous task. The key question for anthropologists is: To what extent can the insights and concepts of institutional economics be applied more generally? To what extent will institutional economics allow anthropologists to explain the complex realities of other societies and cultures? The authors of the essays in this volume have begun to approach this issue, but they have come to no consensus. Some have found the insights of institutional economics helpful in framing questions and interpreting events in the societies they have studied. Others are far less sanguine, and believe that institutional economics is going to have to be substantially modified and extended if it is to be useful in explaining social and economic phenomena in peasant and tribal societies where anthropologists are prone to work. More important, the authors in this volume have come to no definitive conclusions as a group. So little work has been done that no issue has been closed. This volume starts us down a different path. It remains to be seen where it will take us.

Although the "new" institutional economics involves a finite number of key concepts and a common framework, there is no denying that it is a broad field. No single article in this volume is concerned with all aspects of this body of theory. However, a lot of key ideas and themes of institutional economics are woven through these essays. The articles in this volume describe a variety of institutions, and contribute to a number of issues central to the "new" institutional economics. A few of these articles are focused on some of the most central issues in the field.

Most of the articles in this volume are case studies. They describe the interconnections between institutions, decisions, and performance levels in a variety of societies worldwide. The articles by Bates, Colin and Losch, Michie and Wilk are more theoretical in nature. And although these articles are quite different, they all attempt to assess work and ideas connected to institutional economics and anthropology in some fashion. Bates' article is perhaps the most important in that it criticizes some of the most central ideas of the "new" institutional economics, and attempts to chart a new course for research in the field.

Themes and Foci

While the theoretical articles and case studies in this volume go in very different directions, a number of common themes and concepts appear repeatedly.

Transaction costs are a primary concern of the papers by Acheson and Ensminger, and the concept plays a role in the papers by Bossen, Colin and Losch, McGregor, Moberg, Rehfus and Gladwin, Russell, and Wilk. A closely related theme that runs through many articles in this volume is the generation and persistence of inefficient institutions, which North argues characterize

Third World economies. Most notable are: Bossen's description of involution in Chinese farm families; McDowell's article on the institutions generated by the military governments of Guatemala; McGregor's analysis of the role of credit institution in maintaining poverty in Bangladesh; Moberg's article on the self serving activities of agents of the state; and Russell's description of a very inefficient shares system in a Philippine fishing industry. Nor do such institutions exist only in the Third World. Rehfus and Gladwin argue that the medical care system of the United States is marked by high transaction costs and inefficiency. All of these articles describe institutional settings involving the kind of high transaction costs that do not facilitate efficient exchange.

Unfortunately, no paper in this volume focuses on property rights and the effect of property rights on economic decisions. Dr. Edella Schlager and Dr. Sergio Zendejas gave papers on property rights at the 1992 SEA Meetings in Irvine, but neither paper materialized for this volume. However, the establishment and relative security of property rights is a concern of Colin and Losch, Ensminger, McDowell, Russell, and Wilk. This interest is reflected in their papers.

Economists Coase and Williamson are primarily interested in markets and firms, which they see as performing the same functions. Many of the papers in this volume focus on these two institutions. In the peasant world, the units of production are households and not formally chartered firms. Several of the articles in this volume delve into the relationships between household members and the decisions of these small "family firms," including those by Acheson, Bossen, McGregor, Russell and Wilk.

A number of other papers describe various kinds of markets. Marti's paper is concerned with final product markets (i.e. sales to consumers). Other articles are concerned with market relationships between "firms" in the production chain (i.e. intermediate product markets). In this category are the articles by Acheson, Ensminger, Rehfus and Gladwin and Russell.

An important idea in the "new" institutional economics is that non-market institutions are generated under conditions of market failure and inefficiency. Aspects of this idea are examined in the papers by Acheson and Bates.

The "new" institutional economists are much interested in the state and its role in influencing institutions, transaction costs, and the allocation of property rights. These concerns are reflected in many papers. The articles by Bossen and McGregor are concerned with the effect of public policy; while others, such as Marti and Moberg, are primarily concerned with the actions of the agents of the state.

A large number of "new" institutional economists, including Douglass North, are interested in the long-term evolution of institutions (e.g. markets, property rights, legal systems, banking systems, etc.) and their effect on economic development. The papers by Ensminger and McDowell are primarily concerned with the evolution of such institutions and their effect on economic activity at the local level. Bossen is interested in the effect of changes in family structure on economic performance.

Some of the papers in this volume describe institutions that are not considered by "new" institutional economists. The most important of these are the articles by McGregor and Shipton, which describe institutions affecting credit in Third World countries.

Part I contains two articles which give an **Overview** of institutional economics and its connections to anthropology. *Welcome to Nobel Country* by the editor reviews the most important ideas and concepts of both the "old" and "new" institutional economics. The article offers neither a condemnation of institutional economics nor a defense of the field. The key question at this time is: To what extent can the concepts and insights of institutional economics be applied outside the industrialized West? The article concludes with a set of questions that may be of use to anthropologists working in non-industrial settings.

The article by **Robert Bates** provides a broad, and very provocative, perspective on institutional economics, its past and future. Bates is concerned with criticizing one of the most central theories of the "new" institutional economics: the idea that non-market institutions are created in cases of market failure. He argues that this idea is flawed both because it attempts to account for non-market institutions in terms of their consequences, and because it cannot account for generation of "public goods". (As noted in the next essay, *Welcome to Nobel Country*, "public goods" have long posed problems for the "new" institutional economists.) Bates then proposes two alternative approaches to understanding these collective dilemmas, and the generation of institutions which are of benefit to large numbers of people. One he calls an anthropological approach, which is based on the axiom of non-cooperation and the idea that culture can overcome collective dilemmas. The second approach stems from political science and the recognition that the power of the state gives it the capacity to determine transaction costs, and thus motivate people to collective action.

One of the most useful aspects of Bates' article is his delineation of four different types of market failure (i.e. production externalities, public goods, imperfect information, and hidden action), each of which is associated with the creation of a different set of institutions.

The Case Studies

While it is difficult to classify the case studies because so many themes and foci overlap, I have divided them into three different groupings. **Part II** contains papers where the concept of transaction costs and individual decisions play a prominent role.

Ensminger describes the way certain social changes (i.e. establishing weights and measures, literacy and the penetration of Islam) among the pastoral Orma of East Africa lowered transaction costs which, in turn, resulted in economic benefits to both traders and consumers. Her paper underlines the point that the development of markets and economic growth is dependent on institutions that lower transaction costs. In the presence of very high transaction costs, trade is impossible.

Russell's case study analyzes the factors producing and maintaining a very inefficient shares system in one Philippine inshore fishery. Both captains and crew systematically cheat each other and violate the terms of the contract. Crews are not in position to enforce the terms of the shares contract, and thus engage in wholesale stealing of fish. Captains are not in position to enforce the rules against stealing and cannot fire crewmen. They simply estimate the amount of fish the crewman has stolen and then pay him accordingly, regardless of the level of the catch. The massive stealing of fish results in a *de facto* cheating of fish consignors. Russell argues that institutionalized cheating persists in the industry because the transaction costs of negotiating fair and enforceable shares contracts is higher than the transaction costs of allowing the cheating to continue.

This case study poses a dilemma for institutional economists. Oliver Williamson would predict that this kind of rampant opportunism would result in the negotiation of effective and enforceable contracts between captains, crews and consignors. The fact that this has not occurred raises questions about Williamson's hypothesis that high transaction costs due to opportunism lead to a dependence on vertical integration or other kinds of non-market institutions.

Rehfus and Gladwin are interested in the decisions of individual physicians and health care organizations to contract with each other in the United States. In the literature of the "new" institutional economics, contracting is treated as a problem in reducing transaction costs and ensuring property rights through "governance" institutions. Rehfus and Gladwin use a model of decision making that is more sophisticated psychologically and cognitively than the decision models employed in institutional economics as a whole to understand contracts between firms. They demonstrate that the goals of these kinds of firms (i.e. physicians and HMO's and PPO's) are very different, and involve very different kinds of transaction costs. They argue that physicians are willing to put up with high transaction costs to maintain independence. The results are contracts and arrangements that result in high health care costs, a finding which has profound implications for health care policy.

Acheson's study of the furniture industry in a Mexican Indian community emphasizes the strategies local entrepreneurs are forced to use in an environment in which all transaction costs are high. Acheson argues that in these circumstances, local entrepreneurs have no other choice but to resort to two strategies not considered by institutional economists such as Coase and Williamson. First, they have developed a set of relational ties between firms in the production and marketing chain in an effort to reduce risk and uncertainty. Second, they have also devoted a good deal of time and effort to developing two kinds "unions"--units which aid in the production and marketing of furniture.

Bossen's paper describes China's policy shift from collective farming back to the family farm, and questions whether this will result in real development or a return to involution (i.e. growth without development), which has characterized China's farm families for centuries. Her data suggest that men are leaving agriculture for industry, but that a tremendous amount of involution is occurring due to the increased amount of female labor being used in agriculture. Despite the demand for female labor in industry, women are being tied to the family farm by the structure of the rural patriarchal family, and the transaction costs involved in enforcing the legal rights of women.

Part III contains papers devoted primarily to an analysis of the state and its agents, and the role of state power in influencing the generation of institutions.

Marti's case study describes the way women traders in 19th century Mexico City maneuvered to take advantage of government policies regulating vendors and the ways in which they lobbied to change those policies with their own best interest in mind. She points out that the vendors were not merely reacting to regulations; they were operating to make a niche for themselves.

Moberg's paper analyzes four theories of the state. He concludes that the governments of many Third World countries have severe agency problems. That is, state policies are formulated by the agents of the state for their own benefit--and not those of the general public or even the ruling classes. Moberg takes exception to North's assumption that the rulers of states operate to maximize wealth, and thus facilitate the activities of entrepreneurs. Quite the contrary, he points out that leaders of "patrimonial states" use a "spoils bureaucracy" to reward friends, which often results in red tape and huge transaction costs for businessmen. Moberg's analysis gives insight into the reasons that so many governments fail to develop the kinds institutions necessary for a flourishing business community.

McDowell traces the efforts of several Guatemalan regimes to "develop" and "modernize" the country. The result was a set of institutions, reinforced by the Guatemalan military, that gave United Fruit Corporation a monopoly on rail transport, large amounts of land, and an exemption from taxes. These efforts also impoverished the large Indian population by stripping them of property rights. Guatemala inadvertently emerged from these efforts to modernize with a set of institutions designed to maintain its Third World status.

Part IV contains two articles focused on institutions affecting credit and access to credit.

McGregor is concerned with the theoretical perspectives used to understand credit in Third World societies and their policy implications. One perspective emphasizes financial markets and macro level policies by the government. The other focuses on the local institutions surrounding credit. McGregor argues that those viewing credit from the point of view of financial markets overlook the set of social relationships (including patron-client ties) and institutions surrounding credit. These not only affect the flow of credit, but can be manipulated to influence supplies of goods, prices, and ultimately market efficiency. Bankers prefer to loan money through local brokers who are tied into contracts and patron client ties. This not only results in inefficient use of credit, but the continued reproduction of poverty in rural Bangladesh.

Shipton describes the concepts, attitudes and institutions influencing sources of credit and financial practices in rural Gambia. Gambians, he points out, have two legal systems and a variety of financial institutions to choose among and manipulate. Some are of local origin; others are derived from European sources. He is not so much interested in the generation of those institutions as their selection and use by individuals.

Theoretical Papers

Part V contains three papers touching on a variety of theoretical issues of concern to institutional economics. The article by **Colin and Losch** gives an assessment of the work and conceptual commitments of the French development economists working in Africa. They argue that the work of FARE (French Africanist rural economics) has a good deal in common with the "old" institutional economics. It is also clear that the FARE has a good deal in common with anthropology in that both fields are dedicated to describing the complexities of specific cultures and societies. FARE devotes considerable attention to social factors influencing access to resources, the diversity of peasant practices, cultural factors influencing the diffusion of innovations, and the effect of institutional change on production.

This is a demanding article. However, it gives a good deal of insight into the ways that "institutionalism" is developing in France, and an appreciation for its applied possibilities.

Wilk's article develops a set of concepts to understand the management of financial assets within households. He hypothesizes that two ideal types of household exist: the "redistributive household" where most assets are pooled in a general fund and the "reciprocal household" in which most assets are held by individuals in "personal funds" and "obligated funds." Redistributive households allow more flexibility in the use of assets, and lower transaction costs, but they permit less individual autonomy. Reciprocal households involve more transaction costs in negotiations between family members, but allow individual family members more freedom to spend resources with personal goals in mind.

Michie's article is perhaps the most all encompassing. He is interested in examining the history of the debate about economic rationality over the course of the past 40 years, the way in which it has influenced developments in anthropology and economics, and the relationship between these fields. The discussion touches on the ideas and contributions of economists such as Theodore Schultz, Gary Becker, Shaun Heap, Ronald Coase, Douglass North and Oliver Williamson to the work of anthropologists such as Maurice Godelier, Harold Schneider and Sutti Ortiz. He argues convincingly that there has been very little real integration of ideas in anthropology and economics, and that anthropologists have been "talking to themselves." He concludes that the incorporation of an "institutional dimension within mainstream economics" could lead to true cross fertilization between the two fields. Michie does not believe this has occurred yet; and I can only agree.

Summary

Economic anthropology and economics have had all too little effect on each other. Anthropologists have been quick to criticize economics for its unrealistic assumptions, its unwillingness to include social and cultural factors in its models, and its myopic focusing on a few very large industries in the developed world. Economists in the neoclassical mold have responded by ignoring anthropology and virtually all other social sciences.

Institutional economics, may allow some real cross fertilization to take place. It provides a means to integrate the actions of individuals, a wide variety of institutional and cultural factors, and economic performance. Whether the future will see institutional economics providing a bridge between the two fields remains to be seen.

Part I

Overview

1

Welcome To Nobel Country: A Review of Institutional Economics

James M. Acheson

In 1960 Dusenberry quipped that "Economics is all about why people make choices. Sociology (and Anthropology) are all about how people have no decisions to make" (1960). While this comment has a tongue in cheek quality, it did summarize the dominant theoretical niches carved out by these disciplines. The past twenty-five years have seen a substantial merging of the concerns of anthropologists and economists. Anthropologists have become increasingly interested in intracultural variation and individual choices. Such approaches have gone by a variety of names: "action theory," "transactional analysis," "exchange theory," and more recently under the rubric of the theory of "practice" (Kapferer 1976, Ortner 1984, 153ff; Whitten and Whitten 1972, 256). At the same time, there has been a broad revival of interest in institutions in several social science disciplines--especially in economics and public choice. Economists have studied everything from the family (Becker 1981), clubs (Buchanan 1965), and norms (Koford and Miller 1991) to property rights (Demsetz 1967) crime and punishment, and discrimination (Obershall and Leifer 1986, 233)--phenomena that were once solidly in the realm of sociology and anthropology.

In retrospect, it is now apparent that this merging of interests was indicative of a merging of problem as well. Some time in the late 1960s and 1970s, one of the key problems for social science became the relationships between individual choice and social structure (Jenkins 1992, 10). This was the focal point of the work of Fredrik Barth (1963; 1966; 1981). It has continued to be an important concern for Pierre Bourdieu and Anthony Giddens who have had a tremendous impact on sociology, anthropology, geography and political science. In economics this problem has been attacked by the "new" institutional economists. They have attempted to answer two fundamental questions: "How do institutions evolve in response to individual incentives, strategies and choices, and how do institutions affect the performance of political and economic systems?" (North 1990, vi). Despite their common endeavor, the efforts of social scientists in one field are largely invisible to those in another. Hodgson speaks of the "blinkered view of economists" (1988, xvii) who seem oblivious to what is happening in psychology, philosophy, sociology and anthropology. Anthropologists, for their part, are largely unaware that economists have done any work on the generation of institutions, much less have any idea about the analytical insights they have developed.

Institutional economics has burgeoned recently. It has resulted in a number of powerful ideas, which promise to make a permanent impact on the social sciences. The influence of institutional economics within the field of economics is indicated by the fact that the last three Nobel prizes have been awarded to some of the most famous institutionalists (i.e. Ronald Coase in 1991, Gary Becker in 1992 and Douglas North in 1993). In addition, Herbert Simon won the Nobel Prize in 1978. However, the work of the institutional economists remains highly theoretical and has been developed from work done in the United States and other western countries. The institutions of institutional economics are our own. It remains to be seen to what extent the insights and concepts of institutional economics can be applied to other societies.

In this article, my aim is to describe the basic concepts and ideas of institutional economics, concentrating on the "new" institutional economics. My aim is not to criticize. Before anthropologists can assess institutional economics we need to understand the insights and concepts of the field and see to what extent they can be applied to other societies. We have barely begun this task.

The Institutional Approach: Historical Background

The "Old" Institutional Economics

Institutional economics has come to the forefront of economics at two periods. In the interwar years, institutional economics was the dominant theoretical framework when the work of John R. Commons and Thorstein Veblen dominated the field (Hodgson 1988, 21). (We will call this the "old" institutional economics.)

Both Veblen and Commons were essentially concerned with the injustices caused by laissez-faire capitalism in the United States in the late 19th and early 20th centuries. Veblen concentrated on destroying the old economic order; Commons on building a new one. Veblen is best known now for his *Theory of the Leisure Class* (Lerner 1948, 53-196) in which he described the relationships between "conspicuous consumption" and prestige in the wasteful and predatory upper classes. The lower classes were attached to the upper classes "by ties of identification and emulation" (Mitchell 1947, 72-214). However, his most important contribution was his assault on the economics of his day, which he described as nothing short of an ideological buttress for the capitalist system. He ridiculed the idea--then much in vogue--that economic theories were unchangeable "laws", universal and timeless. He said "there are no iron economic laws: there are only man-made institutions" (Lerner 1948, 31). He argued that the destructive and unproductive system created by businessmen and the price system could be changed by a new set of administrative controls (Veblen 1948, 324-348; Mitchell 1947, 423-442).

John R. Commons was a tremendously productive scholar. He wrote on virtually every topic of importance to the economics of his time, ranging from the business cycle and monopoly pricing to social insurance, public utilities, immigration, and tariffs. He did seminal work on the nature of "transactions" (1932, 65-142; 1934). In *Institutional Economics* he distinguished between rationing, bargaining and managerial transactions which occurred in different social situations and under different systems of governance (1934). He had a particular interest in the institutions of working people: trade unions, buying cooperatives and cooperative workshops, etc. Selig Perlman says "Commons was the creator of American Labor History" (1950, 1).

Commons not only saw the great injustices inherent in the capitalist system, he did all he could to cure them. He was very much involved in developing laws and institutions to solve practical problems, working for government agencies and making many appearances before legislatures, congress and the courts. He wrote legislation establishing industrial safety, minimum wage, workmen's compensation, child labor, and health insurance. (His health insurance scheme failed.) He wrote the Wisconsin Civil Service laws. Perhaps his most notable success was the development of the "administrative commission," which allowed government to regulate many different economic activities. He was so effective in helping to develop so many institutions that Kenneth Boulding said his work was the "intellectual origin of the movement toward the welfare state" (1957, 7).

After World War II interest in the "old" institutional economics waned as the neo-classical paradigm came to the fore and has remained the dominant theoretical view to the present.

The "New" Institutional Economics

The second wave of interest in institutional economics--the "new" institutional economics--had its origins in 1937 when Ronald Coase published his landmark article "The Nature of the Firm." Coase's seminal ideas had no "influence for thirty or forty years after they were published" (Coase 1993b, 61). It was only when economists such as Oliver Williamson, Douglass North, Steven H. Cheung (Coase 1993b, 61-73) and others interested in industrial organization expanded on original ideas in the 1970's and 1980's that their value became apparent. Coase was awarded the Nobel Prize in 1991. Like so many other recipients of that prize, Coase was recognized for work done in the past--in this case the ideas developed half a century earlier.

Eggertsson says that "the new economics of institutions is a Tower of Babel, a field in search of a common language" (1993, 1). It is true that it is difficult to attach neat labels to what is occurring. However, this criticism is a little unfair. Institutional economics is moving so rapidly that no commonly agreed on set of principles has emerged. We will be able to talk about periods of development and schools of thought when the pace is less rapid and the situation has jelled.

Essentially the "new" institutional economics refers to the work of a loose collection of economists and political scientists interested in the generation of institutions from the behavior of individuals, and the ways in which those institutions influence the level of productive activity and exchange. Two key concepts are woven through this entire body of literature: property rights and transaction costs.

The work of the institutional economists goes in at least five directions. Some have focused on the institution of property rights (Acheson 1989, 354-357; Bromley 1989, 85-105; Demsetz 1967) and their effect on economic performance. Others are interested in the conditions under which people organize groups to achieve a collective interest, or generate so called "public goods." A third group have focused on the relationship between rules and interaction (Schotter 1981, 1986, 120-21; Bromley 1989; Axelrod 1984). The fourth perspective is that developed by Coase and Williamson and their followers, who have placed emphasis on elementary transactions and the development of various kinds of firms and markets in capitalist societies (Coase 1937, 1993a, 1984; Williamson 1975, 1985, 1986b). Last, another set have developed evolutionary models (Nelson and Winter 1982; North 1981, 1983, 1990) to explain the development of institutions through time.

However, these are not isolated or competing schools of thought by any means. Institutional economists are interested in all of the problems mentioned above; many have worked on so many facets of institutionalism that the work of such individuals is difficult to classify.

The Key Concepts of the "New" Institutional Economics

While the "new" institutional economists come in several different stripes and colors, they share some basic commitments. These are summarized below.

Basic Assumptions of the "New" Institutionalism

Like mainstream economists in the neo-classical tradition, the "new" institutional economists see economizing as central to economic activity. However, the "new" institutional economics is based on some different assumptions. Neo-classical economists view the decision maker as a rational person with perfect knowledge (Hodgson 1988, 98; Littlechild 1986, 28), who is engaged in exchanging homogenous goods, which they own, in competitive markets. They assume that entrepreneurs obtain all the information needed to make all decisions from market prices alone. Institutions are largely ignored since it is assumed they have little to do with markets and choices. If they are considered at all, institutions are seen as impediments or constraints.

The "new" institutional economists have changed all these assumptions. First, they assume a situation of bounded rationality (Simon 1961, xxiv; Williamson 1985, 45), and that knowledge is very costly to obtain (Loasby 1986, 41; MacKaay 1982, Chap 6). Since decision makers do not have perfect knowledge, opportunism (i.e. self interest with guile) can and often does exist (Williamson 1986a, 175). The fact that those engaged in transactions can have incomplete or distorted information increases uncertainty, which leads those entering into exchanges to attempt to obtain as much information as possible from others. The problem of obtaining accurate information is made even more difficult by the fact that goods are highly variable and quality is always a problem. Mary Douglas summarizes these aspects of the "new" institutional economics by saying that the field "characterizes individuals in the market place as weakly rational and weakly moral" (1992, 198).

Exchanges are made even more difficult by the fact that significant market imperfections or outright market failure is common and people do not have exclusive rights to important goods and services. All of this means that there are significant costs to using markets.

Perhaps most important, the "new" institutional economists see the coordination of economic activity as involving more than transactions in markets in which price alone is the sole consideration. A variety of institutions play a role (Langlois 1986, 6) in constraining and presenting opportunities to entrepreneurs (Hodgson 1988, 178). A wide range of social and legal ties can exist between people, which influence the exchanges between them (Williamson 1985, 164). Some of the most important kinds of exchanges are non-market exchanges which take place between people within the same organization.

A key axiom is that institutions have a strong influence on the operation of the economic system. Many of these institutions are the result of political processes. For this reason, much attention has been lavished on the role of the State in influencing the efficiency of markets and the generation of wealth, but there is growing interest in local level governance institutions and stateless systems (Ostrom 1990).

In the past, neo-classical economists have reacted to the assumptions of the "new" institutional economists as if they bordered on heresy. They seem more realistic to most anthropologists.

MacKaay (1982, 16-23) has neatly summarized the difference between neoclassical economics and the "new" institutional economics by pointing out that the neoclassical model does not account for four phenomena: 1. collective goods (free rider problem), 2. significant transaction costs, 3. substantial uncertainty, and 4. imperfect competition. The "new" institutional economics seeks to describe the workings of economic systems taking into account these four phenomena.

Institutions

Institutional economists essentially conceive of institutions as sets of formal rules that can be enforced. North describes institutions as "the rules of the game" (1990, 3). This is the definition that has been used by F.G. Bailey in

Stratagems and Spoils (1969, viii, 20). Institutions influence behavior not only by constraining what people can do, but by motivating certain kinds of actions. Institutions are selected and created by individuals and groups of people who are consciously aware that what they can do and accomplish depends on the institutional framework under which they are working. Jean Ensminger phrases it nicely when she says "The underlying assumption is that institutions directly affect economic outcomes (distribution and growth), that individuals realize this, and that they attempt to change institutions to serve their ends more effectively, whether these ends be ideological or materialistic" (1992, xiii).

Institutions are a substitute for accurate information. In an uncertain world, they provide a basis for making decisions with reasonable assurance because rules help to ensure the behavior of others (Coase 1993a, 57; North 1990, 6, 27). One may not know for certain how to run a particular machine, but one can enter into a labor contract to obtain the services of someone who can. One may not be able to know what the market for one's crops will be at harvest time, but it is possible to sell one's crop on the futures market to obtain a guaranteed price. In a world of perfect knowledge, there would be no need for institutions (Coase 1960).

Institutions do not just constrain choices, they also open opportunities. For example, a contract on the purchase of raw materials at a given price and level of quality is a constraint on both purchaser and supplier. However, an actor might be reluctant to open a business in the absence of such a contract that increases the probability that raw materials will be available on schedule.

Property Rights

Some institutional economists see property rights as the most important "institution" (Eggertsson 1993, 2). Property refers to a bundle of rights held over a resource, which exist in a variety of forms (real estate, currency, intellectual resources, claims on debts, capital assets, services). Property rights are "determined through the political process" and are "assigned" (Libecap 1989, 4) through a series of contracts, which confer some control over the resource. Political maneuvers to change property rights or the system of contracts are bound to be contentious since they will benefit some groups more than others.

To be effective, property rights must be enforced by the state or some other governance institution. However, owners of property never have all of the rights to property (North 1990, 33). Property rights are never perfectly enforced and some rights are always retained by the state or community.

Moreover, "owners" of property often transfer some of their property rights to others, if only temporarily (e.g. rent, hire managers, etc.). Owners can lose property rights by force (i.e. theft or expropriation), or by a lack of information which bestows an advantage to others.

Recently there have been a number of efforts to classify property rights systems. While these systems are simplistic in that they do not convey the complexity of all the combinations of ownership rights possible, they have analytical value. Berkes and Kisliaglu (1992) have produced one that is particularly useful from our perspective. They speak of:

1. Open Access: access to the resource is open to all with no constraints.
2. Communal Property: the resource is held by a community of users different from the government.
3. State Property: the resource is controlled by the central government of national states or sub-units of national states.
4. Private Property: exclusive rights reside with an individual owner, who can trade these property rights with others.

Most important, the type of property rights system, which influences the amount of control that "owners" or "users" of resources have, influences the decisions they make and the way those resources are treated. In Eggertsson's terms, "It is obvious that the nature of control matters for economic actors: short-term control shortens the time horizon; uncertain control discourages potentially profitable projects; lack of control incites costly races for possession; restricted control allocates assets to inferior uses" (Eggertsson 1993, 2).

The effect of property rights on economic decisions has been explored most fully in consideration of the so called "common property problem," which achieved a good deal of attention after Garrett Hardin's (1968) publication of an article called "The Tragedy of the Commons." The theory of "common property resources" asserts that open access resources, such as fisheries, wildlife, parklands, rangeland, air, and rivers, will be subjected to escalating abuse which will cease only after the resource is destroyed economically. When access is open to all and exclusive rights to the resource do not exist, over exploitation is only rational. Why should a fishing boat captain conserve a school of fish when those fish will only be taken by another boat within hours? By way of contrast, privately owned resources will be protected by their owners, who stand to gain by their efforts to conserve (Hardin and Baden 1977; Scott 1955). In addition to causing destruction of resources, a lack of property rights causes high transaction costs, inefficient use of those resources, high external costs, and over capitalization (Acheson 1989, 354-357).

A few years ago, two solutions to the "tragedy of the commons" were advocated: action by a centralized state, or privatization. More recently, a number of anthropologists and other scholars have noted that local level communities can be very effective in generating institutions to manage resources (Acheson 1993; McCay and Acheson 1987; Berkes 1989; Bromley 1992; Pinkerton 1989; Ostrom 1990, 1992; Tang 1992).

Transaction Costs

Perhaps the most important concept of institutional economics is that of transaction costs. Transaction costs refers basically to the effort, time and expense necessary to obtain the "information necessary to make an exchange, negotiate the exchange and enforce the exchange" (Dalman 1979, 149; Goldberg 1989, 21 ff; Hodgson 1988, 201; Williamson 1985, 2). One of the most important components of transaction costs is the cost of obtaining accurate information on markets and prices, business associates, etc. (Williamson 1975, 31-32).

Transaction costs cannot be accounted for in narrow economic terms. They are embedded in the normative system of the society in question (Commons 1934; Granovetter 1985). On the whole, transaction costs will be reduced by all of the myriad of social, technical, and cultural factors that make it easier to gather information (i.e. communications, transportation, literacy, number of people dealing in a market); negotiate and enforce agreements once made (i.e. property rights, contract law, access to courts, standardized weights and measures, standards of honesty and honor, willingness to renegotiate a contract, etc.).

Three factors raise transaction costs. First is *opportunism*, or self interest with guile (e.g. cheating, withholding information, asymmetrical information, etc.). The second is the *frequency* of the exchange. It is much easier to learn about prices, quality of products, etc. if there are a large number of people in the market and large numbers of exchanges are taking place. Last and most influential is *asset specificity* (Milgrom and Roberts 1992, 28-32; Williamson 1985, 15- 42; 52-56). That is transaction costs are high when an exchange depends on a specific person, a specific location, or specific physical assets. In these conditions, one's ability to bargain is low and the chances for opportunism are high.

Transaction costs can be reduced by rules or institutions, which make the activities of others more predictable (Obershall and Leifer 1986, 237; Ouchi 1980, 130 ff). Contracts with suppliers, for example, lower transaction costs by ensuring steady supplies of parts while agreements with unions codify expectations of workers and employers. In the absence of contract law, supplies of raw materials might be impossible to ensure, and the lack of a union contract might result in severe labor unrest and an undependable work force. Moreover, if these institutions are missing and transaction costs are unusually high, business activity is made more difficult if not impossible.

Markets and the Generation of Institutions

According to neo-classical economic theory, competitive markets operate in ways to allocate goods and services produced in efficient ways. Moreover, if markets are working competitively, there should be no divergence between the aims of individuals and the goals of society. Under these conditions, people making decisions in their own best interests will make choices which are socially optimal. From this perspective, efficient markets are the quintessential invisible hand solution.

Unfortunately, markets are rarely perfectly competitive and efficient. Information about goods and prices is often difficult to come by; opportunism is ever present; and enforcement of contracts is always problematic. Moreover, in some cases markets fail completely. There may be no markets for some goods. In other cases, large firms and cartels can charge very inflated prices.

Perhaps the most important insight of the "new" institutional economists is that institutions are formed to facilitate transactions. People use the institution of markets when they work well; but they are able to make arrangements with each other (i.e. non-market institution) to replace the price system when it is not working well.

In the literature of the "new" institutional economics, there are two sets of concepts dealing with the ways in which problems in markets produce institutions. One is concerned with the problem of *market inefficiency* and the development of markets and firms (Williamson 1986b, 88). The other is concerned with the more serious problem of *market failure*, and the actions of the State. These will be discussed in turn.

Markets and Firms

Much of the literature of the "new" institutional economics has been devoted to understanding the organization of industry in the modern West. The emphasis has been on explaining the development of markets and firms of various types since these are the major institutions involved in the production and allocation of goods and services. Many of the key ideas and concepts about the generation of firms and markets have been developed by Ronald Coase, Oliver Williamson, and their followers.

Coase (1937, 21) argues that firms come into being in order to "get around the costs of using the price mechanism" in markets. If markets were completely frictionless and no transaction costs existed, then there would be no need for firms at all. People could obtain all they wanted by entering into a variety of market transactions. But markets are often relatively inefficient, and exchanges may entail large transaction costs. Given the time necessary to obtain information and negotiate enforceable contracts in the market, it is often more efficient to enter into permanent associations with others (i.e. firm or bureaucracy). The distinguishing features of the firm are the "suppression of the price mechanism" and the fact that allocational decisions are made by administrative fiat rather than price (Coase 1937, 20, 27; Hart 1990, 154-159; Masden 1993). In these respects, firms are a type of "non-market institution." While firms are the most important non-market institution, the term can be applied to any entity in which exchanges are not regulated by the price mechanism, including collective farms, cooperatives, households and bureaucracies. Williamson uses the term "hierarchy" to refer to large vertically integrated firms (1975). "Hierarchy" is not used in referring to other "non-market institutions".

From the point of view of Coase and Williamson, both markets and firms (i.e. hierarchies) share many essential traits. They both involve contracts or agreements with other people; and both are alternative organizations through which entrepreneurs can obtain goods and services. Most important, *they are substitutable for each other.*[1] That is, there are two ways in which entrepreneurs can obtain needed goods and services. They can go into the market and buy them from owners of other firms at a negotiated price; or they can produce the needed good or service by expanding their own firm or productive organization. Most entrepreneurs do both (Williamson 1986, 85 ff). Thus they are engaged in transactions within their own firm (i.e. with their own employees), which involves so called "internal transaction costs," and in transactions with owners of other firms, which results in "external transaction costs" (Williamson 1985, 82 ff, 140).

If external transaction costs are higher than internal transaction costs, then entrepreneurs expand the size of their own firms to obtain the desired goods or services by producing it themselves. That is, if it is very difficult to obtain the information necessary to make exchanges with other firms and enforce those bargains, due to *opportunism,* dependency on specific assets, or *a small numbers situation*, one is probably advised to expand one's own firm to provide the needed services internally. However, if internal transaction costs are higher than external transaction costs, the entrepreneur obtains the goods and services needed through the market (Acheson 1982, 1986, 126; Alexander and Alexander 1991; Coase 1937, 20-24; Ouchi 1980, 129; Williamson 1975, 102-105, 117-133, 219 ff; Williamson 1985 chaps 4,5, and 6; Williamson 1986b, 85-99).[2] In summary, the choice of whether to select a market or hierarchy (e.g. large firm) depends on the relative efficiency of exchanges both within and external to the firm. According to the theory, changing the size of one's own firm and the degree of dependence on other firms are the primary tactics used to adapt to transaction costs (Williamson 1975, 26-28; 1985, 94-95).

So far we have viewed exchanges as taking place either between firms (market exchange) or within firms (a type of non-market institution). The situation is more complicated than this. According to Coase and Williamson, people involved in exchanges stand in a wide variety of different kinds of relationships to each other, which are best viewed as falling along a continuum. At one end are large vertically integrated firms or "hierarchies" where the parties to an exchange are organized in a permanent relationship with each other and transactions are regulated by administrative decree rather than prices (Williamson 1975, Chapters 6 and 7). At the other end are spot markets in which price is the best source of information and the relationship is terminated when the exchange is completed. In between are a variety of organizational forms in which the parties to the exchange maintain quasi or fully contractual agreements with each other over the course of time. Franchising is one type of intermediary solution; another is what Macneil calls "relational contracting" (1978). Here parties to exchange are in separate firms or organizations, but establish long term bilateral ties with each other and agree to do business over extended periods. The terms of their agreement may be specified in a legal contract or they may be agreed upon informally. In either case some trust between the parties is called for since contracts are never able to cover all contingencies (Williamson 1986b, 103-104). Prices are an important element in such exchanges although personal ties and non-monetary values influence the bargains struck. Williamson calls all of these various kinds of ties and agreements among and between firms "governance structures;" he has produced a very elaborate analysis of them (Williamson 1975, 1985, Chap 3).

None of these kinds of exchange organizations is unknown to anthropologists. However, anthropologists have paid comparatively little attention to spot markets. The fine work of Geertz (1978) and Bestor (forthcoming) are exceptions. Even less attention has been paid to large firms and trading groups, but there are a few good studies, for example Lomnitz and Perez-Lizaur (1987) and Cohen (1969). What has caught the anthropological imagination is relational contracting which has been reported in a wide variety of cultures ranging from Haiti (Mintz 1964), the Philippines (Spoehr 1980; Szanton 1972), and Indonesia (Dewey 1962) to Nigeria (Cohen 1969) and the United States (Acheson 1985; Ackerloff 1970; Plattner 1983, 1989, 213; Wilson 1980).

Goods and services can also be allocated and distributed by other kinds of non-market institutions, such as the Kula, Potlatch, and direct exchange systems (Bohannan 1955; Leach and Leach 1983; Sahlins 1965). The "new" institutional economists know about such non-market exchange systems, but they have done very little work on them, and have not incorporated them into their models.

Market Failure and the Creation of Public Goods

Market failure involves more serious problems with the price system, and it results in the generation of different kinds of institutions. One source of market failure is that some goods and services have no price. This is the so called *missing market* problem. But the usual cause is *externalities*. "Externalities are the positive or negative effects that one's economic agents have on another's welfare that are not regulated by prices" (Milgrom and Roberts 1992, 77). Externalities result from incomplete ownership rights, which means that firms cannot capture the external benefits they produce, nor can they be charged for the external costs they pass off on others. An industrialist who places a plant in a community which raises property values for all inhabitants cannot charge for his services, nor do heavy industries have to pay for the costs of the air and water pollution produced since air and water are not owned. These costs are borne by other people down-wind or down-stream who are deprived of a clean environment.

Market failure causes resources to be allocated in ways that are both inefficient and not in the best interest of the society. The fact that no practical way has evolved to charge industries for polluting the air not only results in destruction of valuable resources, it also results in a waste of capital since industry has an incentive to build more plants, etc. than they would if they had to pay the full costs of production (i.e. cleaning up the environment) (Acheson 1989, 355-356; Cheung 1970; Scott 1955).

Market failure also results in very high transaction costs. Since externalities result from situations where ownership rights and markets are either flawed or absent, one cannot use market exchanges to solve problems. Since air is not owned, owners of factories are free to use it to carry off noxious emission. They can only be made to cease their activities through the political process, which can take years of effort. Where full ownership rights and efficient markets exist, transaction costs are far less. For example, it is much easier to solve pollution problems concerning land since a well developed market exists. If river front property is damaged by industrial pollution in a river, the owners of the land can be located at relatively low costs. They can then be compensated for the loss of their property rights or the polluter can arrange to buy them out.

One of the results of market failure is the *free rider effect*. That is, flawed markets result in external benefits that can be taken advantage of by people who do not have to pay for them. Such people are getting a "free ride" at the expense of other people or the resource. Where free riders abound, services may not be provided and exchanges may be avoided. Those who are paying the bill may well refuse to carry the burden of those who are not. Thus, market failure can limit the kinds of exchanges that are possible, which, in turn, can have severe consequences for the economy as a whole.

Market failure results in the generation of non-market institutions. Three different processes and types of institutions are involved.

First, market failure can lead to a decision to produce services by the government. In modern industrial countries, it is generally recognized that some services cannot be provided by competitive markets, such as police protection, fire protection and hospitals for the insane. Why should one pay a private company to catch crooks? Those who pay will dispose of the criminals for everyone. Under these circumstances it is illogical for an individual to pay and there are very strong incentives to be a *free rider*. The universal solution to this problem is to have police protection by a government organization.

Second, the problems associated with market failure can be solved by developing more efficient markets. This generally involves activities to lower transaction costs in markets by developing better transportation and communications facilities, along with standardization of weights and measures, etc. One of the very best examples of the way markets are developed has been provided by Jean Ensminger, who describes the process by which markets came about among the Orma, a group of pastoralists in Kenya (Ensminger 1992, 33-108).

Third, still another kind of institution can be developed to solve the problems associated with market failure--namely associations of individuals who cooperate to provide a service. The key question to be answered is when and under what conditions will individuals develop such associations? Generally it is assumed that such services will be provided when their benefits outweigh their costs. Such an approach is very naive. One of the most important contributions to this body of literature has been made by Mancur Olsen (1965), who makes an important distinction between *private goods* and *public goods*. A private good is one that can be restricted to those who have paid for it. Goods in a store can only be enjoyed by those who pay; and the rights to play golf at a private club are reserved for members. A public good is one that must be made available to all regardless of whether they have paid or not. The classic example of a public good is national defense which is made available to everyone in the society, including tax cheats and draft dodgers who have not provided the service.

Olsen's major contribution has been to show that people will not automatically cooperate to provide public goods even if everyone might be better off if they paid their fair share and received the benefits. The problem again is the free rider problem. Everyone in a community might benefit if a waste disposal project is not located in the town limits, and an organized effort to lobby against the project will benefit everyone in town regardless of their contribution to the common cause. Under these conditions there is such a strong incentive for individuals to avoid cooperation that the effort is likely to fail. Olsen concludes that public goods will be provided only if special incentives are involved that in effect do away with the "free rider problem."

In the past few years, a good deal of progress has been made in explaining the conditions under which groups of people cooperate to produce institutions to manage resources on the local level. Elinor Ostrom and her students have done a particularly good job in describing such institutions, and the factors influencing their effectiveness (Ostrom 1990, 1992; Tang 1992). Such institutions are effective because they motivate people to join an association rather than be "free riders."

The State

The neoclassical model of economics assumes that the State has no effect on markets, and thus is largely irrelevant in explaining economic behavior. By way of contrast, institutional economists view the state and governance structures as critical for the operation of the economy.

The state is involved in performing a number of important functions. In cases of market failure, States may provide services directly. It is critical in defining, allocating and enforcing property rights, which affects transaction costs and externalities. Douglass North repeatedly has reminded us that the relative security of property rights has enormous implications for the operation of the economy as a whole (North and Thomas 1973; North 1990, 33-35; 63). In a myriad of ways, governments affect transaction costs in markets. They are instrumental in providing transportation and communication facilities. They provide standards of measurements, and regulate the quality of goods and services. They limit entry into markets through licensing requirements, etc. States operate the central banking system, thus providing a stable medium of exchange. Perhaps most important, states enforce contracts, used by entrepreneurs to gain control over productive assets of all kinds, including labor. There is no problem enforcing contracts when it is in the interests of the parties to live up to them. But inevitably disputes arise, and it is the state that provides the means (e.g. courts, judges, contract law) by which disputes can be adjudicated.

In modern states, governments intervene in the economic sphere in so many ways as to defy description. In the United States, for example, one secret of business success is to have a protected niche, which is usually provided by the government through lobbying activity. The Federal Government has provided an incredible number of subsidies, tax loopholes, protective tariffs, barriers to entry, side payments, research laboratories and "business development" activities. All of these give industries a special advantage. When business failure looms, many very large companies have been able to arrange direct government bailouts (e.g. Penn Central, Lockheed, Chrysler, and the savings and loan industry).

In addition, many valuable resources remain in the public domain. It is worth a good deal of effort to obtain access to them. (See Libecap 1989 for an examination of the ways in which four resources have been allocated and managed in the U.S.)

Are such activities on the part of governments justified? Are they in the best interests of the society as a whole? There is no easy answer because the economic effects of government action can be a double edged sword.

Institutions, Business Activity and Development

Institutions and Business Activity

One of the most important contributions of the "new" institutional economists has been to show that opportunities for individual entrepreneurs as well as the level of economic growth are dependent on the development of institutions, and not just on technological advance. With the right set of institutions transaction costs are lowered, markets become more efficient, and opportunities open.

Institutions play such an important role in business success that industries in the industrialized world lobby intensively at all levels of government to create rules and regulations in their favor.

When the government cannot or will not provide such benefits, businesses will often provide them for themselves. Simis, for example, describes the operation of illegal firms in the Soviet Union and the kinds of rules and procedures these entrepreneurs generated to settle disputes and sell property in a society where such activities were illegal (Simis 1982, 153). In this regard, Abner Cohen gives a marvelous description of the strategies the Hausa migrants of Ibadan Nigeria used to get their own quarter and chief, which were essential if they were to control the cattle and kola trade (Cohen 1969, 71-140).

Does this mean that institutions created by governments and industries are always efficient and lead to growth and opportunities? The answer is clearly no.

In developed countries such as the United States, collusion between industry and government often results in a complicated set of protective tariffs, subsidies, tax incentives, side payments, etc. that are largely designed to protect industries from the full vicissitudes of competition or pass part of the costs of doing business onto someone else--usually the tax payer. The British have become especially adept at subsidizing outmoded, inefficient industries, and in the process, tying up large amounts of capital that could be used to more productive purposes. The massive inefficiencies found in the "old" Soviet Union and Eastern Europe in general have given those countries a standard of living that has not been seen in the West since the great depression of the 1930's if even then.

The situation in the Third World is worse by far. Property rights are insecure, markets are inefficient, officials are corrupt, and powerful oligarchies influence the "Government" with their own benefit in mind. The result can be a set of rules that are so restrictive, unfair and burdensome that ordinary business people are poorly served. Hernando De Soto (1989, 131-187) does a particularly effective job in describing the bureaucratic thicket, and institutional inefficiencies that raise transactions costs to very high levels in Peru. The result is a flourishing "informal economy." Smith (1990) has particularly good coverage of this topic.

A number of forces work to help generate inefficient institutions. North has reminded us that rules are "devised by those with the bargaining power to devise new rules" (1990, 9). It is only to be expected that some very selfish motives will dominate periodically. The agents of the state sometimes make decisions with their own interests in mind rather than the best interests of the public (North 1990, 159). In many Third World countries, corrupt officials are the rule, not the exception. Wade has pointed out that managers often need to be managed (1982; 1987). Finally, the interests of powerful constituencies will come to dominate those of weaker, poorer groups. Olson (1982) argues that special interest groups, which he calls "distributional coalitions," will tend to "rigidify" economies after a time. The result is usually stagnation.

Institutions and Development

Douglass North, an economic historian, and his followers argue quite convincingly that the process of economic development involves replacing inefficient institutions with institutions that promote growth. North himself has done a good deal of work on the development of the institutions of capitalism in Europe and the United States during the past 700 years (1981; 1990, 6). North and his collaborators have carefully traced the development of governments in Western Europe, which they see as strongly connected with the establishment and enforcement of property rights, weights, measures, legal institutions, banking institutions, and capital markets. All of these can affect transaction costs, which affect business activity and the possibility for economic development (North 1981; 1984; 1990, 33, 52-53, 64, 96, 121, 114).

On the whole, institutions that reduce transaction costs are characteristic of advanced societies in the industrialized West and Japan; inefficient institutions are characteristic of the Third World. According to North:

> In consequence institutions were--and are--always a mixed bag of those that induce productivity increase and those that reduce productivity..... But on

balance nineteenth-century U.S. economic history is a story of economic growth because the underlying institutional framework persistently reinforced incentives for organizations to engage in productive activity however admixed with some adverse consequences.

Now if I describe an institutional framework with a reverse set of incentives to those described in the above paragraph, I will approximate the conditions in many Third World countries today as well as those that have characterized much of the world's economic history. The opportunities for political and economic entrepreneurs are still a mixed bag, but they overwhelmingly favor activities that promote redistributive rather than productive activity, that create monopolies rather than competitive conditions, and that restrict opportunities rather than expand them. They seldom induce investment in education that increases productivity (North 1990, 9).

While all "new" institutional economists would argue that development involves the development of institutions that lower transaction costs, there is no agreement on the mechanism by which such institutions come about. Williamson (1985, 404) and Nelson and Winter (1982, 308-322) believe that competition forces out of existence relatively inefficient institutions and firms. Thus the process of evolution is one in which institutions achieve higher levels of efficiency.

North on the other hand believes that evolution does not always favor efficiency. The reason is that "Organizations will be designed to further the objectives of their creators" (1990, 73), and in many cases, inefficiency serves their interests better. We need only think of the opposition engendered by attempts to change featherbedding rules, protective tariffs, and oligopolies to understand his point. North asserts that the primary force behind the evolution of institutions are "increasing returns and imperfect markets characterized by significant transaction costs" (1990, 95). These factors can cause changes in prices for various goods and services, which in turn affect long run choices of individuals and ultimately the institutions. If more efficient institutions result from this process, it is only by accident.

"New" Institutional Economics and Rural Societies

While most of the work in institutional economics has been in the industrial sectors of modern, western societies, a few political scientists, economists and anthropologists have applied these concepts to societies in Third World and rural areas of industrialized nations. While there are not a large number of such studies, they are of obvious interest to anthropologists.

Political scientist Robert Bates has perhaps done more than anyone else to apply the concepts of the "new" institutional economics in a Third World setting. Bates is particularly interested in the role of central governments of Africa in promoting agrarian development and industrialization (1976, 1981, 1989), and the response of the people of tribal societies to these efforts, i.e. cash cropping, migration, and rural protest (1976; 1989, 11-44). He points out that these development efforts have not relied on the generation of efficient markets as much as the development of non-market institutions. In this regard, he writes: "And where one might expect decentralized trading in open markets, one often finds bureaucracies instead" (1989, 73). Bates describes in some detail the marketing boards, development authorities, centrally organized cooperatives, and gigantic, vertically integrated, government sponsored firms, which funnel capital to rural areas, control prices, and market whole crops (Bates 1981, 11-44; 1989, Chap 3).

Jean Ensminger, an anthropologist, has used concepts from the "new" institutional economics to describe the changes in institutions that have occurred among the Orma, a pastoral society in Kenya. She has analyzed the development of private property rights (1991); and the shift in authority from local communities to the state (1990). Her new book *Making a Market* (1992) analyzes the development of a number of institutions among the Orma, including markets, patron-client ties, property; and it includes a section on the role of ideology in institutional change.

A number of anthropologists have used the "new" institutional economics to explain the operation of markets--especially markets for agricultural products and fish. Several have focused on relational markets and the ways in which social ties between buyer and seller reduces risk and uncertainty (Acheson 1985; Finan 1988; Plattner 1989). Still other anthropologists are concerned with the costs of obtaining information in peasant markets and the ways in which prices are established in these markets with high transaction costs (Alexander and Alexander 1991; Cashdan 1990).

Other social scientists have used the concepts of Coase and Williamson to understand the workings of firms and markets in Third World countries. Hamilton and Biggart (1988) have applied them to the organization of firms in Japan, Taiwan and other countries of the Far East. Acheson (1982) uses a transaction cost analysis to explain the size and degree of specialization of small family firms in a Mexican *pueblo*, while Sacks (1983) uses the same set of ideas to analyze Yugoslav self managed productive units. He concludes there are many similarities between capitalist firms and socialist productive units. Bailey (1991) is interested in the transaction costs encountered within formal organizations of all kinds where information is asymmetrical. A small number of social scientists have applied these ideas to problems of economic development (see Nabli and Nugent 1989).

However, the most important concepts anthropologists have borrowed from the "new" institutional economics are those concerning common property resources. There are literally dozens of articles and several books assessing the effects of property rights on exploitation of resources (see, for example: Acheson 1989; Anderson and Simmons 1993; Bromley 1992; Berkes 1989; McCay and Acheson 1987).

Perhaps the most seminal work has been done by Mary Douglas (1992), who brings together a knowledge of both anthropology and the work of Williamson to make a general contribution to the theory of organizations.

Criticisms of Institutional Economics

Economists and other social scientists have reacted strongly to the work of the institutional economists. Marglin (1974, 65ff.) argues that firms are best explained in terms of power rather than efficiency, while Ullman Margalit (1978, 285-6) shows that inefficient structures do occur. Obsershall and Leifer echo this theme, and criticize the tendency to view institutions "as if they were designed by an efficiency expert." They also assert that the institutional economists have ignored power and how "variance of benefits and costs" will differ across participants (1986, 245).

These criticisms are unfair and do not recognize the variations in opinion among the institutional economists themselves. Certainly institutional economists of all varieties recognize the role of power in economic life. The "old" institutional economists recognized that the damaging aspects of laissez faire capitalism could only be alleviated by regulation by the state. Some "new" institutional economists such as North are fully cognizant that the activities of the state in behalf of one or another constituency group can affect economic behavior and distribution of income (North 1984; 1990, 35, 109-112), while Williamson has analyzed the effects of power and governance relationships on various kinds of transactions (1985, 79-79).

There is, however, a difference of opinion about the role of efficiency in generating institutions. Some institutional economists such as Demsetz (1967) do argue that institutions come into being when their benefits outweigh their costs. However, analysts such as North argue strongly that inefficient institutions exist and can even be preferred by various powerful constituent groups. Some "new" institutional economists react with outrage to the idea that they believe that all institutions evolve to increase efficiency, since this assertion suggests that any existing institution is efficient (Eggertson 1993, 10).

Other criticisms by economists need to be taken more seriously. Virtually all of the work of Coase and Williamson and their followers has been in industrialized countries of the West. Their work has not been applied systematically to firms in Third World countries, but some analysts report that their ideas are not very predictive when applied to the organization of industry in the developing world (Acheson 1982, 1984; Hamilton and Biggart 1988, S65-S69). That is, firms are not responding as Coase and Williamson would predict.

Moreover, there is no well developed technique for measuring transaction costs. In addition, "the costs of transacting are not logically distinguishable from other costs" (Milgrom and Roberts 1992, 50). If anthropologists and others are really to use the concept to test hypotheses and describe phenomena on the ground, the concept of transaction costs needs to be operationalized.

Some of the criticisms that have been levelled at the institutional economists by anthropologists and sociologists are even more basic. First, the "new" institutional economists tend to assume that people are free to make rational choices to attain their goals, and are limited only by the problems of obtaining information. Most sociologists and anthropologists would see this as naive. Granovetter points out that the institutional economists assume that actors are "under socialized" and thus are minimally inhibited by cultural and social considerations; in reality, economic relationships are "embedded" in a social matrix, and cannot be understood apart from those relationships (1985, 502-505; 1992, 21-22).

Mary Douglas echos this theme by pointing out that the "new" institutional economics lacks a cultural component. The choices of individuals are strongly influenced by the value system; and the cognitive process by which individuals evaluate decisions has a "social basis" (1986, 11). In speaking of opportunism, she says:

> First, we should observe that opportunism is rarely unlimited. Nor is the boundedness of rationality random. The zone of indifference is not entirely a private matter. What one can safely ignore is largely contained within a boundary etched by a collective process. Regarding opportunism, what counts as responsible initiative is culturally defined. What looks to the outsider like resort to low cunning, lying, stealing, and cheating may be highly prescribed. Moral attributes are really irrelevant (1992, 199).

But how free are humans to make choices? There appears to be no consensus at present. Some social scientists, such as Bourdieu, would argue that the strictures of learned and shared behavior are so tight as to preclude many choices altogether (Bourdieu 1977, 72). For Bourdieu, "rational choice" is highly constrained by habitus. Others take a more intermediate position and argue that humans have some areas where they can make decisions. Well socialized people may be free to select between multiple goals. There are often a variety of conflicting norms which one may select to obey (Obershall and Leiffer 1986, 249). The capacity of the human mind to absorb and process information has not been established, and it has not been determined how many of its operations are overshadowed or determined by social processes. The solution to these problems has considerable import for our understanding of the nature of rationality itself.

Second, Hunt (1993) has pointed out that "new" institutional economists do not distinguish between organizations, rules, statuses and institutions. Eggertsson (1993, 1) would agree. The term "institutions" is used by the "new" institutional economists to refer to formal laws, informal norms, and the congregations of people organized in accordance with these "rules."[3] The distinction between institutions and organizations is critical as Firth (1964, 35) pointed out. People may be able to rationally plan a new organization to accomplish a certain goal in a short time. However, there is general consensus that the process of developing norms and institutions takes decades or even centuries; and this process is not under the rational control of any person or group.

Last, a central concern of institutional economics is the conditions under which people will cooperate in the formation of rules and cooperative groups, and organizations of various sorts (North 1990, 36-43). The institutional economists have had most success explaining the selection of organizational forms when "private goods" are involved and no "free riders" exist. They have had less success in explaining the formation of "public goods" of all types. They do not, in short, have a good answer to the question raised by Margolis (1982)--namely when do individuals allocate time and resources toward their own selfish ends and when to they allocate those resources toward group functions and the development of public goods?

Humans clearly do devote much time and effort to collective activities such as charities, political parties, and efforts to secure collective goods for their community, profession, or other secondary groups--even when they might be "free riders." Such activities appear irrational given the state of economic theory and the assumptions under which the "new" institutional economists work. Several economists and others have pointed out that if economic theory is to be able to account for such behavior, a broader and more accurate understanding of the factors giving people a sense of well being needs to be developed. In short, we need a new "utility function," and the recognition that people's goals can vary considerably from culture to culture, and even within the same culture. The utility function in use now assumes that people "rationally" select between items such as goods, services, and other priced items. This model of human goals and behavior, often labelled "economic man," has justifiably come under a good deal of criticism--particularly from non-economists. Economist A. K. Sen phrases the problem brutally when he wrote "The purely economic man is indeed close to being a social moron" (1977).

Why do people cooperate and sacrifice for the "common good" when it would be rational to be a "free rider"? North's answer is that ideology needs to be taken into account. Ideology, he says, has the capacity to "energize groups to behave contrary to a simple, hedonistic, individual calculus of costs and benefits" (1981, 53). This would seem to take the "new" institutional economics into waters first charted by political scientists and anthropologists who have long understood the importance of ideology in forming identity, building political followings, and manipulating groups (Bailey 1983, 1988; Geertz 1964; Higgs 1987, 35-56).

New Lines of Inquiry

Despite these problems, the "new" institutional economics is enormously stimulating. It has resulted in a number of insights and hypotheses which open some new research areas for economic anthropology.

The "new" institutional economics provides a basic change in orientation from the one provided by the neo-classical school of economics. The "new" institutional economists presuppose: bounded rationality, a lack of perfect knowledge, heterogenous goods and services, and costs associated with market and non-market transactions. Anthropologists see these assumptions as more realistic than those of neo-classical economics. The field is moving so fast in so many directions that its contributions are difficult to assess. But there is no question that it provides a new way of looking at the relationships between economic and non-economic phenomena. It posits relationships between such diverse phenomena as individual decisions, costs of obtaining information, market failure, and the generation of institutions. From my perspective there are a number of basic insights that, I believe, will prove to be fruitful for anthropologists:

1. The problem of obtaining information is central to transactions of all kinds.
2. Institutions are substitutes for a lack of information and are designed to lower risk and uncertainty for their creators.
3. In a world of zero transaction costs, there would be no need for institutions. In the real world, transaction costs and externalities are ever present, which results in rules and institutions to be generated.
4. Entrepreneurs can obtain needed goods and services though market and non-market institutions, such as hierarchies. Which is selected depends on the transaction costs involved, which in turn varies with opportunism and asset specificity.
5. Market failure results in services being provided by the government or by cooperative effort on the local level.
6. Efficient markets depend on secure property rights; the relative security of property rights depends on the ways those rights are allocated and enforced by a governance body.
7. Changes in institutions occur as an evolutionary response to changes in prices which are the result of alterations in the cultural, technical and ecological aspects of the environment.
8. Opportunities for economic actors and ultimately the level of economic performance are determined by efficient institutions in addition to capital, entrepreneurship, and technology.
9. Inefficient institutions are sometimes selected due to self serving activities of agents of the government or special interest groups.

This list suggests a number of interesting questions and areas of inquiry for anthropologists. Five have caught my attention:

1. To what extent can the development of firms and non-market institutions in the Third World be accounted for in terms of market inefficiency and market failure? Does the degree of vertical integration and dependence of firms on markets vary with transaction costs? Does market failure cause the development of "non-market" organizations to provide public goods?
2. How do various societies allocate and enforce property rights? How do these various bundles of property rights influence market efficiency, externalities, and economic choices?
3. What is the effect of the actions of governments on transaction costs and thus opportunities for economic actors at the local level?

4. How and why are inefficient institutions generated in Third World countries? What is the role of agents of the government and other pressure groups in this process?
5. To what extent can long term institutional change be accounted for in terms of a changing environment which produces changes in increasing returns and inefficient markets?

Developments in the Other Social Sciences

Over the past forty years, a number of social scientists who have been working outside the field of institutional economics have dealt with the problem of individual choice and the emergence of rules and institutions. Much of this literature is summarized under the rubric of "rational choice" theory, since it is assumed that institutions are created by individuals who are making maximizing choices to obtain scarce ends by selecting between alternative means.

Exchange theory and other forms of the theory of riskless choice explore the maximizing decisions of individuals operating within fixed parameters; game theory introduces the element of risk which occurs when two or more players are engaged against each other (Heath 1976a, 11-28).

Norms are created, according to the "rational choice" theorists, because they allow individuals to achieve more optimal results than they would have by pursuing their own self interest independently. Thibaut and Kelly argue that norms reduce the costs of transacting by introducing "regularity into the relationship" (Heath 1976a, 68). Homans argues that norms allow people to achieve better results than they would otherwise (Homans 1961, 381-82). Blau (1964, 258) makes the same point through the use of his now famous prisoner's dilemma. His point is that rational behavior in the absence of norms produces poor results for a collectivity. A variation on this theme is found in the literature on the common property problem. In the absence of rules, each villager is motivated to over exploit a pasture held in common. The invention of the institution of private property changes the incentives of individuals and, according to the theory, produces better results for the society as a whole (McCay and Acheson 1987, 2-10.).

Recently there has been an explosion of interest in rational choice theory, which has shed light on a number of persistent problems in the social sciences (Hechter et. al. 1990). The exciting advances being made in this field are thus far unencumbered by questions or contributions from anthropologists. Political scientists Elinor and Vincent Ostrom and their students have explored the circumstances impelling groups to generate rules to manage natural resources.

Much of their work involves "self-governing irrigation systems" (Ostrom 1992; Tang 1992), and draws heavily on the concepts of institutional economics and particularly Olsen's concept of "public goods."

A number of anthropologists in the 1960's and 1970's have written on various aspects of individual action and the generation of institutions. F.G. Bailey (1969; 1977), Raymond Firth (1964), J. Clyde Mitchell (1973) and Jeremy Boissevain (1974) are certainly in this group. As Jean Ensminger (1992, 9-12) points out, the most notable is Fredrik Barth, whose ideas on the relationships between individual transactions and the generation of institutions exhibit considerable overlap with those of the institutional economists.

Barth and the "new" institutional economists can be called "methodological individualists" (Hodgson 1988, 56ff.; Winter 1993, 181-2). Like Williamson and Coase, Barth sees entrepreneurs as making strategic choices to attain culturally determined goals within the confines of the culture (Barth 1966, 1; Heath 1976b). Barth states that there are two essential processes in human relationships, "transaction" and "incorporation" (Barth 1981: 85), which are analogous to Williamson's "market" and "hierarchy." Like North, Barth sees differences in prices as being the engine of change in that they present entrepreneurs with opportunities for innovative action (Barth 1981, 56).

Unfortunately, in the late 1970s anthropological interest in transactional analysis and institutions waned. Anthropologists never did answer the questions posed by Barth, Bailey, Firth, Mitchell et. al. Economists and political scientists pushed forward our understanding of the relationships between individual action and institutions, while anthropologists focused on the problem of deciphering culture through symbolic analysis, hermeneutics, and post modern approaches.

One objective of this book is to introduce economic anthropologists to the central ideas of institutional economics and begin assessing the extent to which that body of theory can be applied to tribal and peasant societies and economies. With fortune, it will rekindle an interest in the issues that Fredrik Barth and Raymond Firth began to address over three decades ago: the relationships between individual choices, institutions and economic performance.

References

Acheson, James M. 1982. Limitations on Firm Size in a Tarascan Pueblo. *Human Organization* 41(4): 323-329.

———.1985.The Maine Lobster Market: Between Market and Hierarchy. *Journal of Law, Economics, and Organization* 1(2):385-397.

———.1986. Constraints on Entrepreneurship: Transactions Costs and Market Efficiency. In Sidney Greenfield and Arnold Strikon, eds., *Entrepreneurship and Social Change*. Monographs in Economic Anthropology No.2. Lanham, Md.: University Press of America.

———.1989. Management of Common Property Resources. In Stuart Plattner, ed., *Economic Anthropology*. Stanford: Stanford University Press.

———.1993. Capturing the Commons: Legal and Illegal Strategies. In Terry L. Anderson and Randy T. Simmons, eds., *The Political Economy of Customs and Culture: Informal Solutions to the Commons Problem.* Lanham, Md.: Rowman and Littlefield.

Ackerloff, George. 1970. The Market for Lemons: Quality, Uncertainty and the Market Mechanism. *Quarterly Journal of Economics* 84: 488-500.

Alexander, Jennifer and Paul Alexander. 1991. What's a Fair Price?: Price-Setting and Trading Partnerships in Javanese Markets. *Man* 26: 493-512.

Anderson, Terry and Randy Simmons. 1993. *The Political Economy of Customs and Culture: Informal Solutions to the Commons Problem.* Lanham, Md.: Rowman and Littlefield.

Axelrod, Robert. 1984. *The Evolution of Cooperation.* New York: Basic Books.

Bailey, Frederick. 1969. *Stratagems and Spoils: A Social Anthropology of Politics*. New York: Schocken.

———.1983. *The Tactical Uses of Passion: An Essay on Power, Reason and Reality*. Ithaca: Cornell University Press.

———.1988. *Humbuggery and Manipulation: The Art of Leadership.* Ithaca: Cornell University Press.

———.1991. Why is Information Asymmetrical? Symbolic Behavior in Formal Organizations. *Rationality and Society* 3(4): 475-95.

Barth, Fredrik. 1963. *The Role of the Entrepreneur in Social Change in Northern Norway.* Bergen: Norwegian Universities Press.

———.1966. *Models of Social Organization. Occasional Papers No. 23* London: Royal Anthropological Institute.

———.1981. *Process and Form in Social Life: Selected Essays of Fredrik Barth, Vol 1.* London: Routledge & Kegan Paul.

Bates, Robert. 1976. *Rural Responses to Industrialization: A Study of Village Zambia.* New Haven: Yale University Press.

———.1981. *Markets and States in Tropical Africa: The Political Basis of Agricultural Policies.* Berkeley: University of California Press.

———.1983. *Essays on the Political Economy of Rural Africa.* Cambridge: Cambridge University Press.

———.1989. *Beyond the Miracle of the Market: The Political Economy of Agrarian Development in Rural Kenya.* Cambridge: Cambridge University Press.

Becker, Gary. 1981. *A Treatise on the Family.* Cambridge: Harvard University Press.

Berkes, Fikret. 1989. *Common Property Resources: Ecology and Community-based Development.* London: Belhaven Press.

Berkes, Fikret and Mina Kislagioglu. 1992. Community Management and Sustainable Development. In J.R. Durand, J. Lemoalle, and J. Weber, eds., La Recherche Face a la Peche Artisanale. *Symposium International.* Paris: ORSTROM-IFREMER.

Bestor, Theodore. Forthcoming. *Tokyo's Marketplace: Culture and Trade in the Tsukiji Wholesale Fish Market*. Stanford: Stanford University Press.

Blau, Peter M. 1964. *Exchange and Power in Social Life*. New York: Wiley.

Bohannan, Paul. 1955. Some Principles of Exchange and Investment Among the Tiv. *American Anthropologist* 57: 60-70.

Boissevain, Jeremy. 1974. *Friends of Friends: Networks, Manipulators and Coalitions*. Oxford: Blackwell.

Bourdieu, Pierre. 1977. *Outline of a Theory of Practice*. Cambridge: Cambridge University Press.

Bromley, Daniel. 1989. *Economic Interests and Institutions*. New York: Basil Blackwell.

———.1992. *Making the Commons Work: Theory, Practice and Policy*. San Francisco: ICS Press.

Buchanan, James. 1965. An Economic Theory of Clubs. *Economica* 32:1-13.

Cashdan, Elizabeth. 1990. Information Costs and Customary Prices. In Elizabeth Cashdan, ed., *Risk and Uncertainty in Tribal and Peasant Economies*. Boulder: Westview Press.

Cheung, Steven. 1970. The Structure of a Contract and the Theory of a Non-Exclusive Resource. *Journal of Law and Economics* 13(1):45-70.

Coase, Ronald. 1937. The Nature of the Firm. *Economica* 4(3):386-404. Reprinted in Oliver E. Williamson and Sidney G. Winter, eds., *The Nature of the Firm: Origins, Evolution and Development*. New York: Oxford. (1993) pp. 18-33.

———.1960. The Problem of Social Costs. *Journal of Law and Economics* 3(1): 1-44.

———.1984. The New Institutional Economics. *Journal of Institutional and Theoretical Economics* 140: 229-31.

———.1993a. The Nature of the Firm: Meaning. In Oliver E. Williamson and Sidney G. Winter, eds., *The Nature of the Firm: Origins, Evolution and Development*. New York: Oxford.

———.1993b. The Nature of the Firm: Influence. In Oliver E. Williamson and Sidney G. Winte, eds., *The Nature of the Firm: Origins, Evolution and Development*. New York: Oxford.

Cohen, Abner. 1969. *Custom and Conflict in Urban Africa*. Berkeley: University of California Press.

Commons, John R. 1932. *Legal Foundations of Capitalism*. New York: MacMillan.

———.1934. *Institutional Economics*. New York: MacMillan.

Dahlman, Carl. 1979. The Problem of Externality. *Journal of Law and Economics* 22: 141-62.

Demsetz, Harold. 1967. Toward a Theory of Property Rights. *American Economic Review* 57:347-59.

De Soto, Hernando. 1989. *The Other Path: The Invisible Revolution in the Third World*. New York: Harper and Row.

Dewey, Alice. 1962. *Peasant Marketing in Java*. Glencoe Illinois: Free Press.

Douglas, Mary. 1986. *How Institutions Think*. Syracuse: Syracuse University Press.

———.1992. Autonomy and Opportunism. In *Risk and Blame: Essays in Cultural Theory*. London: Routledge.

Dusenberry, J.S. 1960. Comments on "An Economic Analysis of Fertility", by Gary S. Becker. In *Demography and Economic Change in Developed Countries*. Princeton: Universities National Bureau Committee for Economic Research.

Eggertsson, Thrainn. 1993. Economic Perspectives on Property Rights and the Economics of Institutions. Paper given at the Beijer International Institute of Ecological Economics. The Royal Swedish Academy of Sciences. Stockholm, Sweden.

Ensminger, Jean. 1990. Co-opting the Elders: The Political Economy of State Incorporation in Africa. *American Anthropologist* 92(3): 662-75.

———.1992. *Making a Market: The Institutional Transformation of an African Society*. Cambridge: Cambridge University Press.

Ensminger, Jean and Andrew Rutten. 1991. The Political Economy of Changing Property Rights: Dismantling a Pastoral Commons. *American Ethnologist* 18(4): 683-99.

Firth, Raymond. 1964. Social Organization and Social Change. In Raymond Firth, ed., *Essays on Social Organization and Values.* London: Althone.

Finan, Timothy. 1988. Market Relationship and Market Performance in Northeast Brazil. *American Ethnologist* 15(4): 694-709.

Geertz, Clifford. 1978. The Bazaar Economy: Information and Search in Peasant Marketing. *American Economic Review* 68: 28-32.

Goldberg, Victor P. 1981. Bridges over Contested Terrain: Exploring the Radical Account of the Employment Relationship. In Gunter Dlugos and Klaus Weiermair, eds., *Management Under Differing Value Systems: Political, Social and Economic Perspectives in a Changing World.* New York: De Gruter.

———.1989. *Readings in the Economics of Contract Law.* Cambridge: Cambridge University Press.

Granovetter, Mark. 1985. Economic Action and Social Structure: a Theory of Embeddedness. *American Journal of Sociology* 91(3): 481-510.

———.1992. The Nature of Economic Relations. In Sutti Ortiz and Susan Lees, eds., *Understanding Economic Process.* Monographs in Economic Anthropology, No. 10. Lanham, Md.: University Press of America.

Hamilton, Gary G. and Nicole W. Biggart. 1988. Market, Culture and Authority: A Comparative Analysis of Management and Organization in the Far East. In Christopher Winship and Sherwin Rosen, eds., Organizations and Institutions: Sociological and Economic Approaches to the Analysis of Social Structure. *American Journal of Sociology* vol. 94: S52-S93. Supplement.

Hardin, Garrett. 1968. The Tragedy of the Commons. *Science* 162: 1243-8.

Hardin, Garrett and John Baden. 1977. *Managing the Commons*. San Francisco: W.H. Freeman.

Harter, Lafayette. 1962. *John R. Commons: His Assault on Laissez faire.* Corvallis: Oregon State University

Hart, Oliver. 1990. An Economist's Perspective on the Theory of the Firm. In Oliver Williamson, ed., *Organization Theory: From Chester Barnard to the Present and Beyond.* Oxford: Oxford University Press.

Heath, Anthony. 1976a. *Rational Choice and Social Exchange.* Cambridge: Cambridge University Press.

———.1976b. Decision Making and Transactional Theory. In Bruce Kapferer, ed., *Transaction on Meaning: Directions in the Anthropology of Exchange and Symbolic Behavior*. Philadelphia: Institute for the Study of Human Issues.

Hechter, M, K. Opp and R. Wippler. 1990. *Social Institutions*. Hawthorn N.Y.: Aldine de Gruyer.

Higgs, Robert. 1987. *Crisis and Leviathan: Critical Episodes in the Growth of American Government*. Oxford: Oxford University Press.

Hodgson, Geoffrey. 1988. *Economics and Institutions: A Manifesto for a Modern Institutional Economics*. Philadelphia: University of Pennsylvania Press.

Homans, George C. 1961. *Social Behavior: Its Elementary Forms*. London: Routledge and Kegan Paul.

Hunt, Robert. 1993. Personal Communication.

Jenkins, Richard. 1992. *Pierre Bourdieu*. New York: Routledge.

Kapferer, Bruce. 1976. Transactional Models Reconsidered. In Bruce Kapferer, ed., *Transaction and Meaning: Directions in the Anthropology of Exchange and Symbolic Behavior*. Philadelphia: Institute for the Study of Human Issues.

Koford, Kenneth J. and Jeffrey B. Miller. 1991. Habits, Customs and Norms in Economics. In, Kenneth Koford and Jeffrey B. Miller, eds., *Social Norms and Economic Institutions*. Ann Arbor: University of Michigan Press.

Langlois, Richard N. 1986. *Economics as a Process: Essays in the New Institutional Economics*. Cambridge: Cambridge University Press.

Leach, Jerry W. and Edmund Leach. 1983. *The Kula: New Perspectives on Massim Exchange*. Cambridge: Cambridge University Press.

Lerner, Max. 1948. *The Portable Veblen*. New York: Viking.

Libecap, Gary. 1989. *Contracting for Property Rights*. Cambridge: Cambridge University Press.

Littlechild, Stephen. 1986. Three Types of Market Process. In Richard N. Langlois, ed., *Economics as a Process: Essays in the New Institutional Economics*. Cambridge: Cambridge University Press.

Loasby, Brian J. 1986. Organization, Competition and the Growth of Knowledge. In Richard N. Langlois, ed., *Economics as a Process: Essays in the New Institutional Economics*. Cambridge: Cambridge University Press.

Lomnitz, Larissa and Marisol Perez-Lizaur. 1987. *A Mexican Elite Family: 1820-1980: Kinship, Class and Culture*. Princeton: Princeton University Press.

MacKaay, Ejan. 1982. *Economics of Information and Law.* The Hague: Kluwer-Nijhoff.

Macneil, Ian. 1978. Contracts: Adjustments of Long-term Economic Relations Under Classical, Neoclassical and Relational Contract Law. *Northwestern University Law Review* 72: 854-97.

Marglin, S.A. 1974. What Do Bosses Do?: The Origins and Functions of Hierarchy in Capitalist Production. *Review of Radical Political Economics* 6(2): 60-112.

Margolis, Howard. 1982. *Selfishness, Altruism, and Rationality: A Theory of Social Choice.* Cambridge: Cambridge University Press.

Masden, Scott. 1993. A Legal Basis for the Firm. In Oliver Williamson and Sidney Winter, eds., *The Nature of the Firm: Origins, Evolution and Development.* Oxford: Oxford University Press.

McCay, Bonnie J. and James Acheson. 1987. *The Question of the Commons: The Culture and Ecology of Communal Resources.* Tucson: University of Arizona Press.

Milgrom, Paul and John Roberts. 1992. *Economics, Organization and Management.* Englewood Cliffs: Prentice-Hall.

Mintz, Sidney. 1964. The Employment of Capital by Market Women in Haiti. In Raymond Firth and B.S. Yamey, eds., *Capital, Savings, and Credit in Peasant Societies.* Chicago: Aldine.

Mitchell, J. Clyde. 1973. Networks, Norms and Institutions. In *Network Analysis: Studies in Human Interaction.* The Hague: Mouton.

Mitchell, Wesley. 1947. *What Veblen Taught.* New York: The Viking Press.

Nabli, Mustapha and Jeffrey Nugent. 1989. *The New Institutional Economics and Development.* Amsterdam: North-Holland.

Nelson, Richard. 1986. The Tension Between Process Stories and Equilibrium Models: Analyzing the Productivity-Growth Slowdown of the 1970's. In

Richard N. Langlois, ed., *Economics as a Process: Essays in the New Institutional Economics*. Cambridge: Cambridge University Press.

Nelson, Richard R. and Sidney G. Winter. 1982. *An Evolutionary Theory of Economic Change*. Cambridge: Harvard University Press.

North, Douglass. 1981. *Structure and Change in Economic History*. New York: Norton.

———.1983. A Theory of Economic Change. *Science* 219: 163-4.

———.1984. Government and the Cost of Exchange. *Journal of Economic History* 44, 225-64.

———.1990. *Institutions, Institutional Change and Economic Performance*. New York: Cambridge University Press.

North, Douglass, and Robert P. Thomas. 1973. *The Rise of Western World: A New Economic History*. Cambridge: Cambridge University Press.

Obershall, Anthony and Eric M. Leifer. 1986. Efficiency and Social Institutions: Uses and Misuses of Economic Reasoning in Sociology. *Annual Review of Sociology* 12: 233-253.

Olson, Mancur. 1965. *The Logic of Collective Action*. Cambridge: Cambridge University Press.

———.1982. *The Rise and Decline of Nations*. New Haven: Yale University Press.

Ortner, Sherry B. 1984. Theory in Anthropology Since the Sixties. *Comparative Studies in Society and History* 26(1): 126-166.

Ostrom, Elinor. 1990. *Governing the Commons: The Evolution of Institutions for Collective Action*. Cambridge: Cambridge University Press.

———.1992. *Crafting Institutions for Self-Governing Irrigation Systems*. San Francisco: ICS Press.

Ouchi, William. 1980. Markets, Bureaucracies and Clans. *Administrative Science Quarterly* 25: 129-141.

Perlman, Selig. 1950. John Rogers Commons. *Preface to the Economics of Collective Action by John R. Commons*. New York: MacMillan.

Pinkerton, Evelyn. 1989. *Co-operative Management of Local Fisheries: New Directions for Improving Management and Community Development.* Vancouver: University of British Columbia Press.

Plattner, Stuart. 1983. Economic Custom in a Competitive Market Place. *American Anthropologist* 85: 848-58.

———.1989. Economic Behavior in Markets. In Stuart Plattner, ed., *Economic Anthropology*. Stanford: Stanford University Press.

Price, John. 1980. On Silent Trade. *Research in Economic Anthropology* 3:75-96.

Sacks, Stephen. 1983. *Self-Management and Efficiency*. London: George Allen and Unwin.

Sahlins, Marshall. 1965. On the Sociology of Primitive Exchange. In Michael Blanton, ed., *The Relevance of Models for Social Anthropology*. ASA Monograph 1. London: Tavistock.

Schotter, Andrew. 1981. *Economic Theory of Social Institutions*. Cambridge: Cambridge University Press.

———.1986. The Evolution of Rules. In Richard Langlois, ed., *Economics as a Process: Essays in the New Institutional Economics*. Cambridge: Cambridge University Press.

Scott, Anthony. 1955. The Fishery: Objectives of Sole Ownership. *Journal of Political Economy* 63: 116-34.

Sen, Amartya. 1977. Rational Fools: A Critique of the Behavioral Foundations of Economic Theory. *Philosophy and Public Affairs* 6:336.

Simis, Konstantin. 1982. *USSR: The Corrupt Society*. New York: Simon and Schuster.

Simon, Herbert A. 1961. *Administrative Behavior*. 2nd ed. New York: Macmillan.

Smith, Estellie. 1990. *Perspectives on the Informal Economy*. SEA Monograph in Economic Anthropology, No. 8. Lanham, Md.: University Press of America.

Spoehr, Alexander. 1980. *Protein from the Sea*. Ethnological Monograph No. 3. Department of Anthropology, University of Pittsburgh.

Szanton, Maria C. B. 1972. *A Right to Survive: Subsistence Marketing in a Lowland Phillippine Town*. University Park, PA: Pennsylvania State University Press.

Tang, Shui Yan. 1992. *Institutions and Collective Action: Self Governance in Irrigation*. San Francisco: ICS Press.

Wade, Robert. 1982. Corruption: Where Does the Money Go? *Economic and Political Weekly* 17(40): 1606.

———.1987. Managing the Managers: Deterring Expropriation or Equity as a Control Mechanism. In Wayne R. Jordan, ed., *Water and Water Policy in World Food Supplies*. College Station Texas: Texas A and M Press.

Wharton, Clifton R. Jr. 1971. Risk, Uncertainty and the Subsistence Farmer: Technological Innovation and Resistance to Change in the Context of Survival. In George Dalton, ed., *Studies in Economic Anthropology*. Washington D.C.: American Anthropological Association.

Whitten, Norman and Dorothea S. Whitten. 1972. Social Strategies and Social Relationships. *Annual Reviews of Anthropology* 1: 247-270.

Williamson, Oliver. 1975. *Markets and Hierarchies: Analysis and Antitrust Implications*. New York: The Free Press.

———.1981. The Economics of Organization: A Transactions Costs Approach. *American Journal of Sociology* 87:548-577.

———.1985. *The Economic Institutions of Capitalism*. New York: Free Press.

———.1986a. The Economics of Governance: Framework and Implications. In Richard N. Langlois, ed., *Economics as a Process: Essays in the New Institutional Economics*. Cambridge: Cambridge University Press.

———.1986b. *Economic Organization: Firms, Markets and Police Control.* New York: New York University Press.

Wilson, James A. 1980. Adaptation to Uncertainty and Small Numbers Exchange: The New England Fish Market. *Bell Journal of Economics* 11: 491-504.

Winter, Sidney G. 1993. On Coase, Competence and the Corporation. In Oliver Williamson and Sidney G. Winter, eds., *The Nature of the Firm: Origins, Evolution and Development*. New York: Oxford.

Notes

1. This is not to suggest there are no differences between markets and firms. Hart (1990) points out that firms are "nexes of property rights" and contracts; and Masden (1993) says that people in firms have very different legal obligations to each other than people exchanging in a market.

Markets involve different degrees of uncertainty and risk as well as different amounts of market power and types of transaction costs (Littlechild 1986, 27-39.) There are also a large number of different types of firms. There is a growing literature on the organization of large firms which can have a variety of organizational types and present unusual governance problems (Williamson 1986b, 32-80.) For example, firms may have centrally organized control structures or may be structured into multidivisional organizations whose units buy and sell to each other via transfer pricing (Milgrom and Roberts 1992, 79). Conglomerates have still different characteristics.

2. Dealing with other employees and units within a firm or organization can involve huge transaction costs. University faculty who have been involved in grievance proceedings or union bargaining know that months of time are involved in such efforts. Department chairs spend enormous amounts of time negotiating within the organization. Recently my department was charged $1814.56 to replace five thermostats in archeology

laboratories. The original thermostats were in good condition and no work order was signed for their replacement. To have this bill rescinded took two months of meetings and letters to the Dean, a Vice President, the President's office, and three functionaries of the maintenance department.

3. Not all institutional economists are equally guilty. North, for example, makes a clear distinction between "institutions," which he sees as rules guiding action, and "organizations," which are collectivities.

2

Social Dilemmas And Rational Individuals: An Essay On The New Institutionalism[1]

Robert H. Bates

The new institutionalism represents an attempt to build a coherent account of institutions from micro-foundations. It attempts to apply to non-market institutions the same form of reasoning that neo-classical economists have applied to the analysis of markets. This paper examines the origins of the new institutionalism, critiques it, and offers two alternatives--one labelled the new anthropology and the other derived from political science.

The Origins

Neo-classical economics seeks to explain collective outcomes in terms of the choices made by rational individuals. Radical individualism constitutes a defining premise for the field. It informs its methodology: market demand, for example, is built up from the choices of individuals who seek to maximize their utility, subject to the constraint of their budgets and in the face of market prices. It also provides its normative core: because Pareto optimality respects the inviolability of the individual's judgment of his or her own welfare, it constitutes the sole ethical criterion that wins broad support among neo-classical economists.

A Crisis of Embarrassment

Given the centrality of radical individualism, it has been profoundly embarrassing to modern economics that in its models market forces did not rest on the choices of individuals. On the side of demand, households made consumer choices; on the supply side, production decisions were made by firms. Neo-classical models analyzed the choices of these entities as if they were made by individuals. But not even Milton Friedman's (1953) spirited defense of "as if" explanations served to paper over the basic reality: that the social science most profoundly committed to radical individualism rested on "collective" foundations.

Despite its unconventional assumptions, Gary Becker's theory of the family therefore won rapid and widespread recognition as a major contribution to neo-classical economics (1981). The reason was obvious: it offered the possibility at last of resting the theory of demand upon the foundations of individual choice. Oliver Williamson (1985) also made notoriously idiosyncratic and unconventional assumptions; but his work, too, rapidly won recognition as a contribution to knowledge, for it too promoted the completion of the neo-classical program.[2] Through the work of Williamson and others, economists thus have begun to build up a theory of the firm, and thus of supply, from the rational choices of individuals.

Embarrassment may not be the mother of invention. But the fundamental embarrassment of neo-classical economics--that of having collectivities where individuals should be--does help to express why the "contributions" of Williamson, Coase and others so quickly became established within the discipline, despite what for mainstream economists were important limitations: their tendency to make unconventional assumptions and their lack of rigorous mathematical foundations.

A Crisis Arising from Triumph

A theoretical deficiency in the existing structure of economics thus provided one source for the new institutional economics. A theoretical triumph provided a second: the codification of the necessary and sufficient conditions for the existence of an equilibrium in a market economy.

The work of Arrow (1951), Debreu (1951) and others proved the conditions under which it would be feasible for prices in markets to shape the decisions of consumers and firms such that all consumers would maximize their utility and all firms would maximize their profits. As this allocation enables all agents simultaneously to maximize, it constitutes an equilibrium; no agent could make himself or herself better off by unilaterally varying his or her consumption or production decisions. In addition, the allocation would be efficient (i.e. Pareto optimal); under the conditions that generate market equilibrium, it would be impossible to improve the utility of any consumer or the profits of any firms without reducing the welfare of another. Insofar as Pareto optimality constitutes a defensible criterion of the social welfare, the Arrow/Debreu conditions thus render the choices of rational individuals consistent with the social welfare.

On the one hand, the proof of the fundamental theorem represented a triumph; it represented the culmination of the quest to substantiate Adam Smith's claims about the properties of markets. On the other hand, it posed a powerful challenge; with the proof of the theorem, market economics no longer was interesting. Economists were compelled to turn from the study of perfect markets to other subjects--ones whose core properties had not yet been formalized and whose characteristics had not been explored using economic reasoning. The study of the conduct of rational individuals under various forms of market failure quickly became a major branch of economic research, and the new institutional economics represents an outgrowth of this new research agenda.

In the sections that follow, I focus on a series of market failures and trace the arguments that attribute to each impetus for the creation of new institutions. This sketch highlights the central role played by social dilemmas. A social dilemma arises when radical individualism becomes inconsistent with the social welfare, i.e. when the choices made by rational individuals yield outcomes that are socially irrational (i.e. not Pareto optimal). Market failures yield social dilemmas. The core argument of the new institutionalism is that institutions provide the mechanisms whereby rational individuals can transcend social dilemmas. They enable individuals to escape the tensions between individual and social rationality created by the perverse incentives that produce the failure of markets.

Sources of the New Institutionalism

Market failures arise when the necessary or sufficient conditions for market equilibrium fail to hold. In the section that follows, we discuss several such "failures" and relate them to the creation of institutions other than markets, such as property rights, contracts, revolutionary parties, and labor movements.

Production Externalities

Production externalities constitute one source of market failure. An externality represents a direct, physical link between the production functions of two or more agents. The activities of one may impose costs on another; the impact of water use by an upstream agent upon the production possibilities of one living downstream furnishes an example. Alternatively, the activities of one agent could confer benefits upon another; firms that provide generalized training increase the productivity of the labor force for all other firms.

In the presence of production externalities, the private decisions of rationally maximizing agents will fail to promote socially rational outcomes; the outcomes will be inefficient. Firms will engage to too great an extent in the activities that generate negative externalities; they will undertake to too little an extent the activities that generate positive ones. There will be too much water use by upstream users and too little job training, in terms of the above examples.

As analyzed in the new institutional economics, the creation of property rights represents a response to the problem of external effects (see, for example, Barzel 1989, Libecap 1989, Ostrom 1990). The assignment of property rights enables markets to span the links created by the physical interdependence of production functions; it therefore promotes the operation of economic incentives, making it in the private interests of maximizing individuals to make socially appropriate production decisions.

When there are negative externalities, for example, the creation of property rights enables the agent incurring the damage to elicit compensation; the resultant economic costs to the producer of the externality provide an incentive for that agent to engage in less of the undesirable activity. In the case of positive externalities, when property rights exist, the beneficiary would have financially to reward the provider of external benefits; and those rewards would create an incentive for the latter to undertake more of the socially desirable activity. As a result of the creation of property rights, then, producers incur financial costs or reap financial benefits; the overlaying of market relationships on top of the physical relationships provides economic incentives for the agents to take into private account the external (or social) impact of their production decisions.[3]

Public Goods

Public goods constitute a second source of market failure. In the case of public goods, interdependence exists not between the production functions of firms but rather between the utility functions of individuals. A good is a public good, as opposed to a commodity, if its consumption by one individual does not diminish the utility derived from its consumption by another: the consumption of the good is non-rivalrous and its provision non-excludable.

Behaving as rational individuals, consumers do not take into private account the benefits that their choices create for others; they fail to take into account the social benefit of their decisions. The private choices of individuals create allocations of resources between private and public goods that are inefficient because, in the presence of public goods, individuals, behaving rationally, will free ride. Rather than incurring the costs of contributing to the creation of a public good, individuals might instead seek to exploit its "non-rivalrousness" and "non-excludability." They might seek to enjoy the benefits for free. When people behave this way, they fail to contribute to the costs of creating public goods. While they might place a high value on the public good, then, they might nonetheless fail to finance as much of it as they truly desire. The equilibrium generated by the private choices of rational individuals thus would be inefficient, given that all might feel better off were each to contribute more of their private wealth to the creation of greater amounts of the public good.

Practitioners of the new institutionalism see in the problem of public goods a reason behind non-market organization. Confronted with unrealized collective gains, they argue, rational individuals create institutions that make it in the private interests of individuals to make socially correct decisions. Political leaders, or political entrepreneurs,[4] create organizations that provide selective incentives, rewarding with private benefits those who contribute to the provision of public goods--and targeting with sanctions those who do not. Popkin, for example, analyzes the strategies of political insurgents who seek to organize peasants in an effort to secure the non-excludable rewards of successful revolution. Participation, he argues, is rewarded with the provision of such benefits as the provision of insurance for oneself and one's family against the risks of poor harvests; access to loans and credit; promotion to positions of greater prestige and higher rank; and protection against violence (Popkin 1979). These benefits can be given to the faithful and withheld from those who seek to free ride on the efforts of the cadres; and political leaders carefully orchestrate them in an effort to rally the peasantry to the revolutionary cause.

Mancur Olson underscores the role of "selective incentives" in collective action by workers (1965). Given the incentives to free ride--i.e. to act as strike breakers or scabs--it is difficult for workers to secure higher wages through collective bargaining; strikes will collapse and worker threats will therefore not be credible. But when organizers can successfully intimidate strike breakers, then they weaken the incentives to free ride; collective action can succeed; and they gain the power of collective bargaining. One conclusion is that it is a mistake to see in labor violence evidence of lack of support for workers' movements; given the incentives to free ride, even supporters of the labor movement might agree to allow themselves to be coerced by its leaders. A second conclusion is that in situations where decentralized decision making might fail, such as in the provision of public goods, then the purposive organization of such non-market phenomena as coercion might create mechanisms for rational individuals to make choices that enhance their collective welfare. Given such targettable incentives, people might elect, as a matter of their own self-interest, to make choices that lead to the provision of public goods: a world without landlords, in the case of peasants, or a world with higher wages, in the case of workers. The organization of incentives and constraints; the manipulation of bribes, and of violence--these forms of non-market behavior can correct for the failure of decentralized choices to supply collective goods.

Imperfect Information

Information constitutes a third source of market failure. The acquisition of information is costly; individuals might therefore rationally chose to be imperfectly informed. Several implications follow.

For the fundamental theorems to hold, all economic agents in a market must confront the same set of prices. Only in this way will utility and profit maximizing choices lead to similar ratios of marginal utility across all consumers and similar ratios of marginal value products across all factors of production. Without these equalizations, Pareto optimality does not hold. When agents are imperfectly informed, however, then their estimates of prices will differ. Poorly informed consumers will pay higher prices than will those with better information, for example. In the presence of higher prices, the poorly informed consumers may cease consumption at a point where the marginal valuation of his or her expenditure is higher than that of the better informed consumer. The result is a failure to achieve Pareto optimality.

Leadership, persuasion, influence: these phenomena represent social processes whose origins may lie in efforts by people to compensate for the imperfection of information. For given imperfect information, economic actors may not know their best choices. In seeking to determine where their interests lie, they may seek to acquire information from persons whose tastes could be presumed to resemble their own, but who for a variety of reasons could be expected to be more knowledgeable. The possession of (slightly) greater amounts of education,[5] superior exposure to specialized media and sources of information, or greater experience becomes sufficient, in environments of imperfect information, to render a person influential: an "opinion leader," in the jargon of studies of the phenomenon (see: Katz and Lazarsfeld 1964).

Uncertainty about price is not the sole means whereby costly information generates market failures and the use of non-market information. So too is uncertainty about the choices or intentions of other actors and about future contingencies.

Hidden Action

High information costs limit the ability of people to monitor the choices of others. An example is provided by someone with land and capital who seeks to secure labor services. Were the landlord able to monitor labor effort and output at low cost, then the landlord could simply pay the laborer the value of the marginal product of labor. But when it is difficult accurately to gauge effort or to monitor the relation between effort and output, then it is also difficult to reward labor in a way that maximizes the returns to both parties. The result is the substitution of contracts for spot exchanges of money for effort. One contract might be a wages contract: paying the laborer a fixed wage, with the landlord securing all the surplus--but also absorbing all the risk. This form of contract provides weak incentives for altering the intensity of effort, however, as in response to changes in the weather or to the incursion of pests. A rental contract provides an alternative option: the laborer could pay the landlord a fixed amount for the use of the land and capital, and retain all the surplus (and accept all the risk). Where variability in output arises from the use of land and capital equipment, however, this form of contract will provide insufficient incentive; not being the residual claimant, the landlord possesses few incentives to increase the quality of land or to vary the use of capital--the factor inputs she or he owns--so as to increase total profits. Under these circumstances, then, the best form of organization--given the high costs of monitoring--might be one in which the landlord and the laborer reward themselves for their inputs of land, capital and labor by dividing the total output. Neither accepts a fixed payment; nor does either become the sole residual claimant; rather, they share the total output--and thus the risk--of rural production. Incentives arriving from the costs of information thus can structure the contractual relationship between the owners of land, capital and labor in rural societies (see discussion in Barzel 1989; also Stiglitz 1986).

Hidden Type

Uncertainty about prices or choices is not the sole source of non-market organization; so too is costly information and the resultant uncertainty about "type:" the quality of a good or the capabilities or intentions of another. This information is often asymmetrically held; an agent may know his or her own type, even when others cannot. The magnitude and structure of such uncertainty may make it costly for maximizing agents to make valuable transactions. The resultant losses of welfare can also motivate the use of non-market institutions.

Labor markets once again provide an example. Consider the problems of an employer facing a pool of potential employees. To secure the services of able workers, the employer would offer a high wage. But ability is difficult to measure. One response might be to offer a wage that represents the average ability of the pool of applicants. The job applicants know their own abilities, however; and those with above average abilities will find the wage too low while those with low abilities will find it attractive. The result then is a shift downward in the average quality of the applicant pool. And should the employer respond by revising downward his or her assessment of the average quality of the job applicants and adjust the wage offer accordingly, the process will simply repeat itself. In Akerloff's famous phrase, the result is the creation of a "market for lemons:" a market in which workers of high quality fail to offer themselves, even though employers desire their services and would be willing to reward them for their superior skills (1970, 1984).

In such a situation, people possess incentives to engage in "non-market" activities. One way of transcending the dilemma is for employees to invest in signals that reveal their hidden type. If the costs of the signal is less for those who possess higher abilities,[6] then employers could select for ability by choosing those who emit strong signals. Education constitutes an obvious illustration. Insofar as ability lowers the costs of academic attainment, then employers, by paying a higher wage to those with more schooling, can transcend the dilemma generated by costly information, asymmetrically distributed in the labor market.

The problem of costly, asymmetric information concerning "type" reappears in a wide variety of settings and the institutional responses to it assume varied forms. Employers can encourage employees to reveal their type by offering a spectrum of contracts, in which those with high ability (or high preference for risk) will select one form of contract and those with lower abilities (or lower preferences for risk) will select another. To prevent the degeneration of markets as a result of adverse selection, people may also find other ways of signalling. They may, for example, incur costs that would reveal their type. Those seeking to convince insurers that they are good risks may, for example, chose higher deductibles. Or, in intertemporal settings, people may offer collateral or post bonds to signal their good faith. Offering "hostages" provides evidence of one's intentions; it enables one to commit credibly to a course of behavior.

Preferences are difficult to measure. Because opportunism often pays, verbal protestations provide unreliable evidence of true intentions. The consequence is that many desirable agreements can not be arrived at. In such a world, people possess incentives to engage in behavior that reveals private information. They possess incentives to engage in costly acts that reveal their type. By doing so, people provide the information needed for others to detect their type, such that they may take part in transactions that should otherwise be infeasible. People engage in these non-market forms of behavior in order to escape the imperfections of markets.

Unforseen Contingencies

There is a third source of imperfect information: that arising from the inability of human beings to foresee future states of the world. This source of uncertainty also motivates the creation of institutions other than markets.

As noted by Arrow, were people able to foresee all possible states of the world, then they could use the market to insure themselves against risk (1971a). They could trade contracts in which they promised to exchange commodities or services whose prices, quantities, or type varied according to specific circumstances. By buying or selling such contingent claims, they could optimally adjust their holdings so as to assure themselves of a level of utility that reflected their assessment of the probabilities and their preferences for risk.

In practice, of course, not all contingencies can be foreseen; it is prohibitively expensive to write contracts that completely specify actions to be undertaken under all possible states of the world. As a result, the insurance market is not complete and people therefore cannot use the market to maximize their welfare. In response, they employ other institutions.

One class of such institutions are those that offer "generalized reciprocity:" institutions in which people invest resources, not in expectation of specific recompense, but rather in an effort to create a general fund of good will which can subsequently be tapped should a specific need arise. Families constitute the most striking example of such institutions. And, as argued by Posner (1980), Binswanger (Binswanger and Rosenweig 1984), myself (Bates 1989,

1990), and others, the structure and organization of families reflects the degree of risk, the structure of risk, and the availability of other instruments for coping with it. Families become larger--blending virtually into lineages--the greater the level of risk; the greater the ability of the family to diversify it; and the scarcer or more costly alternative mechanisms for coping with uncertainty.

The inability to foresee and "contract around" future contingencies affects most directly capital markets. When investors invest, they put themselves at risk; they sacrifice present consumption out of a desire for future gains. Insofar as they cannot foresee the future and trade contracts that generate rewards or incur obligations depending upon the contingencies, they are unable to insure against losses from their investments. As argued by Williamson (1985) and others (see: Putterman 1986), the result is the creation of non-market institutions. Williamson calls these "governance structures." Given their inability to foresee all possible contingencies, the suppliers and demanders of investments may instead form long-term relationships through which to renegotiate and adjust their obligations in response to changing circumstances. In particular, they may withdraw decisions from the realm of the market and instead lodge them in firms.

The inability to foresee future contingencies leads to the creation of other forms of non-market organizations. As noted in the literature on bureaucracy, one way of dealing with specific forms of unforeseeable risk is to hire the services of specialists: people who possess expertise in the sensitive area or records of performance that reveal success in coping with such issues in the past. The costs of their services constitute, then, costs of insurance; such contractual relationships represent the substitution of organizations for markets. Contracts for such specialists are, of course, subject to the sources of welfare loss discussed above: adverse selection, insofar as their expertise may be difficult to measure; or moral hazard, insofar as their choices are difficult to monitor. Specific organizational forms then arise to deal with such problems: hiring on the basis of credentials or records, the use of apprenticeships and probationary periods, and the construction of "fire alarms" so as to alert principals when their agents have failed to perform.[7] The form, as well as the fact, of organization can thus be analyzed as a response to risk arising from costly information. There are other sources of the market failure--such as non-convexities and scale economies--and these too have been analyzed and related to the creation of institutions. Rather than extend the discussion on the new institutionalism, however, I now turn to a characterization and critique of its central arguments.

Discussion: The New Contractarianism

As this overview suggests, a common form of reasoning underlies much of the new institutional economics. It is perhaps best summarized by Kenneth Arrow: "When the market fails to arrive at an optimum state, society will, to some extent at least, recognize the gap, and non-market social institutions will arise attempting to bridge it" (Arrow 1971b, as quoted in Przeworski 1991, 109).

The origins of non-market institutions, it is thus claimed, lie in the failure of markets. Persons in decentralized settings encounter social dilemmas, i.e. circumstances under which their individually rational choices fail to elicit allocations of resources that maximize the social welfare. By providing forms of pre-commitment, altering individual incentives, generating governance structures, and so forth, non-market institutions provide mechanisms that enable individuals to transcend the dilemmas and attain higher levels of collective welfare.

As noted at the outset, one of the goals of the new institutionalism in economics was to complete the neo-classical program by "reducing" social organization to the choices of rational individuals. As will be highlighted here, however, two major failures bedevil its efforts. Taken together, they reveal that this attempt to extend the neo-classical paradigm founders on a contradiction: it violates the very premises of neo-classical reasoning--a commitment to the individual as the unit of analysis and to rational choice as a theory of decision.

As can readily be seen in Arrow's formulation, the new institutionalists locate the causes of non-market forms of organization in their consequences: i.e. in their ability to solve market failures. This form of reasoning suggests a deficiency in the attempt thus to extend the neo-classical paradigm; for it leaves the level of explanation at the social rather than the individual level. The approach is functionalist (see: Stinchcombe 1968, Elster 1978). It is the needs of society--deficiencies in the social welfare--that call forth non-market organization. This form of reasoning therefore abandons the individual level of explanation and bases its explanations on the welfare of society; and the explanations advanced by the new institutionalism thus depart from the standard form of explanation used in neo-classical economics. Rather than representing an extension of the paradigm, they represent a departure from it.

The new institutionalists' "account" of the origins of institutions also violates the assumption of rationality. By their reasoning, should people encounter a social dilemma, they would forge new institutions in an attempt to transcend it. But, given that the new institution would make all better off, the institution constitutes a public good. Would not the act of its provision itself generate incentives to free ride? And why, then, would individuals, behaving rationally, be willing to pay the costs of its provision? Viewed in terms of the incentives faced by individuals, then, it appears that the demand for institutional solutions to collective dilemmas does not imply their supply; the solutions themselves pose collective dilemmas.[8] Individuals, behaving rationally, would fail to provide them.

The approach thus appears to founder on a basic contradiction. Devised to extend neo-classical reasoning outside of the realm of markets, it violates the axioms of neo-classicism. In the face of such contradictions, we can move in two directions. One is toward a "new anthropology." The other is toward politics.

A New Anthropology?

Rather than emphasizing "hard" incentives, such as monetary inducements or legal sanctions, the "new anthropology" emphasizes "soft" phenomena, such as social reputations and cultural symbols. In doing so, however, it remains "within the church" of rational choice theory. To communicate and explicate this form of analysis, we begin with a canonical social dilemma: the two-person prisoners' dilemma, presented in strategic form:[9]

A prisoners' dilemma constitutes a social dilemma when it is played one time. Refer, for example, to Figure 2.1, which exhibits a one sided, single shot prisoners' dilemma game. Look at the choices facing B. Clearly, given the payoffs contained in this figure, B will abuse A's trust, for B thereby guarantees herself 15 units instead of 10. Knowing that, A will therefore not trust B; A thereby guarantees herself 0 instead of the -5 that B will inflict upon him by abusing his trust. The result of the two players' choices is the payoff of (0,0) instead of the (10,10) that both would prefer. Given the structure and incentives of the game, each, behaving rationally, thus chooses in a way that generates a collectively irrational outcome.

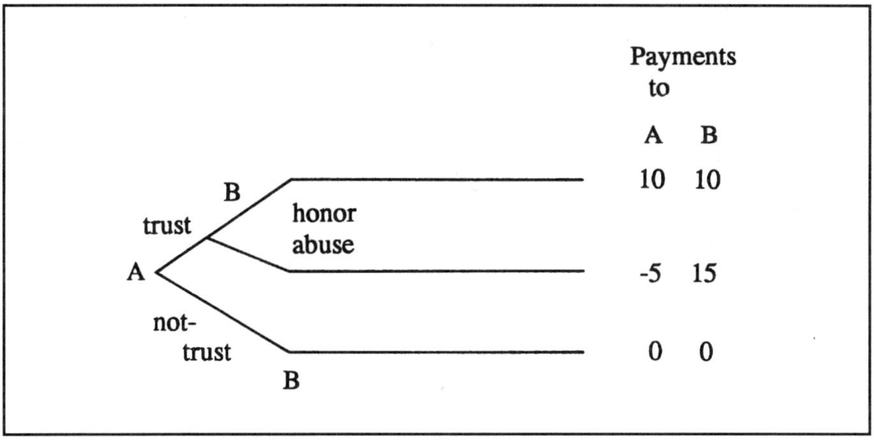

Figure 2.1: A One-Sided Prisoners' Dilemma

What would happen, however, were the game to be repeated? At first glance, repetition would appear to offer promise. For, given repetition, people could make use of the information provided by the past choices of actors; additionally, they could reward or punish other players, contingent upon their past behavior. A player could, for example, adopt a trigger strategy in which she distrusts forever someone who has, in a previous play, abused her trust. Faced with the prospect of punishment for the rest of the game, a player might find the initial gain of 5 units [i.e. the traitor's payoff of 15 compared with the cooperator's reward of 10] not worth the subsequent loss of 10 units in every future play of the game [i.e. the 0 inflicted by the trigger strategy of never again trusting, by comparison with the 10 that could be secured each round, had A's trust not been abused].

The problem is: were the game repeated a finite number of times, its outcome would be identical to that achieved when it is played but once. In computing their best strategies, players reason backward; they therefore concentrate on the last round of the game. The last round embodies incentives precisely similar to those of the one shot game; in the last round, B, behaving rationally, will abuse trust. A, knowing that, will distrust B. When the players infer their best strategies in each previous round of the game, the possibility of cooperation unravels. With both players choosing rationally, mutual trust is not achieved.

How, then, might this social dilemma be transcended? Face to face contact, knowledge of past histories, signalling and social experimentation--these social mechanisms, so often studied by anthropologists, can be seen to play a powerful role in underpinning socially desirable behavior, particularly in the face of imperfect information.

Were, for example, the agents unable to forecast the end of the game, they might guess that at each play of the game there would be, say, a .8 probability of the game continuing one more round. Were A employing his trigger strategy, B would therefore compare the 5 units to be gained by abusing A's trust and the 0 resulting from her subsequent punishment with the rewards to be secured from continuing to honor A's trust and the .8 chance of enjoying those 10 units in the subsequent round. For a plausible range of discount rates, not abusing A's trust will thus remain B's best strategy. Even more interesting is a second possibility. Say, for example, that A could not know for certain B's type; that A felt that B was "trustworthy," with probability equal to .001. Under these circumstances, even were the game played a finite number of rounds, were there many rounds to go, A might chose to risk 5 units by trusting B in order to determine whether B were trustworthy or not. The payoffs to A would be a loss of 5 units with a probability of .999 but a possible gain (with a probability of .001) of 10 units in all remaining rounds. Consider, too, the calculations of B. Were she to abuse the trust, she would receive 15; were she to honor it, she would receive 10 units per period for many plays of the game. With many rounds remaining in the game, then, when A is uncertain of B's type, it pays A to test B by trusting her--and B to honor that trust, *regardless of her true type.*

The prisoners' dilemma game stands as the archetype of the social dilemmas that have motivated the new institutionalism. Given its structure and incentives, individuals, choosing rationally, secure outcomes that no one prefers. These outcomes are socially irrational. The contractarian solutions posited in the new institutional economics themselves pose collective dilemmas, if only because they are subject to free riding. In this section, however, we have noted conditions that might promote the resolution of the prisoners' dilemma. They include: repeated face-to-face interactions; the use of history; the ability to infer information regarding other people by remaining in contact with them and observing their behavior; the ability to experiment with people and to test them out; and the ability to respond to such tests, to give assurances, and to communicate one's type--and therefore one's intentions. People dwell in contact with others over time; they do not live as isolated individuals or for single periods. The insight of this section is that these simple facts may provide mechanisms that better account for the creation of institutions that enable human beings to solve social dilemmas than would the contractarian logic offered by the new institutionalists. And these are precisely the properties of human communities most deeply investigated by anthropologists.

What, however, if social ties were not dense; what if people did not repeatedly meet each other face to face? Under such circumstances, communities would not provide an adequate mechanism; "anthropological" solutions would not work. Rather, people would have to employ mechanisms that would operate even in the absence of primary, face-to-face contact. Let us briefly turn to some recent work that addresses this problem, using the kind of reasoning that we have just presented.

In a fascinating article, Milgrom, North, and Weingast (1990) analyze a social mechanism that facilitates trust and promotes welfare enhancing exchanges: the Law Merchant, a form of customary law developed in Medieval Europe. Under this system, a trader can secure a judgment against another who has betrayed a trust, provided that the plaintiff had earlier queried the Law Merchant regarding previous complaints about the defendant. For a well defined structure of fees (for making such an inquiry), fines (for having breached a trust), and losses (generated by breach of contract), the authors show, there exist equilibria under which the merchants find it in their interests to place their conduct on the public record; having done so, they then find it in their interest to honor contracts, for fear of being boycotted by persons who learn of previous dishonest acts. For the benefits gained by a single fraud could be offset by the losses incurred as a result of the unwillingness of others to deal with a merchant possessing a sullied reputation.

What is remarkable about this result is that it does not depend on repeated play. That is, the merchants could be "Townsend matched," such that they came into contact but once in their lifetimes. Under such circumstances, trigger strategies would not work; personal histories then could not provide resources for making it in the personal interest of merchants to make socially desirable choices. The system of the Law Merchant fills this gap by providing an institutionalized history: an archival record and a fee structure that makes it in the interests of players to contribute to--and draw from--this record for their own benefit, which happens to coincide with the interests of other merchants.

The movement from a 2-person to an n-person setting, with the resultant possibility of anonymity, thus provokes a search for mechanisms other than face-to-face community that provide a means for transcending collective dilemmas. One possibility, as we have seen, is legal institutions. Further work by Weingast suggests a second: culture, by which is meant shared definitions of appropriate behavior. Those who stress the significance of culture often focus on its role in primary, face to face communities. But, as argued by Weingast, culture may in fact be of even greater significance in large, n-person communities, where the past histories of individuals may be costly to obtain and trigger strategies therefore of little use in shaping their behavior.

To illustrate the way in which culture can assist in transcending dilemmas, consider, once again, an n-person setting: one in which a single person, A, confronts a multitude of other persons, whom I shall refer to as Bs. In this setting, what are the motivations for A to behave honorably? Say that A behaves dishonorably toward one of the many Bs. A's chances of encountering that particular B again are sufficiently small that a trigger strategy would offer insufficient incentive to elicit honorable behavior. Rather, the history of B's encounter would have to contribute to the creation of A's reputation, so that the behavior of other Bs, acting in a coordinated manner, would provide that incentive.

A key to making such collective behavior work is the creation of a shared definition of honest behavior. Say that A were to harm a particular B: without some widely shared definition of what constitutes a dishonorable act, other Bs will not be able to judge A's behavior and thereby implement their trigger strategies. By the same token, A will not be able to build a reputation for honesty; working with private definitions of honorable acts, the actions of A vis-a-vis one B would be of no significance for others. As noted by Weingast in the essay from which these arguments are drawn:[10]

> What is needed to restore cooperation is a mechanism that coordinates the reaction of [the multiple Bs]. ...[B]y providing a shared belief system among [the Bs], it coordinates their interpretations of [A's] actions in different circumstances and ensures that deviations--as defined by the belief system--will be punished (1990).

This portion of the paper has considered an alternative to the "new institutionalism" which I have called the "new anthropology." The approach stays within the church of neo-classical reasoning; it is based upon the individual as the unit of analysis and the premise of rational choice. But rather than seeing society's interests as driving the behavior of institutions, as does much of the new institutionalism, it instead builds its analysis upon the theory of non-cooperative behavior.[11] To motivate the presentation, I have explored an archetypical model of a social dilemma--the prisoners' dilemma--and analyzed it in strategic form. In 2-person form, it suggests that community can provide an alternative to the contractarian theory of the resolution of social dilemmas so often--indeed, too often--advanced in the new institutional economics. With increases in social scale, however, community cannot work: repeated, face-to-face encounters are less likely, and reputation can play less of a role in triggering punishments for opportunistic behavior. Rather than the solution of community, what appears needed are the solutions of customary law and normative order, with legal institutions and shared standards of correct behavior. It should be noted that this analysis thus supports the theory of others--most notably Durkheim--who stressed the significance of explicit legal frameworks and shared, cultural values as sources of social order as societies moved from small, face-to-face communities to large, anonymous communities i.e. from the "stage" of mechanical to organic solidarity (Durkheim 1959).

The Role of Politics

There is a second alternative to the new institutionalism and this is the treatment of institutions from the point of view of political science. The "Coase Theorem" stands as one of the classic texts in the new institutional economics. It serves to motivate this presentation.

Consider a situation in which a single railway line runs through a valley populated by a multitude of small farmers. Each train run through the valley generates revenues; it also inflicts costs, in the form of soot, smoke, and noise. One of Coase's fundamental contributions to the new institutional economics was to demonstrate that property rights--any form of property rights--would make it in the private interests of the operators of the railroad to make efficient use of the railway. In the absence of property rights, the railways would run trains until the revenue from the next train equalled the costs to the railway of running one more train. With a system of property rights, however, the railways would run fewer trains, for it would then have to take into account the full social cost, including the costs imposed upon the farmers. Should the structure of property rights favor the farmers, then the owners of the railway would have to compensate the farmers for the external costs imposed upon them. Should the structure of property rights favor the railways, then the farmers, in an effort to reduce the externalities inflicted upon them, could in effect "bribe" the railway to run fewer trains; they could compensate the railways for their loss of profits from running fewer trains. Either system of property rights thus creates incentives for the railways to reduce the number of trains out of a regard for the value of the negative externality inflicted upon agriculture.

As summarized, then, the "Coase Theorem" suggests the power of an institution--in this instance, property rights--to control a social dilemma: the tendency, under conditions of externalities, for individually rational acts to generate collectively irrational outcomes. But, in such a situation, where is the legal system--the solution itself--likely to come from? In addition, which legal system is likely to prevail: that favoring the rights of firms or that favoring the rights of the railways?

As we have repeatedly stressed, the new institutionalism's answer to the first question is fundamentally flawed. There is a second possible answer, however: that the origins of institutions lie in politics. As a new institutionalist, Coase answered the second question by stating: it would depend upon the costs of transacting. Once again, there is a second possible answer: that it would depend upon the structure of politics. For the origin of the legal system is the state. And the nature of the costs of guaranteeing and structuring property rights is determined in large part by the nature of political institutions. In the state, then, and in the study of politics, we can find answers to both questions.

The new institutional economics is profoundly a-political. Institutions represent agreements or conventions chosen by voluntarily transacting parties in efforts to secure mutually welfare enhancing outcomes. Each agent is assumed to be autonomous; each agreement, voluntarily entered into by mutually assenting parties. The emphasis is upon choices, not constraints; even slave "contracts" are analyzed from the framework of Pareto optimality (see: Barzel 1989).

What is omitted from the accounts of the new institutionalists, then, is that institutions impose constraints; that institutions are often imposed rather than chosen; and that, being backed by the power of the state, institutions provide means whereby agents can extract involuntary transfers of resources. The sort of marginalist choices studied by the new institutionalists take place within structures. They may yield Pareto optimal outcomes, given the constraints imposed by these structures (including the initial endowments that each actor is allowed to bring into the social arena). But when social dilemmas are solved and non-market solutions chosen, some people benefit more than others; indeed, some may benefit at the expense of others. These are key features of outcomes which the voluntaristic and marginalist approach cannot explain. Explaining them requires political, not economic, analysis.

By way of illustration, return, once again, to the discussion of the "Coase Theorem." Consider a world in which elections are banned, the state rules by decree, and laws are made by bureaucrats after consulting with major economic interests. One could easily infer that in a political system thus structured, the structure of property rights would favor the railway. Indeed, political theories based upon the very reasoning explored in this paper would predict that outcome. For the railway is the more highly concentrated interest;

given its level of concentration, it stands to capture privately the full social benefits of lobbying and therefore encounters weak incentives for free riding. By comparison with the farmers, the railways would therefore be the superior lobbyist (see: Olson 1965). And the state, structured so as to respond to interest groups, could be expected to be biased in its favor.

Now consider another state: one in which politicians make the laws, but only after capturing a majority of the votes in competitive elections. Provisioned with additional assumptions--about the number of rural dwellers voting in the electoral district containing the railway and the proportion of rural as opposed to urban districts in the legislature, for example--one could easily infer an alternative outcome: one in which property rights would favor the farmers as opposed to the railway. In electoral systems, numbers count; political incentives spur efforts by politicians to secure majorities; and politicians will champion laws that favor the numerous small, even sometimes at the expense of the "big interests."

The structure of the political system therefore shapes the choice of institutions. One consequence is that the structure of the state helps to determine the particular form in which collective dilemmas are solved. Another is that the structure of the state generates involuntary transfers of resources; as illustrated above, in the absence of elections, payments flow from farmers to the railway, and in their presence, they flow in the opposite direction. Flows in either direction will create incentives for individuals to use resources in ways that, while privately profitable, are collectively optimal; that is the message of the new institutional economics. Left out is the difference that the institutional forms induce in the resultant distribution of income.

Indeed, we can think of institutions as wealth. For they create entitlements to streams of income. The opportunities that they create represent assets that yield flows of payments over time. In this sense, they create endowments that shape the life chances of individuals.

Politics involves coercion; the state, in Weberian phrasing, is the human institution that possesses a monopoly of violence. The institutions that promote social rationality are generated and put in place by the state. The structure of political institutions affect which economic institution is chosen. Behind every Pareto optimal outcome, then, arrived at by marginal adjustments among maximizing agents choosing between alternatives, lies an act of coercion: the creation of an institutional framework that restricts alternatives, structures incentives (and thus the flow of payments), and determines the distribution of wealth that will prevail in the resultant social order.

Using the bloodless language of the new institutionalism, Coase was right: which institution is chosen depends upon the structure of transaction costs. It is the state that determines the allocation of these costs, however. The costs of agreement among the multitude of farms are lower, for example, if vote seeking politicians help them to organize in opposition to the railway. Once politicians are seen as determining the magnitude and distribution of these transaction costs, then a different vocabulary becomes relevant: that of political science. And the problem itself acquires a different coloration. It is no longer one of pure economics. Nor is it one amenable to solutions via communities, nor law, nor normative order. Rather, the way in which rational individuals transcend dilemmas and secure collectively rational outcomes, becomes a problem in politics.

Conclusion

This paper, then, has provided an introduction to the new institutionalism. It has presented it as an attempt to extend the neo-classical program and to build upon the concept of market failure. Examining a series of imperfections in markets, it has illustrated the central focus on social dilemmas: situations in which, because of perverse incentives, rational individuals are unable to attain socially rational outcomes. The paper then critiqued the theory of the origins of institutions contained within this literature and stressed the utility of alternative approaches: one based on anthropological notions, such as community and trust, and others on political notions, such as coercion and constraint.

References

Arrow, Kenneth. 1951. An Extension of the Basic Theorems of Classical Welfare in Economics. In J. Neyman ed., *Proceeding of the Second Berkeley Symposium* on Mathematical Statistics and Probability. Berkeley: University of California Press.

———.1971a. *Essays on the Theory of Risk Bearing.* Amsterdam: North Holland.

———.1971b. Political and Economic Evaluations, Social Effects and Externalities. In Michael D. Intriligator, ed., *Frontiers of Quantitative Economics.* Amsterdam: North-Holland.

Barzel, Yoram. 1989. *Economic Analysis of Property Rights*. Cambridge: Cambridge University Press.

Bates, Robert H. 1989. *Beyond the Miracle of the Market.* Cambridge: Cambridge University Press.

———.1990. Capital, Kinship and Conflict: The Structuring of Capital in Kinship Societies. *Canadian Journal of African Studies* 24(2): 151-164.

———.1988. Contra-contractarianism: Some Reflections on the New Institutionalism. *Politics and Society* 16: 387-401.

Becker, Gary S. 1981. *A Treatise on the Family.* Cambridge: Harvard University Press.

Binswanger, Hans P. and Mark R. Rosenzweig. 1984. Behavioral and Material Determinants of Production Relations in Agriculture. Research Unit, Agriculture and Rural Development, World Bank, Report No. ARU 5.

Coase, Ronald. 1960. The Problem of Social Costs. *Journal of Law and Economics* 3:1-44.

Cornell, Stephen and Joseph Kalt. 1991. Where's the Glue? Institutional Bases of American Indian Economic Development. John F. Kennedy School of Government, Harvard University, Working Paper Series, March, 1991.

Debreu, Gerard. 1951. *Theory of Value.* New York: John Wiley and Sons.

Durkheim, Emile. 1959. *The Division of Labor in Society.* Trans. by George Simpson. Glencoe, Ill.: The Free Press.

Elster, John. 1978. *Logic and Society.* Chichester: Wiley.

Friedman, Milton. 1953. *Essays on Positive Economics.* Chicago: University of Chicago Press.

Frohlich, Norman and Joe A. Oppenheimer. 1978. *Modern Political Economy*. Englewood Cliffs, N.J.: Prentice Hall.

Katz, Elihu and Paul F. Lazarsfeld. 1964. *Personal Influence*. New York: The Free Press.

Kreps, David. 1990. Corporate Culture. In James E. Alt and Kenneth A. Shepsle, eds., *Perspectives in Posititve Political Economy*. Cambridge: Cambridge University Press.

Libecap, Gary D. 1989. *Contracting for Property Rights*. Cambridge: Cambridge University Press.

Luce, R. Duncan and Howard Raiffa. 1957. *Games and Decisions*. New York: Wiley.

McCubbins, Matthew D., Roger G. Noll and Barry R. Weingast. 1987. Administrative Procedures as Instruments of Political Control. *Journal of Law, Economics, and Organization* 3(2): 243-277.

———.1989. Structure and Process, Politics and Policy: Administrative Arrangements and the Political Control of Agencies. *Virginia Law Review* 75(2): 431-482.

———.1990. Slack, Public Interest and Structure Induced Policy. *Journal of Law, Economics, and Organization* 6: 203-212.

Milgrom, Paul R., Douglass C. North and Barry R. Weingast. 1990. The Role of Institutions in the Revival of Trade: The Law Merchant, Private Judges, and the Champagne Fairs. *Economics and Politics* 2(1): 1-22.

O'Halloran, Sharon and Roger Noll. 1991. Institutions as Congressional Precommitments: International Trade Policy In the Postwar Liberal Era. Paper Prepared for the SSRC Conference on Congress and Foreign Policy, April 21-22.

Olson, Mancur. 1965. *The Logic of Collective Action*. Cambridge: Harvard University Press.

Ostrom, Elinor. 1990. *Governing the Commons: The Evolution of Institutions for Collective Action.* Cambridge: Cambridge University Press.

Popkin, Samuel L. 1979. *The Rational Peasant.* Berkeley and Los Angeles: University of California Press.

Posner, Richard A. 1980. A Theory of Primitive Society with Special Reference to the Law. *Journal of law and Economics* 23: 1-52.

Przeworski, Adam. 1991. *Democracy and the Market.* Cambridge: Cambridge Universtiy Press.

Putterman, Louis. 1986. *The Economic Nature of the Firm.* Cambridge: Cambridge University Press.

Stiglitz, Joseph. 1986. The New Development Economics. *World Development* 14(2): 257-65.

Weingast, Barry R. 1990. A Rational Choice Perspective on Shared Belief Systems. Manuscript. Stanford University: The Hoover Institution.

Notes

1. I wish to thank Alberto Diaz, Catherine Elkins, Brian Loynd, and Beatrice Magaloni, and participants in seminars at Rutgers University, Haverford College, and the Society for Economic Anthropology, for their comments on an earlier version of this paper.

2. This literature builds as well on the work of Friedrich Hayek, Ronald Coase, and Frank Knight. See the useful overview contained in Louis Putterman (1986).

3. It should be noted that flows of payments from the person who is harmed by the infliction of negative externalities would also work. Such "protection money" would provide a benefit that would make it in their financial interest to refrain from inflicting external, physical costs. For an elaboration, see the classic article by Ronald Coase (1960).

4. The phrase is from Frohlich and Oppenheimer (1978).

5. Too great a differential in education would suggest a difference in preferences, rendering the source of information an unreliable guide to appropriate decisions.

6. If the signal were cheaper for those with lesser abilities, less able workers would disguise themselves.

7. For an elaboration of this argument, see the works of the notorious "McNollgast" (McCubbins, Noll and Weingast 1987, 1989, 1990; O'Halloran and Noll 1991).

8. For a fuller discussion, see Bates (1988) and Ostrom (1990).

9. This discussion follows the superb analysis by David Kreps (1990).

10. See as well Cornell and Kalt (1991).

11. One of the most lucid discussions of the distinction between cooperative and non-cooperative game theory remains (Luce and Raiffa 1957).

Part II

Case Studies: Transaction Costs, Individual Decisions and Economic Performance

3

Transaction Costs Through Time: The Case Of The Orma Pastoralists in East Africa

Jean Ensminger

Institutions matter to new institutional economists because they directly affect cooperation.[1] They are our informal norms of behavior and the formal rules by which we live; they add predictability to human behavior. Because institutions affect the level of cooperation in society, they affect the gains we can reap by such cooperation, which ultimately affects the economic performance of society. The outcomes that result from different institutional arrangements may serve select individuals, or special interest groups, and do not necessarily serve the needs or best interests of society as a whole. In other words, governments do not always behave in ways that promote better economic performance. For their own reasons, people in the position to exert pressure on institutions may not push for changes that are good for society as a whole, but rather, for changes that shift distribution in their favor (Knight 1992, Ruttan 1989). Nevertheless, sometimes governments make institutional changes that do yield economic benefits, though these may be far from optimal, and by no means equally shared. This is one such story.

One way in which institutions matter to the economy is by affecting the costs associated with exchange of all sorts. Since Adam Smith, economists have argued that economic growth stems from the gains from trade and increasing specialization and division of labor. In other words, if one group can raise cattle more cheaply than its neighbor, which can raise rice more cheaply--they may both be better off specializing and exchanging. The insight from transaction costs economics is that such exchange may *not* be cost-saving if the transaction costs eat up all the savings from specialization. Transaction costs include the costs of gathering information, negotiating, monitoring, and enforcing property rights and contracts. These are incurred whenever people try to measure the prices and quality of the goods and services that they want, to monitor the performance of employees, to find trading partners, or to enforce property rights and contracts. When transaction costs are high they serve as a disincentive to exchange.

In the small-scale societies typically studied by anthropologists, most exchange occurs among people known to each other, and often linked through numerous cross-cutting ties.[2] As the substantivist economic anthropologists of the 1950s and 1960s (see especially Polanyi 1944 and Dalton 1967) so well articulated, and Granovetter (1985 and 1991) has recently elaborated, economic relations are embedded in social relations in such societies. Trust may be great, and exchange is less of a problem within the domain of one's own society and networks. Trust (based in part upon readily available information about reputations) and cross-cutting ties that facilitate enforcement (should a rare breach of contract occur), contribute to lowering transaction costs in such societies.

Problems typically arise in the developing world in the process of transition to larger spheres of exchange where individuals must deal with people outside their own ethnic group, often in exchange relationships with no repeat dealing. Under such circumstances altogether different institutions must be established to reduce information costs, ensure trust, and provide reliable enforcement mechanisms that help ensure the sanctity of contracts. One of the important functions of states is the supply of institutions that are recognized by the many sub-populations that make up the state. This is especially critical for new states in Africa which are made up of as many as several hundred recently autonomous societies with unique institutional structures. But governments cannot unify the institutional structure by fiat. While governments can control the formal codes of behavior--through the executive, the legislature, and the judiciary--these alone do not ensure low transaction costs. Also important are people's ideas about the justness of the formal code and the means by which it is enforced, as well as the pattern of informal behavior, which may change far more slowly than the formal code (North 1993). Where state institutions are found wanting in the eyes of the population, a legitimacy problem arises that may seriously undermine the system and bring such discontinuity between the formal and informal norms of behavior that unpredictability is increased and high transaction costs result (see Cornell and Kalt 1989).[3] The state may also have to use a "go slow" process in the gradual take-over of enforcement mechanisms if it desires to maintain legitimacy (North n.d.).

In this particular paper I am not addressing the supply of institutional changes offered by the state. That is, I am not examining why some measures were enacted by the government of Kenya and not others (for such a discussion of African institutions see Bates 1981 and 1989, and more generally on institutional supply see Ruttan 1989). Rather, here I treat these processes as exogenous, and examine the impact of given policies upon transaction costs among a rural pastoral Orma population in northeastern Kenya.

As has been noted elsewhere, measuring transaction costs is exceedingly difficult (see Wallis and North 1986, for a rare attempt). I do not attempt to measure transaction costs in this paper, but rather to build a strong circumstantial case for their reduction over time. Further, without direct measure of this crucial variable I can only speculate that the drop in transaction costs is the cause of the more favorable turn in terms of trade for the Orma. I maintain that no other explanation can as satisfactorily account both for the improvement in the terms of trade and for the increase in trade over time.

In the case study below I address the following questions: 1) What did policies more favorable to trade look like in the African context? 2) What might the consequences of such changes have been for economic performance? 3) And how might the economic effects have been distributed among the population? In the course of this analysis I focus specifically upon transaction costs, and examine longitudinal data from Orma pastoralists in Kenya.

The Case Study

The Orma are pastoral cattle, sheep and goat herders in northeastern Kenya. The Galole Orma, the subgroup with which this study deals, inhabit the geographic center of Orma territory, just west of the current district headquarters at Hola. The data presented here are of two types from two different periods. Those from the period 1920 to 1980 are based largely upon archival and oral history. For this period there are no household-level data, but some district-level data exist. Due to the absence of household-level data it is not possible to address the effect of changes in transaction costs on producers as opposed to traders. The second dataset (1980 to 1987) derives from household economic data on many of the same households over time. These data allow us to see how changes in transaction costs affected Orma producers directly.

Like the rest of Kenya, the homeland of the Galole Orma (current day Tana River District) became a British Protectorate in 1895. This point was actually a low period for trade between the Orma and neighboring peoples. There was also only limited long distance trade going on within Orma territory, as the Orma had a reputation for fierceness that kept even the Arabs out of the interior. By the 1920s this had substantially changed, and Arabs were trekking up into Orma territory to buy cattle for cash. The Orma had to go themselves to trading centers to use the cash, however, as there was an absence of shops in the interior. In the 1930s this also changed. The first Orma trader (named Shambaro) began to bring goods to trade in the Galole Orma interior.

Shambaro worked as an agent for Arab traders in the south. He took trade goods such as salt, oil, and cloth from his agent in the south, moved them north by canoe up the Tana, transferred them to donkeys, and trekked westward to the interior. There he exchanged his goods for cash and ghee, which he took back down south. In the 1940s trade increased as he opened his first permanent shop at Wayu. By this time, sugar, tea, and tobacco were significant trade items, as well as maize during times of drought. By this time he no longer needed to go in person to get the trade goods; Shambaro was minimally literate and his Arab agent sent goods at written request. Credit was now playing a significant role in his business. By 1945 Shambaro also began to receive a lot of cash from his agent, with which he bought cattle in the north. This represented a standard Islamic partnership known as the *commenda*. By 1948 Shambaro had purchased the first African owned vehicle in the district, which he used for his trade; by the late 1940s he also had three shops. Obviously, the volume of interior trade had increased substantially over this period.

Why Did Trade Increase?

It is often argued that colonial trade in Africa was spurred by taxation necessitating cash, and not by the advantages of trade. In fact there is ample evidence to support this position in many parts of Africa. The hut tax, for example, was imposed and manipulated in many areas in order to drive more African labor into the market to work at cheap wages on white farms (see, for example White 1987). Among the Orma, however, the argument that taxes spurred exchange does not appear to hold up so well. While trade was increasing significantly after 1920, taxes were actually declining (Ensminger 1992). A second explanation for increased trade is that the costs of trade itself were declining, thus providing an increasing economic incentive to specialize and exchange. I shall argue that many different factors contributed to the declining costs of exchange, including conversion to Islam, literacy, standardization of weights and measures, improvement in roads, telecommunications, and the presence of more and better qualified government civil servants.

The first major boost to trade may well have been conversion to Islam.[4] The Orma converted to Islam between 1920 and 1940. Shambaro, the first Galole Orma shopkeeper, was a very early convert. Islam may well have helped ensure good faith between Shambaro and his Muslim agents. Among other things, it represented an overarching set of institutions (legal and otherwise) to which both parties agreed to abide. One such set of institutions was the *commenda* partnership arrangement used by Shambaro from the earliest days. As elsewhere all over the Muslim world, this arrangement allowed for a partnership between one party who fronted the capital and the other who carried out the actual trading, with an agreed upon division of the profits. This facilitated the extension of considerable credit to Shambaro, thus providing him with a competitive edge against other traders who merely visited the area and were not resident there.

A second factor facilitating trade was literacy. Shambaro was minimally literate, but even this was an enormous help to his business. As a consequence, he was able to communicate with his suppliers in writing, thus reducing the necessity to travel in person each time he needed goods and cash. This meant that he could spend a greater amount of time on site managing his shops. Indirectly, literacy thus facilitated specialization in the division of labor by allowing Shambaro to focus on sales transactions while lower cost hired labor transported the goods.

Other factors, such as the standardization of weights and measures, improvement in roads, telecommunications, and upgrading of civil servants, also had an effect on declining transaction costs and fall into the sort of categories we usually associate with transaction costs. The first such measure was the imposition of standardized weights and measures in 1937. The annual district reports give clear evidence of how great the impact of this legislation was in the area. Prior to the legislation, we find the following in the Tana River District Report of 1936.

> Yet another cause of discountent is that all produce, again excepting cotton, is sold by volume, and the measure used is varied to suit the shopkeeper's pocket. If a standard Government "pishi" [8 lbs.] were introduced, it would be enthusiastically received by the cultivators and better class traders, who are constantly petitioning for the standardization of the measure (TRD Annual Report 1936, 18).

In 1937 and 1938 respectively, we find the following two reports indicating the positive impact of the weights and measures legislation, which was passed in 1937.

> The most important piece of legislation immediately affecting the natives was the application of the Weights and Measures Ordinance to the Coast Province and the establishment of the half-bushel measure and subdivisions thereof as compulsory dry measures. This was very popular with the natives and with the better class of traders, as the situation had become chaotic with each person using his own measure, with no two measures holding the same quantity (TRD Annual Report 1937, 5-6).

> The introduction last year of the Standard Dry measures, the use of which is compulsory, has proved of considerable benefit to the natives, and also to the less intelligent traders, in preventing frauds.

> The traders have willingly brought their measures to be stamped, and although some illegal measures may still be in use, their use is becoming increasingly risky (TRD Annual Report 1938, 14-15).

Another major issue affecting transaction costs is roads. Poor transportation adds not just to the cost of delivering goods, but also to the costs of information. The first truck did not arrive in the district until 1929 and then could not really penetrate due to the absence of roads. By 1955, however, there were 11 trucks owned by traders in the district. As in all exchange, the value of information is crucial in cattle marketing. Arguably this is even more true in the case of cattle trading than it is for agricultural commerce. Information about supply and demand and price are crucial prior to moving cattle, but so also is information about cattle diseases. Great losses may be associated with moving cattle to market over long distances only to learn upon arrival that all buyers have left, that the price is far lower than expected, or that the area is infested with a cattle disease. Transportation enormously facilitates the rapid dispersal and competitive flow of information.

Similarly, telecommunications provide the same information benefits to trade as those associated with roads.[5] One example of the costs of poor communications comes from the district records of 1954. It describes the costly effects of a garbled telegram.

> The wire as sent reported an epidemic among Somalis at Walu, but as received read as the report of an epidemic among cattle at Wayu. This led to a considerable dislocation of the stock movement and a special trip by air to be made by the Provincial Veterinary Officer to contact the writer on safari and straighten out the tangle (TRD Annual Report 1954, 19).

Over the course of the entire period from 1923 to 1987 there were substantial improvements in telecommunications.

A final area of development in the district that arguably contributed to the declining costs of exchange was the posting of increasing numbers of civil servants and agricultural specialists. Most certainly, government institutions and personnel can also have the effect of increasing transaction costs, and many such cases could be cited for Africa. Marketing boards, corrupt licensing bureaus, and overregulation are typical examples (see Bates 1981). Nevertheless, many of the measures undertaken by the government in Tana River District appear to have actually had a net beneficial effect on local exchange. Among these one can point to widespread cattle inoculations, locust eradication, and the development of centralized auction houses.

Further evidence that these declining transaction costs were correlated with an increase in trade comes from the data on the number of traders working in the district. The Tana River District reports of 1923 (pp. 5-6) and 1929 (p. 5) complain of too few traders in the district and the presence of a monopsony. The TRD report of 1949 (p. 13), however, complains of too many traders.

Data on Transaction Costs for the Period from 1980-1987

The author conducted fieldwork among the Orma from 1978 to 1981, and again in 1987. Large quantitative household economic surveys were carried out on both occasions and provide considerable data on many of the same households in 1980 and again in 1987. Both surveys were of the population living in the exact same locality, with controls built in to account for biases associated with population movements in and out of the area (for more details see Ensminger 1992).

Over this period a number of significant changes occurred which affected transaction costs. For the first time, the chief began to notarize legitimate livestock traders and the ownership of stock. While seemingly insignificant, this procedure was aimed at reducing the sale (and possible forfeiture) of stolen cattle. Police forces in the area were also increased fourfold in an effort to reduce the level of banditry, a chronic problem in this sparsely populated and difficult to patrol area. The government continues to regulate weights and measures, including annual validation of all instruments.

One of the most dramatic changes over this period was the opening of the first bank in the district. While the bank has had little impact yet on the availability of credit to small-scale producers, it has had a major impact upon the way in which business is carried out in the district. Its presence reduces the need to carry large quantities of cash within and between districts. This obviously reduces the security risk of vulnerability to armed bandits, a real threat in the district, especially prior to the increased police presence.

Between 1980 and 1987 there were marked improvements in the roads and bridges in the district, with much construction on-going in 1987 that would directly impact the Orma in the interior. Bridges under construction over a major river that floods the territory twice yearly and cuts off the interior for weeks at a time will enormously facilitate the stocking of local shops in the interior during the rainy season. They will also allow the cattle traders better access to the area during the period when most cattle sales take place (during the rains). With every landrover and lorry that gets through in the wet season arrive 10 to 30 people also bringing information from all corners of the district.

During the 1980s the district headquarters significantly upgraded their telephone exchange, linking many government departments and local shops for the first time. It is no longer necessary now, as it was in 1980, to send a runner each time a message needs to be delivered between the administrative offices and the commercial district (as much as 4 kms. away). Communications with the outside were also vastly improved, better affording communications between merchants and their wholesalers outside the district.

The Kenyan government's national plan to decentralize the administration (District Focus for Rural Development) also had significant effects upon the local civil service. The central government did not increase the size of the civil service so much as they set about posting people out of the capital and into the rural countryside. This decentralization initiative resulted in an increase in staff and upgrading of the level of virtually all government ministries in Tana River District over this period. This included the veterinary office, health clinics, schools, and the development office. These staffing increases were apparent both in the district headquarters, and even more so in the rural hinterland where the Orma live and herd their cattle. For the first time a district veterinary officer was actually posted to an Orma town (where the cattle are) rather than the district headquarters. Health, teaching, and civil service staff similarly increased. Another example was the posting of the first adult education teacher. The result of initiatives like these is seen in the data on school enrollments. In 1980 4% of the school-age female population were attending school, while 26% of the boys were attending. The comparable figures for 1987 were 30% and 50% respectively. These are enormous gains over only a seven-year period. It now remains to be seen what effect these factors that reduced transaction costs have had on the economic fortunes of Orma producers.

Effects of Declining Transaction Costs on Orma Producers

The best data available to document the effect of declining transaction costs upon Orma producers comes from the data on terms of trade over time for 1923 to 1987. These data indicate that traders themselves did not consume all of the benefits of declining transaction costs; some filtered down to Orma producers. In Figures 3.1, 3.2, and 3.3 I present data on the terms of trade for cattle, the key commodity produced for sale, against the major consumption items (maize, rice, sugar, cloth, paraffin and cooking oil).

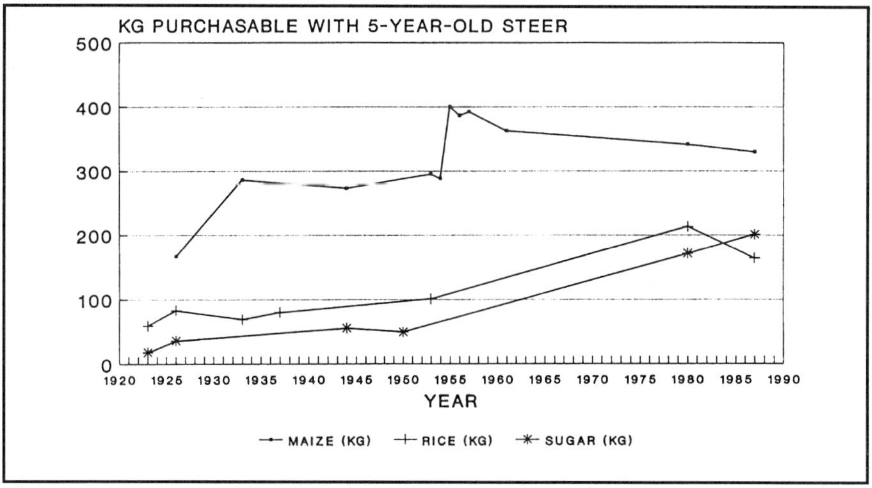

Figure 3.1: Terms of Trade: Cattle, Maize, Rice, and Sugar

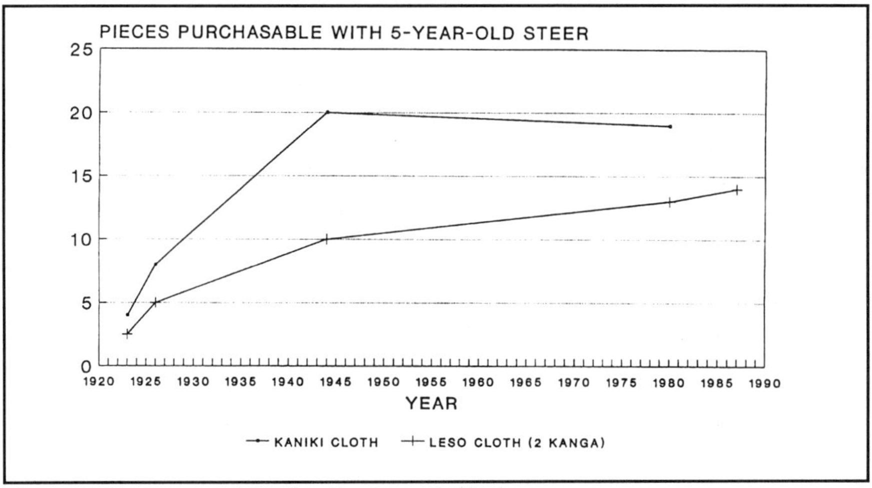

Figure 3.2: Terms of Trade: Cattle and Cloth

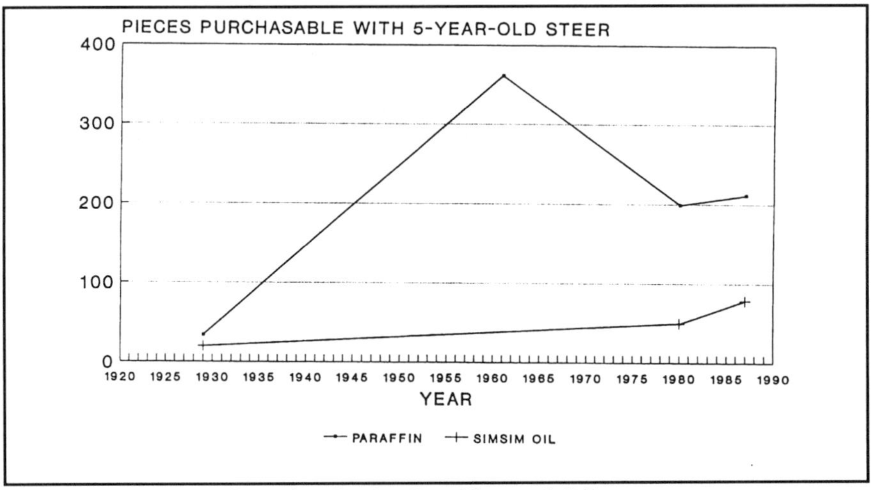

Figure 3.3: Terms of Trade: Cattle, Paraffin, and Oil

The figures show graphically the increasing quantities of each commodity that could be purchased with a five year old steer (the major marketable item of the Orma). In all cases, there have been substantial gains in terms of trade for the Orma over time, from 1923 to 1987.

For the period from 1980 to 1987 we have far more detailed data based upon a household survey of 52 households (in 1980) and 90 households (in 1987) from exactly the same area. In Table 3.1 we see the data on terms of trade weighted by the percentage of production and consumption for each commodity in actual household budgets. Here we are able to weigh the cattle sales by the actual percentage of sales in each age group, and figure the inflation rate on all purchased commodities weighted by the percentage of the budget spent on each. While one notes some loss in terms of trade with regard to particular commodities (a slight loss against maize flour, and a major loss against rice), the overall data again show a marked gain for the Orma between 1980 and 1987. While their major source of income (cattle) shows a gain of 116% for the period, their basket of consumption goods shows an overall increase in cost of only 93%. All food commodities together show even smaller increases, at 89%. Their net gain overall in purchasing power is on the order of 23%.

Commodity	1980	1987	% increase, 1980-7
Price to Orma producer			
Cattle: 1-2 years	366	787	115
Cattle: 3-4 years	753	1741	131
Cattle: over 5 years	988	2072	110
All cattle sales[a]	NA	NA	116
Price to Orma consumer			
Sugar (1 kg)	5	9	80
Maize flour (2 kg pkt)	5	11	120
Tea leaves (50 grams)	1/50	1/90	27
Simsim oil (700 ml)	12	16	33
Rice (1 kg)	4	11	175
Kanga cloth	65	130	100
Paraffin (700 ml)	3	6	100
All food	NA	NA	89
All commodities[b]	NA	NA	93

Note: The exchange rate for Kenyan shillings in 1980 was 8 shillings to the dollar and in 1987 it was 16 shillings to the dollar.

[a] Weighted by the proportion of sales in each age category.

[b] Weighted by the proportion of the household budget spent per commodity.

Table 3.1: Terms of Trade for the Galole Orma at Wayu (in Kenyan shillings), 1980 to 1987

A final piece of data is perhaps the most compelling of all in making the case that significant reductions in transaction costs occurred between 1980 and 1987. It is typical for all households, but especially the poor, to take food from the local shops on credit throughout the dry season and sell cattle to the shopkeeper when the rains begin in order to clear the debt. Economic necessity drives most poor households to engage in such debt bondage. Interest rates for the two periods (1980 and 1987) were calculated comparing the difference between the price one receives for cattle sold to the local shop to clear one's debt, compared to the price received for cattle sold to outside traders to whom one was not indebted. In 1980 the effective interest rates were 37% for one season, or approximately 87% for the year. Surprisingly, in 1987, the effective interest rates were 5.6% per season, or approximately 12% per year. In both cases, these rates are net of inflation. North (1990) argues that interest rates are one of the most telling indicators of transaction costs, and this being the case, these data appear consistent with the other data that the trend for real economic benefits accruing to the Orma from declining transaction costs begun in 1923 was continuing in the 1980s.

Transaction Costs and Monopoly Rents

While one could argue that even small-scale producers gained from declining transaction costs over time, there certainly were greater advantages realized by some individuals. Each change in government policy and institutions, including those reducing transaction costs, also potentially opens a window of opportunity for the collection of monopoly rents. Beginning with Islam and literacy, we find that in 1920 few Orma had converted, and fewer yet were literate. Thus, Shambaro was in a decidedly advantageous position. With time, these advantages eroded as more and more people shared these qualities.

Next came the standardization of weights and measures. Initially, the high costs of officially sanctioned weights and measures may have kept some people out of trade, thus giving an advantage to those already established and those who could afford the costs of such overhead.

Roads and telecommunications offered advantages to those who happened to be in the right place at the right time, or who were influential enough to see to it that roads and telegraph and telephone lines passed their way.

Perhaps more than any other advancement, transportation confers enormous gains selectively and has tremendous exclusionary power as a consequence of the great expense of purchasing and maintaining a vehicle. Until at least 1987, no African traders except Shambaro have been able to crash this barrier. While even those who do not own vehicles benefit from the greater flow of information resulting from increased traffic, clearly those owning the transportation have greater access. Lack of access to transportation may well be the main reason that Africans have not been able to break the Arab monopsony on wholesale marketing in the district.

Finally, the greater presence of civil servants, government licensing, and regulation provide more opportunities for bribery and favoritism. It is likely that those who begin with greater financial resources and influence will attempt to use new government institutions to perpetuate such influence (see Knight 1992). The more successful they are, however, and the more profitable their enterprise, the greater the incentive for other entrepreneurs to break into their territory. But this may take a long time once a powerful player is entrenched.

Formal Versus Informal Norms of Behavior and the Problem of Legitimacy

One of the least researched areas to date in transaction costs analysis is the interface between formal and informal norms of behavior. Changes in government policy are likely to have significantly less success in reducing transaction costs if informal norms of behavior are not consistent with the formal codes and if ideological support is not also present. One of the reasons that the policy changes discussed in this paper were successful in reducing transaction costs is because they were imposed gradually, and usually not before the majority of the population were prepared to accept them.

The two areas where government institutions have been resisted to some degree are education and the transfer of legal affairs from the council of elders to the state. These two issues are worth examining briefly because the manner in which they were handled has implications for the bridging of formal and informal norms and the creation of legitimacy.

Education was controversial from its very origins in the district in the early 1950s. However, at that time it was not compulsory, so after some airing of grievances with the then chief, the elders who were opposed to it tolerated its presence so long as they could refuse to send their own children. The main problem for the opposition elders was that male children were crucial for cattle herding, and they perceived education as a threat to their livelihood. Education became controversial again in the 1970s when primary school became compulsory in Kenya. However, such a stringent change of policy was *not* implemented among the Orma, where only 26% of boys and 4% of girls attended in 1979. To have insisted upon compulsory schooling overnight would have created severe disruption of the economy and of ideological support for the state. Instead, the chief *gradually* increased pressure on households he knew could afford to send some children to school. The result was a vast increase in enrollments by 1987. What is more, by 1987 many of the very same elders who were outspoken against education in 1979 then viewed education as the future.

A similarly slow process has unfolded as the chief (a government civil servant) increasingly hears more and more legal disputes formerly brought before the elders. This process has played itself out fairly smoothly and naturally without need of proclamations mandating the transition. As people learn the biases of the state courts versus the elders, those disputants who perceive that the state favors their side are likely to choose to have their cases heard there rather than by the elders. Eventually, precedent dictates that all cases of a given nature are handled by the state. In this way the state has managed to assume most legal authority in the area.

One reason that the other topics discussed in this paper have not been particularly controversial for the Orma and have met neither ideological resistance nor intransigent informal norms, is that most did not directly have obvious redistributive consequences at the time of implementation. It is often redistributive consequences that engender strongest opposition. So, for example, the fact that roads and telecommunications benefit some more than others may not have been the focus of perception, so much as the fact that all would benefit a little bit from cheaper and more frequent transportation and a more regular supply of goods to the local shops.

Not all institutional changes affecting transaction costs are as free of controversy. One subject not discussed here, but one almost always accompanied by opposition, is changes in property rights.[6] Since property rights so obviously redistribute resources, they are almost invariably the subject of contention, and are very difficult to alter. This is a particularly crucial area for more study of the relationship between formal and informal norms and legitimacy.

Conclusions

The importance of transaction costs for development can certainly be exaggerated; they are not the entire solution to poor economic performance. However, as I hope to have demonstrated in this study, they do represent a legitimate and important area of attention for development planners and their reduction can yield significant economic benefits. One of the lessons of transaction cost analysis is that there is no such thing as *the* optimal set of economic institutions. In the absence of legitimacy and compliance through informal norms, the most "perfectly" designed institutions yield poor results. For this reason, transaction costs research is a natural arena for the combination of economic and anthropological methods and understandings.

References

Bates, Robert H. 1981. *Markets and States in Tropical Africa: The Political Basis of Agricultural Policies*. Berkeley: University of California Press.

———.1989. *Beyond the Miracle of the Market: The Political Economy of Agrarian Development in Kenya*. Cambridge: Cambridge University Press.

Cornell, Stephen and Joseph P. Kalt. 1989. Culture and Institutions as Public Goods: American Indian Economic Development as a Problem of Collective Action. Harvard Project on American Indian Economic Development, Malcolm Wiener Center for Social Policy. John F. Kennedy School of Government, Harvard University.

Dalton, George ed. 1967. *Tribal and Peasant Economies: Readings in Economic Anthropology*. Garden City, NY: The Natural History Press.

Ensminger, Jean. 1992. *Making a Market: The Institutional Transformation of an African Society*. Cambridge: Cambridge University Press.

———.n.d. *Explaining Conversion to Islam: Evidence from Africa*. Unpublished manuscript.

Ensminger, Jean and Andrew Rutten. 1991. The Political Economy of Changing Property Rights: Dismantling a Pastoral Commons. *American Ethnologist* 18(4): 683-699.

Granovetter, Mark. 1985. The Strength of Weak Ties. *American Journal of Sociology* 78(6): 1360-1380.

———.1991. The Nature of Economic Relationships. Paper presented at the Workshop on New Institutional Theory, sponsored by the Comparative Societal Analysis Program November 8-10, Department of Sociology, Cornell University, Ithaca, New York.

Greif, Avner. 1992. *Cultural Beliefs and the Organization of Society: A Historical and Theoretical Reflection on Collectivist and Individualist Societies.* Unpublished manuscript, Stanford University.

———.1993. *On the Nature and Evolution of Political and Economic Institutions: Commitment, Reputation, and Self-enforcing Institutions in Late Medieval Genoa.* Unpublished manuscript, Stanford University.

Knight, Jack. 1992. *Institutions and Social Conflict.* Cambridge: Cambridge University Press.

Nabli, Mustapha and Jeffrey B. Nugent. 1989. The New Institutional Economics and Its Applicability to Development. *World Development* 17(9):1333-1347.

North, Douglass C. 1981. *Structure and Change in Economic History.* New York: Norton.

———.1990. *Institutions, Institutional Change and Economic Performance.* Cambridge: Cambridge University Press.

———.1993. *The New Institutional Economics and Development.* Paper prepared for the Conference on Public Choice and Development: The New Institutional Economics and Third World Development, London, September 16-18, 1993.

———.n.d. *The Paradox of the West.* Unpublished manuscript.

Norton, Seth W. 1992. Transaction Costs, Telecommunications, and the Microeconomics of Macroeconomic Growth. *Economic Development and Cultural Change* 41(1): 175-196.

Polanyi, Karl. 1944. *The Great Transformation.* Boston: Beacon Press.

Pollak, Robert A. 1985. A Transaction Cost Approach to Families and Households. *Journal of Economic Literature* 23: 581-608.

Ruttan, Vernon W. 1989. Institutional Innovation and Agricultural Development. *World Development* 17(9): 1375-1387.

Shipton, Parker. 1988. The Kenyan Land Tenure Reform: Misunderstandings in the Public Creation of Private Property. In R. E. Downs and S. P. Reyna, eds., *Land and Society in Contemporary Africa*. Hanover, NH: University Press of New England.

Wallis, John Joseph and Douglass C. North. 1986. Measuring the Transaction Sector in the American Economy, 1870-1970. In, S. Engerman and R. Gallman, eds., *Long-term Factors in American Economic Growth*. Chicago: University of Chicago Press.

White, Landeg. 1987. *Magomero: Portrait of an African Village*. Cambridge: Cambridge University Press.

Notes

1. The research on institutional change by new institutional economists (particularly that of economic historians such as Douglass North 1981, 1990 and Avner Greif 1992, 1993) has direct relevance to the concerns of anthropologists. Modifications of the perspective (such as that of Jack Knight 1992) that address the issue of distributional consequences and the role of power in institutional change also have considerable relevance for anthropologists. See Nabli and Nugent 1989 for a brief summary of the applications of the new institutional economics to development concerns.

2. See Pollak (1985) for a discussion of the economic limitations of this form of exchange.

3. Shipton (1988) provides a perfect example of informal practices and norms undermining formal codes in his discussion of Luo land tenure practices which undermine the Kenyan government's policy of land privatization.

4. For a detailed discussion of this argument see Ensminger (1992) and (n.d.).

5. See Norton (1992) for a discussion of the importance of telecommunications in reducing transaction costs.

6. For a discussion of changes in Orma property rights see Ensminger and Rutten (1991) and Ensminger (1992).

4

Institutionalizing Opportunism: Cheating On Baby Purse Seiners in Batangas Bay, Philippines[1]

Susan Russell

Introduction

Agricultural sharecropping contracts between landlords and tenants often have been viewed as relatively efficient institutions for spreading risk between labor and capital. Some scholars also argue that sharecropping lowers the transaction costs associated with the supervision of labor by bestowing tenants a higher share for increased labor input (e.g., Reid 1976; Bardhan 1980). Labor monitoring costs are especially high when production uncertainty makes it difficult to infer input from output (Bardhan 1980, 87) or when the quality of labor (pace, efficiency, timing) is critically important for productive success (Wells 1984, 7). Despite these observations on why share contracts may be preferred to other forms of labor payment, Cheung (1969) and Robertson (1987) argue that the transaction costs of negotiating, managing and enforcing sharecropping contracts tend to be higher than those associated with fixed rent or wage labor arrangements. While any given state of risk dispersion may not be ideal for both parties, share contracts still may be preferable to other contractual arrangements as long as the transaction costs are at least compensated for by the gain from risk dispersion (Cheung 1969, 69). In Cheung's work, as others have noted (e.g., Hart 1986; Bhardan 1989), the higher labor supervision and enforcement costs of share contracts are left essentially unexplored.

Very little has been written about either the efficiency or the nature of transaction costs in fishing enterprises characterized by share contracts between boat owners and crew members. Acheson's review (1981, 278) observes that share contracts in fishing are widespread in order to reduce the risk for boat owners of having to pay fixed wages when catches are poor. He notes that maritime share contracts tend to have two effects that may contribute to inefficiency. First, they may contribute to high turnover of crew members, since crew will seek to work on the most successful boats. Second, they may inhibit capital investment since crew members share in increased profits without having to contribute to the cost of new technology. Alexander (1982) argues that share systems in Sri Lankan beach seining over time have become both inefficient and inequitable in terms of rewarding labor as rural capitalists disrupted the pattern of joint ownership of nets. It also has been observed that maritime share institutions may persist long after their efficiency in regard to the wider economy has been diminished. In New England, for example, high prices have tended to reward workers in the fishing industry more so than in other sectors of the economy, thereby compensating fishermen at higher levels than are needed to maintain a labor supply. Also, when returns from fishing are high, profits that could provide new investment capital are siphoned off into wages. When returns are low, declines in wages stabilize falling profits, which inhibits reductions in the number of firms engaged in fishing (Doeringer, Moss and Terkla 1986, 79-80).

One of the most comprehensive and in-depth studies of how the earnings from fishing are distributed is Firth's (1966) study of Malay fishermen. He observes that the shares allotted to labor and capital vary by the type of fishing and are fairly complex, but in general the largest share accrues to the owner(s) of capital. In artisanal fishing without motors, the net often comprises the most important capital item. The proportion returned to capital and labor largely correspond to the degree to which each contributes to the total yield, e.g., the higher the amount of fixed capital required for a particular type of fishing, the higher the share received by the owner (ibid: 256; Acheson 1981; Bailey 1983; Vercruijsse 1984). Yet in his description of share systems in Malay seining, he remarks on their "bewildering complexity" that at first glance appears inexplicable (Firth 1966, 256). He notes that the formal division of shares between the boat and the crew gives little clue to the complexities involved since it "leaves unstated all the special allowances for the wide range of functions and services which are taken into account" (ibid, 236).[2]

In fishing communities, informal codes of conduct include practices wherein owners of boats often distribute shares so as to reward crew members selectively according to their extra effort, skill or even need (e.g., Firth 1966; Carsten 1989). Carsten also observes that owners often reduce the share normatively allocated to the boat when the catch is small. This practice is especially likely to occur when the owner is also a crew member and when he and the crew are co-villagers or close kin. In addition, most fishing studies stress that the owners of boats usually allow crew members to take some fish home for consumption after each trip.

In most descriptions of maritime share systems, it is difficult to ascertain the degree or frequency with which boat owners in any one community deviate from the formal rules of sharing the catch, vary among each other in terms of how formal rules are structured, or change the rules from season to season. Some studies, however, reveal a surprising amount of diversity in the formal rules of dividing the catch within any one peasant community (e.g., Alexander 1982; Villafuerte and Bailey 1982). In some cases the formal rules may be less significant in determining actual share payments than informal bargaining between boat owners and crew (e.g., Orbach 1977, 185; Firth 1966, 256).

The nature of transaction costs in maritime share systems has received little direct discussion, yet it is likely that these institutions have even higher transaction costs than agricultural sharecropping systems owing to the the greater risk and uncertainty surrounding the timing and amount of the 'harvest' and because of the much greater frequency with which shares usually are divided throughout a fishing season. This uncertainty surrounding the frequency and amount of fish which will be caught poses heavy demands on share contracts in areas undergoing marine resource depletion, particularly when the number of crew members is large and fishing is their primary form of income generation. In these circumstances, share systems must often be renegotiated during a fishing season or perhaps balanced over several seasons in order to support the needs of both boat owners and crew. Bray and Robertson (1980) argue that in horticulture, for example, the frequency of harvesting tends to complicate the sharing process, and hence in horticulture transaction costs may be lower with wage contracts or fixed rent tenancy. Cheung (1969, 64) also notes that transaction costs increase as the number of participants and contractual exchanges increase.

Coase (1960) observes that when it is costless to transact, competitive efficiency through the operation of the market will occur regardless of the institutional environment. Vertically integrated firms or other relational contracting arrangements may arise in the presence of high transaction costs, which are often brought about by opportunism (Williamson 1975, 26-34). The new institutional economics takes the position that the purpose of organizations, firms or other institutions, then, is to reduce transaction costs and uncertainty in human interactions. Yet as Bardhan (1989, 1391) notes, this approach has not always come to terms with the "enormity of the collective action problem that limits the ability of potential gainers to get their act together in bringing about institutional changes."

In this paper, I discuss the history and nature of maritime share contracts in a Southern Tagalog baby purse seining fleet in Batangas Bay, Luzon. These contracts in the past may have operated relatively efficiently, but in recent years a pattern of institutionalized cheating has emerged which raises the transaction costs for everyone concerned. This paper seeks to explain why the share arrangements that have evolved over the last century operate less effectively today, and why boat owners and crew members are constrained from negotiating a new share system which would reduce certain inefficiencies that now characterize these institutions.

The Evolution of Share Systems in Baby Purse Seining

Since the late 1800s, Tagalog fishermen in Batangas have been using seining nets of one form or another to catch tuna, mackerel, round scad, anchovy, and a number of other pelagic fish. Beach seines, lift nets, small purse seines, and ring nets are all in use today (see Szanton 1971; Spoehr 1984). In this paper, I focus on *panmumukot*, or 'baby' purse seining.[3]

In the first half of this century, the seiners of San Andres fished with 25-30 crew members on large outrigger canoes equipped with oars and sails. These were much larger canoes (14-20 meters in length) than those used in other kinds of fishing, owing to the need for extra room to haul the huge seining net (350 meters long, 35-45 meters deep) and the large amount of fish in the bottom of the boat. Fishing was done during the day up and down the coast of Batangas, and then the fish were brought back to shore. Once on shore, they were cooked and salted, and later taken by oxcart to markets in nearby towns for retailing. The price of fish was very low at that time, and crew members were easily recruited from the nearby area.

The crew structure of seining boats has changed only slightly over the years. The owner of the boat (*nagmamandas*, or 'the one who commands') accompanied his boat to sea, but did little manual labor. His primary responsibility on the boat was to scan the surface of the sea for schools of fish, pilot the boat, and give the order for when to set the net. The *magdadala*, 'the one who carries' the boat, was responsible for hiring the crew, diving into the sea to make sure the net was in proper position, and covering the fish in containers after a catch. There was also a rudder man (*timonero* or *manenemon*), a second diver (*manunugbo*), a master net mender (*maghahayuma*), a crew responsible for throwing the net (*tagahulog*), a water bailer (*tagapaglimas*), and the primary crew who commands the group pulling the rope which closes the seine net (*tagabirador*). Individuals who are very experienced are collectively referred to as the *mamumutot* (the ones who get the 'last piece' from the bottom of the boat). The entire crew is referred to collectively as the *barkada* (group or gang who travel together), or more often, simply as 'the people' (*ang tao*).

The customary practice of sharing was one where the owner received half of the catch, and the crew received the other half (*hatian*, or 'halves'). Each regular crew member on the boat also received a 'share for the body' (*ang tumpok ng katawan*). The owners received three shares from the crew's share to pay for the expenses of the boat and net, and the *magdadala* also received three shares. The master net mender and the second diver each received one and a half or sometimes two shares.

In the 'old style' of sharing, the crew received their shares in money only once a year or sometimes every two or even three years. Hence, the actual sharing system was comprised primarily of the fish received at the time of the catch, and loans of money made to crew members by the owner. The loans of money were taken from the gross sales of the boat that the owner kept. The system of paying cash shares once a year or every two years allowed owners to adjust share payments with their expenses for the boat and with the amount of fish caught over the course of a whole ten month fishing season, or even several fishing seasons.

During this period, catches were often large but prices for fish were low, so boat owners usually allowed crew members to get extra fish during big catches to make up for delayed payment of monetary shares and to reduce the need to constantly make small loans to crew members. This is the original meaning of the term *delihensiya*, a pattern of bonuses or give-aways during large catches. As an institution, *delihensiya* has become elaborated and is now a significant component of sharing practices.

Around 1960, the owners of seining boats adopted motors. Today, the boats are equipped with second-hand diesel truck engines from South Korea or Japan that have been adapted for marine use. As a result of the overfishing of tuna in the Philippines in the 1970s, the fish catch per boat also has decreased. Tuna became heavily overfished in most Philippine waters during the 1970s, and most commercial canneries today catch yellowfin tuna and make up for local shortfalls in skipjack through fishing in other South Pacific waters. The decrease in overall catch has been accompanied by higher prices for fish.

There are currently two ways by which fishermen generally market their catch. Fishermen who are indebted to a fish consignor are required to sell them all of their fish and pay a 10 - 20 percent commission rate of the total price offered. If they are out of her jurisdiction when they sell their catch, they are obliged to remit this same commission rate to their fish consignor. In order to monitor client fishermen who may try to renege on the terms of these contracts, the largest fish consignor relies on a system of 'spies' (local informers) in various coastal towns.

The second method of marketing the catch is to sell fish at sea. The pattern of spies used by the fish consignor who independently financed the expansion of this baby purse seining fleet in the 1980s was partly in response to the growth in the number of small retailers operating from boats. These retailers hover around the bays wherever they see seining boats fishing, waiting to see which boats will catch fish. Sometimes, if the captain wishes to set the net immediately to try and catch some more fish, he will sell all of the catch at sea. Since retailers at sea do not charge a commission rate, nor charge for transportation and labor to market the fish, they also represent a very attractive alternative market outlet to traditional fish consignors.

With the adoption of motors, the crew structure and the share system of seining also changed. Originally, boat owners always were captains, whereas owners now are captains on only one-third of the boats. A majority of the 62 seining boats in San Andres have adopted a system of sharing based on thirds (*sikatlo*) where the owners get two parts of the catch (one part for the expenses of the boat, one part for owning the boat and gear) and the crew receive one part to be divided among them. In this system, most boat owners deduct the cost of the fish consignor's commission, marketing costs, and food for the crew when they are fishing far away before the shares are divided. Hired captains usually receive 10 percent of the catch after expenses are deducted. Most owners try to pay a cash share to crew either after every catch or every two weeks when they dry dock the boat. A few older boat owners, however, retain the traditional practice of paying cash shares irregularly.

Crew recruitment patterns also have changed. The Southern Tagalog region of Batangas is now the most highly developed area of the Philippines outside of Metropolitan Manila. It has become more difficult to recruit crew members locally, as corporations and migration abroad represent more attractive employment opportunities. Therefore, some boat owners have turned to hiring Bikol or Visayan crew members from poverty-stricken areas of the central

Philippines by paying their costs of transportation to San Andres, and by providing them free food and housing. Also, casual laborers (*mananamahan*) and young boys form a larger percentage of the crew of seining boats today. Because there are now at least 62 seining boats in the village, crew members also have the option of changing boats often unless they are indebted to a boat owner.[4]

The Institutionalization of Small-Scale Cheating

Cheating in seining is a widely tolerated, if not sanctioned social norm and a common topic of discussion in the village. One afternoon while talking to a retired fisherman who owns a seining boat, I was startled to hear his daughter start needling her brother about cheating their family by selling fish at sea without their father's knowledge. Her brother was defending himself by explaining that sometimes he had no money for expenses, but she wasn't buying his explanation. As their discussion grew more heated, the boat owner leaned over to me, smiled, and said "Cheating is the twin of the pukot boat" (*Ang pangdaraya na ay kakambal ng pukutan*). "Doesn't it bother you that the crew are cheating you?" I asked. "Well, even if they hide fish, even if they sell fish on the outside, it's okay; they're my children," he said.

If cheating is the twin of seining, there is no doubt in everyone's mind that cheating has become a much more serious problem nowadays. Boat owners are surprisingly tolerant of cheating by their own sons, but some owners whose captains are not their children complain bitterly about how their crew are secretly selling fish at sea without their knowledge. They complain even more often that some of their crew are 'stealing' too many fish, and that it causes rivalry and dissension with other crew who were not able to steal as much.

How did things ever get to be this way? Firth (1966) makes no mention of cheating or stealing in his study of net fishermen in Malaysia in the 1930s, instead noting that everyone seemed satisfied with the way the captains divided up the catch in their own highly variable ways. Szanton (1971) later, however, found that fishing in the central Philippine town of Estancia resembled a kind of 'economic warfare' between boat owners and crew members as a result of conflict over changes in the share system initiated by boat owners (also see Alexander 1982).

While there are many kinds of cheating in seining, the most frequent form of cheating and the one which most directly affects share systems today revolves around the original custom of *delihensiya*. As described earlier, this term originally referred to a system of bonuses and give-aways by the boat owner to the crew during large catches. Today, however, the term has been expanded to include the practice of *dampot*, or 'fish grabbing'.[5]

Because seining boats are large in terms of the number of crew, some crew members grab fish and secretly stash them in their shirt or pockets, or hide them around the canoe. The actual amount they take depends on the individual (some are more agile and quick at this than others) and whether the owner or captain of the boat sees them doing it. If he does not see them grabbing the fish, then an adept crew member easily can get around 10 small fish. Once the boat docks and the captain can see how many surreptitiously gathered fish the crew member has, it is too late for the owner to do anything about it. As one older boat owner explained, "Once he has it, I cannot do anything because I did not see him steal it. I am ashamed to ask for it back." If the owner or captain does see a crew member grabbing some fish and trying to hide it, then he sometimes allows it up to a point, and other times scolds the person to stop.

The origin of 'fish grabbing,' or *dampot*, probably arose with the adoption of seining and larger boats. It is a practice initiated by crew members and generally tolerated by boat owners due to the low income of crew. This practice has its basis in the customary and much more widespread right of various individuals (including the crew) in almost all kinds of fishing in the Philippines to bring home *pangulam*, or 'food that is eaten with rice,' every time the boat catches fish (see for comparison Firth 1966, 254-256). In fact, the 'share of the body' discussed above implies a share of food, and therefore each crew member has the right to an equal amount. As one boat owner said, each crew member's "stomach is the same size," therefore *pangulam* should be given equally to all.[6] Over time, fish grabbing became an established customary right (*ang karapatan*) of the seining crew in the overall catch. The practice itself is not found in other forms of small boat fishing--although it is common in lift-net fishing with large nets. It is only in the larger, more complex forms of fishing like seining where the boats are big enough for crew to hide fish on them, and where the crew size and coordination required to haul the net allows for surreptitious stashing of fish without the owner or captain being aware of it. The fish that get caught in the net close to where the crew member is hauling it aboard are the original source of fish that are stashed (and regarded as *swerte*, or a crew member's 'luck'). In big catches, there is a more direct form of grabbing when the main bunt of the net is pulled into the boat.

In a big catch, say over 200 kilograms, the power that most captains have over crew members is minimal. On most boats, the crew initiate the activity blatantly. Crew members often work in pairs, with one guarding the fish that the other one is grabbing from the net with one hand as he hauls it in with the other hand. In a small catch, where the captain is more vigilant, fish grabbing is far more surreptitious, as the more agile crew tend to stick them in their pockets, inside their pants, into their shirts, under their hats, or toss them into corners of the boat. It is the captain's job to supervise as best he can the amount of extra fish crew members are grabbing. On the one hand, he can allow all or certain favorite crew members to get more than others by simply looking the other way--wherein *dampot* becomes a form of crew-initiated share or bonus payment. If the catch is very small, say 40-50 kilograms or less, then captains sometimes just yell "*Pangulam lang*" (meaning there is only enough for food) and crew members rush to the center of the boat to receive a handful of fish from the captain. Hence, fish grabbing today is an alternative to fish given by the captain to crew members. If the crew manage to snatch a lot of fish, then they do not receive a separate share for food. As will be discussed below, however, and which is untrue of the past, if the crew snatch too many fish, then they may also not receive any fish from the captain in the next catch. They may also not be given any cash share at all.

Prior to the 1960s, the degree to which crew members may have tried to get extra fish was constrained by the very low prices that could be obtained and the difficulties of marketing the fish. Most crew members (or their wives) just marketed whatever fish they and their kin group could not consume by walking house to house in nearby areas. During this period, in other words, it cost the owner very little to allow crew to take extra fish. Since boat owners were at that time and even today much wealthier than crew members, it would have been more costly in terms of local social norms to scold crew members for stealing a few fish than it was to simply look the other way. As a result, the practice was tolerated. At the same time, a crew member's incentive for getting a large number of extra fish was minimal owing to marketing difficulties and low prices.

Today, seining is riskier by far than any other form of fishing in Batangas Bay. Small fishermen catch some fish almost every time they go fishing, whereas seining boats may go for days without any catch at all. In the last three years, seasonal returns from fishing have been very poor. The situation is now one of high uncertainty as to whether there will be a peak season and when it will occur. With the overfishing of tuna, whose seasonal migratory movements are little understood in this region of the Pacific, neither boat owners nor crew members can predict what their likely income will be.

Therefore, the circumstances in which fish grabbing operates have changed enormously. What once may have been some fish of inconsequential value is now often a significant portion of the value of the catch since the price of fish is far higher now than before. Grabbing fish is now a profitable way for crew to supplement their meager income during low catches, and represents a loss of important income for cash-strapped boat owners, who often refer to it as 'cheating' (*nanandaya*) or, less charitably, 'stealing' (*nagnanakaw*).[7]

Cheating in this manner is ubiquitous with seining, but how significant is the value of fish crew members stash? If a boat is really hitting it, say getting a haul of 100 bins of fish, (each bin holds the rough equivalent of 40-45 kilograms), the cost to the boat owner is not too high and so captains tend to be lenient in supervision. Crew members typically can snatch 10-25 kgs each under these circumstances. If many boats catch fish at the same time, then the price might be around 200 pesos [27 pesos = 1 U.S. dollar] per bin. On a boat with 20 crew members, then, the loss to the boat owner is roughly equivalent to 2,000 pesos if the average is 20 kilograms per crew. Hence, the crew are basically 'allowed' to take around one tenth of the catch since, as Szanton (1971, 45) observes, captains are practically powerless to stop it. In a good fishing season, this amount is not considered exceptionally high by captains, especially if the boat is catching fish every day and everyone is having fun.

During the low season, however, the price of fish is much higher and snatching fish is surreptitious. Boats are often lucky if they catch only two bins of fish, and crew may only be able to snatch the equivalent of one kilogram each. (In reality, of course, the amount each one gets is variable; some get a lot and others get none.) If the price is 1,800 pesos per bin, then the gross value of the catch is 3,600, minus the 20 kilograms stolen by the crew. In this case, they have taken the equivalent of 900 pesos, or 25 percent of the gross sales value. Even in a good fishing season, this is considered a high amount. It is also a main source of tension between boat owners, captains and other crew.

Share Systems and Informal Codes of Conduct

In San Andres today, the most common method of sharing the catch on seining boats is the *sikatlo*, or 'thirds' system described above. In the 1991-92 fishing season, boat owners seldom paid cash shares to crew members that corresponded with the formal labor agreement (such as two and a half shares to the rudderman or two shares to the diver). Most boat owners alternated between (1) merely giving crew members pocket money and/or fish to take home for consumption; and (2) paying cash shares which were either evenly divided among all crew members or rewarded proportionately to long-term (or 'core') crew members versus those who were still new. Boat owners claimed that given the low and sporadic catches, the common welfare of all crew members should take precedence over special individual allocations for extra work performed. Crew members on most of these boats supplemented their meager cash shares through fish grabbing and fish given to them for food by the captain, in addition to engaging in other, small-scale forms of fishing.

What are the different transaction costs in this system of share payments? For the bulk of owners using the *sikatlo* system, and who do allow *delihensiya* on their boats, there are some obvious problems associated with attempts to reward individual crew members according to the skill and effort each crew expends.[8] The crew most active in grabbing fish are those who have the least work to do on the boat. The core crew (*mamumutot*) are busy in the center of the boat, hauling up the bunt of the net, laying it in place, and scooping fish into the hull, where it is covered in bins. The least experienced crew are at the ends of the net, relatively far from the watchful eye of the captain, and have the most opportunity to grab fish. Whereas the captain tries to make up the difference by giving the core crew the last pile of the fish after all the covering is finished to make up for the difference, crew members often quarrel over the inconsistency of the amount of fish each one received, especially if they feel their work effort was greater than that of another crew member. Boat owners and captains have to resolve these problems with disgruntled crew after each catch by trying to make it up in the distribution of shares.

If the hard feelings are not evened out among the crew, then the owner faces one or more of his crew leaving. Therefore, *delihensiya* is a crucial aspect of the share system insofar as it determines the amount the boat owners decide to pay crew in cash, whether they pay them anything at all, and how much each crew receives. While he has ultimate (and unchecked) authority to decide expenses and the payment of cash shares, a boat owner also has to manage the finances of the boat and crew in a rather haphazard manner that leaves long term financial planning extremely difficult.

In a big catch, the difficulties of rewarding crew members according to their work effort are even worse. Boat owners complain that some crew only "work for their *delihensiya*," thus allowing fish to escape the net by not pulling as hard and fast as they should. Instead, their attention is divided between hauling in the catch and piling up fish, as described earlier. Compared to a small catch, the control of a captain in a big hit is weak owing to several factors: the presence of numerous small fishermen who are begging for handouts, and the practice wherein individual crew are simultaneously selling their legitimate as well as clandestine 'share' in fish to retailers at sea. As

Szanton (1971, 45) describes, these sales to retailers are almost impossible for the captain to prevent during a large catch even if he tries. The various exchanges of fish that occur during a large catch literally prevent a captain from ascertaining the exact volume of fish that were hauled up.

Most boat owners in San Andres pursue a combination of strategies to reduce problems of crew recruitment and small-scale cheating. These strategies include the practice of becoming godparents to their crew members, feeding and housing crew members when necessary, drinking with their crew, performing rituals together to increase the luck of the boat in fishing, offering secret bonuses to their long-term crew members, and offering no interest loans to crew. For those owners who are also captains, instilling crew loyalty is easier owing to their participation in the work process and general conviviality on board the canoe. Those owners who are too sickly or too old to captain their own boat generally rely on their captains to perform these same forms of social control.

One strategy captains use to instill loyalty in their crew is to give them their share in fish to sell at sea. This pattern was uncommon until around 1980 when the *pukot* fleet expanded, as there were fewer retailers at sea. Before that time, boat owners paid shares to crew from the fish they sold to fish consignors. But now they have reverted back to paying crew sometimes a large part of their share in fish in order to avoid passing on the cost of fish consignors' commissions and other charges to the division of the catch. In this way, the crew do not have to pay for the commission rate that the boat owner's fish consignor would charge. While this is another way of cheating the fish consignor, it is very popular with crew. It also increases, however, boat owners' uncertainty over how much additional fish were sold at sea under the guise of crew payments.

Transaction Costs and Constraints on Institutional Change

Transaction costs are high in seining not only because of the opportunities for crew and captains to cheat boat owners by grabbing or selling fish at sea, and boat owners to cheat their fish consignors the same way, but also because of the nature of the sharing institutions and informal property rights in the catch that have evolved in San Andres. In the past, when fish were plentiful and a slack labor market in fishing existed, the market structure did not provide the opportunities for cheating the way it does today. Since crew and owners were well-known to each other, share contracts were enforced more by informal moral codes of conduct. The 'moral economy' of fishing at this time provided on the boat evolved. In this environment, the wealth of pukot boat owners compared to crew members sponsored patterns of patron-client relationships.

While these informal rights and codes of conduct persist today, the environment has become more complex and the motivation of actors has changed. The primary factors which explain why the formal share system is less closely followed today and why 'cheating' has increased have to do with the declining returns from baby purse seining (described above) and the changing nature of the labor force.

Owing to the declining catch and the increase in the number of alternative employment opportunities in this region, the nature of crew composition has changed dramatically in recent years. First, almost all boats depend on recruiting at least some crew members from poorer, less developed regions of the Philippines.[9] Many of these crew members do not know either the captain or the boat owner personally when they are hired. New recruits from Bikol and the central Philippines are only minimally conversant in the local dialect. Hence, it is not surprising that while share systems still reflect the older institutional codes of conduct and informal constraints, the changes in the environment and actors means they function less well.

Second, many crew members are teen-agers or in their early 20s, unmarried, and not ready to commit to being a long-term crew member of one boat.[10] Instead, they prefer to move around periodically to experience different sharing systems and to 'change their luck'. In effect, they engage in a search that eventually provides them sufficient (however incomplete) information to make a long-term commitment to one boat. The same is true of casual crew members, who form an important part of the crew these days, but who rarely stay longer than a month with one boat.

For the many young and casual crew members who do not know the owner or captain personally, the only way to acquire accurate knowledge about the way he distributes shares to less important crew or disperses favors such as interest free loans is to experience it. In the short run for these crew, 'cheating' through grabbing fish or shirking tend to loom as having a higher payoff than relying on experience alone.

Grabbing fish is a crew member's immediate reward; it's money in his pocket, or food. It's also a hedge against the risk that a boat owner will not pay an adequate cash share, or will not pay one at all. In effect, it's a short-run risk premium extracted in fish. The price crew members pay for this activity is low in the sense that it has traditionally evolved as an informal property right of the crew in the catch, and hence the costs of changing these rules or enforcing new informal restrictions are large. The common practice of boat owners allowing their crew to sell fish at sea in order to avoid paying the high commission to fish consignors also increases the opportunities for some 'hidden' sales by crew members.

Norms of behavior, mutual trust, and paternalism still characterize the relations between boat owners and their core crew (*mamumutot*) on seining boats in San Andres, at least for those owners who have managed to retain a core of important crew members over a fairly long period of time. In these cases, the core crew are usually kin or neighbors of the owner. Enforcing the rules of the boat with these individuals is not nearly as difficult as on the boats that have not managed to maintain a core crew over a long period. In these cases where mutual trust prevails, long-term crew have acquired a great deal of information over the years as to how fair or generous the owner will be in evening out their seasonal share of the catch, how easy it will be to get loans for food during the low season, how often and how selectively secret bonuses will be dispensed, and how flexible the repayment periods for loans will be.

While long-term crew may believe that in a normal fishing season their overall returns will be fair, in current conditions a high degree of uncertainty exists over whether a boat owner will be able to live up to previous cash payments. Many boat owners have lost money for several seasons in a row and are heavily in debt. Traditional secret bonuses and loans are not nearly as common as they once were. Therefore, small-scale cheating, at least through surreptitious fish grabbing, is now often regarded by even loyal crew as a low-cost way to ensure a minimal return. These newer perceptions owe much to the more heterogeneous composition and motives of crews today, which lessen the likelihood that mutually reinforcing social sanctions will prevent the free rider problems associated with fish grabbing.

The conditions surrounding the sharing of the catch in San Andres would seem a ripe setting for the negotiation of a new share contract that better serves the interests of both boat owners and crew members. The crew relies on cheating owing to the absence of regular share payments by boat owners and suffer from the inequities that arise over their differential ability to snatch fish. In response to the cheating and also to the low catches, boat owners seldom pay shares according to the formal agreement. Instead, they rely on rough estimates of the value of fish crew members have taken (both legally and 'illegally') when they do pay shares and strive to even out disputes over equity among their crew after each catch. They also experience labor shortages that arise from their crew's dissatisfaction with their management of shares. Clearly, this is a share system that is in serious distress.

Two interrelated issues concern the nature of enforcement costs surrounding the current share system, and the constraints on negotiating a new, more realistic share system in line with the declining catches. Why can't boat owners and captains prevent the crew from cheating? Boat owners grumble about the amount of fish that crew members sometimes take and the time required to even out the conflicts that arise. Yet both owners and captains are reluctant to introduce restrictions on the traditional right of crew to appropriate some of the catch due to the high cost of monitoring compliance and the difficulty of enforcing stricter rules on the boat. Boat owners and captains are restrained by the likelihood that they will alienate a large number of their crew members and thus not have an adequate number of men to go fishing. Some boats regularly must stop fishing because they do not have a minimal number of ten crew. As a result, nobody ever fires crew members. Even drunkards tend to be maintained, as long as they are not the pilot of the boat and so do not endanger other crew. A very erratic record of showing up at the boat for fishing also is insufficient reason to fire a crew member.[11]

Boat owners also are not motivated to collective action because the 'costs' of cheating are not evenly spread among them. The costs of cheating vary according to the overall seasonal value of fish caught by each boat; a loss of 1,000 pesos is minimal for a boat owner who caught 50,000 worth of fish that season, but huge for one who caught less than 10,000 pesos worth. Since there is great variability in the overall catch among boats, the costs of cheating versus the costs of challenging the rights of crew to appropriate fish are too unevenly dispersed to sponsor any collective effort to bring about major changes. Those owners striving to alter the existing right of crew to appropriate part of the catch would likely bear a disproportionate share of the cost of bringing about such a change since they are powerless to enforce uniform compliance among all boat owners.

Why do crew members lack sufficient collective power to enforce correct and regular share payments by boat owners? First, the higher bargaining power of crew that has arisen with the tightening of the labor market has been accompanied by an increase in other labor tying arrangements. Many crew members--including all of those who have migrated to this region--depend on boat owners for housing. San Andres is a densely packed area of settlement, and roughly half of present crew members live either with the owner or in small barracks on his property. Many of these individuals also depend on the boat owner for daily food rations. Their reluctance to challenge boat owners in a face to face confrontation is due to their role as strangers in the community and their nearly complete subsistence dependency on one family.[12]

Second, crew members are divided among themselves. Many local Tagalog crew members are not dependent on a boat owner for housing and food. Their relatively greater autonomy means they are the most outspoken in demanding changes in the share system. Their local status as native residents and lack of dependence on boat owners, however, is a source of conflict between them and immigrant crew members. These disparities in status and ethnic background further hinder any collective action among crew members to force share system changes.

Third, even if collective action by crew members resulted in a concerted demand for share system changes, it is not at all clear that it would succeed. Most boat owners today in San Andres are not solely dependent on income from fishing. Many have at least one child working abroad or in another local occupation who contributes money to the household budget on a regular basis. A temporary lack of sufficient crew to go fishing is a common occurrence in this area, but boat owners' financial ability to withstand such periods diminishes their need to change the system of share payments. Instead, they usually respond to labor shortages by enticing additional crew members from other boats by offering to provide housing, food, or by paying off a crew members' existing debt to another boat owner, or by mounting a recruiting expedition to hire crew members outside the region.

In short, enforcing the rules of the formal share system through collective action is restricted by the 'free rider' problem facing both boat owners and crew members. Boat owners do not experience the costs of cheating evenly, and so have differing incentives to challenge the existing system. Whoever incurs the initial cost of attempting to challenge the crew's right to appropriate fish at sea is likely to bear a disproportionate share of the costs that will arise should his crew abandon his boat or quarrel among themselves over contract renegotiations. Other boat owners will profit from these initial efforts to restrict the various rights of crew if contract renegotiations on a few boats succeed, but they will not have to bear a similar share of the costs. It is in their interest to wait and let someone else engage in these initial efforts. In fact, some boat owners may profit disproportionately if contract negotiations stall or break down and a larger than normal number of crew become available for hire.

Crew members, in turn, are divided among themselves in terms of their dependency on a particular boat owner for food and housing. The more independent crew members have more incentive and ability to withhold their labor to try and force compliance among boat owners to uphold formal share payments, but crew who are dependent on boat owners for food and housing face the potentially higher costs of collective protest.

Conclusion

Institutional economists have come to view the costs of transacting as the key to the performance of economies. There are always obstacles to capturing the gains from trade, and institutions exist in order to provide the norms and incentives to help individuals forego opportunities to cheat, steal, or engage in opportunistic behavior. As North (1990, 25) observes, this does not imply that the institutions which evolve are necessarily efficient. Inefficient institutions may persist for political reasons, such as the inability of rulers to offend powerful constituents, or simply because people generally have access to less than perfect information about how to devise more efficient institutions. Institutions themselves constitute a "mixed bag composed of those that lower costs and those that raise them" (ibid, 63).

The opportunistic behavior of the seiners of San Andres has much in common with the behavior of fishermen elsewhere in the Philippines (e.g., Szanton 1971) and thus should not be considered unique. The traditional share systems found among the larger indigenous forms of fishing in Southeast Asia have several factors in common that promote opportunistic behavior. The monitoring of crew behavior at sea is both expensive and complicated, property rights in the catch tend not to be exclusive by force of custom, and both boat owners and captains are under pressure to reorganize payments to labor or raise wages owing to the increased uncertainty in the seasonal returns from fishing. In these circumstances, a certain amount of 'cheating' and opportunism may become prominent features of a particular institutional structure as long as they occur within certain tolerable limits, simply because the cost of changing the rules or enforcing existing rules is perceived as being higher than not changing the rules by all parties concerned.

While it may be tempting to characterize the system of sharing found in San Andres as another example of an inefficient institution that contributes to or typifies the underdeveloped economies of many Third World countries, a closer understanding of the nature of contract renegotiation and enforcement costs suggests that the current system may in fact be more efficient than it appears at first glance. Besides the various problems discussed above that limit the ability of boat owners and crew to act collectively, there also exist serious bargaining problems over how income should be shared in current economic conditions. Any public forum of debate is likely to lead to disputes wherein the coordination necessary for efficient fishing activities is disrupted. The generalized nature of the informal rules surrounding fish appropriations by the crew hinder effective renegotiation of the share system. As Cheung (1969, 64) notes, different sets of stipulations require varying efforts in enforcement and negotiation. The share contracts in San Andres have never precisely delineated the distinction between a crew member's right to 'a share for the body', his right to snatch fish as a circumstance of 'luck' or as a reward for extra effort, and the crew's right to initiate wholesale appropriations of fish as bonuses in large catches. The current system of small-scale cheating evolved gradually as the result of the pursuit of individual interest, not as the direct outcome of conscious contractual bargaining. Boat owners allowed the custom of ensuring crew a right to a share of food from the catch to blend into their right to snatch fish--perhaps because it was cheaper than negotiating a guaranteed 'minimum wage' in the event of poor seasons of fishing and because of the difficulties of quantifying the exact volume of the catch.

Even if boat owners and crew could overcome the problems of free riders, the need to make conceptual distinctions concerning the conditions under which crew have a right to appropriate fish and how much each one can appropriate in any given catch are very costly, especially since the amount they are allowed to appropriate varies with the value of the species. Boat owners and captains are typically more lenient with crew when fish are of smaller size and lower value. The costs of gathering the information necessary to monitor whether each crew member who appropriates fish has done so within the limits set by newly specified rules, or has transgressed these limits are also comparatively high. While the simplest solution might seem to be for boat owners to increase the shares allotted to crew and then pay them on a regular basis in return for a no-cheating clause, these days many boat owners would simply be unable to comply owing to the high cost of fishing expenses (acquired through loans) relative to the low value of the catch.

In circumstances such as these, maritime share institutions could well use multiple 'famine' clauses, wherein crew members can expect to receive a specified but reduced share payment when the overall catch for that month or season is exceeded by high operating costs. Yet the transaction costs of renegotiating appropriately lower and higher payments with a large number of crew according to the amount and value of the catch, degree of work effort, and amount of accumulated fishing expenses are relatively high, since these vary throughout the season. Moreover, these costs loom especially high relative to the low value of the catch in recent years. Should the monthly or even seasonal returns from fishing suddenly increase in size and consistency, then both boat owners and crew members would face a realigned incentive structure for contract renegotiation.

Given the currently low returns from fishing and the fact that many boat owners are perpetually short of cash, however, it is simply cheaper for them to make rough estimates of how much each crew member snatched (legally and 'illegally') and then adjust share payments in acordance with the overall returns that he receives. While crew members periodically overstep the bounds of what individual boat owners consider to be fair appropriations of fish, there is still a certain 'honor among thieves' that prevents the cheating from getting too out of hand. In other words, in the absence of more consistent fishing success, 'cheating' persists as an alternative solution for all concerned.

References

Acheson, James. 1981. Anthropology of Fishing. *Annual Review of Anthropology* 10:275-316.

Alexander, Paul. 1982. *Sri Lankan Fisherman: Rural Capitalism and Peasant Society*. Canberra: Australian National University.

Bardhan, Pranab K. 1980. Interlocking Factor Markets and Agrarian Development: a Review of the Issues. *Oxford Economic Papers* N.S. 32(1): 82-98.

———.1989. The New Institutional Economics and Development Theory: A Brief Critical Assessment. *World Development* 17(9): 1389-1395.

Bailey, Conner. 1983. *The Sociology of Production in Rural Malay Society*. Kuala Lumpur: Oxford University Press.

Bray, F. A. and Robertson, A. F. 1980. Sharecropping in Kelantan, Malaysia. *Research in Economic Anthropology* 3:209-244.

Carsten, Janet. 1989. Cooking Money: Gender and the Symbolic Transformation of Means of Exchange in a Malay Fishing Community. In J. Parry and M. Bloch, eds., *Money and the Morality of Exchange*. Cambridge: Cambridge University Press.

Cheung, S.N. 1969. *The Theory of Share Tenancy*. Chicago: University of Chicago Press.

Coase, Ronald H. 1960. The Problem of Social Costs. *Journal of Law and Economics* 3:1-44.

Doeringer, Peter B., Philip I. Moss, and David G. Terkla. 1986. *The New England Fishing Economy: Jobs Income, and Kinship*. Amherst: University of Massachusetts Press.

Firth, Raymond. 1966. *Malay Fishermen: Their Peasant Economy*. Hamden, Connecticut: Archon Books.

Hart, Gillian. 1986. Interlocking Transactions: Obstacles, Precursors or Instruments of Agrarian Capitalism? *Journal of Development Economics* 32: 177-203.

North, Douglass C. 1990. *Institutions, Institutional Change, and Economic Performance*. Cambridge: Cambridge University Press.

Orbach, Michael K. 1977. *Hunters, Seamen, and Entrepreneurs: The Tuna Seinermen of San Diego*. Berkeley: University of California Press.

Reid, Joseph. 1976. Sharecropping and Agricultural Uncertainty. *Economic Development and Cultural Change* 24: 549-76.

Robertson, A.F. 1987. *The Dynamics of Productive Relationships: African Share Contracts in Comparative Perspective*. Cambridge: Cambridge University Press.

Spoehr, Alexander. 1984. Change in Philippine Capture Fisheries: an Historical Overview. *Philippine Quarterly of Culture and Society* 12: 25-56.

Szanton, David L. 1971. *Estancia in Transition: Economic Growth in a Rural Philippine Community*. Quezon City: Ateneo de Manila University Press.

Vercruijsse, Emile. 1984. *The Penetration of Capitalism: A West African Case Study*. London: Zed Books.

Villafuerte, E. D. and Bailey, Conner. 1982. Systems of Sharing and Patterns of Ownership. In Conner Bailey, ed., Small-Scale Fisheries of San Miguel Bay, Philippines: Social Aspects of Production and Marketing. *ICLARM Technical Reports 9*. Quezon City: University of the Philippines in the Visayas, International Center for Living Aquatic Resource Management, United Nations University.

Wells, Miriam J. 1984. The Resurgence of Sharecropping: Historical Anomaly or Political Strategy? *American Journal of Sociology* 90(1): 1-29.

Williamson, Oliver. 1975. *Markets and Hierarchies: Analysis and Antitrust Implications.* New York: Free Press.

———.1985. *The Economic Institutions of Capitalism.* New York: Free Press.

Notes

1. I would like to thank the National Science Foundation (Grant Nos. 9009745 and 9107136) and the Fulbright-Hays Foundation for their financial support of this research project in the Philippines. I also thank James Acheson for his careful comments and suggestions on an earlier draft of this paper.

2. Firth (1966) spends 23 pages describing share systems; here, I emphasize only a few general themes, but Tagalog share systems in seining are as equally complex as those of other Malay peasant fishermen.

3. Technically, the only difference between a purse seine and a ring net in the Philippines is that the bunt of the net is in the center in a ring net. The baby purse seiners described here use such a net, but the boats, number of crew, and power of their engines are far larger than that of other ring netters (locally called *barongis)* who operate close to shore. Hence the term 'baby' purse seiner, a term which primarily denotes the labor-intensive nature of this type of seining, where catches are small and neither mechanization nor radar are involved. Seining is referred to as *panmumukot,* whereas *pukot* refers to a seine net.

4. The most common reasons that crew give for changing boats are to *pahiyang* ('change our luck'), a dislike for the rules and regulations of the boat's share system, or because the owner scolded them publicly once too often about their *delihensiya.* In fact, the practice of stealing another boat's captain by offering higher shares or percentage of the catch became so problematic in San Andres that boat owners publicly held meetings to disallow such practices unless the new boat promised to pay off the captain's loans with his former boat. Both Orbach (1977) and Firth (1966) also remark on the tendency of seining crews to frequently change boats, but in San Andres this has become exacerbated in recent years.

5. *Dampot* is a noun which literally refers to the act of picking something up from the floor or the ground.

6. On a wider scale, however, many more people can claim a portion of the catch for the same reason. Whenever a *pukot* boat comes in to shore, villagers line the beach in hopes of a handout. If it is a big catch, then small fishermen and other pukot boats similarly may ask for a share of fish even before the boat returns to shore. The largest portion of fish are actually given away at sea, but shore distributions are spread among a much larger number of households.

7. There are numerous Tagalog terms for cheating (*nandadaya),* and they are often used interchangeably. Despite the use of terms that refer to cheating and stealing, however, in seining contexts they do not imply as serious an offense as accusing someone of stealing money from your house or swindling you in gambling. Fish are still food, and since the crew has a right to a share of food from the catch, boat owners tend to be culturally constrained from preventing it. Instead, it is supposed to be the captain's job to see that it does not get too out of hand, and the boat owner's job to take the 'cost' of cheating into account in the way he distributes shares.

8. In the absence of a system other than wage payments, of course, it is difficult to discuss whether a share system is 'inefficient'. Here I only discuss some obvious inefficiencies that arise in association with the *pukot* share systems in San Andres.

9. Around 20 percent of the crew members on seining boats in San Andres are migrants from either Bikol or the Visayan areas of the Philippines (n=192).

10. Of the full-time crew members on seining boats in San Andres, 14 percent are teenagers and 41 prcent are 25 years old or less (n=192). These figures exclude the large number of casual crew, most of whom are teenagers.

11. The absence of an institutional mechanism for firing crew members is reinforced by the nature of informal cultural constraints which govern interpersonal relations on the boat. Scolding crew members in front of others elicits 'shame' *(hiya)* and engenders lasting personal resentment. Since it is so easy for crew members to change to another boat if they have not incurred debts, many captains are inhibited from orally disciplining their crew when they see them shirking or even stealing fish. In fact, being 'scolded' is as common a reason for crew members changing to another boat as is their personal dislike for the way shares are distributed.

12. In fact, the boat owners whom crew privately claim have the most onerous share system rely exclusively on recruiting crew members from the central Philippines. All crew are housed and provided food in the walled compound on these boat owners' property. These boat owners experience a high turnover in crew with many simply leaving the community altogether in order to escape their debts after one or two seasons. Nevertheless, poverty in many coastal areas of southern Luzon and elsewhere ensures their replacement (though not without substantial recruitment cost to a boat owner).

5

Individual Choice and Institutional Constraints: The New Organization of Health Care In The USA

Melissa Rehfus and Christina Gladwin

The "new" institutional economics has stressed the necessity of integrating individual choices with the constraints institutions impose on choice sets (North 1990; Ensminger 1990, 1991). In this body of literature, institutions are defined as the framework within which human interaction takes place, and may consist of formal rules that human beings devise or informal conventions or codes of conduct. Institutions "include any form of constraint that human beings devise to shape human interaction" (North 1990, 4).

Nabli and Nugent (1989) describe three characteristics of institutions: their rules and constraints "nature," the ability of their rules and constraints to govern the relations among individuals and groups, and the predictability of the rules and constraints in repeated and future situations.

Ostrom (1986, 5) has defined these rules and constraints as "prescriptions commonly known and used by a set of participants to order repetitive, interdependent relationships. Prescriptions refer to which actions are required, prohibited or permitted." It is important in terms of institutional analysis to consider configurations of rules rather than single rules separately. It is as sets or configurations that rules are considered as basic characteristics of institutions (Nabli and Nugent 1989, 8).

This definition of institutions allows the "new" institutional economists to include organizations such as labor unions and employers' organizations as institutions because they provide sets of rules governing the relationships both among their members and between members and non-members. Markets--"be they stock exchanges, labor markets, credit markets, wholesale markets or traditional bazaars" are also institutions (Nabli and Nugent 1989, 8). Contracts, explicit or implicit, are also institutions because they lay down rules; cultural rules and codes of conduct are institutions because they constrain the relationships between different individuals and groups.

Defining institutions in this way serves two functions. First, it "makes the definition complementary to the choice theoretic approach of neoclassical economic theory" (North 1990, 5). This makes the "new" institutional economics an approach which is increasingly palatable to "structuration" theorists who have reached a consensus that **structures don't change structures; people change structures** (Giddens 1979). In the postmodern, post cold-war age, it is finally recognized that the individual actor has an important role to play in changing structures, no matter whether he/she is totally rational or limited to "bounded rationality" (Simon 1986), no matter whether the government is socialist or capitalist.

Institutions are a creation of human beings. They evolve and are altered by human beings; hence our theory must begin with the individual (North 1990, 5).

Second, "building a theory of institutions on the foundation of individual choices is a step toward reconciling differences between economics and the other social sciences" (North 1990, 5). For too long, social scientists--psychologists, anthropologists, sociologists, experts in artificial intelligence--have critiqued *rational choice theory* and the underlying behavioral assumptions underlying the choice theoretic of neoclassical economics to no avail (Simon 1957, 1986; Tversky 1972; Kahneman and Tversky 1972, 1982; Newell and Simon 1972; Etzioni 1988; Hodgson 1988; Smelzer 1990). In his Nobel Prize address, Simon reported that he had despaired of changing neoclassical economists' "cognitively-unrealistic" behavioral assumptions of how people with "bounded rationality" make real-life choices. Anthropologists studying indigenous knowledge systems have agreed with Simon and so have long used less-restrictive cognitive assumptions to predict real-life decisions of indigenous actors in many different cultures. Sociologists and political scientists also have argued that many human actions must be understood in terms of *social norms* rather than individual rationality; they are performed out of habit, tradition, custom, or duty (Bourdieu 1977; Elster 1986; Smelzer 1990) and should be represented by "scripts" which tell the actor what to do and say in a routine situation--rather than decision models per se (Schank and Abelson 1977).

The Cognitive Revolution

What is shared knowledge among "other" social scientists, i.e., other than economists, is a belief in the importance of **cognitive science** and "the cognitive revolution" which since the 1950s has shaken the foundations of six social sciences: artificial intelligence, anthropology, linguistics, neuroscience, psychology, and philosophy (Gardner 1985). They realize that the ability to predict individuals' decision making depends on the underlying assumptions that are made about **cognition**, i.e., the thought process itself. These assumptions changed drastically with the cognitive revolution. Before the cognitive revolution, decision models--both economic and psychological--were mathematically sophisticated, with risk-aversion often being measured by the sign of the second differential; after the cognitive revolution, simpler problem-solving and decision rules replaced optimization of a continuous, twice-differentiable function normally found in standard micro-economics texts (Henderson and Quandt 1958).

Scientific assumptions about cognition were radically changed in 1956 with the publication of a seemingly-innocuous article entitled, "The Magic Number Seven, Plus or Minus Two" by the psychologist George Miller (1956). Miller's new idea was that the human computer is of limited capacity, unlike a real computer; its short-term memory is limited to roughly five to seven items at a time. Indeed, people seem to categorize or discretize variables, rather than deal with continuous quantitative variables as a real computer does. People use logic rather than perform complicated mathematical operations as a real computer does. The limited "rehearsal buffer" of humans affects the way people organize their language and thought processes, such that they are "hierarchically" organized (Miller, Galanter, and Pribram 1960).

This revolutionary idea was taken up by the linguist Noam Chomsky, whose "trees" or transformational grammars could be applied to the analysis of most known languages around the world, as well as to structural models in psycholinguistics (Chomsky and Miller 1963; Boyd and Wexler 1973). In the field of artificial intelligence, it stimulated scientists to invent computer programs called "expert systems" which mirrored the way humans think, rather than expect humans to think like sophisticated computers. In psychology, the revolution stimulated new theories of problem solving (Newell, Shaw, and Simon 1958; Newell and Simon 1972) and plans or scripts (Schank and Abelson 1977), and caused the abandonment of decision making models of "expected utility" in favor of theories of "elimination-by-aspects" and "preference trees" (Tversky 1972; Kahneman and Tversky 1972, 1982; Tversky and Kahneman 1981).

In anthropology, it resulted in the spread of cognitive models of taxonomies, schemas, and decision processes which replaced the use of culturally-specific "personality traits" and psychological tests to explain cultural differences. Given the aims of ethnographers to model the insiders' point of view and knowledge, it was not surprising that the cognitive revolution found the field of anthropology a fertile ground to grow in. The products of cognitive anthropology can now be seen in frame analysis (Frake 1964), taxonomic analysis (Berlin and Kay 1969), componential analysis (Romney and D'Andrade 1964), schemas or folk models (D'Andrade 1981, 1984; H. Gladwin 1974; Quinn 1989), plans or scripts (Werner and Schoepfle 1987), a theory of arithmetic practice in the supermarket (Lave 1988), as well as decision trees or tables. During the 1970s and 1980s, "ethnographic decision tree" modeling became fashionable and actually predicted indigenous decisions made by native actors in many different cultures (Gladwin 1989).

Beyond Cognition, Toward Institutional Linkages

What was still missing in these ethnographic models of individual choice, however, was *a link, an interface* between the individual choice model and institutional behavior. Totally ignored was the role of institutions which were affecting the individual decisions being modeled, and the complex way in which the individual making the decision (to sell fish in a market, or to grow subsistence vs. cash crops, or to buy a car, or to adopt fertilizer, or to cut back production and sell land) interacted with the organization(s) imposing constraints on his or her decision process. True, the constraints were listed and these organizations were often described; but no formal method *linked* decision making *within the organization* with the constraints on the individual choice being modeled. As a result, the picture painted was that of individuals who merely reacted to the policies or constraints imposed by an organization; they were not seen as interacting with the organization or negotiating with it in any kind of empowered way. Neither was the decision-making of the organization explored in any rigorous way. As a result, the picture painted was too often that of an all-powerful, unresponsive organization incapable of reacting to individuals in any reasonable way.[1]

The purpose of this paper is to fill that gap, and present both a model of individual choice and a model of organizational decision making, and show how both link up and interact with each other in a highly-complex way. In the case of this study, the choice context is the rising cost of health care in the United States, something with which we are all familiar. The individual choice being studied is that of *primary care physicians* (here defined as physicians in general practice, family practice, or pediatrics) who routinely have to decide whether to join or contract with managed care plans--typically, Preferred Provider Organizations (PPOs) or Health Maintenance Organizations (HMOs). PPOs and HMOs operate as independent companies, or often are programs offered by insurance companies as alternatives to traditional health insurance products. The organization that interacts with the individual physician is the PPO or HMO.

The structure of the rest of this paper is as follows. The first section describes the choice context, the changing health care environment. The second section describes the decision process for 1) individual physicians deciding whether or not to contract with a PPO or HMO; and 2) one insurance company which operates both a PPO and an HMO (the company prefers to remain anonymous).[2] In conclusion, the last section spells out the linkages between the two decision-making processes.

The Choice Context: The Changing Health Care Environment

The rising cost of health care has focused interest on factors which affect the cost of care, including the role of physicians. There are unavoidable factors which contribute to rising costs, such as the aging of the American population, technological advances which make complex and expensive services for diagnosis and treatment widely available, the dramatic increase in malpractice litigation and therefore premiums for malpractice insurance, and the general price inflation which affects all goods and services in the United States. However, there are also a number of avoidable factors which inflate the cost of care. Regarding physician services, these factors include the high degree of specialization among physicians, the tremendous and problematic variations in practice patterns (and therefore costs), and the incentives in the fee-for-service payment system for physicians to provide a high volume of services, and to "game" the billing system. It is factors such as these which have led many to the conclusion that, while we are spending more on health care, a significant portion of our health care dollars may be buying waste and inefficiency. Moreover, while the major portion of each health care dollar is spent on inpatient hospital services, awareness has been growing that physicians control the provision of services and therefore have significant influence on health care costs. As Eisenberg (1986) points out, physicians both organize and direct the production of health care services, as well as provide some of the services. The result is that while physicians fees account for approximately 20 percent of health care expenditures, *the services that they directly prescribe make up as much as 80 percent of health care costs* (Gibson et al. 1983; Eisenberg 1985).

Concern about rising costs and the efficiency of our health care system has led to efforts to control the cost of health care and improve the effectiveness of the health care system. These efforts have taken several directions, including 1) establishing controls over the price paid for care; 2) better managing the use of health care services; and 3) developing alternatives to the traditional system for financing and delivering health care in the United States. The third approach, alternative health care delivery systems, is the most comprehensive, and usually incorporates some aspects of the first two.

Health maintenance organizations (HMOs) and preferred provider organizations (PPOs) are types of alternative delivery systems. These organizations attempt to control health care costs by better managing patients' use of health care services and by providing care more efficiently. Hence, these types of organizations are generally referred to as **managed care plans**. However, HMOs and PPOs use very different methods to control costs and achieve efficient medical care.

HMOs represent a more dramatic change from the traditional health care system than do PPOs, from both the physician's and patient's perspective. HMOs are designed to control health care costs in several ways. First, to provide incentives for efficiency, HMOs usually establish a different payment method for physicians than fee-for-service (salary; or capitation--that is, payment per member of the plan). Thus, in an HMO the physician's income may no longer be directly calculated according to the number and type of services he provides. Rather, he/she is paid the same amount no matter what services are provided, removing the incentive to provide more services in order to increase income. In addition, HMOs usually share some of the financial risk for care with physicians, providing physicians with further incentives for efficient practice methods. Second, to manage patients' utilization of health care services, HMOs rely on the gatekeeper concept. Every HMO member has a primary care physician, who is the "gatekeeper" to health care services.

Visits to specialists cannot be initiated by the patient, but must be set up by the primary care physician. In order to keep the system as cost-effective as possible, patients are restricted to using physicians and hospitals which contract with the HMO, and which have agreed to follow the HMO's rules and requirements. Third, HMOs often monitor physician cost and use performance and give feedback to physician participants so that inefficient practice methods can be improved. Finally, HMOs have a philosophy of preventing illness and promoting health. HMOs tend to provide more preventive services than do traditional health care plans.

There are three basic types of HMOs: staff, group, or independent practice association (IPA) (Thorpe et al. 1986). They are distinguished by the way physician services are organized and by the method used to pay physicians. The amount of direct control the HMO exercises over physician behavior decreases from staff to group to IPA model of organization. In a staff model, physicians are employees of a health plan, serve the plan's customers exclusively, and are paid a salary, or sometimes a capitation rate. In a group model, the HMO contracts with a physician group to provide services to its members, and physicians, who may have patients other than plan members, are paid by capitation. In an IPA, physicians in their own solo or group practice settings contract to see HMO patients in addition to their fee-for-service patients. Most often, they are paid on a fee-for-service basis; primary care physicians may be paid by capitation.

In contrast, PPOs are more similar to the traditional health care system. As Rice et al report, "PPOs began in the early 1980s as a means of allowing employees to retain choice of provider--albeit with some additional costs if that provider did not belong to the PPO--and still allow employers to exercise some control over costs" (1989, 367-8). Physicians are paid under a fee-for-service method, although usually at a discount from their regular fees. They often must comply with utilization management programs, such as those which require them to receive certification to admit a patient to the hospital. They must admit patients to hospitals contracting with the PPO. From the patients' perspective, as members of most PPOs they can see any physician they choose. However, they receive better benefits or incur lower out-of-pocket expenses if they use the PPO providers. Ideally, PPOs increase efficiency, and therefore control costs, by identifying and contracting with the efficient providers in a community, and by employing utilization management programs.

Managed care plans are relatively new health care organizations in many areas of the country. However, their origins lie in the prepaid group health plans established in the 1920s, 30s, and 40s. Due mainly to the opposition of organized medicine, this type of practice did not flourish, although a scattering of prepaid plans were established and became quite successful, still operating profitably today (for example, Group Health Cooperative of Puget Sound, the Kaiser-Permanente health plan, and the Health Insurance Plan of New York). Historically, physicians have opposed any organized form of private medical practice other than fee-for-service solo practice. Fee-for-service solo practice has been and continues to be the predominant form of medical practice in the United States (although changes have been occurring over the past decade, and new changes are on the horizon, which may alter this situation). Physicians favor this practice form because it secures autonomy for the individual practitioner and resists control by any other entity (whether the government, corporations, hospitals, or consumer groups) over physicians.

The growth in market share of managed care plans over the past decade has been impressive. Concurrently, the involvement of physicians with managed care plans has also increased rapidly. In the research area, HMOs and PPOs began to operate in 1984 and 1985. They have become a significant part of the health care system in the community over the past five years. Physicians and other providers are learning how to work with them and how these plans impact their practice of medicine.

Individuals' and Organizations' Decisions

The Physicians Decision Process

This section describes a primary care physician's decision process regarding whether or not to contract with the PPOs and IPA-type HMOs in one community. The decision tree presented here is a composite model, representing the input of thirty physician consultants. It is a descriptive model, as it has not yet been tested for predictive ability on a unique sample of physicians.

The research reported here concentrated on the decision of physicians to contract with a managed care plan. However, during the course of the study it became apparent that there was a prior decision: whether to set up a traditional private practice or to become a salaried employee of a clinic or managed care plan. Only those in private practice face subsequent decisions about contracting with managed care plans. In the research area, there is only one staff model HMO, with physicians as salaried employees. Thus, the norm for physicians in this area, as in most areas of the United States, is to maintain an independent practice and contract their services to managed care companies. This study focused on physicians who have already chosen an independent private practice setting, and who must decide whether to contract with the IPA-type HMOs or PPOs in their community.

Contracting with managed care plans is one of the main business decisions for many physicians. Contracting with managed care plans has also made the business of medicine more complex. Managed care plans require more overhead, as physicians keep track of the various rules and requirements for each plan, and take on filing patient claims. Financial analysis and planning are more complex because physicians must deal with different payment methods and payment levels for different plans. Some physicians feel that contracting with managed care plans requires a computerized accounting system, which in itself is expensive, and which requires staff trained to operate it.

All the physicians reported that they evaluate each managed care plan on its own merits for contracting. They do not compare two or more plans simultaneously and then select the "best" one with which to contract. This is partly because of the manner in which physicians are solicited to join plans. Contracting opportunities occur sporadically, and a physician rarely has two contracts to consider at the same time. More importantly, each plan has its own benefits to offer. One may have a higher fee schedule, another may have a larger number of the physician's patients as its members, and so on. Each plan is evaluated as a separate case, and most physicians contract with several plans.

Figure 5.1 displays the primary care physician's contracting decision tree model. This model describes the decision process of a physician as he/she decides whether or not to contract with a managed care plan. The physician's choice alternatives in this model are "contract" or "do not contract." A physician answers the set of questions (the decision criteria) which form the nodes of the tree. The starting point is criterion number 1 at the top of the tree. The physician's responses send him or her "down" the tree on a path to a particular outcome. Thus, if the physician's responses send him down a path to the outcome "do not contract," the model predicts that the physician will not or did not contract with the managed care plan.

The first four criteria in the physician's contracting model are constraints which determine that the physician is interested in contracting with a managed care plan and has the authority to make the contracting decision. The remaining criteria define the characteristics which physicians find critical for contracting with a managed care plan. Because physicians consider each plan on its own merits, the decision model does not include comparative evaluation with other plans. It is, rather, a fairly simple model which evaluates a single plan against a physician's contracting criteria.

To reach the outcome "contract," the physician must be interested in contracting with managed care plans in general, either because he/she needs the patient volume plans offer; or because he/she feels managed care plans are here to stay and physicians need to learn to work with them. The physician also must verify that the plan has a payment *method* with which he is comfortable (regardless of the payment *level*), and that joining the plan will improve his practice, not endanger it. Finally, the plan under consideration must pass profitability, referral, contract, and ease of administration constraints.

The Insurance Company's Decision Process

This section describes the decision processes of an organization regarding 1) contracting with physicians to provide services to its managed care customers; and 2) negotiating with physicians for modifications to standard contracting arrangements. While the previous section discussed the contracting decision of primary care physicians, this section presents the other side of the contracting equation, modeling the decisions of an organization which contracts with physicians to support its managed care plans.

The organization whose decisions are modeled here is a health insurance company which markets both an IPA-type HMO and a PPO in the research area. The HMO and the PPO differ in general structure and operations.

The company's HMO and PPO contract with selected hospitals, physicians, and other health care professionals to provide services to their customers. The company's staff in the research area has responsibility for working directly with customers, physicians, hospitals and other health care providers in the region. The company consultant who provided information on the contracting and negotiating decision processes manages the unit responsible for physician contracting.

Due to the differences in the structure and organization of its HMO and PPO, the company has different decision processes related to each of these managed care plans. That is, the company approaches contracting and/or negotiating with physicians differently, depending on whether it is considering a physician for the HMO physician network or the PPO physician network. The company consultant identified the decision criteria for contracting and negotiating with *primary care physicians* for *each* network. As a result, there are two decision tree models related to contracting, one for the HMO and one for the PPO; and two decision tree models related to negotiating. Like the physician contracting decision model, these company decision models are descriptive--they have not yet been tested for their predictive success.

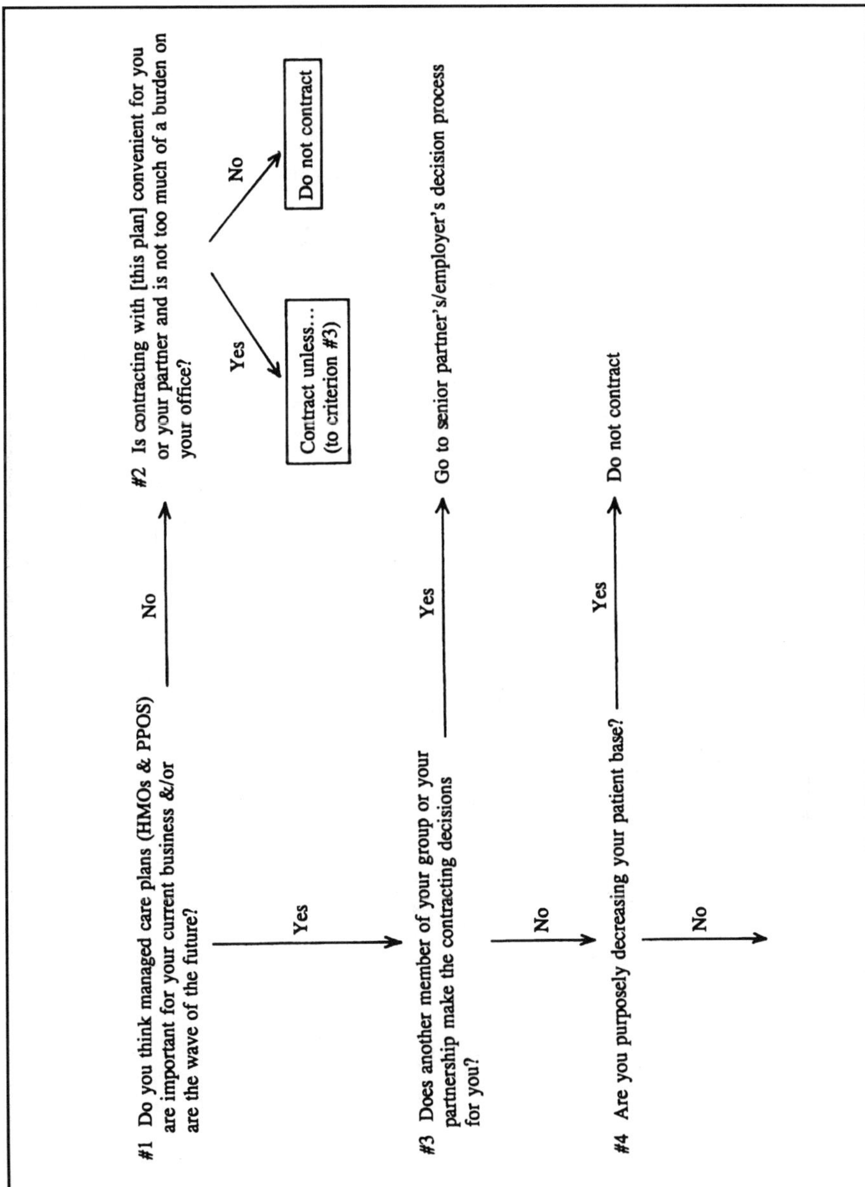

Figure 5.1: Physicians' Contracting Decision Tree Model

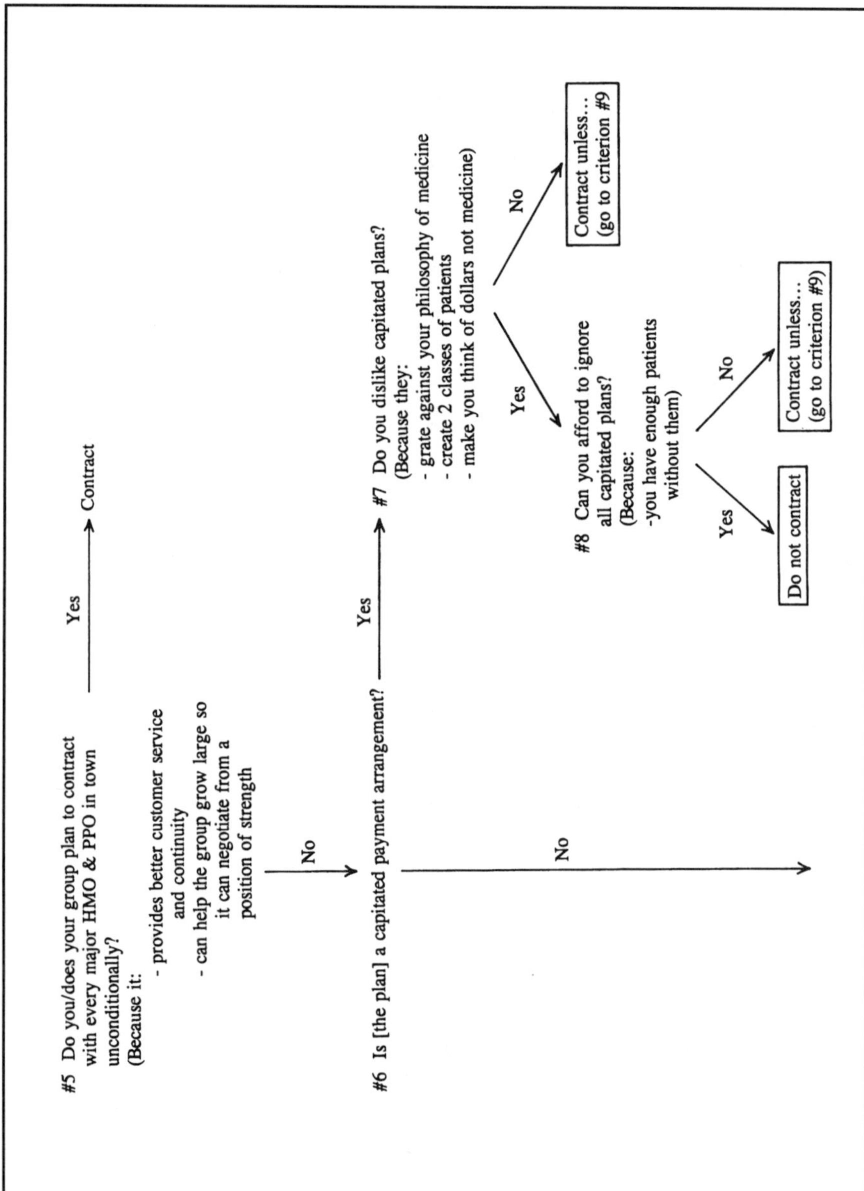
#5 Do you/does your group plan to contract with every major HMO & PPO in town unconditionally?
(Because it:
- provides better customer service and continuity
- can help the group grow large so it can negotiate from a position of strength
Yes
Contract
No
#6 Is [the plan] a capitated payment arrangement?
Yes
No
#7 Do you dislike capitated plans?
(Because they:
- grate against your philosophy of medicine
- create 2 classes of patients
- make you think of dollars not medicine)
No
Contract unless...
(go to criterion #9
Yes
#8 Can you afford to ignore all capitated plans?
(Because:
-you have enough patients without them)
No
Contract unless...
(go to criterion #9)
Yes
Do not contract

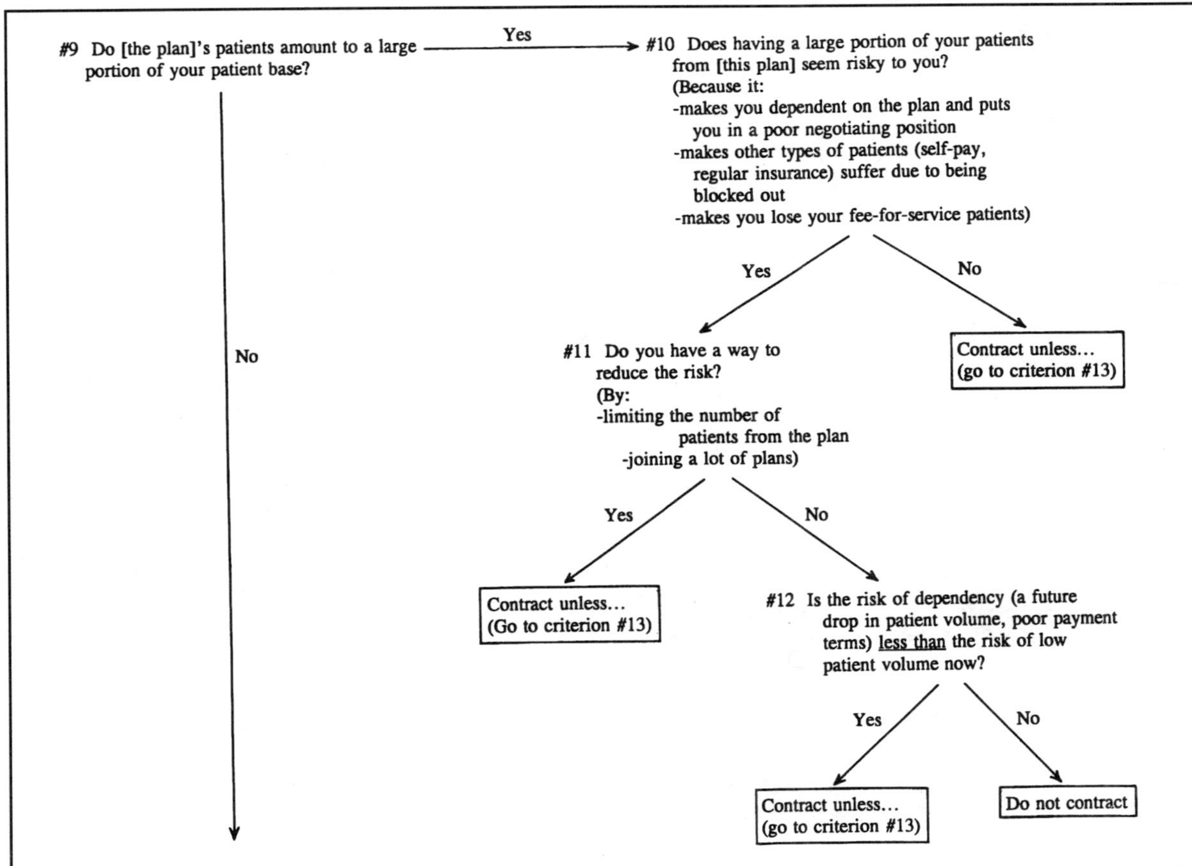
#9 Do [the plan]'s patients amount to a large portion of your patient base?
Yes
No
#10 Does having a large portion of your patients from [this plan] seem risky to you?
(Because it:
-makes you dependent on the plan and puts you in a poor negotiating position
-makes other types of patients (self-pay, regular insurance) suffer due to being blocked out
-makes you lose your fee-for-service patients)
Yes
No
Contract unless... (go to criterion #13)
#11 Do you have a way to reduce the risk?
(By:
-limiting the number of patients from the plan
-joining a lot of plans)
Yes
No
Contract unless... (Go to criterion #13)
#12 Is the risk of dependency (a future drop in patient volume, poor payment terms) less than the risk of low patient volume now?
Yes
No
Contract unless... (go to criterion #13)
Do not contract

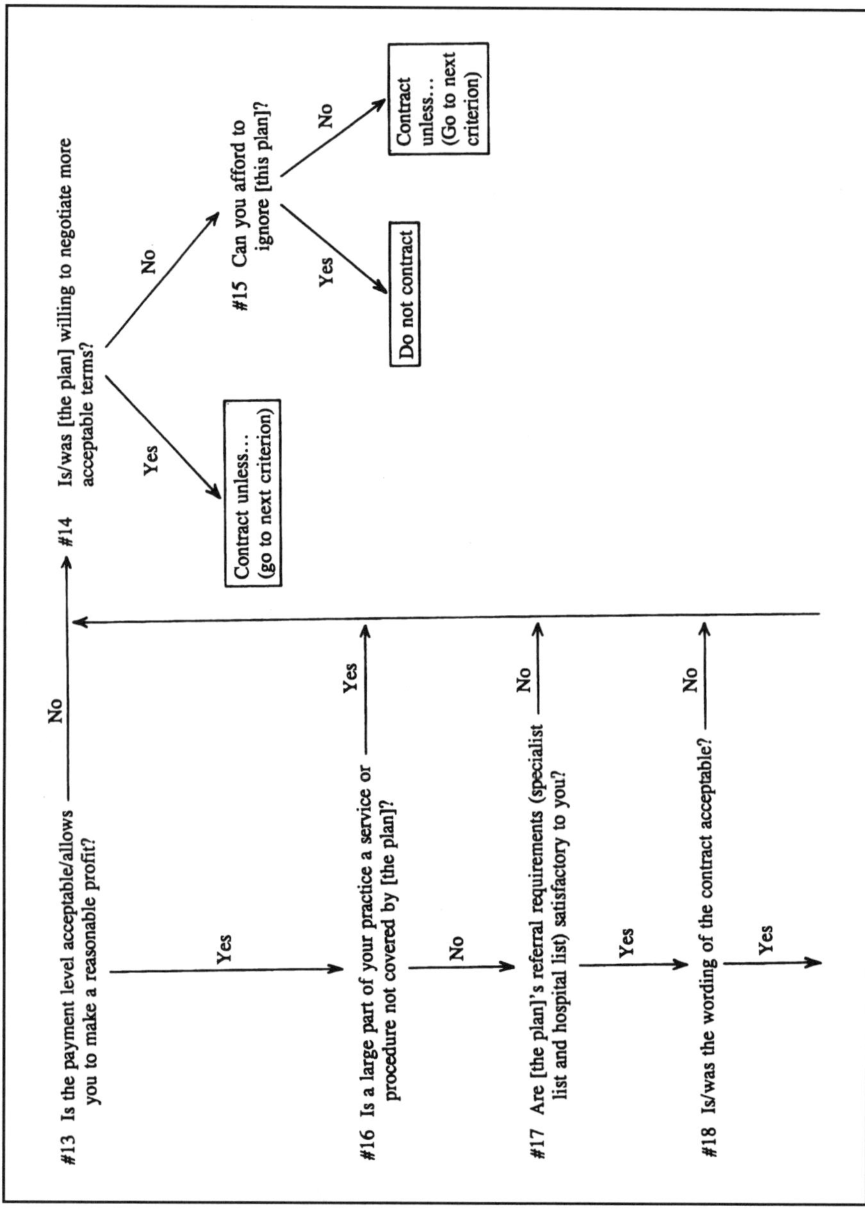
#13 Is the payment level acceptable/allows you to make a reasonable profit?
No
Yes
#14 Is/was [the plan] willing to negotiate more acceptable terms?
Yes
No
Contract unless... (go to next criterion)
#15 Can you afford to ignore [this plan]?
Yes
No
Do not contract
Contract unless... (Go to next criterion)
#16 Is a large part of your practice a service or procedure not covered by [the plan]?
Yes
No
#17 Are [the plan]'s referral requirements (specialist list and hospital list) satisfactory to you?
No
Yes
#18 Is/was the wording of the contract acceptable?
No
Yes

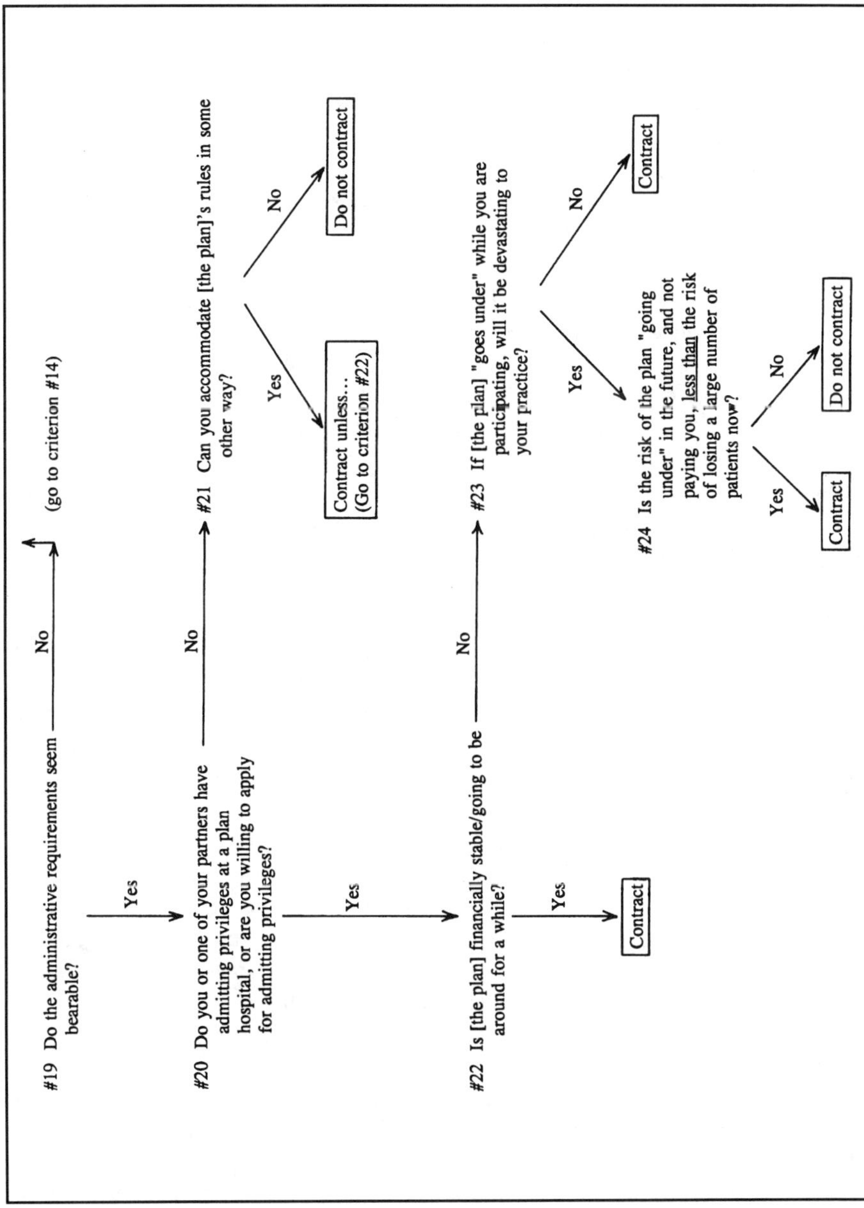
#19 Do the administrative requirements seem bearable?
Yes
No
(go to criterion #14)
#20 Do you or one of your partners have admitting privileges at a plan hospital, or are you willing to apply for admitting privileges?
Yes
No
#21 Can you accommodate [the plan]'s rules in some other way?
Yes
Contract unless... (Go to criterion #22)
No
Do not contract
#22 Is [the plan] financially stable/going to be around for a while?
Yes
Contract
No
#23 If [the plan] "goes under" while you are participating, will it be devastating to your practice?
Yes
No
Contract
#24 Is the risk of the plan "going under" in the future, and not paying you, less than the risk of losing a large number of patients now?
Yes
Contract
No
Do not contract

Figures 5.2a and 5.2b display the company's decision tree models for contracting and negotiating with primary care physicians. For both types of decisions, the model for the HMO decision and the PPO decision are contained in the same figure because they share the same initial criteria. However, both the contracting and negotiating decision trees split, separating the HMO and PPO decision processes.

In the contracting decision process, the company's choice alternatives are "contract" or "do not contract". The company consultant answers the set of questions (the criteria) which form the nodes of the tree. The starting point is criterion number 1 at the top of the tree. The consultant's responses send her down the tree on a path to a particular outcome. In sum, if the consultant's responses send her down a path to the outcome "do not contract," the model predicts that the company will not or did not contract with the physician.

For the negotiation decision process, the company's choice alternatives are somewhat more complex than in the previous decision tree models. The choice alternatives for the negotiation decision process are "negotiate, and contract"; "do not negotiate, and (attempt to) contract;" and "do not negotiate, and do not contract." As in the other decision tree models, the company consultant answers the set of questions at the nodes of the tree. The starting point is criterion number 1 at the top of the tree. The consultant's responses send her down the tree on a path to a particular outcome.

The criteria in the contracting decision process ensure that the company contracts with physicians who fulfill the needs of the company's customers for certain types of physicians, in convenient locations, who are respected practitioners in the community. Contracting physicians should also meet the needs of the company for efficient, high quality physicians, whose practice patterns will help the company control health care costs for its customers.

From the perspective of the HMO or PPO, the negotiation decision process occurs following the contracting decision process. That is, a physician must pass the contracting criteria before the HMO or PPO considers negotiating with him/her. In some cases, a physician is already contracting with the HMO or PPO and asks to negotiate a change. Even in this situation, the first step in the negotiation decision process is to verify that the physician still meets contracting requirements.

The first criteria in the negotiation decision process are constraints which establish that the physician has met contracting requirements, is asking for changes which are negotiable, and is important to the plan. In general, the HMO will consider negotiating changes in certain aspects of the contract if the changes are consistent with the design of the HMO, and allow efficient, accurate administration of the program. The PPO negotiates few changes: of

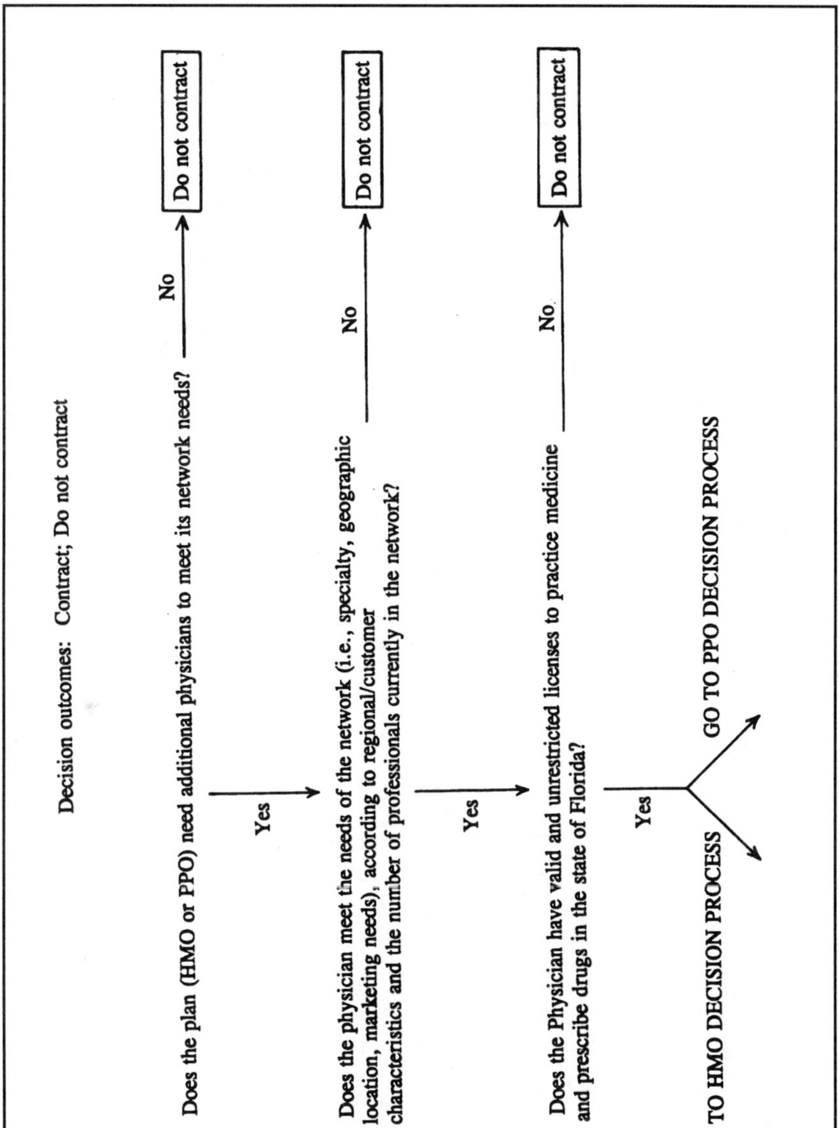

Figure 5.2a: Company's Decision to Contract

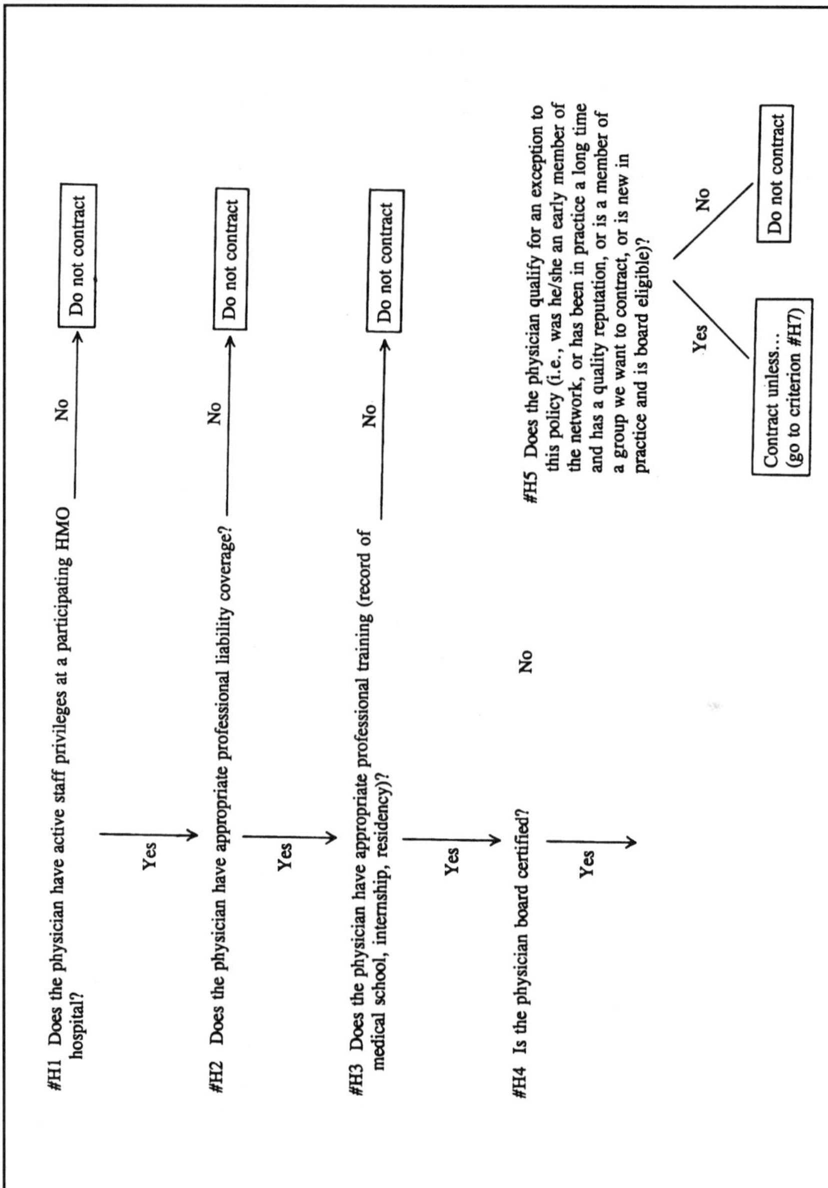

HMO Contracting Decision Process

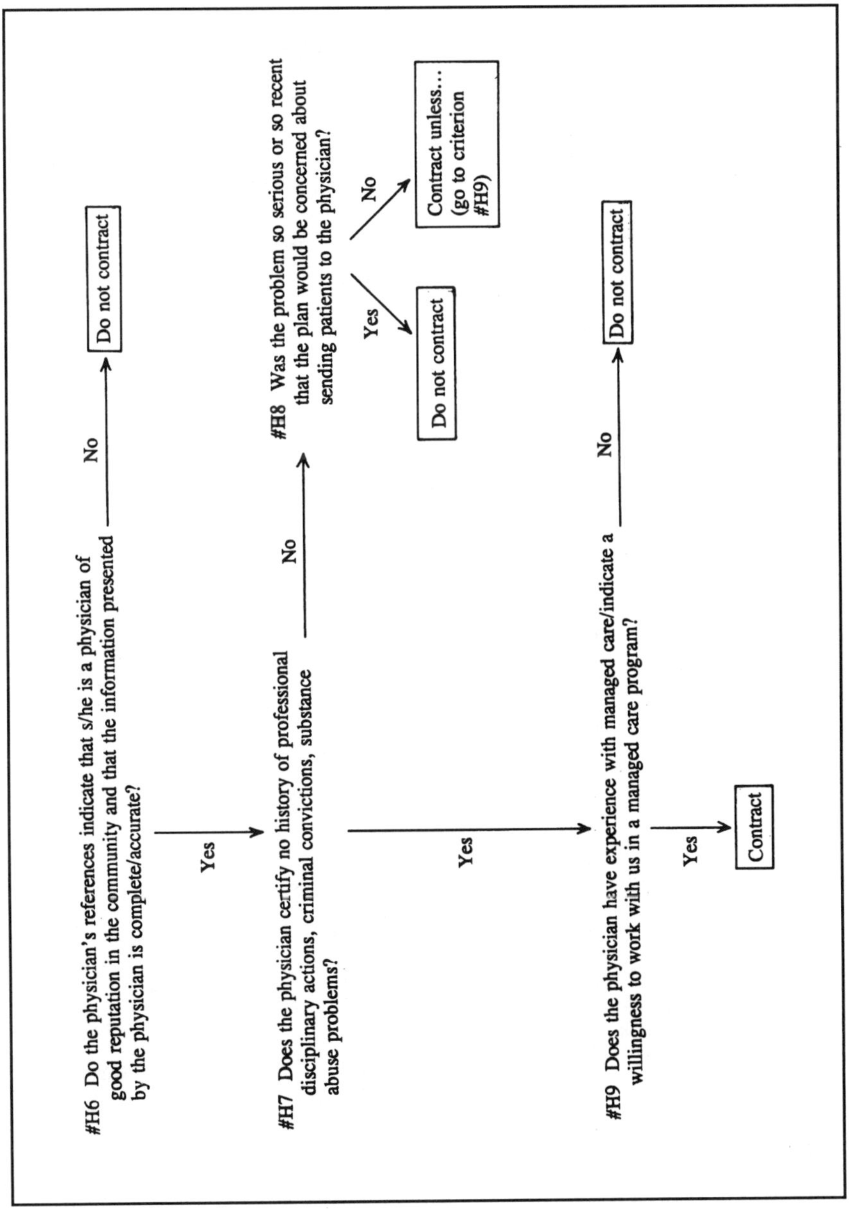
#H6 Do the physician's references indicate that s/he is a physician of good reputation in the community and that the information presented by the physician is complete/accurate?
No
Do not contract
Yes
#H7 Does the physician certify no history of professional disciplinary actions, criminal convictions, substance abuse problems?
No
#H8 Was the problem so serious or so recent that the plan would be concerned about sending patients to the physician?
Yes
Do not contract
No
Contract unless... (go to criterion #H9)
Yes
#H9 Does the physician have experience with managed care/indicate a willingness to work with us in a managed care program?
No
Do not contract
Yes
Contract

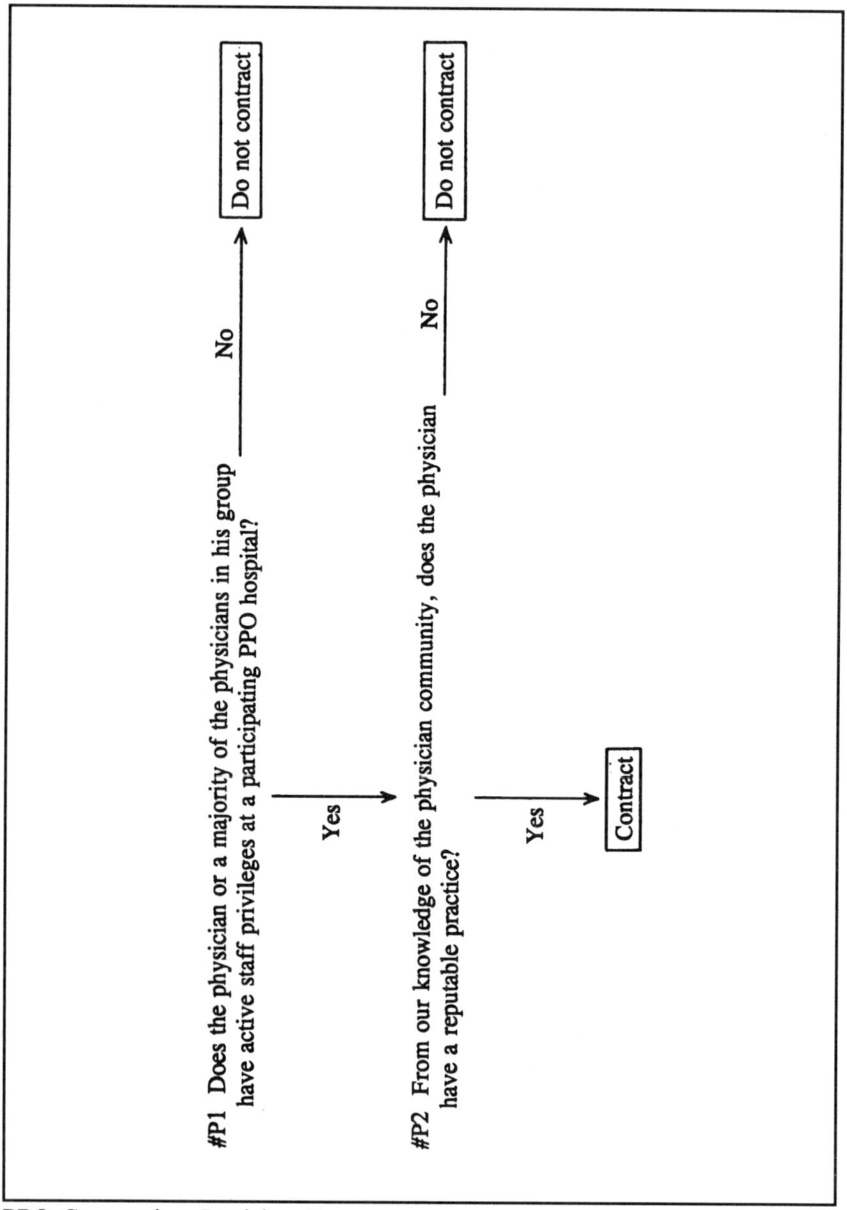

PPO Contracting Decision Process

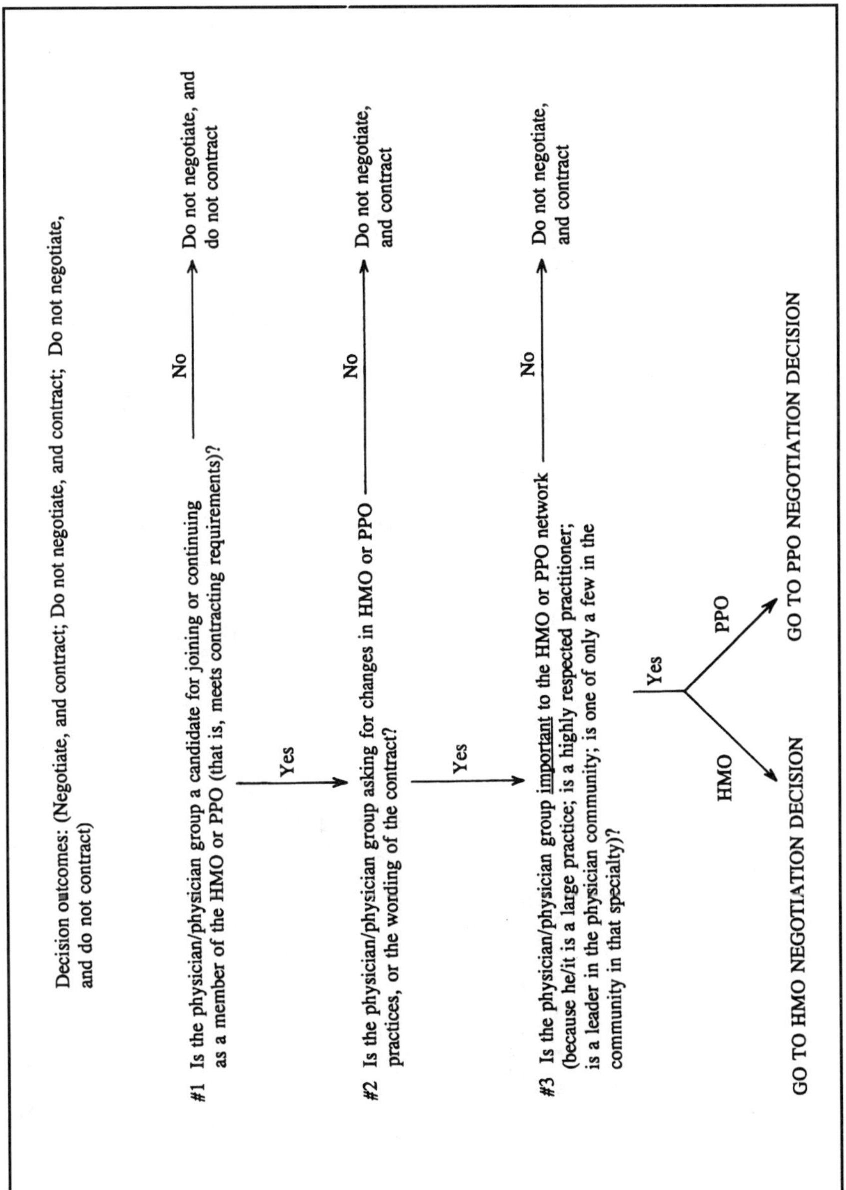

Figure 5.2b: Company's Decision To Negotiate

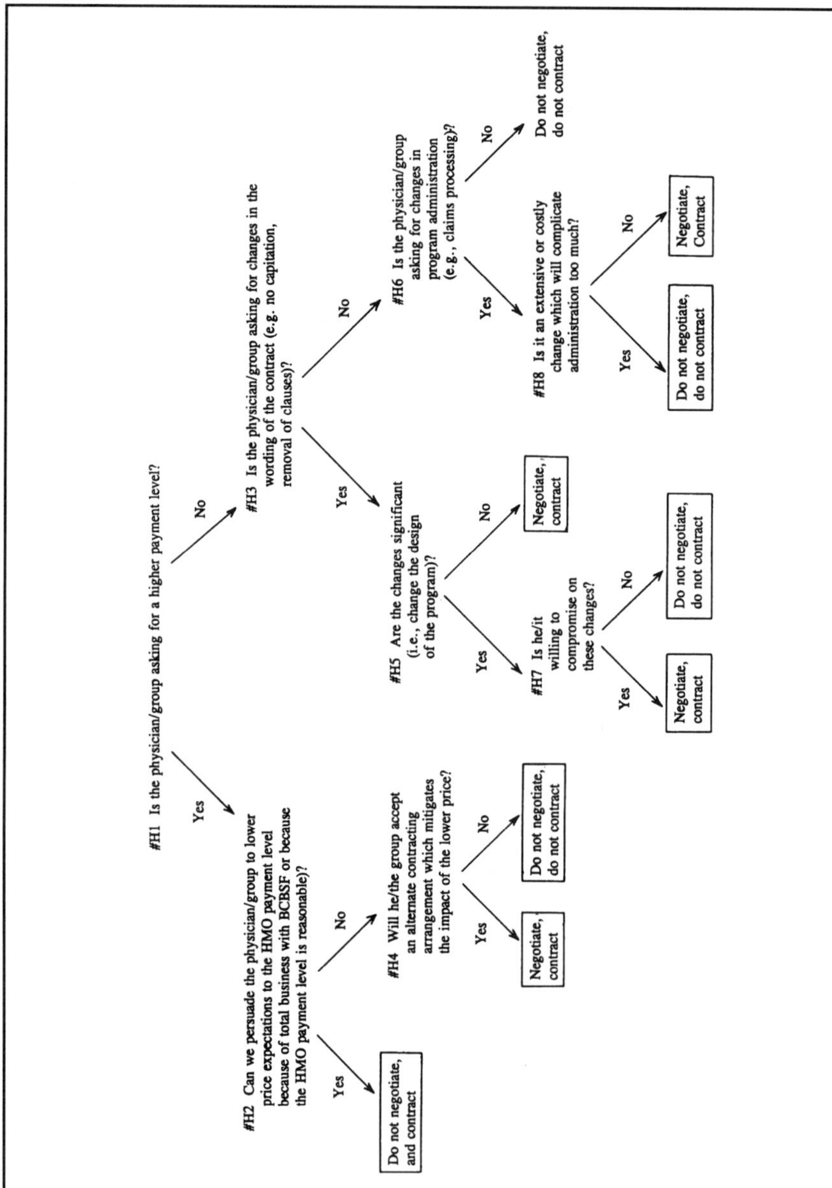

HMO Negotiation Decision Process

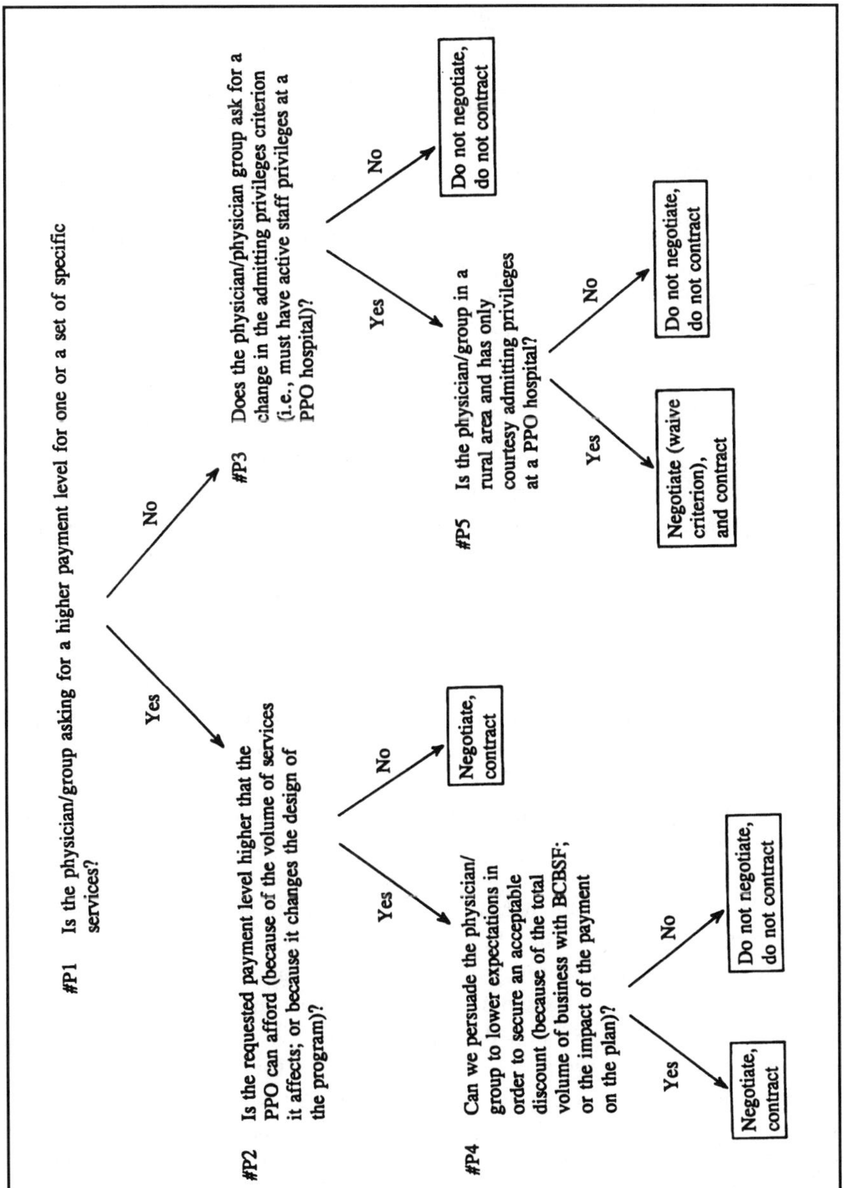

PPO Negotiation Decision Process

the PPO's few requirements, most are customer service components, which are not negotiable.

Conclusion: Links Between Individual and Organizational Choice

This research was conducted among primary care physicians and an HMO and a PPO. It provides information about the decision making of physicians regarding contracting with the HMOs and PPOs in their community. It also provides information on two managed care plans' decisions to contract and negotiate with physicians. Together, the two sets of players are shaping the health care environment in their community.

Economic Organizations and Individual Behavior

The contracting decision processes documented in the decision tree models shed much light on the interactions between the contracting parties. These models demonstrate that there are significant differences between physicians and the managed care plans with regard to their contracting goals, and the understanding and acceptance of the roles defined by the contracts. These differences, and the players' responses to them, have significant results for the health care system in the community.

Physicians face a dilemma. There are very high transaction costs related to contracting with managed care plans. In many respects, contracting with managed care plans contradicts their views (and, perhaps not surprisingly, the traditional views of organized medicine) about the practice of medicine. First, these physicians are very concerned about maintaining independence in the way they practice medicine. Most resent the managed care plans' attempts to impose controls on their practice patterns. Managed care plans tell them where to send patients, have standards on appropriate treatment patterns, and state what services can or cannot be provided by the primary care physician (at least, for which the plan will pay). These rules and regulations often do not coincide with the physician's usual practice methods--the way he/she operationalizes being a "good doctor." Second, physicians feel that managed care plans and employers have come between the doctor and the patient, interfering with the doctor-patient relationship. They point out that patients no longer choose their own physicians; employers direct physician choice when they purchase managed care plans. Also, HMOs make the physician responsible for some financial aspects of medical care. As a result, the physician may have to discuss financial issues with the patient. This is a situation in which both patients and physicians are uncomfortable, and which may strain the physician-patient relationship. Physicians feel these factors (along with others, such as fear of malpractice suits) have contributed to an erosion of loyalty and trust between physicians and their patients. Finally, for many physicians, having to deal with the requirements of managed care plans increases the business aspect of medical practice. This takes time away from patient care and clinical activities. Most physicians resent this intrusion of business into their work, and strongly feel that practicing medicine is more important than business.

Given these high transaction costs, the physicians' decision model offers a number of insights into *why* physicians contract with managed care plans. Most physicians contract with managed care plans to maintain and/or build their patient base. More and more employers are trying to control health care costs by moving their employees into managed care plans. For physicians, this means that increasing numbers of patients are directed to physicians contracting with managed care plans. Thus, the emphasis here is on "maintain." That is, many of these physicians are contracting so as not to *lose* their current patients.

Some transaction costs, however, are too high. Many physicians prefer not to contract with capitated plans--and can still afford not to. Also, while payment is one of the criteria all physicians consider, acceptable payment is not in itself enough if some of the other criteria are not met. For example, most pediatricians will not sign with a plan that does not allow them to refer to certain pediatric specialists, no matter how well the plan pays. "Good" payment is also offset by complex administrative rules which require the physician's office staff to spend a great deal of time complying with them.

In sum, physicians contract because their patients are increasingly restricted, or given strong financial incentives, to seek care from physicians allied with managed care plans. While most feel they must contract with some managed care plans, which involves high transaction costs, physicians do try to limit the transaction costs by staying away from certain types of plans. Nevertheless, physicians are willing to pay high transaction costs in order to maintain as many aspects of traditional medical practice they can, especially independence in the way they practice medicine.

While physicians are looking for the least intrusive or least restrictive plans, the company approaches the task of contracting with physicians for its managed care plans with two different goals: achieving a competitive advantage, and enhancing marketability. To achieve a competitive advantage, the company must market products with competitive prices and other value-adding characteristics. Therefore, the IPA-type HMO and PPO are interested in contracting with efficient physicians, who can provide quality care while minimizing costs. To enhance marketability, the company tries to contract with the physicians who are respected in the community. In the HMO's case, the decision criteria select respected practitioners who show a willingness to work with the plan to achieve its managed care goals. The HMO relies on the financial incentives of capitation and the gatekeeper role of primary care physicians to achieve efficient medical care for its customers. In the PPO's case, the decision criteria select respected practitioners, but do not include specific criteria related to efficiency. Rather, the PPO relies on discounted fees to achieve lower costs for its customers.

Managed care plans design their programs (rules, payment methods, etc.) to achieve more efficient care. Because of their control over patient volume, the plans have been able to contract with physicians and other providers. However, the plans rely on the independent physicians' and other providers' cooperation and support to achieve their cost containment goals. Thus, physicians' attitudes toward and interaction with HMOs and PPOs can either limit or enhance the effectiveness of these programs. In the research area, primary care physicians are adapting to the new emphasis on managed care in a very specific way. Most physicians who contract with managed care plans are not changing the way they practice medicine. Physicians are contracting with a number of managed care plans in order to limit their risk of dependency on any one plan, and to sustain their patient base. Nevertheless, they are practicing medicine, in terms of their treatment decisions, as they always have. The rules of the plans are simply overlaid on their usual practice routine--and physicians rely mainly on their office staffs to ensure they comply with the referral or other requirements of a particular patient's health care plan.

The result is that to date physicians in this community are limiting the effectiveness of the IPA-type HMOs and PPOs in achieving their cost containment goals. The HMOs are hampered because most primary care physicians have not accepted the gatekeeper role. They are uncomfortable, as are many of their patients, with their responsibility to manage care, guided by the goal of efficiency. Primary care physicians cannot embrace the payment arrangements and the gatekeeper concept until their, and their patients', view of the physician's role changes. The gatekeeper is crucial to the effectiveness of HMOs in increasing the efficiency of medical care and thereby lowering or restraining the rise in medical costs. Unless physicians are more effective gatekeepers, HMOs cannot realize their cost containment potential. While companies offering managed care plans work to educate physicians about HMOs and their role in them, and to enforce rules and regulations, these activities drive up administrative costs for the IPA-type HMOs.

The ability of PPOs to contain health care costs is likewise problematic. PPOs employ the fee-for-service payment method, which is one of the major factors contributing to rising costs. Further, to achieve cost containment, PPOs must rely to a great extent on selectively contracting with efficient providers. Both of these conditions severely limit the effectiveness of PPOs. Physicians themselves stated that PPOs are ineffective at controlling costs. They noted that physicians can offset discounted fees by providing and/or billing a higher volume of services and more expensive services. And while theoretically PPOs can achieve their cost containment goals through selective contracting with providers identified for their efficient practice patterns, in practice this is not yet possible. There is little agreement in the field of medicine on what services should be provided in which situations. Therefore it is difficult to identify practice patterns which represent efficient diagnosis and treatment.[3] The company operates utilization management programs (for example, pre-admission certification and case management) to try to minimize overutilization or gaming of the billing system in its PPO. However, these programs are not a great solution to the problem; they place the managed care companies and their contracting physicians in adversarial roles, and add significant administrative expense to the PPO's operations.

In sum, the company experiences high transaction costs in contracting for services with independent physicians for its HMO and PPO. Because of their control over patient volume, the plans have been able to contract with physicians and other providers. However, the plans spend significant administrative dollars trying to gain compliance and cooperation with their cost containment efforts.

Institutional Framework: The Rules of the Game and the Evidence From This Research

IPA-type HMOs and PPOs in the research area are not fulfilling their cost containment potential. The effectiveness of managed care plans is limited by physicians' behavior, which is based in physicians' beliefs and values regarding the practice of medicine. These limitations will persist until physicians and managed care plans begin to share more of the same goals, and have closer agreement on the medical practices which can achieve those goals.

Both physicians and managed care companies face high transaction costs in the current system in the research area. Economists predict that when external transaction costs are high for both parties, then vertical integration is a more desirable organizational structure for both parties (Williamson 1979).

Vertical integration would bring physicians and managed care plans into arrangements where goals are shared, removing at least some of the barriers to controlling medical costs. Why, then, is there little vertical integration taking place in the research area? The answer is that while some vertical integration has occurred (that is, the one staff model HMO in which physicians are employees of the managed care plan), the physicians in the community are still willing to pay high transaction costs to retain their independence. Managed care companies would be moving very quickly toward greater vertical integration of the system if physicians were more willing to move in that direction. How likely are physicians' beliefs about the physician's role to change, leading to changes in behavior? Further, how quickly might change occur? Several authors' work is helpful here. Cancian (1975) points out that social rules can change very rapidly. The attributes which characterize a "good doctor" could change very rapidly. However, there would have to be some compelling need to stimulate such change. North (1990) offers further insight in this regard. He distinguishes between institutions and organizations. In explaining this distinction, he employs a game analogy. The institutions are the rules which define how a game is played, while organizations are the teams or players who play within that set of rules to win the game. Organizations, in North's definition, include political, economic, social and political bodies. They are "groups of individuals bound by some common purpose to achieve objectives" (1990, 5).

Institutions and organizations are constantly evolving. Organizations and institutions interact to guide this change process: "Institutions, together with the standard constraints of economic theory, determine the opportunities in a society. Organizations are created to take advantage of those opportunities, and, as the organizations evolve, they alter the institutions" (1990, 7). North asserts that institutions typically change incrementally, and thus slowly, rather than in a discontinuous manner. Organizations effect change by altering some aspect of the institutional framework. Entrepreneurs in organizations work to alter the existing institutional framework based on perceptions that they could operate more profitably or efficiently.

North's concept of institutions is related to the concept of cultural knowledge, in that it is the culture members' *knowledge* of formal and informal constraints which guides their actions and understanding of events. In this sense, the shared beliefs among doctors and patients about how a good doctor should practice are a set of institutional constraints on physicians' behavior. That is, these constraints limit the choices available. In North's terms, businesses such as managed care plans are economic organizations. As health care costs have risen, pressure on the health care industry to become more effective at controlling health care costs has increased. New organizations called managed care plans have emerged to offer different approaches for financing and delivering health care services. The existence of these plans has begun to change our understanding of the role of physicians and how the health care system should operate. This change will take place over time, as more and more physicians and patients adapt to the new managed care environment.

Change is already accelerating, because compelling reasons for change have developed or are anticipated. As Medicare implemented its payment reforms, physicians became more eager to attract private-pay patients, and are increasingly willing to accept alternative payment arrangements such as capitation to secure their private patient base. More recently, the Clinton administration has made health care reform a major goal. Currently, managed care plays a major role in the administration's discussions of how to reform the health care system. New laws or regulations for a health care system emphasizing managed care will help to speed change among physicians regarding their relations with managed care plans.

References

Berlin, Brent, and Paul Kay. 1969. *Basic Color Terms*. Berkeley: University of California Press.

Bourdieu, Pierre. 1977. *Outline of a Theory of Practice*. Cambridge: Cambridge University Press.

Boyd, John, and Kenneth Wexler. 1973. Trees with Structure. *Journal of Mathematical Psychology* 10: 115-47

Cancian, Francesca. 1975. *What Are Norms? A Study of Beliefs and Action in a Maya Community*. Cambridge: Cambridge University Press.

Chomsky, Noam, and George Miller. 1963. Introduction to the Formal Analysis of Natural Languages. In R.D. Luce, R.R. Bush, and E. Galanter, eds., *Handbook of Mathematical Psychology*. New York: John Wiley.

D'Andrade, Roy. 1981. The Cultural Part of Cognition. *Cognitive Science* 5: 179-95.

———.1989. Folk Models of the Mind. In Dorothy Holland and Naomi Quinn, eds., *Cultural Models of Language and Thought*. Cambridge: Cambridge University Press.

Eisenberg, J. M. 1986. *Doctor's Decisions and the Cost of Medical Care*. Ann Arbor, Michigan: Health Administration Press.

Elster, Jon. 1986. *Rational Choice*. New York: New York University Press.

Ensminger, Jean. 1990. Co-Opting the Elders: The Political Economy of State Incorporation in Africa. *American Anthropologist* 92 (3): 16-29.

———.1991. The Political Economy of Changing Property Rights: Dismantling a Commons From Within. *American Ethnologist*.

Etzioni, Amitai. 1988. *The Moral Dimension: Toward a New Economics*. New York: The Free Press.

Gardner, Howard. 1985. *The Mind's New Science*. New York: Basic Books.

Gibson, R. M., D. R. Waldo and K. R. Levit. 1983. National Health Expenditures, 1982. *Health Care Financing Review* 5: 1-33.

Giddens, Anthony. 1979. *Central Problems in Social Theory: Action, Structure, and Contradiction in Social Analysis*. Berkeley and Los Angeles: University of California Press.

Gladwin, Christina. 1976. A View of the Plan Puebla: An Application of Hierarchical Decision Models. *American Journal of Agricultural Economics* 58(5): 881-87.

———.1979a. Cognitive Strategies and Adoption Decisions: A Case Study of Nonadoption of an Agronomic Recommendation. *Economic Development and Cultural Change* 28(1): 155-173.

———.1979b. Production Functions and Decision Models: Complementary Models. *American Ethnologist* 6(4): 653-674.

———.1989. On the Division of Labor Between Economics and Economic Anthropology. In S. Plattner, ed., *Economic Anthropology*. Stanford: Stanford University Press.

———.1989. *Ethnographic Decision Tree Modeling*. Sage Qualitative Research Methods Series, No. 19. Newbury Park: Sage.

Gladwin, Christina, and John Butler. 1984. Is Gardening an Adaptive Strategy for Florida Family Farmers? *Human Organization* 43(3): 208-216.

Gladwin, Hugh. 1972. Semantics, Schemata, and Kinship. Paper presented at the annual meeting of the American Anthropological Ass'n, November 20.

Gladwin, Hugh, and Michael Murtaugh. 1980. The Attentive/Pre-Attentive Distinction in Agricultural Decisions. In P. Barlett, ed., *Agricultural Decision Making*. New York: Academic Press.

Henderson, James, and Richard Quandt. 1958. *Microeconomic Theory*. New York: McGraw-Hill.

Hodgson, Geoffrey M. 1988. *Economics and Institutions*. Philadelphia: University of Pennsylvania Press.

Kahneman, Daniel, and Amos Tversky. 1972. Subjective Probability: A Judgment of Representativeness. *Cognitive Psychology* 3: 430-54.

———.1982. The Psychology of Preferences. *Scientific American* 246: 160-173.

Lave, Jean. 1988. *Cognition in Practice*. Cambridge: Cambridge University Press.

Miller, George. 1956. The Magic Number Seven, Plus or Minus Two: Some Limits on our Capacity for Processing Information. *Psychological Review* 63: 81-97.

Nabli, Mustapha K., and Jeffrey B. Nugent. 1989. The New Institutional Economics and Economic Development: An Introduction. In M.K. Nabli and J.B. Nugent, eds., *The New Institutional Economics and Development*. Amsterdam: North-Holland.

Newell, Allen, J.C. Shaw, and Herbert Simon. 1958. Elements of a Theory of Human Problem Solving. *Psychological Review* 65: 151-66.

Newell, Allen, and Herbert Simon. 1972. *Human Problem Solving*. Englewood Cliffs, N.J.: Prentice-Hall.

North, Douglass C. 1990. *Institutions, Institutional Change, and Economic Performance*. Cambridge: Cambridge University Press.

Quinn, Naomi. 1989. Metaphors of Marriage. In Dorothy Holland and Naomi Quinn, eds., *Cultural Models of Language and Thought*. Cambridge: Cambridge University Press.

Rehfus, Melissa. 1991. The New Organization of Health Care in the United States: Decision Making of Physicians and Managed Care Plans. Ph.D. Dissertation, Northwestern University.

Rice, Thomas, Jon Gabel and Gregory de Lissovoy. 1989. Do Physicians Induce Demand for Medical Services? *Journal of Health Politics, Policy and Law* 14(2): 367-382.

Schank, Roger, and Robert Abelson. 1977. *Scripts, Plans, Goals and Understanding*. New York: Wiley and Sons.

Simon, Herbert A. 1957. *Models of Man*. New York: John Wiley.

———.1986. The Failure of Arm Chair Economics. Interview in *Challenge* November/December: 18-25.

Smelzer, Neal. 1990. Rational Choice Theory: A Critique. Paper presented in the Sociology Dept., University of Florida, March.

Thorpe, K. E., J. L. Thorpe and N. Barhydt-Wezenaar. 1986. Health Maintenance Organizations. In S. Jonas, ed., *Health Care Delivery in the United States*. New York: Springer Publishing Company.

Tversky, Amos. 1972. Elimination by Aspects: A Theory of Choice. *Psychological Review* 28: 1-39.

Tversky, Amos, and Daniel Kahneman. 1981. The Framing of Decisions and the Psychology of Choice. *Science* 211: 453-458.

Young, James C. 1981. *Medical Choice in a Mexican Village*. New Brunswick, N.J.: Rutgers University Press.

Werner, Oswald, and G. Mark Schoepfle. 1987. *Systematic Fieldwork*, Vol 1 and 2. Newbury Park, CA: Sage Press.

Williamson, Oliver E. 1979. Transaction-Cost Economics: The Governance of Contractual Relations. *The Journal of law and Economics*: 233-261.

Notes

1. This was not the case in at least one instance, the case of the Puebla Project studied by Gladwin (1976, 1979a, 1979b). The Puebla Project planners were in fact very interested in how Poblano farmers were making their decisions about adoption or non-adoption of the project's recommendations. Partly based on Gladwin's decision-tree results, the Plan Puebla changed at least one of its agronomic recommendations, to fertilize at planting.

2. For legal and ethical reasons, the insurance company in this study prefers to remain anonymous. The major author of this paper was a full-time employee of the company during the time the ethnographic fieldwork was performed, and still is.

3. Research over the last decade on the wide variations in practice patterns for similar populations has helped identify the extent of this problem. To improve this situation, much research on appropriate clinical parameters and treatment outcomes has been initiated in the past several years, funded by both private and public agencies.

6

Transaction Costs And Business Strategies In A Mexican Indian Pueblo[1]

James Acheson

Introduction

As the tentacles of modernization and the global economy reach back into what were isolated peasant communities, local economies and productive units are being changed in ways that would be difficult to predict even a few years ago. The strategies being tried by peasant entrepreneurs are producing changes in both the households and the industries of which they are part.

In this article, I describe the changes that have occurred in the organization of the furniture industry of Cuanajo, Michoacan, Mexico over the past 25 years, a period when the industry expanded in response to changing markets both within Mexico and internationally. In Cuanajo, the number of carpentry shops has increased greatly. The amount of furniture sold, and the range where it is sold have increased dramatically. Nevertheless, production takes place in household firms which have remained small, even though they are increasingly specialized. No large vertically integrated firms have been formed. However, firms in the furniture making industry are not autonomous either. Firms in the production chain have developed bilateral ties involving a commitment to do business with each other in the long run. In addition, two "unions" (part cooperative, part business association) have been developed to aid in the production and marketing of furniture.

In this article, I argue that these are not discrete events. The size of firms, their interconnections, the degree of specialization, and the characteristics of the markets they face are all interconnected. The relationships between these seemingly isolated events can be understood by using concepts developed by Coase (1993) and Williamson (1975; 1985; 1986a; 1986b), who have developed a body of ideas that has been used with great success in explaining strategies of firm owners, and the ways in which industries are organized in the industrialized West (Williamson and Winter 1993).[2] As we shall see, these concepts will shed a great deal of light on the situation in Cuanajo. However, this perspective has its limitations when applied to communities such as Cuanajo and others in the Third World.

The essential argument of the institutional economists is that "organizations will be designed to further the objctives of their creators" (North 1990, 73). Coase and Williamson hypothesize that firms are created by entrepreneurs as a means of coping with transaction costs. In a world with no transaction costs, there would be no need for firms (Coase 1937; Milgrom and Roberts 1992, 38-39). Owners alter the size and degree of specialization of their firms depending on the types of transaction costs involved (Acheson 1982; Williamson 1975, 8; 1985, 85-130). Owners can alter the size, degree of vertical integration and dependence on other firms for component parts and services. According to the theory, they do not attempt to influence the wide variety of social, cultural and economic factors influencing transaction costs in the first place. They respond to these transaction costs; they do not attempt to organize a movement to change them.

The problem is that in Cuanajo all transaction costs are high. This has meant that the firm owners have resorted to a much larger variety of strategies than the Coase and Williamson model would predict. This is not to suggest that peasant entrepreneurs are irrational or that the Coase, Williamson model is completely inapplicable, but that it may need to be modified and extended if it is to be applicable to the Third World.

Thirty Years of Change in Cuanajo and Its Furniture Industry

Cuanajo is located in the state of Michoacan, a fertile, well watered highland area of West-Central Mexico. In 1991, the community contained approximately 5166 people organized into 1066 households. The vast majority of the people over the age of 40 are bilingual in Spanish and Purepeche, but an increasing number of young people are now monolingual in Spanish. Like all Purepeche speaking communities, Cuanajo was an agricultural community with a strong craft tradition. In this case, the craft is woodworking. People in Cuanajo have made furniture, from local pine, since at least 1789 (West 1948, 58-59). In 1961, the power line reached the community; and in 1963, the first carpentry shop was equipped with machinery powered by one to five horsepower electric motors (Acheson 1972, 1154-55).

In the past 30 years, agriculture has declined in importance, while the furniture industry has expanded very rapidly.[3] Both the number of shops and the capital employed have gone up. In 1967, there were 89 carpentry shops. Fifty-six of these shops had no machinery at all, and typically employed a man, and perhaps one of his sons, who produced furniture only during the agricultural off season. The 23 mechanized shops employed an average of three or four people, who worked in carpentry most of the year (Acheson 1972). In 1991, there were 238 shops, all of which had some electric powered machinery, and which employed the vast majority of all adult men in the pueblo and some of the women throughout the year.

During this same time span, the amount of capital employed in the average shop increased from about $300.00 U.S. to over $2000.00 in constant U.S. dollars as the quantity and sophistication of machinery was increased. In the early 1960's a well equipped mechanized shop would have nothing more than a small table saw with an attached drill to make joists and a 3 H.P. electric motor. In 1991, a moderate sized shop would typically have several motors, a table saw, a lathe, a band saw, and two types of planing machines. Some shops would have much more equipment.

The source of this capital has changed somewhat. In the 1960s much of the machinery was purchased using credit extended by companies selling machinery in nearby cities such as Morelia and Celaya. Much of it is still purchased in this way. However, the late 1970s and 1980s saw Mexico in a period of financial crisis, with very high inflation and a resulting drying up of credit. As a result, a higher percentage of machinery and shop capital is provided by savings, land sales etc. (see Acheson 1993).

The quality of furniture has increased, and markets have expanded. In the 1960's, shops were producing cheap pine furniture, which was sold to peasants in the markets of the cities of central Mexico. By the early 1970s, many shops still produced pine furniture for the peasant market, but others had begun to specialize in more sophisticated pine furniture, called *muebles artisanos*, which featured a good deal of carving and lathe work. This furniture was sold in the cities of central Mexico to townsmen and city dwellers who had higher incomes (Acheson 1988, 134-137). By the 1990s, a few shops had begun to producing mahogany and oak furniture, which was both well made and well finished.

Thirty years ago, all of the wood for Cuanajo's shops was supplied by farmers from nearby *ranchos* who cut lumber on a part-time basis. Much of the pine is still supplied in this manner. In the past few years, some pine is being trucked to Cuanajo from sawmills in other parts of the state; and the hardwood is transported to Cuanajo by truck from the east and west coasts of Mexico.

More important, the markets have changed. In the 1960s, the furniture was bought by local "Indian" salesmen, who sold it in the markets of the cities of central Mexico. In the past few years, Cuanajo's furniture is being sold all over the republic and increasingly is finding its way into the international market through the efforts of cooperatives and private firms. (These will be discussed in detail below.)

The expansion of the industry is due to the fact that a number of factors created opportunities, and Cuanajo's carpenters were able to take advantage of them. Demand for furniture rose in the past several decades as population and average income in Mexico generally went up. Electric power was made available to the *pueblo*; transportation possibilities increased as the road and bus service were improved; and the machinery companies made credit available. Some of the established carpenters were generally responsive to the possibilities opened for them, and there has been a good deal of entry into the industry by people who hitherto had earned their living in other occupations such as agriculture.

However, it is important to note that despite this expansion of furniture production, no vertical integration of the industry has occurred. The carpentry shops remain relatively small, and specialized in the production of furniture.

Organization of the Industry

There are three kinds of firms in the production of any piece of furniture: wood supplier, carpentry shop, and sales specialist. The nature of these three kinds of firms and the relationships among them need to be discussed.

Firms and Families

Some of the carpentry shops are essentially embedded in household units and are run by the man of the house assisted by perhaps one or two of his sons. In such households, no sharp distinction can be drawn between household and shop activities. The shop is located in the home; the personnel are all members of the household; and the money earned is pooled in one general account and is used for both capital and consumption needs (Acheson 1993). Other carpentry businesses have expanded to the point where they can be considered small family firms. The largest shops have 12 employees, not all of whom are kinsmen; the household of the owner and the shop have different accounts; and in some of these businesses the shops and household of the owner are located in different places.[4]

In all cases, the shop owners make all decisions concerning purchases of capital equipment and wood; they also sell the furniture. However, in the small shops the owner is a carpenter first and foremost. The owner maintains the tools and machinery, and spends most of his time making furniture. In the largest shops, the owner is much more a manager and salesman. He might spend relatively little time actually making furniture and doing maintenance work. These tasks are left to a foreman, who is usually, but not always, a close kinsman.

In all shops there is a strong preference for hiring kinsmen. Owners feel obligated to hire kinsmen if possible. Moreover, they feel that kin are more reliable and trustworthy. In addition, in times of emergencies, kinsmen are expected to work longer hours if necessary and even without pay. Moreover, owners do not mind training close kin since they are ostensibly less likely to leave the firm at short notice.

The owners of the vast majority of shops have only a few years of education at the most so that record keeping is minimal. However, the owners of some shops are far better managers than others, and are able to expand their businesses. The businesses of more inept managers remain small. (The relationship between shop financial management and business success is the subject of another paper. See Acheson 1993.)

Wood Supply

The farmers, who supply the pine lumber used to make most of the furniture in Cuanajo, live on the edge of Cuanajo itself or in the small *ranchos* within a few miles of the center of town. They transport logs to

Cuanajo by dragging them with a team of oxen; boards are brought to town in carts.

Most of this lumber is illegally cut. It is illegal to cut any trees in Mexico --even trees on one's own land--without permission from the Federal Forestry Agency, *FORESTAL*. Cuanajo's wood suppliers never have permission. In addition, some of the pine logs are stolen from land owned by other people. At any given time, one or two of these wood suppliers are in serious difficulty with the law. Over the course of the last several years, literally dozens have been fined, and a number have served jail sentences. In December of 1991, two wood cutters were in jail and another 20 had recently been arrested for illegally cutting wood.

Under these conditions, it is not surprising that carpenters are not willing to talk about their sources of lumber. However, the general outlines of the trade are clear. Carpenters generally obtain lumber from a small number of suppliers with whom they have been doing business for some time. They rarely obtain all of their lumber from just one person since they do not want to be dependent on a single source, but they do not depend on an open, free market for lumber either. A farmer does not sell logs to a stranger who offers a high price. Some degree of trust needs to be established before an exchange can take place. Given their dependence on each other, both carpenters and wood suppliers may sacrifice price for other considerations.

When a carpenter needs lumber, he generally goes to one or more of the people who have been supplying him with wood and places an order. The price to be paid is generally agreed on, but is not specified exactly since the price will depend on the size of the trees delivered. The "farmer" then cuts the trees and delivers them to the carpenter as quickly as possible. Teams of oxen can be seen bringing logs into town during the day, but a sizeable proportion of the loads arrive late in the afternoon or after dark as well--times when forestry inspectors are less likely to be present. The carpenter and "farmer" negotiate a final price, and then the wood is brought into the shop where it is cut up and dried in a smudge fire kiln with little delay.

The relationship between wood cutters and carpenters is symbiotic but marked by plausible deniability. Farmers clearly depend on the carpenters to buy their logs, dispose of the evidence with dispatch, and protect them from inquiries from the inspectors of *FORESTAL*. The carpenters, for their part, are very dependent on these farmers for a supply of wood. They are particularly vulnerable to the whims of weather and wood suppliers since they do not dare to stockpile a large supply of pine.

In the working relationship between carpenters and wood suppliers, both take some pains not to be too familiar with each other. One carpenter said, "I find it convenient not to know too much about the source of the lumber I use. I am not even sure where some of these *rancheros* live or what their names are."

The long term ties built up between carpenters and the "farmers" who supply them wood make the trade in pine possible. Without such relationships, it is doubtful if such a trade would exist. Nevertheless a number of factors make supplies of lumber uncertain. Relationships between "farmers" and carpenters can be difficult. Most of the "farmers" are mestizos, who consider themselves superior to "Indian" carpenters. Problems in negotiations are common. The prospect of problems with inspectors and the ever present threat of fines and arrest make deliveries even more uncertain. The problem is exacerbated in the summer when rains and mud make it difficult to transport heavy loads.

The hardwood is generally purchased legally from lumberyards, which buy it in the hot country on the east and west coasts of Mexico. It is transported to Cuanajo by truck.

Here again problems with delivery have been reported. Sometimes, the hardwood is simply unavailable, but no one can do more than guess at the reasons.

Markets

In the 1960s and 1970s, all of Cuanajo's furniture was sold by "Indian" salesmen from Cuanajo, who transported loads of furniture to markets on the top of the buses. These salesmen generally sold in one or two city markets, which they know very well. A good deal of the furniture made in town is still sold in this fashion.

Carpenters generally sell their furniture to one or two salesmen with whom they have established a long term relationship. When a salesman is planning a trip, he goes to the carpenters with whom he does business and orders a specific lot of furniture which he believes will sell in his particular market. This means he orders furniture of a particular type, quality and style, to be delivered at a certain date. Few orders are the same. It is customary for the salesman to give the carpenter an advance for the furniture ordered--usually one half of the final negotiated selling price--to ensure that the deal will be consummated. Such agreements add a measure of security for both. If carpenters value the business and the security of the advance, they will make a real effort to live up to their part of the bargain. Of course, the fact that the salesman has put up an advance ensures he will return to purchase the furniture he has ordered.

When carpenters and salesmen have been doing business for many years, bonds of trust are built up, and business deals between the two are generally uneventful. But all too often there are problems with quality; furniture is not picked up by the salesman or delivered by the carpenter on time. Since no legally enforceable contracts are used, there is little one can do to enforce deals except to wait in frustration. Sometimes the waits are not inconsiderable. I know one salesman who gave a substantial advance for a load of furniture. After three years, he is still waiting for it to be delivered.

Despite the problems, these ties between salesmen and carpenters do appear to facilitate exchange. Some salesmen try to buy furniture on the open market either because they do not have the money for advances or because they have had several unfortunate experiences. At times, these men are able to get the kinds of furniture they want on a schedule; but all too often they have major difficulties.

In the cities, salesmen sell most of their furniture in organized markets, or in informal markets, called *tianguis*; and a considerable amount is sold by salesmen literally hawking their wares through the streets of residential districts. A small amount is sold to owners of furniture stores and urban wholesalers with whom the salesman has established a long standing relationship.

Selling furniture in the cities of Mexico takes the kinds of skills and knowledge that can only be built up over time. Experienced salesmen know the times of year when demand is high in "their markets" due to the fiesta cycle, harvests, etc. They also gain an understanding of the transportation system, locations and markets where furniture will sell, the police and market officials, vendors' unions, hotels and inns, and people who will give them trouble.

Salesmen also face a large number of problems in the cities where they sell furniture. Some have been robbed; loads of furniture have failed to arrive at the train station. Many have had trouble with police, market officials, and local salesmen's unions who exclude the furniture salesmen from Cuanajo from selling in official city markets.

In addition, prices and demand can vary considerably and with little warning. Some of the price variation can be traced to the fact that there no coordination among and between salesmen working in the same market. Five men from Cuanajo might be selling furniture in a market one day, and none the next. As a result, gluts, shortages and price fluctuations are the rule.

Salesmen will sometimes talk knowledgeably about what will sell in "their" markets, but their efforts have a hit or miss quality which is unmistakable. Many salesmen have miscalculated what can be sold in a given length of time, and have either had to sell at bargain basement prices or return home with part of the load of furniture. Wives rarely know exactly when to expect them home. The kinds of problems Cuanajo salesmen experience is similar to those documented in markets of other Third World cities. (See, for example, Clark 1988; Smith 1989, 304-305.)

In the past ten years, other ways of selling furniture have come on the scene. Approximately ten shop owners have opened small stores in Cuanajo where they sell small amounts of furniture to the occasional tourists who happen to come to Cuanajo. More important, three other organizations have begun to purchase substantial amounts of furniture in Cuanajo. Approximately 45 carpenters have formed a union called *UNIAMICH* which is affiliated with the State Artisan Agency *La Casa de Artisanias*. *UNIAMICH* is a local union which has its own officers and meetings; but it operates as an arm of the *Casa de Artisanias* which is a Federal and State agency charged with aiding local craft unions to preserve traditional crafts. The *Casa de Artisanias* is dedicated to perpetuating small craft shops rather than promoting large units and efficient, high volume production. The *Casa de Artisanias* not only buys furniture from these union members, which it markets widely from its store in the capital city of Morelia; it also gives technical help and small loans to its members. Most of the furniture bought by *La Casa de Artisanias* is high quality pine furniture made in traditional styles. *UNIAMICH* also formally registers carpentry shops with the "Government" and thus gives the existence of these shops legitimacy in the eyes of at least one government agency. It has also been known to intercede with *FORESTAL* in the interests of its members.

Another 35 people have begun to sell very high quality pine furniture to a privately owned firm in nearby Erongaricuaro, where it is expertly sanded, painted and finished, and then sold on the international market. This firm has developed its own designs and it has trained this group of carpenters to produce this furniture. When this firm places an order with a carpenter, the amount, type and quality of furniture is specified. Such agreements almost approximate a "putting out system" described in other Mexican Indian communities (Stephen 1991, 125; Waterbury 1989, 244 ff.), save for the fact that the wholesale firm does not supply the raw materials, and the carpenter can and does sell to other people. Another wholesale firm in nearby Patzcuaro has begun to buy furniture from 12 carpenters in Cuanajo, which it then ships to the United States. This firm places orders with the carpenters with which it does business, and there is a verbal contract specifying amount and style of furniture, price and delivery date.

Again, the relationship between the carpenters of Cuanajo and these organizations is not trouble free. The carpenters complain about irregular orders and excessive quality demands; the wholesaling organizations are quick to complain about poor quality and unmet delivery schedules.

Another type of organization was on the horizon in December of 1991 when I last left the *pueblo*. For a period of months, another group of some 40 carpenters was forming a union, which has no official name, but was known as the "private union." This union is an association of carpenters and had no affiliation with any government agency. The primary aim of this group is to borrow a very large amount of money from *FIRA*, an agency of the Central Bank of Mexico (*Banco de Mexico*) to finance the construction of a large building to house a number of carpentry shops, a central marketing unit, a large wood drying kiln, and a machine shop. In addition, this union is seriously exploring ways to import a large amount of wood legally into the pueblo from legitimate saw mills in other parts of the State and central Mexico.

This union has gone beyond the talking stage. Its members have been meeting and planning every week for over six months. In addition, the officers have made contact with the Bank of Mexico concerning the loan and a feasibility study was scheduled for the spring of 1992.

The officers of this union are an unusual group. The president is a man from the community who has an engineering degree and works in the nearby State of Guanajuato; the vice president is a very energetic local man, who is one of the local school principals. The driving forced behind this union is the son of a very successful local businessman who has moved to the nearby City of Patzcuaro where he has built up a sizeable business. All of these men and their followers would like to expand economic opportunities in Cuanajo.

This second union does not have the universal support of the entire community by any means. Many people feel the second union would evolve into a social class system with a big factory owned by a small influential elite which would reduce a large number of now independent carpenters to the status of laborers.

It is not at all clear if this second union will succeed in its aim of establishing a large production, and marketing unit. But if such a development does take place, then a significant step toward vertical integration of the furniture industry would have been taken since manufacturing of wood, furniture production and marketing would have been combined in the same organization.

Institutional Economics and the Behavior of Firms

The past 25 years has seen the development of what has become known as the "new institutional economics." Essentially institutional economics is concerned with the generation of institutions and the effects of those institutions on economic decisions and economic performances. Coase, Williamson and other institutional economists interested in the nature of elementary transactions have developed a body of theory that appears to be relevant to understanding the events that have taken place in Cuanajo. Coase points out that the owners of firms can obtain the services and goods they need either by buying them from other firms in the market or by producing them in their own firms. The owners of most firms do both. This means they are engaged in two kinds of transactions: transactions within their own firm which produce "internal" transaction costs, and transactions with other firms which involve "external" transaction costs (Williamson 1975, 82-132).

Internal transaction costs are affected by variables influencing exchanges with employees and units within the same firms such as union rules, levels of education, accounting practices, the honesty and reliability of the work force, etc.

External transaction costs depend on the ease with which owners of firms can get accurate information on prices, supplies, and markets, and can negotiate enforceable contracts with each other (Williamson 1975, 82ff.;1986a). It is also influenced by market efficiency, which refers to the degree to which consumer preferences are reflected in the amounts and prices of goods offered on the market. If markets are inefficient, producers of products do not enter the market with the mix of goods demanded, and gluts, shortages, and rapid price fluctuations result.

The size and degree of specialization of a firm depends on the relative size of internal vs external transaction costs. If internal transaction costs are higher than external transaction costs, then entrepreneurs obtain the services and goods they need from other firms. This results in small, specialized firms. If internal transaction costs are lower than external transaction costs, then owners will expand their own firms to produce the goods or services they require. This can result in very large, specialized firms (Acheson 1982; Williamson

1975, 208ff; Chandler 1977, 209ff) Large firms then are the result of high external transaction costs, which often are the result of inefficient markets.

Internal and external transaction costs are influenced by two sets of factors. First is the type of market. Two types of markets exist along the marketing chain: intermediate product markets which refer to exchanges between firms producing and consuming component parts of a good; and the final product market, the market between the person selling the completed product and the ultimate consumer. Both of these types of markets have different effects of size of firms and the degree of specialization.

If intermediate product markets are relatively efficient, firms can buy and sell to each other with minimal costs. Under these conditions, it costs little to obtain component parts and goods from other firms. Thus, there will be a tendency for firms to be small and specialized in production. Market inefficiency will result in a tendency for firms to expand and perform more tasks for themselves, including the production of more component parts. The efficiency of final product markets, if anything, has even more effect on the configuration of firms. If final product markets are efficient, then firms will receive steady, predictable orders. This makes it possible to have long production runs, use specialized labor and machinery, and enter into long-term contracts with employees. Efficient final product markets can have a great effect on the size of firms. In the United States, firm size expanded greatly when mass marketing techniques made it possible for firms to sell large amounts of standardized goods. Inefficient final product markets mean that it is difficult to sell to consumers. Under these conditions, there would be a tendency for firms to expand forward into the marketing of its products.

Both internal and external transaction costs are influenced by business skill and organizational ability. Literacy and knowledge of accounting techniques and business law make it easier to deal successfully with government officials, bankers, owners of other firms, union leaders, and one's own employees.

For our purposes it is critical to note that according to the Coase and Williamson perspective, owners expand or contract their firms to avoid high transaction costs. They do not attempt to influence the myriad of social, cultural and economic factors that produce such costs in the first place.

Transaction Costs in Cuanajo's Furniture Industry

There can be little doubt that all transaction costs are high in Cuanajo's furniture industry. Several factors make internal transaction costs high. Local entrepreneurs have little education, and no training in law or accounting. They typically operate the business and household from a single general account;

there are no funds set aside for working capital, repairs or business emergencies. These practices not only make it difficult for them to know where their money is being spent, but the lack of working capital often causes delays for days on end when any kind of problems appear. In addition, shop owners find it difficult to enter into contracts with their own employees. The lack of education increases the costs of training. Mexicans also sometimes do not make the most reliable and honest employees. Many do not show up for work and are careless in their use of tools. Wood and tools tend to disappear. There are instances where laborers have borrowed money from employers with the understanding that they would pay back the debt out of their earnings and then have used the money from the loan to finance a trip to the United States. In Robert Hunt's terms, "Mexicans regard jobs as licenses to act in ways which Americans call stealing" (1965, 61).

In addition there is a general shortage of experienced labor in Cuanajo. This is not only due to the rapid expansion of the industry, but also to the strong value placed on independence and autonomy. Once a man has the experience to operate his own shop, with all that indicates about skills in maintenance, supervision and carpentry, he is very likely to do so. As a result, there is a constant turnover of experienced workers, and it is virtually impossible to hire people to supervise others. Why be a foreman when one could own one's own shop? Both of these factors increase internal transaction costs further (Acheson 1982, 326-27).

External transaction costs are high as well. Agreements between firms are purely verbal; legally binding agreements are virtually unknown. People in Cuanajo do not use lawyers and contracts. Moreover, it is considered a serious breach of local norms to take another townsman to court regardless of what agreements he may have violated.

In addition to these general problems, the deals between carpenters and wood suppliers are further complicated by the fact that much of the wood supply is illegal. In an atmosphere where stealing, stealth and problems with law enforcement officials are ever present, shortages and unstable prices are the rule.

The entire furniture sales operations appears to be plagued by timing problems. Not only are schedules and orders not met, but gluts, shortages, and fluctuating prices are the rule.

The inefficient final product markets cause problems for the producers. Since salesmen want to take to market a variety of types of furniture which they feel will sell in their markets, they order small, heterogenous lots of furniture from carpenters. This means that carpentry shop production runs are very short and thus the degree of possible specialization is limited. A laborer cannot specialize in using one machine to produce one component part day after day when the shop owner has only small irregular orders. He must be prepared to make any kind of furniture for which orders can be obtained.

Problems with wood supplies and labor result in carpentry shops being unable to meet orders, which in turn can put salesmen off schedules and result in the kinds of gluts, missed sales, and price fluctuations characteristic of inefficient final product markets.

The ability of the shop owners of Cuanajo to gain access to large amounts of capital is limited by the prejudice against "Indians", which is compounded by their poor Spanish, lack of education, and lack of network ties to national lending institutions. Very few "Indians" have been able to negotiate sizeable loans from banks. In addition to cultural barriers, the lack of secure deeds to houses and land means there is nothing that banks will regard as "collateral." To be sure, some of the machinery companies have extended enough credit to make it possible to purchase small motors and machinery parts on credit, but the amount of credit that these firms will extend is strictly limited.

Dealing with the government is perhaps more difficult.[5] Corruption and inefficiency are rife. Here again "Indians" with their lack of education and "proper Spanish" do not do well.

In summary, internal transaction costs are high due primarily to lack of organizational skills which make it difficult to deal with employees, handle finances, maintain working capital, etc. These costs are exacerbated by the inability to hire managerial personnel; and the small, unpredictable orders which make it difficult to have long production runs and limit the possible specialization of labor. External transaction costs are high because of inefficient final product markets which make it difficult to sell large amounts of furniture on a predictable schedule; and because supplies of wood are so uncertain which means that a critical intermediate product market is inefficient as well. It is also difficult to gain access to capital, which is traceable in large part to low levels of organizational skills.

Responses to High Transaction Costs

According to institutional economists, firms should expand or contract to take advantage of high transaction costs. Unfortunately, all transaction costs are high in the case of Cuanajo's furniture industry. Owners can take advantage of neither high nor low transaction costs. How do these owners operate in this confining environment? I argue that they are using three different types of institutional arrangements in an effort to reduce transaction costs.

Reducing Internal Transaction Costs

The primary ploy used to lower internal transaction costs is to hire kinsmen whenever possible. Kinsmen usually make more trusted and reliable employees and they can be counted on to sacrifice for the family firm should necessity dictate. Hiring kinsmen reduces the kinds of internal transaction costs associated with hiring non-family members. This is not to suggest that there are no transaction costs involved in hiring kin. It may be very difficult to fire kinsmen, for example. More important, kin have a claim on family income. A spouse with a drinking problem or spendthrift tendencies can cause havoc with the family and business budget. Some successful entrepreneurs have solved this problem by setting up obligated funds dedicated to the needs of the business and completely under the control of the person in charge of the business (Acheson 1993).

Reducing External Transaction Costs

There are two kinds of institutions that are being used to lower external transaction costs. The first is what Ian Macneil (1978) calls "relational markets;" the second is the development of intermediary organizations to aid in the production and marketing of furniture.

1. *Relational markets*: Cuanajo's furniture industry is characterized by small firms, linked to each other through "relational market" ties. No large vertically integrated firms have developed, which are involved in all phases of the business from cutting trees to selling furniture in distant markets. Yet the owners of these small businesses do not operate in an open market, buying and selling to the highest bidder, with economic optimization the sole concern. Rather, they have established long term ties, and a relationship of some trust with the firms with which they do business. The reasons for this pattern can be understood by considering the transactions involved in other options.

No carpentry firm has expanded into the production of wood, despite the fact that wood shortages are a constant problem. Going into the wood business means trouble with the law and landowners. Yet carpenters cannot get wood easily by operating in the open spot market since "farmers" prefer to sell wood to people who can be trusted to maintain their anonymity. The result is that carpenters have a strong tendency to obtain wood from a few "farmers" with whom they have built up a relationship of trust.

In a similar vein, no carpenter has attempted to expand his own firm by hiring salesmen and setting up a sales department.[6] Selling furniture, after all, involves a good deal of knowledge and experience. Rather, they have attempted to overcome the high transaction costs associated with selling furniture by developing long term ties with salesmen which are reinforced by verbal contracts to ensure that the interests of both parties are protected.

The kinds of bilateral ties owners of carpentry shops have with the owners of the two wholesaling firms involve more commitments on the part of both parties. These agreements specify an advance, price, and delivery schedule, and the particular designs to be used. The benefits of dealing with these two private wholesaling firms is a higher price per piece of furniture. These firms sell Cuanajo's high quality furniture in international markets to which local salesmen do not have access.

2. *Intermediary organizations*: The second kind of institution that has been developed to reduce external transaction costs are intermediary organizations, which are essentially associations of carpenters. *UNIAMICH* assists in marketing furniture, increasing quality of the product, obtaining credit, and running interference with government agencies. The private union promises to be a vehicle for obtaining a good deal of credit, which will be spend on capital assets to increase production. In time, it may aid in marketing. The unions undoubtedly help to reduce the high external transaction costs associated with selling furniture. They also cut the costs of dealing with the government.

Conclusion

Cuanajo is not in the modern industrialized world and thus it is not surprising that firms in this community do not behave as do the firms described by Coase, and Williamson. However, the intellectual tools developed by these institutional economists shed a good deal of light on what has occurred in the development of Cuanajo's carpentry industry and the reasons for these changes. Most important, Coase and Williamson and their followers are assuming a situation in which some transaction costs are higher than others. However, in Cuanajo **all transaction costs are high.** This leads to some strategies not considered by the institutional economists and an industry that has some unusual features.

First, the high transaction costs environment has resulted in small, unspecialized and relatively unprofitable firms. The reason for this can be understood by considering the options open to owners of firms. In Cuanajo, external transaction costs are high. Under these conditions, one would expect the owners of these firms to expand their own firms backward into the production of component parts and forward into marketing. However, internal transaction costs are high as well, which make it very costly or impossible to expand. In short, the owners of these businesses are caught between the proverbial rock and a hard place. The result is the kind of "small scale" firms with "short time horizons and little fixed capital" that North says are typical of firms in the Third World in general (North 1990, 67).

Second, the very high transaction costs environment results in the furniture industry developing a set of intermediary institutions which lie somewhere between a market on the one hand and a hierarchy on the other.

Again the reason for this development can be understood by considering the organizational enigma the carpenters face. Relations between carpenters and wood suppliers and furniture salesmen exhibit a good deal of "asset specificity" (Milgrom and Roberts 1992, 30-31). That is, carpenters are very dependent on certain people with whom they have built up relationships of trust. It is in these situations that it makes most sense to establish a firm to incorporate all of these interdependent people (Williamson 1985, 52-56). However, expanding a firm to take over the wood cutting operation and marketing functions make little sense from if one wants to avoid trouble with the law; and the specialized knowledge and risks of marketing would make the selling operation very difficult to administer as part of a large firm. The result is a dependence on long term ties (i.e. relational markets) and intermediary organizations (the unions) which avoid the high transactions costs of organizing large "hierarchies" (i.e. vertically integrated firms) or spot markets. Relational markets have been commonly observed in Third World Countries (Finan 1988; Mintz 1964; Plattner 1986); fewer intermediary organizations have been described, but they have been noted in Third World situations (Brautigam 1991, 17-18). I hypothesize that the dependance on these intermediate institutions stems from situations in which both internal and external transaction costs are high.

Third, the high transaction costs have resulted in a good deal of effort being expended on developing new organizations and institutions to lower them. Internal transaction costs are lowered by hiring kin, and use of "obligated funds;" external transaction costs are lowered by the use of long term bilateral ties linking firms in the production chain, the development of intermediary firms run by outsiders, and the development of the "unions."

These responses would not have been predicted by the work of Coase and Williamson. According to the theory, firms do not attempt to lower transaction costs by changing the cultural and institutional framework in which they exist; rather they respond to the transaction costs produced by those cultural and institutional factors by altering the size of the firm and the number of functions it performs for itself. If your firm needs paint, and your employees are dishonest, you do not attempt to organize a paint factory and hire a clergyman to change the attitudes and values of the crew. You simply buy paint at the hardware store. What the owners of shops in Cuanajo have done is analogous to hiring the priest. That is, they are devoting a good deal of effort to developing local institutions and organizations to create a more favorable business climate. **The lesson from Cuanajo appears to be that in an environment in which all transaction costs are high, owners of firms have little choice but to cooperate in developing institutions to lower them.**

Last, in Cuanajo, internal and external transaction costs are high due to high organizational costs. Williamson mentions organization costs obliquely when he speaks of "human factors" (Williamson 1975, 8) and "verification" problems, but this is not a central concept or issue. However, the data from Cuanajo suggest that the furniture industry is limited in large measure by high organization costs, and that these costs could be lowered by increases in literacy, and training in business law, accounting, finance, and personnel management. If this is true, then the keys to the development of poor countries do not lie in the transfer of technology, additional capital or increases in amount of land. They are to be found in education, and the development of institutions which permit the lowering of very high transaction costs.

References

Acheson, James M. 1972. Limited Good or Limited Goods?: Response to Economic Opportunity in a Tarascan Pueblo. *American Anthropologist* 74(5): 1152-1169.

———.1985. The Maine Lobster Market: Between Market and Hierarchy. *Journal of Law, Economics, and Organization* 1(2): 385-398.

———.1982. Limitations on Firm Size in a Tarascan Pueblo. *Human Organization* 44(2): 202-2-3.

———.1988. Tamaño de las Empresas e Inovacíon en un Pueblo Tarasco. In Guillermo de la Pena, ed., *Antropologia Social de la Region Purepeche.* El Colegio de Michoacan and the Government of the State of Michoacan. Zamora: Colegio de Michoacan.

———.1993. *Household Budget Structures and Business Success in a Mexican Indian Pueblo* (Unpublished Manuscript).

Benedict, Burton. 1968. Family Firms and Economic Development. *Southwest Journal of Anthropology* 24(1): 1-19.

Brautigam, Deborah. 1991. Governance and Economy: A Review. Working Paper of the Policy and Review Department of the World Bank. WPS 815. Washington, D.C.: The World Bank.

Chandler, Alfred D. 1977. *The Visible Hand: The Managerial Revolution in American Business.* Cambridge, Mass.: The Belknap Press.

Clark, Gracia. 1988. *Traders Versus the State.* Boulder: Westview.

Coase, Ronald H. 1937. The Nature of the Firm. *Economica* 4: 386-405.

Cook, Scott. 1984. *Peasant Capitalist Industry.* New York: University Press of America.

Cook, Scott and Leigh Binford. 1986. Petty Commodity Production, Capital Accumulation and Peasant Differentiation: Lenin vs. Chayanov in Rural Mexico. *Review of Radical Political Economics* 18(4): 1-31.

de Soto, Hernando. 1989. *The Other Path: The Invisible Revolution in the Third World.* New York: Harper and Row.

Ellis, Frank. 1988. *Peasant Economics: Farm Household and Agrarian Development.* Cambridge: Cambridge University Press.

Finan, Timothy. 1988. Market Relationships and Market Performance in Northeast Brazil. *American Ethnologist* 15(4): 694-709.

Gudeman, Stephen and Alberto Rivera. 1990. *Conversations in Columbia: The Domestic Economy in Life and Text.* Cambridge: Cambridge University Press.

Hart, Gillian. 1992. Imagined Unities: Constructions of "The Household" in Economic Theory. In Sutti Ortiz, ed., *Understanding Economic Process.* Lanham, Md.: University Press of America.

Hunt, Robert. 1965. The Developmental Cycle of the Family Business in Rural Mexico. In June Helm, ed., *Essays in Economic Anthropology*. Proceedings of the American Ethnological Society. Seattle: University of Washington Press.

Johnson, Allen W. 1971. Security and Risk-taking Among Poor Peasants: A Brazilian Case Study. In George Dalton, ed., *Studies In Economic Anthropology.* Washington, D.C.: American Anthropological Association.

Macneil, Ian. 1978. Contracts: Adjustments of Long-Term Economic Relations Under Classical, Neoclassical and Relational Contract Law. *Northwest University Law Review* 72: 854-97.

Milgrom, Paul and John Roberts. 1992. *Economics, Organization and Management.* Englewood Cliffs, N.J.: Prentice-Hall.

Mintz, Sidney. 1964. The Employment of Capital by Market Women in Haiti. In Raymond Firth and Basil S. Yamey, eds., *Capital, Savings and Credit in Peasant Societies*. Chicago: Aldine.

Netting, Robert Mc. 1989. Smallholders, Householders, Freeholders: Why the Family Farm Works Well Worldwide. In Richard Wilk, ed., *The Household Economy*. Boulder, Colorado: Westview Press.

———.1993. *Smallholders, Householders: Farm Families and the Ecology of Intensive, Sustainable Agriculture.* Stanford: Stanford University Press.

North, Douglass. 1990. *Institutions, Institutional Change and Economic Performance.* Cambridge: Cambridge University Press.

Plattner, Stuart. 1989. Economic Behavior in Markets. In Stuart Plattner, ed., *Economic Anthropology*. Stanford: Stanford University Press.

Rothstein, Frances Abraham, and Michael L. Blim. 1992. *Anthropology and the Global Factory*. New York and Westport: Bergen and Garvey.

Sahlins, Marshall. 1972. *Stone Age Economics*. Chicago: Aldine Atherton.

Smith, Estellie. 1989. The Informal Economy. In Stuart Plattner, ed., *Economic Anthropology*. Stanford: Stanford University Press.

Stephen, Lynn. 1991. *Zapotec Women*. Austin: University of Texas Press.

Waterbury, Ronald. 1989. Embroidery for Tourists: A Contemporary Putting-Out System in Oaxaca, Mexico. In Annette B. Weiner and Jane Schneider, eds., *Cloth and Human Experience*. Washington: Smithsonian Institution Press.

Wharton, Clifton. 1971. Risk, Uncertainty and the Subsistence Farmer: Technological Innovation and Resistance to Change in the Context of Survival. In George Dalton, ed., *Studies in Economic Anthropology*. Washington, D.C.: American Anthropological Assn.

West, Robert C. 1948. *Cultural Geography of the Modern Tarascan Area*. Smithsonian Institution, Institute of Social Anthropology Publication No. 7. Washington, D.C.: U.S. Government Printing Office.

Williamson,Oliver E. 1975. *Markets and Hierarchies: Analysis and Antitrust Implications*. New York: Free Press.

———.1979 Transaction-Cost Economics: The Governance of Contractual Relations. *Journal of Law and Economics* 22: 233-60.

———.1985 *The Economic Institutions of Capitalism*. New York: Free Press.

———.1986a. The Economics of Governance: Framework and Implications. In Richard N. Langlois, ed., *Economics as a Process: Essays in the New Institutional Economics*. Cambridge: Cambridge University Press.

———.1986b *Economic Organization: Firms, Markets and Policy Control*. New York: New York University Press.

Williamson, Oliver and Sidney Winter, eds. 1993 *The Nature of the Firm: Origins, Evolution and Development*. New York: Oxford.

Notes

1. This paper is based on data gathered in 1990 in the course of a field project sponsored by the National Science Foundation. Special thanks are due to Jean Ensminger, James Wilson and a reviewer who commented on an earlier draft of this paper.

2. There is no well developed body of theory in anthropology to explain these developments. Much of the problem is conceptual. Industries, after all, are composed of production units, usually firms, which are linked by some means--usually through markets. The anthropological literature on households focuses on internal organization of these households (Ellis 1988; Hart 1992; Hunt 1965; Sahlins 1972), and their production decisions (Benedict 1968; Gudeman and Rivera 1990; Johnson 1971; Netting 1989, 1993; Wharton 1971). As Wilk (1984) points out in this volume, even this body of literature gives a very inadequate picture of the way resources--especially financial resources--are managed. The literature on peasant involvement in markets goes in very different directions (see Plattner 1989 for a review of this literature). There have been few attempts to bring these two bodies of literature together.

3. The expansion of the furniture industry is due to a large number of changes both inside and outside the *pueblo*. In this article, the focus is on the organization of the industry and changes in firms. Nevertheless, it must be recognized that the opportunities in the furniture industry would not have existed were it not for many changes in infrastructure, such as the construction of roads, electric power facilities, and the development of the transportation system, etc. (Acheson 1972). In addition, the level of education has increased as the Federal Government built schools in large numbers of remote pueblos including Cuanajo. Finally effective demand for furniture increased as the population increased and levels of income in Mexico went up.

4. The fact that a range of household types can exist in the same Indian community and that some of these have at least some of the characteristics of "firms" has been noted by at least two other ethnographers. Cook has described how "peasant artisan household enterprises" move to "petty capitalism" (Cook 1984; Cook and Binford 1986), while Stephen describes the differentiation of Zapotec weaving households into four types, including "independent weaver households workshops" and "merchant workshops with hired laborers" (1991, 124).

5. The high transaction costs involved in dealing with Latin American bureaucracies are best exemplified by the work of Hernando de Soto, a Peruvian economist of some renown, who organized a research team to go through the procedures necessary to set up a small business. It took 289 days of work to get through the red tape (de Soto 1989, 134).

6. A few carpentry shop owners have opened small stores in Cuanajo and sell a small amount of their output to the Mexican tourists who drive into town.

7

The Household Economy In Rural China: Is The Involution Over?[1]

Laurel Bossen

China's History of Involutionary Family Farming

China's post-Mao reforms which began in the 1980s and continue into the 1990s have generated attention primarily as a shift from socialist economic planning toward a market system. A key element of this reform policy, referred to as the Household Responsibility System, permits individual households to manage land and labour, retaining and marketing their surpluses once government quotas are met. The institutional transformation that accompanies this shift, the revival of China's rural households as core economic institutions, has received less attention.

With a rural population currently estimated at 70 percent of its total population, any explanation of China's economic development and/or stagnation must look at these institutions and the way they (and their members) behave. Following China's dramatic shift from collective back to family farm management, many scholars have been concerned with the capacity of China's rural household economies to develop. The central question is whether China has now chosen a new road to development after decades, or centuries, of involutionary growth without development, or whether China has returned to the long trodden path of labour-intensifying involutionary family farming.

In this paper, I intend to review some of the theoretical arguments in Philip Huang's provocative study, *The Peasant Family and Rural Development in the Yangzi Delta, 1350-1988* (1990) regarding China's long history and recent reforms. In so doing, I wish to emphasize that consistent with Huang's commitment to studying regional variations in China's rural economies, I see China's rural village and household economies as institutions which exhibit a great deal of local and regional variability--and about which we still know very little. While idealized patterns of Chinese family organization and the widely disseminated national administrative policies for collective and household institutions are well studied, the actual local adaptations that are emerging through recent research prove challenging to our general theories.[2] My discussion of Huang's theory, then, will use an alternate set of local data from Henan province to contrast to his interpretation of the recent reforms in the Yangzi Delta.

Philip Huang (1990) argues that China's peasant households have experienced over six centuries of commercialization and economic involution. Countering the theory that commercialization leads to dissolution of the family farm, he believes that in China commercialization led to its strengthening. He argues that historically population pressure caused peasant families to intensify labour "by resorting to ever greater use of auxiliary household labour for low returns" (1990,11). Huang emphasizes the interaction between population pressure and commercialization as producing intensification or involution. Involution "actually comes to obstruct the development of wage labour-based production by virtue of its ability to sustain labour input at returns that are below market wages"(13).

> One of the consequences of a high level of *involutionary commercialization* sustained by *the familization of rural production* was that family farming outcompeted wage labour-based managerial agriculture, for the simple reason that managerial enterprises had to **rely mainly on adult male labour paid at prevailing market wages** [emphasis added]. A family farm that used spare-time and auxiliary household labour at net returns well below the prevailing market wages could sustain much higher levels of labour intensification (14).

As Chinese peasants experienced population growth and diminishing returns to labour on a relatively unexpandable land area, they spent more time working and switched to more labour intensive activities. This expanding work effort was organized not by a labour market, but by the family economy. The unpaid "auxiliary labour" of women and children increased, contributing to a process that Huang calls the "*familization*" of labour. Huang describes this pattern as one of economic growth without development, also called involution. That is, the total output of the population and of the household increases, but the returns per unit of labour decline. Huang does not explore how and why the labour of women was segregated from the labour market, questions which point to the need for historical analysis of the changing ways Chinese patriarchal families operated as economic institutions.

Huang's review of the economic history of the densely populated Yangzi River Delta during the Ming and Qing dynasties (1350-1911) outlines several ways in which China's rural involution occurred. These include switching from grain crops to more labour intensive commercial crops such as cotton and mulberry leaves for silkworms, and adding household production of labour intensive commercial crafts such as cotton and silk textiles. Underlying these innovative responses is the pressure of population growth upon already densely populated cultivated land and the possibility of trading cash crops and crafts for grain.

Huang argues that involutionary familization of rural production continued, although restructured, under the influence of international capitalism of the republican period (1911-1949), and was followed, under the postrevolutionary state (1949-1978) by collectivist involution (1990, 5-16). Under the leadership of the Chinese Communist Party, collective farms were to replace family farms and organize labour into large scale units with greater economies of scale. Families were not dissolved as units of residence, consumption or biological reproduction, but their rights to control land and labour were transferred to government collectives. These rural collectives were territorially defined institutions managed according to state and local plans that directed the entire labour force. These collectives eliminated leisure and unemployment by spreading agricultural labour tasks more evenly among the rural population. The collectivist institutions, Huang correctly argues, maintained the "tolerance for surplus labour" characteristic of the peasant household. It was only in the 1980s, that there was finally a significant change in direction that allowed labour to be allocated more flexibly.

> The rural change of the greatest long-term import was the de-involution in crop production that came with the diversification of the rural economy, and not the turn to marketized farming in crop production, as is commonly assumed....To put it bluntly, marketized farming in the 1980s did no better in crop production than it did in the six centuries between 1350 and 1950, or than collective agriculture did in the preceding three decades.

> The crucial development in the delta...came not from the "private" crop production and petty commerce that were given so much press, but rather from rural industry and new sidelines. It was rural industrialization and side-line development that finally contrived to lower the number of labourers sharing in a relatively fixed crop-production pie and reverse the centuries old pattern of involution....the record shows that the truly transformative development is rather de-involution in farming through *rural industrialization and sidelines development, mostly under collective units* (Huang 1990, 17-18) [emphasis added].

In Huang's view, the Yangzi Delta's rural involution ended with the reforms not because the household system of *farming* was more efficient than the collective one, but because the greater local autonomy which accompanied the return to family farming freed some labour to pursue more productive activities in towns and rural industries. Productivity of labour within farm households increased when underemployed labour was finally released.

For Huang, the end to Chinese farm involution is not simply the effect of family farm incentives producing innovations leading to greater productivity. Most of the innovations were introduced in the preceding period, but failed to have a transformative effect until surplus labour was permitted to leave. Although acknowledging weak incentives for labour quality under the collectives, he dismisses this as a central problem on the argument that labour rewards in the work teams were always tied to output. The following extended quotation presents the gist of his analysis, based on research on peasants in Huayangqiao, a brigade in Songjiang county in Shanghai municipality.

> ...there can be no mistaking the difference between the earlier pattern of growth without development in crop production and the new pattern of development without growth [in crop production]. In the one, absolute output increased, as did the state's take in taxes and procurement, but farm labour productivity and peasant incomes stagnated. In the other, crop yields have stagnated, as has the state's take in taxes and procurement, but farm labour productivity and peasant incomes from farming have risen dramatically. Nor can there be any mistaking the cause of the change: it comes not from any dramatic breakthrough in crop yields as a result of the supposedly superior incentive power of marketized family farming, but rather from diversification of the rural economy and the diversion of surplus labour from farming into off-farm employment (1990, 246).

Significantly, Huang refers to income distribution to a smaller number of farmers, not to a rise in *total village income* from farming. As he explained,

> although crop yields in the village dropped that year [1983], the *gongfenzhi* [work point value] jumped dramatically, breaking clearly away from the one yuan value of the preceding decades. Why? Because, as Gao Youfa explained, "the year before each family got to send one worker to the brigade factory. Thus the number of people who shared in the total agricultural output decreased" (1990, 45).

In other words, family farming per se is not what bailed these rural households out of involution, but rural industries, even collective ones, which attracted labour away from the family farm. What is not explicitly answered, however, is if, why and how the marketplace and larger firms are now able to "outcompete" the peasant household after they failed to do so during the many previous centuries of commercialization and commoditized peasant family farming.

Sociologists Victor Nee and Su Sijin see China's reforms differently. Using institutional theory, they maintain that the transition from the redistributive collective economy to the market economy is linked to the question of transaction costs which shape incentives (1990, 3).

> In the analysis of economic action, institutional theory maintains that institutions in the aggregate result in higher or lower transaction costs (i.e., costs over and above production costs) and thereby shape the structure of incentives. In an economy, the higher the cost of transaction, the lower the level of its efficiency and performance (1990, 3).

In this view, "direct bureaucratic microintervention is an important cause of higher transaction costs" (1990, 4).

There is no question that China's rural collectives were insular and bureaucratically administered. Officials maintained rigid bureaucratic boundaries with high transaction costs between urban and rural sectors. In general, market activity was curtailed. For example, farmers could not respond to market price signals about what urban consumers wanted to buy, but had to obey bureaucratic decrees about what and how much to produce, as well as where and when to deliver it and for what price (Skinner 1985, 27). Moreover, people could not change their place of residence or the place of work without obtaining permission from local officials in both their natal community and their new community. For those registered as rural residents, such transfers generally could take place only at marriage and only within the rural sphere. Migration to urban jobs and assignments of housing were all bureaucratically controlled.[3] The transaction costs for an "illegal" or unregistered "immigrant" wanting to come to the city to work or to sell produce, when neither food, jobs nor housing were legally available in a free market, must have been forbidding indeed and certainly served to dam up the flow of urban migrants. For most of the collective period beginning in the 1950s to the reforms of the late 1980s, the price mechanism for informing and mediating supply and demand, hallmark of market efficiency, was severely suppressed. This was particularly true during the more radical phases of the Great Leap Forward (1958-1960) and the Cultural Revolution (1966-1976) when the number and frequency of markets and trade fairs across the country dramatically declined (Skinner 1985, 7-32).

The reforms of the 1980s have reduced national and local level cadre control by breaking up the collectives, returning "responsibility" for agricultural production to households and allowing them to sell their surplus on the free market rather than solely to state agencies. The ongoing reforms increasingly allow market competition to lower many, but not all, of the transaction costs and bureaucratic barriers to the movement of goods, information and people. In the early 1990s, peasant markets continue to grow and multiply, and villagers are beginning to ignore the household registration system, changing residence without changing registration. In the last decade, state propaganda has been increasingly eclipsed by competitive product advertising on television, billboards, and in newspapers. As a result of the removal of internal trade barriers and bureaucratic transaction costs, the incomes of rural producers have risen, and their access to industrial inputs and consumer goods has improved dramatically.

In developing a theory of market transition, Victor Nee proposes three interrelated theses concerning power, incentives and opportunities. The first is that in the transition from redistribution to market exchanges producers gain more control over resources and price negotiations. The second is that prices for labour are no longer set by administrative fiat at lower than market-determined prices, and producers have a right to withhold labour power until mutual agreement is reached. The third is that "rather than focusing exclusively on access to and mobility within the redistributive sector, market opportunities open up alternative avenues of socioeconomic mobility" (Nee 1989, 666-667).

Taking these three related theses right to the heart of the family economy and the question of familization, I see the peasant family itself as, in most cases, a redistributive institution--not a market one. Those who must labour within it (but are not entitled to manage it) have less power, incentive, and opportunities than those who are free to venture outside it. This goes back to the question of Huang's interpretation of China's historical involution, and why the peasant household was able to "outcompete" those entrepreneurs who sought to hire labour through the market mechanism. Huang indicates that there was a market for *male labour*, but that the *family* was able to take advantage of increased intensity of labour by its female and child members--those who were powerless to negotiate their own wages or withhold their labour for better incentives or look for better opportunities. My goal here is not to explore Huang's historical argument as much as to ask if we can discover what may or may not be different this time around, and specifically to ask that question as it applies to the *female producers* who are so crucial to the *familization thesis*.

Coase (1937) asked why, if market mechanisms are efficient, is it profitable to establish a firm? In this case, I ask why is it profitable or efficient to restore the family farm as the unit of agricultural production as opposed to managing village lands as competitive enterprises which hire agricultural labour? Coase suggested that

> there is a cost of using the price mechanism. The most obvious cost of "organizing" production through the price mechanism is that of discovering what the relevant prices are...The costs of negotiating and concluding a separate contract for each exchange transaction which takes place on a market must also be taken into account (1937, 336).

Clearly, there are "costs" associated with using the price mechanism for some of the activities, particularly human reproduction itself, which are performed by the household as an institution. In farming, one of the chief transaction costs is searching for and securing labour during brief, but urgent "peak periods" such as harvesting and planting. At such times, if labour is neither available in the village nor congregating at the local market place, farmers cannot afford to take time to travel about to other villages looking for unemployed labourers willing to work very hard for a short period. Family farms as institutions tend to keep at least some family members tied in year round to have them available at peak periods. But for those who are subject to household economies operating with a patriarchal redistributive structure, a transition to "market mechanisms"--in other words, greater choice--could surely bring benefits similar to those seen for the peasant sector as it is released from the redistributive control of the collective. These questions about redistributive and market mechanisms require us to press further into the issue of the nature and extent of the market for female labour in contemporary China, and how it is related to the Household Responsibility System.

Involution and Agricultural Productivity: Where and How Is The Involution Ending?

Huang's analysis of the recent "end to involution" in peasant farming is based on research in China's Yangzi Delta, in the vicinity of Shanghai and Suzhou, one of the most prosperous urban-industrial regions of China, with highly valuable real estate near one of China's three great port cities (Tianjin, Shanghai, and Canton). His theory needs further examination and testing in *other settings*, where transportation and distance from major metropolitan markets are *not* at the most favourable end of the national scale.

In assessing China's rural reforms, one can distinguish between their impact on rural households as diversified small enterprises and their impact on family agriculture. Here, I also want to distinguish between the farming of staple grains and cotton--in which the state has long taken a regulatory interest--and the farming of other cash crops, such as vegetables which are sold independently on open markets. While Huang has suggested that labour productivity increased in crop production with the withdrawal of labour, it is important to ask whether the current system retains involutionary institutional features which cause peasants to continue allocating labour to activities where their marginal product is close to zero.

Huang's historical and contemporary analysis of involution explicitly considers the sexual division of labour within the rural household economy. Given the general tendency of historians to accept the stereotypic view of rural Chinese women as traditionally locked in the house, inconspicuously consuming much and producing little, it is refreshing that Huang pays considerable attention to the historically changing productive roles of women, particularly with the expansion of cotton production. He not only recognizes that the roles of peasant women were changeable, he also integrates them (albeit using the peculiar tag, "auxiliary labour") into his analysis of economic involution. Yet there are still many questions about rural women that need to be answered before the processes of stagnating involution and transformative development are understood.

My objective here is not to address Huang's analysis of historical involutionary development in the Yangzi Delta. It is to address his analysis of the de-involution of the 1980s. How valid and widespread is the evidence that the involution in *farming* per se has ended, or is ending in rural China? Is a *de-familization* of farming taking place? Has the involutionary use of female labour in the rural household economy ended, or at least been reversed? If it is ending, what kind of institutional transformations have made this possible? How is this related to the restoration of the *family farming system*, that is, the Household Responsibility System, in the 1980s? Here I review some of the evidence that the involutionary growth in the farm sector is reversing and the productivity of farm labour is increasing.

Female Labour in the Yangzi Delta Sample

In Huang's case study of Huayangqiao, the exodus from farming to off-farm jobs appears to be gender neutral, but selective by age.

> By 1985, more than half of the labourers in the Huayangqiao villages had come to be employed in rural (commune town and village) enterprises. And by 1988, only those villagers above age fifty still remained entirely in farmwork; all the younger men and women were working in higher-paying and less strenuous off-farm jobs....Thus, even with the diversion of more than half of the full-time labour force from farming, crop yields were maintained at levels close to the collectivized years. The results were a sharp rise in the cash value of the workday equivalent in farming (Huang 1990, 245).

Yet earlier, Huang describes a more complex situation, acknowledging gender stratification in the feminization of farming as one pattern, and implying that a second pattern, with a similar exodus from farming by both sexes, is equally significant.

The *first pattern* is one of part-peasant part-worker households illustrated by the Huayangqiao villages, at least up to 1985. Noting that half of all the full-time labourers were employed off-farm, he stated that

> the vast majority were men...In all, men outnumbered women two to one in off-farm employment.
>
> By the mid-1980s, in fact, the rural cadres were inclined to joke about how farming was being done mainly by the "Three Eight Team" (*sanba duiwu*)--a reference to March 8, Women's Day (Huang 1990, 213, see also Table D6, p. 353).

Furthermore, in describing intravillage and intrafamily stratification, Huang discussed villagers who worked only in farming as forming the bottom strata of village society: "Two-thirds of them women, usually the middle aged and older women, were at the bottom" below urban registrants with state jobs living in the villages, and below those employed in commune, town, or village factories (297).

The *second pattern*, illustrated by Shenxianglang village of Fengqiao commune, "on the outskirts of Suzhou city, however, suggests that the 'feminization of agriculture' does not completely capture the direction of change" (213).[4] In Fengqiao, the economy has been transformed from one in which agriculture and "hand-produced sidelines" accounted for 83% of output in 1958 (note that even with 1958 as a baseline year, the proportion of nonagricultural employment is unclear), to one in which industry accounted for 83% in 1984. Huang suggests that this "pattern typifies the sidelining of agriculture, not its feminization." He reports that in 1985 "*nearly all* the village women, as well as the men, had off-farm jobs. And farming had become, not women's work but simply spare time work" (214). He makes a similar statement about Huayangqiao:

> According to my peasant informants, by 1988 every male and female labourer under fifty in Huayangqiao was employed outside of agriculture; only older people still remained in farming (256).

This suggests that in three years, pattern one (half-nonfarm, primarily male employment) in Huayangqiao had been transformed into pattern two (all nonfarm, equal male and female employment). Given the prominence Huang gives to the Shenxianglang example and to several informants' statements[5] about female nonfarm employment, it is unfortunate that for neither the industrial village of Shenxianglang nor Huayangqiao in 1988 are precise employment figures made available. The informants' statements about women in the workforce at present and in the past remain unconfirmed.

Similarly, Huang lacks comparable measures of actual labour expended in agriculture between earlier and later periods, or of how prevalent the two "new" patterns may be in the context of the Yangzi delta, as well as more widely in China. Surely, location on the outskirts of a flourishing industrial-textile city, famous for its silks, is far from a typical farming situation. Combined with the evidence from 1936 on the absence of women from farming and the importance of cottage and incipient industrial textile production in this region (Fei 1939), it is hard to accept this case solely as a convincing example of the recent sidelining of agriculture in the reform period, and a newly instituted process of de-involution.

Beyond these questions about temporal change and geographic specificity, another reason for caution in accepting Huang's thesis is that contemporary farm labour is only **partly** free to leave the involutionary farm sector. The reforms are, as Victor Nee (1989) says, "partial reforms." They only move part way toward a market economy. Land, housing, and labour are still to a large extent under the control of the redistributive state sector. This sector has been shrinking in relative importance, but it is not yet out of the picture. Labour, and especially married female labour, is still constrained by the redistributive mechanisms which continue to allocate many of the better industrial jobs, urban housing, and residence rights. If rural labour seeking nonfarm employment does not have access to truly open labour and housing markets, both institutional and neo-classical economic theory predict that it would remain in an involutionary, and in some respects involuntary, manner on family farms.[6] The extent to which the reintroduction of market mechanisms to the allocation of labour reduces involution might seem to be implicit in Huang's assessment of the reforms, but it is not a point that he chooses to make.

A Henan Village Study

I reexamine the issue of involution using fieldwork data from the village of Yancun collected in 1989 in Henan Province.[7] Yancun is located north of the Yellow River in a densely populated part of the North China plain. It is only an hour or so from a major city and from major railway lines. Yet it is reached by a dirt road, and has very minor local "industry" (a flour mill that serves the village). Has the familization (or feminization) of farming declined? Has the total labour input decreased in relation to grain output? Has the surplus labour traditionally tolerated in the involutionary collective and on the involutionary family farm found new sources of employment? If so, it would suggest that the farming portion of the rural household economy is at least reducing its involutionary tendencies.

Table 7.1, based on my sample from Yancun, shows that 71% of the adult women participate in farming as their major occupation (usually in conjunction with domestic responsibilities), as do 43% of the men (of whom half, in turn, have other part-time pursuits.)

Table 7.1. Yancun (Henan) Occupations by Sex, 1989

Occupation	Men (%)	Women (%)[1]	Number	Percent
Farming[2]	43	71	94	57
Industry	20	3	20	12
Construction	22	0	18	11
Housekeeping	0	16	13	8
Other	13	5	14	8
Retired/ill	2	5	6	4
Percent	**100**	**100**		**100**
Number	**(N=82)**	**(N=83)**	**(N=165)**	

[1]This table excludes 10 women who were aged 70 and over. There were no men in that age category in the sample.
[2]Just over half of the male farmers engage in additional seasonal occupations, often outside the village.

Note: The category of construction for men includes about 40% subsidiary farming, and the industry category includes some officially retired workers (such as railway workers) who continue to hold jobs after retirement, and have a pension. The housekeeper category for women includes some women temporarily withdrawn from fieldwork due to recent birth or small children, or withdrawn due to age and childcare needs of grandchildren.

This clearly looks more like Huang's pattern one, the feminization of farming, than pattern two, the sidelining of agriculture.

How Productive is Yancun Farm Labour

Looking solely at the *principal grain crops*, calculations of total time spent in fieldwork by both sexes show that women perform approximately half of the fieldwork under the Household Responsibility System. In a sample of 42 households, the average number of labour days reported for each sex in wheat production (33 days) was essentially the same, for a total of 66 days.[8] Similarly, in rice production villagers reported that there were 29 days per household by women, and only 23 by men. For those growing corn (a rather minor crop) the average number of labour days was 6 days for women and 5 for men (see Table 7.2).

Table 7.2. Yancun: Average Household Allocations of Labour Days to Grain Production by Sex, 1989.*

Crop	Men	Women
Wheat	33	33
Rice	23	29
Corn	5	6

*N = 42 households for wheat and rice production. For corn production N = 23 since many households do not plant corn.

Family farming is, of course, a complex occupation involving a variety of activities centering on plant and animal care. A full comparison of changing farming productivity involves so many variables that it is daunting to contemplate. However, if I simply attempt to compare the current to earlier productivity of land and labour in Yancun staple crops, this can supply provisional tests of the de-involutionary hypothesis.

In Yancun, the average household sampled farmed 9.1 mu of wheat with 66 days of labour, for an average of 7.3 labour days per mu. The output per mu was 544 jin (1 jin = 500 grams), or 74 jin per day. The figures for rice and corn can be seen in Table 7.3.

Table 7.3. Average Amounts of Land, Labour, and Their Productivity in Yancun 1989

Crop	N	mu	labour days	output (jin/mu)	days/mu	jin/day
Wheat	42	9.1	66	544	7.3	74
Rice	42	3.4	52	728	15.3	48
Corn*	35	1.2	11	696	9.2	76

*Output measures were only available for 23 households.

How do the Yancun output/input figures in Table 7.3 compare to earlier periods? To answer this question, one needs first to determine which periods are relevant. Because Huang has convincingly argued that China's agriculture was highly involutionary throughout the collective period, it is useful to compare its current productivity to the pre-revolutionary period. I examine some of the relevant productivity estimates that can be gleaned from Huang's discussion of agricultural change, and from John L. Buck's study from the 1930s. It is a risky exercise to use data from a different data base as a baseline from which to measure change, but it does provide at least some indication of the magnitude of change.[9]

For rice, Huang's informants reported yields of 320 to 480 jin per mu in 1939. Elsewhere, Huang refers to Buck's estimates of 10.5 days of labour per mu for the Yangzi region in the 1930s (Huang 1990, 103, 84). This yields a ratio of 30.5 to 45.7 jin/day in the 1930s, which at the high end is not terribly different from the ratio of 48 jin/day for Yancun reported in 1989.[10] For wheat and corn, there seems to be a more dramatic improvement in productivity. Yancun village informants' recollections are consistent with Buck's survey describing yields in the 1930s; wheat yields were significantly lower in the past. For China as a whole, and for the wheat region, Buck reported wheat yields of 145 jin/mu and 136 jin/mu, respectively, and corn yields of 178 and 162 jin/mu, respectively (1937, 224-225).[11] Labour requirements for wheat in a village in north China were about 7.8 days per mu in 1937 and for maize they were 9.1 days per mu (See Table 7.1 in Huang 1990,125). Thus, in the 1930s, the output of wheat was approximately 17 to 19 jin per day, and for corn 17 to 20 jin per day (see Table 7.4).

Table 7.4. Crude Estimates of Labour Productivity (output in jin per labour day) in Grain Crops

Crop	1930s[1]	1989[2]
Rice	31-46	48
Wheat	17-19	74
Corn	17-20	76

[1]Estimates for China, and for wheat region, based on Buck (1937).
[2]Based on sample from Yancun in Henan.

This suggests that the productivity of labour in these two crops has increased enormously. Even though the amount of labour applied per mu of land is not much changed, the yields are now much higher per mu. At the same time, with a rapidly growing population since the 1930s the number of mu per household is much decreased. While these measures are admittedly quite crude, they suggest de-involution is taking place in two crops, wheat and corn, but not in rice.[12] In terms of the history of Yancun, as one particular case, agriculture has been transformed by major investments in irrigation and soil improvement since the 1930s. In the 1930s, Yancun villagers did not grow rice at all, but grew cotton instead. Today they scarcely grow any cotton, remarking on the low government prices for that crop. It should also be noted that cotton is generally an even more labour intensive crop than rice.

How Productive Is Yancun Farm Labor at the Margin?

Another way to evaluate involution is to ask whether the quantity of labour dedicated to farm work per household bears any significant correlation with reported grain output. Taking Yancun households' reported yields of each crop, the area of field they cultivated, and the amount of labour they contributed, I statistically tested the relationship between grain output, land and labour. I found that variation in the quantity of land was a significant predictor of grain production, but that the variation in the quantity of labour, many days or few, male or female, had no statistical significance as such a predictor.[13]

My data on grain farming in Yancun seem fully consistent with the general view that Chinese farms still contain vast amounts of underemployed labour. Here I use the accepted economic definition of underemployment as a situation in which men and women may be working hard and long hours, but adding little or no additional output compared to what could be achieved with fewer workers. By this criterion, the use of family labour in farming under the Household Responsibility System in rural Henan is still involutionary. What seems to be different compared to historical reports of northern farming is that men now do a smaller proportion of the farming, and women do as much as men or more.

While Yancun women are taking to the fields, they seem to be doing so under conditions where there may be fewer productive alternatives for their labour than there are for male labour, or where prevailing institutions and associated transaction costs restrain their participation in more productive areas. If this pattern turns out to be widespread in rural China, we may need to reassess the household de-involution raised by Huang, and its gender neutrality.

Huang saw the household historically involuting when it increased the labour time of women in labour intensive cash crops and cottage industries, particularly in hand spinning and weaving of cotton. He did not examine the conditions under which women accepted this exclusion from the market. Now, he sees involution ending as more people work off farm. Off-farm activities, especially industry, can draw surplus labor to sectors that are more productive than farming. The former familization of spinning and weaving to produce domestic commodities has been eliminated with market access to more efficiently produced industrial textiles. This has reduced a substantial part of the involutionary domestic work that used to employ rural women. In response, many women have now shifted more of their labour to the family fields, while some family members migrate to seek better employment. Is it increased productivity of family labour in small-scale agriculture that can reverse the China's historical penchant for involution, or is it the productivity of hired labour in new industrial and commercial sectors? If the nonfarm sectors account for the main productivity increases, then can we see the growing concentration of women in farming as as evidence of persisting involutionary institutional barriers? Perhaps we can.

Institutional economist Douglass North asked "how do we account for the survival of economies with persistently poor performance over long periods of time?" (1990, 92) The first part of his answer is that "history matters." More specifically, North argues that institutions, as complex systems of incentives, provide increasing returns over time. Initial set-up costs, learning costs, coordination costs and diffusion of experience all result in increasing returns to a given institutional complex and thereby inhibit shifts to systems that may be more efficient or more productive (1990, 95). The second part of his answer blames the persistence of inefficient institutions on "imperfect markets characterized by significant transaction costs" (1990, 95). These include "the costliness of information" and the "costs of protecting rights and policing and enforcing agreements" (1990, 27).

My suggestion, drawing on this institutional approach, is that a shift from a redistributive system of family labour toward one of individuals allocating labour according to market demand is not solely a function of the "productivity" of labour or wage levels in the market sector. It is affected both by institutional "lock in" and by transaction costs. Incentives for women to migrate to new industries and urban jobs are countered by the disincentives and costs associated with patriarchal family institutions. Women have more limited rights both to the real estate of the patriarchal family, which reserves land only for sons, and to bureaucratically allocated rental housing of state industries. In addition, the weak legal system often leaves women's rights subject to local patrilineal and/or patriarchal interpretation and control.[14] Thus, the costs of obtaining information about their rights, and enforcing and policing agreements remain far higher for women in patriarchal rural China than they are for men. The traditions of rural law enforcement continue to provide men with rights that women can't claim and that money can't buy. As a result, rural women are more likely to remain wedded to the involuted, low productivity family farm, abiding by traditional family policies, where their labour is not highly valued but their claims, as farm wives, are upheld by custom.

In sum, it is not my contention that women are being completely "excluded" from opportunities to work in the industrial and urban sectors or that there is no market for female labour. Quite the contrary, women's labour is being sought in many areas, albeit at lower average wages. Nor is it that women do not find even the low wages rather attractive. Rather, in the aggregate, I believe the data indicate that women who seek alternatives to the (involutionary) farm face greater risks and barriers than men. As I have argued elsewhere (Bossen n.d.), China is still an economy where housing is not yet generally accessible in open rental or real estate markets, and where women's legal claims to real property have little force against patriarchal family customs in rural areas.

The National Perspective on Development and the Feminization of Farming

In this last section, I attempt to look beyond small village samples, whether coastal or inland, and discover the overall direction of change as reflected in national employment (1982-1987). Analyzing the increase in the national labour force in farm and nonfarm sectors, it is no great surprise that over five years the absolute increase in the farm sector has been slightly less than the growth in nonfarm employment; this is surely a good sign (See Table 7.5).[15] On the other hand, an analysis of the sex ratio shows an alarmingly unbalanced pattern. Almost two-thirds of the increase in male employment was in the nonfarm sector, whereas for female employment the proportions were nearly reversed; nearly 60 percent of the women entered the farm sector. These findings are clearly disturbing for the thesis that the familization of farming is ending, and the sidelining of farming is occurring. After all, the population employed or underemployed in farming still grew by 30.5 million over this five year period, and nearly two-thirds of that growth was in female labour.

Table 7.5. Absolute and Percentage Increase in Farm and Nonfarm Employment by Sex, 1982-1987[1]

Sector	Female (mill.)	Female (%)	Male (mill.)	Male (%)	Total (mill.)	Total (%)
Farm	19.0	58.6	11.6	37.9	30.5	48.3
Non-farm	13.4	41.7	19.0	62.1	32.5	51.5
Total	32.4	100.3	30.6	100.0	63.1	100.0

[1]Totals may not add due to rounding.

Source: All China Women's Federation Research Institute and Research Office of Shaanxi Provincial Women's Federation. *Zhongguo funu tongji ziliao (1949-1989)*. China Statistical Publishing House. 1991. Tables 3-23 and 3-24 (pp. 274, 280).

Moreover, the "breathtaking speed" of growth in the value of agricultural output from 1980-1984 had slowed to three percent in 1988. As Bruce Reynolds observed:

> In addition, production of the three key staple crops--grain, oil seeds, and cotton--fell sharply in 1988. In fact, for grain and cotton the decline began in 1984. Some analysts view the past four years of stagnation in grain and cotton output as a sign that agriculture is once again becoming China's Achilles' heel (1989, 31).

Table 7.6, below, indicates how China's agricultural labour force compares to other sectors in terms of gross returns to labour.

Table 7.6. Returns to Labour by Economic Sector, 1984-85

Economic sector	Gross return in ¥/unit of labour input
Crop farming	4.9
Animal husbandry	4.4
Processing agricultural products	8.4
Commerce & catering	8.6
Transport & industrial processing	15.0

Source: Andrew Watson, "The Family Farm, Land Use and Accumulation in Agriculture." In *China: Modernization in the 1980s*, Joseph Y.S. Cheng, ed. Hong Kong: The Chinese University Press, 1989, 389-423. Data are based on a survey of 28 provinces and 232 villages in 1984-85 (Watson 1989, 302).

Of course, government price controls distort the returns compared to what they might be given market-driven prices. But given these figures, it is not surprising that labour should be switching out of agriculture. From the perspective of gender, this means that the feminization of farming and animal husbandry concentrate women in a sector with the lowest returns to labour. The data on labour productivity from the national 1984-1985 survey[16] showed:

> net income per mu for grain crops in 1984 was ¥ 85. For "economic crops," it was ¥ 172. Clearly, peasant producers have a strong incentive to move out of grain production and this may well have been a major factor in the decline in grain output in 1985 (Watson 1989, 395).

Questions about China's involutionary family farming and the ways women have been retained within this sector are far from answered. The reforms of a decade are still "partial reforms," with the state sector still restraining labour, land, and output markets. The constraints that keep so many people, and particularly women, in the low productivity farming sector have not vanished. Indeed, the problems of the farm sector are the subject of much debate. Anyone who follows China's rural economy in the press encounters daily reminders of the slowdown in agricultural productivity, the saddling of agriculture with state-fixed prices, the periodic threat of payment in IOUs, and of the desperate desire of many farmers to leave the farm.[17] Huang's argument that China's familization of labour and tolerance for surplus labour are central features to China's involutionary past, grows more intriguing when we realize that it is again female labour that appears to be less free to compete in the wider labour market, somehow remaining more tied to the farm despite its involutionary drawbacks.

Earlier I asked, is it really different this time around? Today, it seems highly implausible that family farms, using surplus labour at below-market rates of return, would be able to "outcompete" more specialized firms and industries responding to market incentives, using more productive technologies and more efficient forms of organization. The explanation for their persistence to date lies rather with institutional constraints which continue to promote family farms. Yet despite their disproportionate concentration in family farms, women are also gaining access to urban and industrial labour markets in increasing numbers. Younger generations of women, better educated and better informed about their rights and options, should face lower transaction costs should they opt for hired labour in preference to unpaid farm labour.

The involution that Huang maintains persisted over six centuries surely had some "blips." By 1990, can any change that begins only in the 1980's be judged, with confidence, as more than a historical blip? Much as one hopes Philip Huang is correct about China's reversal, there is no guarantee that China has finally turned the corner and that the centuries' old trend of administrative redistribution and involutionary family farming is finally over. After a review of six centuries of involution and one decade of development, considerable caution is warranted before claiming a significant shift. However optimistic the current outlook seems, it is too soon to tell. As in many other parts of the world, vested interests and resistance movements to protect the institution of the family and the family farm may arise. Even if Deng Xiaoping is correct, and current policies hold for "one hundred years" (*Renmin Ribao* 1992), it remains to be seen whether the involutionary characteristics are being reversed only in the villages surrounding port cities and special economic zones of the coast such as those studied by Huang and Nee, or across the heavily populated hinterlands as well.

References

All China Women's Federation Research Institute and Research Office of Shaanxi Provincial Women's Federation. 1991. *Zhongguo Funu Tonji*

Ziliao: 1949-1989. [*Statistics on Chinese Women: 1949-1989*]. China Statistical Publishing House.

Bossen, Laurel. n.d. Chinese Rural Women: What Keeps Them Down on the Farm? Paper presented at Harvard University-Wellesley College Conference on "Engendering China." John Fairbanks Center, Cambridge, Mass. Feb 7-9. 1992.

Buck, John L. 1937. *Land Utilization in China*. Shanghai: University of Nanking.

Coase, R.H. 1937. The Nature of the Firm. *Economica* 4: 386-405.

Cohen, Myron. 1992. Family Management and Family Division in Contemporary Rural China. *China Quarterly* 130: 357-377.

Fei Xiaotong [Fei Hsiao-Tung]. 1939. *Peasant Life in China: A Field Study of Country Life in the Yangtze Valley*. New York: Dutton.

———.1983. *Chinese Village Close-Up*. Beijing: New World Press.

Huang, Philip C.C. 1990. *The Peasant Family and Rural Development in the Yangzi Delta, 1350-1988*. Stanford University Press.

Huang Shu-min. 1989. *The Spiral Road: Change in a Chinese Village Through the Eyes of a Communist Party Leader*. Boulder, CO: Westview.

Judd, Ellen. 1992. Land Divided, Land United. *China Quarterly* 130:338-357.

Massell, Benton. 1968. Economic Variations on a Theme by Schneider. In E. LeClair and H.K. Schneider, eds., *Economic Anthropology: Readings in Theory and Analysis*. NY: Holt, Rinehard, Winston.

Nee, Victor. 1989. A Theory of Market Transition: From Redistribution to Markets in State Socialism. *American Sociological Review* 54(5): 663-681.

Nee, Victor and Su Sijin. 1990. Institutional Change and Economic Growth in China: The View from the Villages. *The Journal of Asian Studies* 49(1): 3-25.

North, Douglass. 1990. *Institutions, Institutional Change, and Economic Performance: Political Economy of Institutions and Decisions.* Cambridge: Cambridge University Press.

Potter, Sulamith and Jack Potter. 1990. *China's Peasants: The Anthropology of a Revolution.* Cambridge: Cambridge University Press.

Renmin Ribao. 1992. Laolao bawo dang de jiben luxian--bainian bu dongyao [Firmly hold to the Party's basic line--for 100 years it will not change]. Headline, Friday, March 13, 1992.

Reynolds, Bruce. 1989. The Chinese Economy in 1988. In Anthony J. Kane, ed., *China Briefing, 1989.* Boulder: Westview.

Skinner, William. 1985. Rural Marketing in China: Revival and Reappraisal. In Stuart Plattner, ed., *Markets and Marketing.* Monographs in Economic Anthropology. NY: University Press of America 7-48.

Watson, Andrew. 1989. The Family Farm, Land Use and Accumulation in Agriculture. In Joseph Y. S. Cheng, ed., *China: Modernization in the 1980s.* Hong Kong: The Chinese University Press, 1989: 389-423.

Whyte, Martin K. 1992. Introduction: Rural Economic Reforms and Chinese Family Patterns. *The China Quarterly* 130: 317-322.

Notes

1. This paper has benefitted from the encouragement and criticisms of James Acheson and Nathan Bossen, as well as from the Society for Economic Anthropology which provides a serious and supportive forum for anthropologists interested in the study of economic change. My research on China has been generously supported by a Canada Research Fellowship and Research Grants from the Social Sciences and Humanities Research Council of Canada.

2. In the introduction to an important set of recent work on Chinese family patterns, Martin K. Whyte emphasizes the difficulty of generalizing in the face of growing knowledge of regional variation and advocates "a research agenda calling for dozens of new local ethnographic studies across China, designed to reveal the evolution of rural family patterns in historical depth and...contemporary variations and processes of change" (1992, 321).

3. There is an extensive literature on the inefficiencies, shortages and planning blunders that characterized China's periods of cadre control over the collectives. Potter and Potter (1990), Fei Hsiao-Tung (1983) and Huang Shu-min (1989) are among the many anthropologists who have described the economic problems Chinese peasants faced under the planned economy, when the cost of deviating from the plan was being labeled a counterrevolutionary and facing, among other penalties, ostracism, torture, and labour reeducation.

4. This commune was not part of Huang's sample of eight villages in the Yangzi delta, where it appears he did not find the "second pattern."

5. It appears from Huang's reference section that this information came from a maximum of six informants, all male, of whom only two are representing the team level. Given my own experience with enormous inaccuracies in official statements that are not backed up by statistical evidence, I am inclined to discount undocumented statements about the prevalence of women in public positions. While an actual but undocumented 20-30 percent participation rate may "seem" like evidence of equal female participation to a local official who sees women's participation as an all or nothing question, it would be evaluated differently by those concerned with the persistence of social and cultural barriers to women.

6. In another paper, "Chinese Rural Women: What Keeps them Down on the Farm?" (n.d.), I explore some of the institutional factors which constrain rural women's (particularly married women's) access to the labour market and the idea that women are "married to the farm."

7. These data are based on fieldwork conducted in Henan Province in 1989. Some of the data included here have been presented in 1989 in a paper titled "Farm Women in Northcentral China." The village name is a pseudonym. I revisited this village in 1993, and by this time the village could be reached on an asphalt road to its local administrative center which, unfortunately, is located in the opposite direction from the main highway connecting to the big urban markets.

8. The 1989 sample of 42 households showed an average of 66 days of labour for an average area of 9.1 mu in wheat, or approximately 104 days per hectare. (One hectare equals 15 mu.) J.L. Buck's (1937, 314) figures for Henan provincial locations include total labour days (recalculated as man-labour which reduced women's day by 20 percent) per hectare. Buck's survey data showed wide local variation in the number of labour days (from 28 to 117) needed to farm one hectare of wheat (see Table 9, p. 314).

9. I looked in vain for comparable output (jin)/input (labour days) figures in Huang's analysis for wheat and corn. Huang generally offered estimates of labour days per mu for various crops and illustrated involutionary crop choices according to prevailing prices at the time. Thus, the choice between two crops, one of which involved more days per mu and higher net income would be taken as evidence of involution if the increased income of the more labour intensive crop brought a lower *cash* income per day of work. Since prices are so unstable historically, I have chosen to measure output by weight (jin), leaving government intervention in pricing as a separate issue.

10. Huang (1990, 89) presents a table showing estimates of similar rice yields per mu going back to the Song dynasty, and suggesting that labour intensive methods of rice cultivation in the Yangzi delta had probably nearly reached the point of diminishing returns long ago.

11. Buck reported yields in bushels and I used the following conversion rates to jin per mu: 1 bushel of wheat = 60 lbs, 1 bushel of rice = 45 lbs, 1 bushel of maize = 56 lbs, based on conversions used by *The Economist.* Other conversion rates used were: 1 mu = 1/6 acre and 1 jin = 1.1 lbs.

12. The increased output of grain per unit of labour here may be deceptive with respect to the benefits to the producer, especially if grain prices are controlled by the state. Under a regime of prices below market value, the benefits of increased productivity are not the farmer's. There may well be a connection between the controlled prices in agriculture and the increased participation of women in farming when men leave for sectors that are more productive in *monetary terms.*

13. Specifically, I tested by multiple linear regression a Cobb-Douglas type production function which specifies the degree to which increases in the factors of production, inputs such as land or labour, will produce increases in total production. For each grain crop--wheat, rice, and corn--I ran a multiple linear regression using a Cobb-Douglas production function and in each case, the quantity of land cultivated was a very significant predictor of total output, but labour days (total, male or female) had no predictive value. My results take on added plausibility as they also suggest approximately constant returns to scale for the inputs taken together. For further discussion of this methodology, see Massell (1968).

14. See Bossen (n.d.) where I discuss difficulties women face in securing property rights. The weak property rights of rural women in the reform period are also discussed by Cohen and nicely illustrated in a case where a sister "of her own accord" renounces her right of inheritance and assigns her share to her brothers (1990, 368, 374-375). Judd also refers to the persistence of preferential male rights to land and the "erosion of women's rights to land" (1992, 346, 356).

15. Data for Shanghai both confirm Huang's image of the sidelining of agriculture, and indicate how atypical this region is. Whereas almost half of new employment nationally was in agriculture, for the Shanghai municipality such employment *declined* by over 40 percent from 1982 to 1987 (source as for Table 5, in text).

16. I assume these data come from the 1984-1985 survey, although Watson does not explicitly state the source when he refers to them.

17. The *South China Morning Post*, Dec. 9, 1992, featured articles illustrating these difficulties.

Part III

Case Studies: Institutions and The State

8

Vendors And The Government: A Case Study In Institutional Economics

Judith E. Marti

Traditional economic approaches to the study of urban markets and the municipal governments of the 19th century portray their relationship as static and unidirectional, with market regulations and laws as fixed by a governmental action that restricts vendors. In other words, governments act and vendors react. Research into 19th century Mexican markets, public vendors and the municipal governments of Mexico City and Guadalajara during the Porfiriato (1877-1910) indicates that the relationship between these parties is an ongoing reciprocal process. The evidence shows that mechanisms for vendor input, and thus for governmental change, were built into the system, and that if vendor behavior was shaped by the constraints of municipal policies and regulations, the market regulations and government policies themselves also changed as a response to vendor pressure.

This evidence is in line with the institutional economics approach, which portrays the economic system as an evolving process, embedded within a larger socio-political structure; and the relationship between the economy and the government as both processual and reciprocal.

I will first give an historical background to the period of early industrialization for 19th century Mexico. The study is placed in the wider economic and political context--extent and nature of market regulations, identification of buyers and sellers, etc. I then examine the evidence and contrast traditional approaches with that of institutional economics. It is the relationship between municipal government that regulated vendor activity and the vendors who provisioned the industrial workers that interest me here. My approach is to use several case studies from 19th century Mexico to verify the conclusions of institutional economics.

Historical Background

For the thirty-three years between 1877 and the 1910 Mexican Revolution, a period known as the Porfiriato, the Mexican government adopted a series of measures aimed at pushing the nation toward industrialization. Essential to the program was a large pool of workers at accessible urban locations. To create this labor force, the government encouraged a massive labor migration to the cities. Largely poor, uneducated and rural, this population relied on street and market vendors to supply them with cheap basic subsistence goods. Thus, unwittingly, market and street vendors became factors in a national policy of development.

Throughout the period prior to the push for modernization and industrialization, Mexican society was characterized by a lack of political, social and economic stability. From the end of the War of Independence (1821) to the ascension of the Porfirio Díaz government (1877), Mexico witnessed over sixty changes of government, 800 revolts, and five foreign wars (Bazant 1979; Cumberland 1968; Vanderwood 1981). Wars, rebellions and an unstable national government, combined with dismal roads, unnavigable rivers and canals, and rural lawlessness, contributed to regionalism and fragmentation (Coatsworth 1973). When Díaz came to power in 1877, Mexico "was still very much a plural entity...a land segregated by economics, and local sovereigns..." (Benjamin 1984, 9).

Industry was small and centuries behind the times. For example, in 1870, there were only fifty-two mechanized spinning mills that could not even supply enough for domestic consumption (Cumberland 1968). Agriculture, subsistence based, still used digging sticks and ox-drawn wooden plows (Meyer and Sherman 1979). To make matters worse, the national treasury was empty, and there was little incentive to attract foreign investors. Those who attempted found that the investment in modern technology generally led to bankruptcy.

The population figures for this period are tenuous at best, but rough estimates put the 1875 national population at 9.5 million (García Cubas 1876), and the 1869 urban populations of Guadalajara at 65,000 and for Mexico City 230,000 (García Cubas cited in INEGI 1985).

After 1877, the national government adopted policies directing production for export and projected an economic growth based on foreign investment and trade. Compared to the stagnation of the 1821-1877 period, this rate of growth was staggering. The fastest economic development occurred during the relative stability of the early Díaz rule (1877-1900). But even during the following ten years of economic crisis and social unrest, the Mexican economy continued to grow.

The development of a national transportation system is a good indicator. Mexican railroad lines increased from 640 kilometers in 1876 to 13,540 kilometers by 1900 (Calderón 1974). The output of manufactured goods doubled, and by 1902, there were 5,500 manufacturing industries (Bazant 1979). The growth was largely due to the influx of capital from Germany, the United States, France and Britain which was attracted as much by natural resources such as silver mining and petroleum as by government incentives, such as tax exemptions for foreign investors.

The political, economic and social changes Mexico experienced during the Porfiriato had a direct impact on the growth of its two largest cities, Mexico City and Guadalajara. It has been estimated that from 1877 to 1910, the national population rose to 15.1 million, or 62.9 percent. Mexico City and Guadalajara also had enormous population increases. The population of Mexico City has been estimated to have increased by about 104.8 percent; that of Guadalajara (including the adjoining villages of Zapopan and Tlaquepaque) by between 68.9 percent and 94.9 percent (Marti 1990). This growth can be accounted for in terms of the urban migration of workers.

Buyers and Sellers: The Marketing Chain

Nineteenth century urban markets in Mexico can be classified into three groups. First are the public markets proper--large, permanent structures that housed rows of fixed *puestos* (shops), most of which could be closed and locked. Many of these buildings also had fixed central tables or patios for selling goods. In addition, extra tables were added for selling seasonal products. The second group are the *tiendas* (small stores) that lined the colonnades or covered walks throughout the commercial areas of the cities. These stores were so tiny that it was not unusual to find more merchandise displayed outside the shops than inside. In addition, the portal columns held *alacenas* (box-like stands) for selling goods, which could be locked at night

(BPE, *El Paladín* 23 September 1900; AHMG, *Mercados*, exp. 4, 1893; photographs, AHF/INAH, Muriá 1981). The third group are the open air markets generally found in plazas across the city. Here merchandise was displayed from blankets on the ground, or from portable tables sheltered from the sun by covers supported by makeshift poles. Although many of these markets met daily or on a specific day throughout the year, they proliferated during annual fairs, or civil and religious holidays (AGN CF, C.B. Waite, cat 42, fol. 4: 33; Bárcena 1954 [1880]; Bribiesca 1896, 1901).

The items sold in the markets were usually basic necessities: fruits, vegetables, grains or cereals, beans, fresh and dried meats (goat, chicken, tripe), coffee, eggs, potatoes, cheese. Some markets also sold prepared foods--tacos, tamales, flavored waters, sweets. Non-edible goods sold in public markets included new or used clothes worn principally by the indigenous population--*rebozos* (women's shawls), *huaraches* (open leather sandals)--and various sized blankets, clay pottery, etc. Medicinal herbs, tables, flowers, soap, notions could also be found. There were also specialty markets, selling flowers, second hand goods and non-foods such as books, furniture, or ironware (for a more complete list of goods sold in specific markets in Mexico City and Guadalajara, see Marti 1990).

A fourth class of vending, ancillary to the markets were the street vendors. Many of these were *vendedores ambulantes*, free agents who roamed the streets, selling everything from foods to water and charcoal. Others sold from fixed stands or *puestos* in streets, plazas, parks, in front of markets, and portals. From the documents it is not always possible to distinguish between the market and street vendors who sold goods they produced and middle-men, those who bought the goods they sold. A traveler to Mexico City describes the farm produce brought into Mexico City by mules and sold by producer/peasants in the main square of the city. Flowers, on the other hand, were often sold by middle-men. Peasants grew flowers on *chinampas* (floating gardens) in neighboring Xochimilco, and brought them into the city early in the morning by boat via the Canal de la Viga. Vendors sold these flowers in public markets, from flower kiosks in the Plaza Mayor, and in the streets (Brocklehurst 1883).

In a letter of complaint to the government, it is clear that some street vendors misrepresented themselves as producers and that many market vendors were not selling goods they themselves produced. Twenty-one "*comerciantes establecidos*" (established merchants) from the Mercado Corona in Guadalajara complained to the government that other market vendors from the market were selling their goods in the streets just outside the market. These vendors are actually market vendors, they wrote, who "love to go to the street outside the markets because they believe that they sell more, and they trick the people, *making them believe that they are peasants who just come and sell their own things* they say that they can sell for lower prices, and, as people in general believe everything you say, they believe it...[in fact they are] selling [goods] that are more expensive" (AHJ, *Gobernacion*, n/c, "*Señor Gobernador: Los Subscritos*," 1910, author's italics).

Public market customers came from all income levels, but descriptions, photographs and other evidence suggest that the majority were not affluent. Brocklehurst describes Indian women carrying children in rebozos as they shopped (Brocklehurst 1883). And photographs show market customers in typical indigenous dress ("*Mercado de la Merced*" 1903, in González Navarro 1985, opp. 145). The type and quality of goods sold in the market also indicates limited income. In a typical factory worker's budget, many items are products invariably found in public markets: beans, coffee, clothes, etc. (González Navarro 1985; Muriá 1981).

Housekeepers from the wealthier homes came to the markets for fresh local produce and low prices. Brocklehurst reports that in the market "Most things are extraordinarily cheap. A Mexican lady gave me a list of...prices which she said her housekeeper never exceeded" (Brocklehurst 1883, 54). And local restaurant owners chose only the best. The owner of a Mexican City restaurant famous for its English dinners and its "Kid a la Concordia" shopped in the public market for the finest local potatoes. But for the more expensive, imported goods and meats, the affluent patronized specialty shops and butcher shops. Luxury items, such as wines from France and the United States, were advertised in contemporary newspapers and magazines. Gibbon described the items one could find in Guadalajara shops, from English Waltham watches to Swiss sausages (Gibbon 1893).

Market Regulations and City Administration

The municipal governments of Guadalajara and Mexico City were responsible for the administration and regulation of public markets and street vendors. Buildings, expenses and revenues came under the department of markets and other agencies within the municipal government. Thousands of employees were involved. Each market had an administrator, caretaker (keeper of the market keys), night-watchmen, janitors. Engineering inspectors employed by the department of markets supervised construction and repairs. In addition, there were market inspectors, scribes and tax collectors (AHCM, *Boletín*

Oficial, various years; AHMG, *Mercados*, various documents, 1893), as well as all the municipal government personnel involved in market administration. The extent of this involvement can be documented by tracing internal government memos and correspondence dealing with street and public market vendors.

In disputes, market and street vendors usually petitioned the president of the city government. Matters would be decided by members of the *cabildo*, the meetings' records kept by the secretary of the *ayuntamiento* and copies of rulings sent to the vendors and the appropriate government departments (see various documents in AHCM, Gobierno Del Distrito, Mercados, tomo 2, vol. 1728, 1901: AHJ, Gobernación, n/c, 1910: AHMG, Mercados, exps. various, 1893). Financial matters, such as tax collecting, were sent on to the *tesorero municipal* (city treasurer) (AHMG, Mercados, exp. 16, 1893); problems with sanitation involved the *Consejo Superior de Salubridad del Estado de Jalisco* (Superior Council of Public Health, State of Jalisco) (AHMG, Mercados, exp. 6, 1893); questions about weights and measures could originate, for instance, at the *Jefatura Política del ler Canton* (Political Headquarters for the First Ward) (AHMG, Mercados, exp. 5, 1893).

Market regulations covered the types of goods that could be sold, food quality, the use of coloring and dyes in foods, fees charged for *puestos*, standardization of weights and measures, market building codes, etc. Yet, regulations were often unenforceable because of lack of manpower, ambiguities in the letter of the law, or were plainly out of date. Thus, problems were not addressed until a case or question came up that required a ruling. Food spoilage and poorly maintained markets are examples of this. Regulations required a standard of cleanliness for foods and the markets in which they were sold, but the documents show difficulties in enforcing them. On daily inspection in the public markets, Guadalajara officials reported throwing out rotting vegetables and fruits, putrefied fish and diseased meats. Conditions persisted, however. As a Guadalajara editorial complained, there just weren't enough foods inspectors for the job (BPE, *La Gaceta*, 1 July 1900). As for the physical upkeep of market structures, the number of repairs reported in the *Boletín Oficial* attest to the fact that regulations requiring safety standards for markets were also not enforced. Although the Mexico City Ayuntamiento made an effort to keep the facilities in good condition, markets were in constant need of repair. The *puestos* in the Mercado Martínez de la Torre were in shambles, but it was only when a hailstorm destroyed the ceiling that monies earmarked for another market were diverted to rebuild the damaged structure (AHCM, *Boletín oficial*, various dates; BPE, *La Gaceta*, 1 July 1900; AHMG, Mercados, exp. 7, 1893; Gallo Pérez 1986).

Two specific cases illustrate the problems concerning market regulations. One deals with the use of food coloring in sweets, the other with the standardization of weights and measures. When a health inspector noticed the sudden appearance of very deep yellow colored sweets for sale in the *alacenas* of the portals, he suspected at first they might be dyed with a poisonous substance, "*cromato de plomo*" (lead chromate). When the health codes were consulted it was discovered that Artículo 67 which "prohibited the use of poisons or toxic substances for dying, painting, coloring or packaging foods or beverages" had been replaced by *Artículo* 4, "all dispositions and laws related to the subject are out of date and need to be updated." This temporary order which rescinded *Artículo 67* had, in effect, left the city without a health code or an answer to the question of the colored sweets. The sweets were confiscated as a prudent move until the *Consejo do Salubridad* could make a ruling. Two months later, the sweets were tested and the dye found to be saffron, a harmless substance. A ruling was made allowing the sweets to be sold, but no mention is made of the article under which this decision was made, if any (AHMG, Mercados, exp. 6, 1893).

In another instance, government officials were pressed for the standards for weights and measures used in markets. They did not know if any existed or where to find them. The *Jefatura Política* sent a memo to the president of the *Ayuntamiento*. The *Secretaría del Supremo Gobierno*, reads the memo, has inquired if there is a "standard accurate official measurements for measuring length and for weights that are used in the markets." After several departments were consulted it was discovered that, indeed, there was such a set of standards, located in the municipal treasury (AHMG, Mercados, exp. 5, 1893).

Regulations could also go out of date, or be selectively enforced, especially since the types of goods sold changed gradually throughout the Porfiriato, with the municipal government being sometimes responsible for the changes. For example, in 1901, Mexico City market regulations required that in some markets only "genuine market products" be sold--daily food needs and perishables with a one-day shelf life, such as vegetables, fruits, seafood, eggs, milk products, game, etc. The rationale was not to allow markets "to become bazaars" that sold baskets, fabrics, pots, drugstore items, and other durable goods considered unsuitable for a market (AHMC, *Boletín Oficial*, 29 September 1905). Nevertheless, regulations were sometimes reinterpreted to allow the sale of non food items. This comes across clearly in the case of the cloth merchants from Au Bon Marché, Al Puerto de Marsellas, and three other large stores located near the Mercado San Cosme, in Mexico City, who petitioned the municipal government to remove the vendors that sold percale and other fabrics similar to theirs (AHMC, *Gobierno del Distrito*, Mercados, *tomo* 3, vol. 1732, 1906). An earlier memo from the secretary to the Ayuntamiento, Juan Bribiesca, to the governor of the Distrito Federal, shows that the Ayuntamiento concurred with the merchants' reading of the market regulation that "forbids the existence of *puestos* that sell anything other than basic foodstuffs" (AHMG, *Gobierno del Distrito*, Mercados, *tomo* 2, vol. 1728, 1901). Here, the Ayuntamiento chose to reinterpret the law and give another reading to market regulations: "The law does not prohibit the selling of clothing and fabrics in the markets, rather it gives preference to foodstuffs but, since this market is very large, it has enough room for everyone who wants to sell foodstuffs" (AHMC, *Gobierno del Distrito*, Mercados, *tomo* 3, vol. 1732, 1906). The market vendors were allowed to continue selling cloth over the objections of local merchants.

Institutional Economics

In his preface to *Institutional Economics*, Gordon sets down the basic premise of this approach and the aim of his book: "This work is a survey of economics, done from the perspective of the institutional approach. This approach centers on ongoing process. How did we get this way? What are the influences which guide or control the economy as it evolves from a vaguely known past to an uncertain future" (Gordon 1980, ix). The idea of the economic system as an "evolving, developing process" can be traced to Thorstein Veblen (Gruchy 1990, 362). It was taken by Gruchy: "the substance of institutional economics is a concern with the reality of the economic system as historic-cultural phenomenon, an evolving process" (1990, 368); and echoed by William Dugger, "Institutionalism is a processual paradigm, emphasizing social process, not market equilibrium" (1988, 983).

Central to the institutional economic approach is the cultural anthropology paradigm that the economy is embedded in the larger social and political system, with the relationship between sub-systems as processual and changing over time (Gruchy 1987). Adams has stressed the reciprocal nature of the government-economy relationship: the "role of the government in society and economy...is very complex, first, and second, it is reciprocal; forces in society and economy effect politics and governance, forces in politics and governance effect economic behavior and performance..."(1990, 849).

According to Adams, interest groups are an important factor in this process. "Power and interest groups are important elements in shaping the economy and its outcomes...groups formed for special purposes around rather narrow interests" (1990, 849). These interest groups can differ greatly as to "interest, size, organization and style of operation" (Anderson 1979, 42), and need not have great influence, resources, or a large membership. Lindblom defines interest-group activity "very loosely" to mean "all interactions through which individuals [of wealth and connections] and private groups not holding government authority seek to influence policy" (1980, 85).

In this paper, I focus on the reciprocal nature of the relationship between the vendor sector of the economy and municipal governments in Guadalajara and Mexico City, during the 19th century. I see this relation as a process, a phenomenon changing over time, with institutions influencing how individuals make decisions, yet changing as a result of individual actions. Market vendors petitioned the government (a) as a group (for instance, Martín Rodríguez, Guadalupe Torres and twenty other market vendors from the Mercado Corona in Guadalajara complained to the Governor of Jalisco that vendors selling outside the market were unfair competition (AHJ, *Gobernación*, n/c, "*Señor Gobernador*: *Los Subscritos*," 1910). They (b) also petitioned as individuals, albeit in terms of hundreds of complaints, and argued to narrow interest such as lowered fees, not to be moved from a location, permission to sell cloth in a market which is designated as a food market or to remove street vendors from selling in front of the market (Sra. Dolores Acosta of the Mercado Alcalde was one of hundreds of individual vendors who petitioned the city government for a reduction in fees, AHMG, Mercados, exp. 12, 1893). In both cases, they acted as interest groups and influenced government policy.

Traditional research on 19th century Mexican vendors often studied markets as autonomous entities, for instance Cosío's monumental *Historia Moderna de México* (1974). These studies view government as static, and government regulations and laws as fixed. When they portray the interplay between the government and vendors, it is one of action on the part of the former and reaction from the latter. As a rule, vendors were at the mercy of municipal government policies and measures.

The view that vendors were pawns of larger forces can, in part, be explained as adherence to a particular theoretical framework. Power, especially in non-industrial nations, is always concentrated on a governing elite or an oligarchy at the top. While this might be true for ruling, it need not hold in all economic relations.

This view is also an artifact of the documents. Traditional research relies heavily on official publications, newspaper accounts, etc. In the case of Mexico during the 1890s, these accounts reflect the rhetoric and goals of the Porfirio Díaz government: goals that were expressed in terms of progress, modernization and a strong centralization. These views are echoed even in the official municipal publications. Although local government had some autonomy in deciding on matters of immediate concern, such as dealing with market vendors, local officials still depended on the national government's patronage. Thus, we see the posturing of municipal governments that wanted to appear strong and as a result, talk tough to market and street vendors who, after all, hardly fit the image of a modern nation.

Case Study Approach in Institutional Economics

There exists a large base of documents, even official publications, including municipal records, correspondence between vendors and city government, etc., that give us another picture. These documents are often inaccessible, poorly classified, and housed in local archives, thus making them difficult to find. These documents show vendors to be active participants, not just passive victims. Municipal government put restrictions on vendor behavior, and also allowed their input, even their political pressure. Government policies and actions are then seen to be initiated or changed, at least in part, in response to vendor pressure.

The advantage of using a broader base of evidence can best be illustrated by comparing how the two sets of documents present similar events. In the following cases, one set of documents is largely made up of the more commonly used official publications and newspaper accounts, while the broader set includes letters, complaints, minutes of city council meetings, the daily workings of municipal governments recording their decisions and discussions.

In one case, the *Portal de San Agustín*, a public market in Guadalajara, was selected for demolition. Throughout the 19th century market activity was constant. New structures were built, moved or removed, and more often repaired, and its vendors temporarily relocated. As a result, conflicts arose between the municipal government and vendors. In this case, the municipal government claimed that the destruction of this market was a step toward beautification and modernization of the city: removing the market cleared the view of the magnificent *Teatro Degollado*, then obscured by the *Portal*. The editorial pages of *El Paladín*, a local newspaper, portrayed market vendors as victims of government policies and actions. The government plan for removal was, according to the fiery editorials, a deliberate move against the vendors. The newspaper argued that the city planned to devalue the property by first removing the portal and columns, and thus pay vendors less indemnity (BPE, *El Paladin*, 23 September 1900). The editorials clearly marked the vendors as being on the receiving end of harmful actions and policies originated by the municipal government.

A study of internal government memos, correspondence between vendors and city government, etc. gives us another picture. As the market demolition proceeded and the old shop localities were destroyed, the municipal government gave the vendors new localities in compensation. In fact, the vendors carried out an active campaign of petitions, complaints, and appeals that won them further compensations and even better concessions, even reductions in fees. One of the actors was Sra. Luciana Padilla, one of several market vendors who petitioned the government for compensation when the market location was demolished. Twice she asked for reductions in stall fees, and twice the government ruled in her favor. She was an active player, not passive pawn; and in the process, her actions influenced changes in government regulations and interpretation of market law.

As demolition proceeded, Sra. Padilla's shops number 1 and 1½ were removed and the city relocated her to numbers 9 and 18. She complained to the municipal government of Guadalajara that she was being charged too much for the new shops, a larger sum than for the original shops, even though the new shops were of equal size and value to the old ones. "The law," her petition read, "does not take into account corner shops such as [mine]." And here she quotes market regulations: "you will see on page 533 of volume 14 of the laws of the state in which it says that the Illustrious Ayuntamiento 'will receive per month as rent the quantity of 1 *peso per vara de frente*' [the length of the front of the shop]." The treasury had sent an agent to measure the front of shop number 18, she relates, "but as it is in a corner, one side measured 6 *varas* and the other 6 more, so [the treasury] charged 12 pesos." Sra. Padilla requested that the Ayuntamiento charge her only 6 pesos for the frontage of shop number 18 and 5 pesos for shop number 9, to "have my taxes lowered so they will be in proportion to what I earn." The municipal government agreed with her recommendations. In addition, it directed the treasury to change its policy and count only the front of corner shops in the future when fixing public market fees (AHMG, Mercados, exp. 14, 1893).

Success encouraged Sra. Padilla and she filed yet another petition. This second petition eventually brought about a reinterpretation of market law.

After thanking the city for reducing her payments, so the petition goes, she feels the need to complain once again. Her business has suffered from the move, her new shops are not of equal worth to the old ones, even with the reduction of fees, "I just have money for living [expenses]." In an interdepartmental memo the Ayuntamiento states that although a second reduction is not possible within the limits of the law, there is a way around it. There would be no "legal objections" to allowing her to pay a reduced fee against what she owes (AHMG, Mercados, exp. 14, 1893). In this second petition, market law was reinterpreted rather than officially changed. Eventually, and under the weight of hundreds of similar petitions from market vendors requesting fee reductions, such reinterpretations became the norm rather than the exception. Thus vendors, working within the constraints of government bureaucracy, policies and rules, actively contributed to the shaping of these policies and rules.

In the case of Sra. Padilla, and many others, we see the governmental restrictions under which vendors make rational decisions and, how, at the same time, these constraints on individual choice provide the opportunity for vendor pressure. It is important to note that I am not speaking of rational decision-making in the sense of acting according to a particular theory. Rather, I am positing a person who acts rationally as one who knows how to manipulate the environment, give and take, initiate change--though not always effectively--someone approximating Williamson's "human agent" who is "subject to bounded rationality" (Williamson 1981, 553). Williamson's "boundedly rational agents" have "limited competence." They "experience limits in formulating and solving complex problems and in processing...information" (Simon 1978, quoted in Williamson 1981) but "they otherwise remain 'intendedly rational'" (Williamson 1981, 553). To explore the opportunistic side of human nature that Williamson also posits is beyond the scope of this paper.

Governmental constraints on vendor decision-making included the costs of petitioning the government, the stamps that must accompany official petitions, the services of a scribe (most vendors appear to be illiterate, usually the calligraphy of the letter is well executed but not the signatures), the time taken from work, etc. The large number of successfully argued vendors' petitions that have survived attests to the fact that when these constraints were perceived as too limiting, vendors resorted to pressure.

Government constraints take other forms. Institutions also influence how individuals make choices. Market vendors argued within the framework of governmental policy--stated and unstated--and market regulations. This was the approach in the case of the cloth merchant's unsuccessful petition. And from her approach and mode of arguing, it is evident that Sra. Padilla understood the framework of governmental policies and argued within its precepts. She knew how to work within the bureaucratic system.

Some Concluding Remarks

Unfortunately, the relationship between vendor and government is more complex than just outlined, and many questions remain unanswered. How much influence did vendors actually have to effect change? Was reinterpretation of law in order to reduce vendor's fees, for example, due solely, or even principally to vendor pressure? I argue elsewhere that by reducing vendors' fees the government was, in effect, subsidizing vendors under a government policy to keep them viable and provisioning a growing population of impoverished factory workers--the backbone of an industrializing nation (Marti 1990). Were fee reductions, then, a result of vendor pressure or of government policy? Both appear to be the case.

Another question is whether fee reductions and opportunity for vendor pressure could be explained as measures taken by government to provide an outlet for growing discontent among an increasingly impoverished urban population. That is, were these measures taken to prevent rebellion? Even with fee reductions, market vendors barely made a living and would be considered members of the urban poor. And these were the years just preceding the Mexican Revolution of 1910.

What of governmental constraints on vendors, such as the petition fees? Could the petition fees be explained as measures taken by a government hard pressed for funds? And the opportunity such measures gave for vendor pressure only the unintended consequence of these actions? At the end of the 19th century, Guadalajara was hard pressed to provide services to a rapidly growing population. From 1885 to 1910 Guadalajara grew from approximately 90,000 to 120,000 (INEGI 1985). In 1895, when the local poll tax was abolished, "the municipality had no money for lights, police, schools...not even for sending a document in the mail" (BPE, *El Correo de Jalisco*, 15 June 1895: 1-2). A city so strapped for funds could be expected to charge a tax for every document filed by its citizens.

Factors other than vendor pressure no doubt influenced government actions. We have entertained a few possibilities. Nonetheless, it appears (1) that vendors did, to some degree, have an influence on government policy and actions; (2) that government constraints on vendors also provided opportunities for vendor pressure; (3) that the interrelationship between vendors and government was one of give and take--i.e. it was reciprocal; (4) that the result of these interrelationships was change; and (5) that the relationship between vendors and municipal government was an ongoing process.

Archives

MEXICO CITY

AGN -- Archivo General de la Nación, México
AHCM -- Archivo Histórico del Ayuntamiento de la Ciudad de México

GUADALAJARA, JALISCO

AHJ -- Archivo Histórico de Jalisco
AHMG -- Archivo Histórico Municipal de Guadalajara
BPE -- Biblioteca Pública del Estado de Jalisco

References

Adams, John. 1990. Institutional Economics and Social Choice Economics: Commonalities and Conflicts. *Journal of Economic Issues* 24 (3): 845-859.

Anderson, James E. 1979. *Public Policy-making. 2nd edition.* New York: Holt, Rinehart and Winston.

Bárcena, Mariano. 1954 [1880]. *Descripci ón de Guadalajara en 1880.* Biblioteca Jalisciense. Guadalajara, Jal.: Ediciones I.T.G.

Bazant, Jan. 1979. *A Concise History of Mexico from Hidalgo to Cardenas 1805-1940.* Reprinted with corrections. Cambridge: Cambridge University Press.

Benjamin, Thomas. 1984. Introduction: Approaching the Porfiriato. In Thomas Benjamin and William McNellie, eds., *Other Mexicos: Essays on Regional Mexican History, 1876-1911.* Albuquerque: University of New Mexico Press.

Bribiesca, Juan. 1896. *Discurso del C. Ingeniero Sebastian Camacho, Presidente del Ayuntemiento de 1895, al instalarse el de 1896.*

Contestación del C. Gobernador del Distrito Federal, Gral. Pedro Rincón Gallardo y Memoria Documentada de los trabajos municipales de 1895. Mexico City: Imp. y Lit. "La Europa", de Fernando Camacho.

———.1901. *Discurso del Señor Don Guillermo de Landa y Escandón, Presidente del Ayuntamiento en 1900. Discurso del Señor Don Ramón Corral, Gobernador del Distrito Federal, y Memoria Documentada de los Trabajos Municipales de 1900.* Mexico City: Tip. y Lit. "La Europea" de J. Aguilar Vera y Compañía (S. en C.).

Brocklehurst, Thomas Unett. 1883. *Mexico To-Day: A Country with a Great Future, and a Glance at the Prehistotic Remains and Antiquities of the Montezumas.* London: John Murray.

Calderón, Francisco R. 1974. Los ferrocarriles. In Daniel Cosío Vegas, ed., *Historia Moderna de Mexico: El Porifiriato* la Vida Economica vol. II, Tomo I. 2nd edition. Mexico City: Editorial Hermes.

Coatsworth, John Henry. 1973. Impact of Railroads on the Economic Development of Mexico, 1877-1910. Ph.D dissertation, Department of History, University of Wisconsin. Ann Arbor, Michigan: University Microfilms.

Cosío Villegas, Daniel. 1974. *Historia Moderna de México: El Porifiriato, la Vida Económica.* Mexico City: Editorial Hermes.

Cumberland, Charles C. 1968. Mexico: The Struggle for Modernity. *Latin American Histories.* Oxford: Oxford University Press.

Dugger, William M. 1988. A Research Agenda for Institutional Economics. *Journal of Economic Issues* 22 (4):983-1002.

Gallo Pérez, Celia Guadalupe. 1986. Una visión de la Guadalajara de fines de siglo XIX y principios del actual. *Colección Temática Jaliscience* 14. Guadalajara, Jal.: Gobierno del Estado de Jalisco, Secretaría General de Gobierno, Unidad Editorial.

García Cubas, Antonio. 1876. *The Republic of Mexico in 1876: A Political and Ethnological Division of the Population, Character, Habits, Costumes, and*

Vocations of its Inhabitants. G. F. Henderson, transl. Mexico City: "La Enseñanza" Printing Office.

Gibbon, Eduardo A. 1893. *Guadalajara, la Florencia Mexicana*. Guadalajara, Jal.: Imprenta del Diario de Jalisco.

González Navarro, Moises. 1985. Trasfondo humano. In Daniel Cosío Villegas, ed., *Historia Moderna de Mexico: El Porfiriato, la Vida Social*. 4th edition. Mexico City: Editorial Hermes.

Gordon, Wendell. 1980. *Institutional Economics: The Changing System*. Austin: University of Texas Press.

Gruchy, Allan G. 1987. *The Reconstruction of Economics: An Analysis of the Fundamentals of Institutional Economics*. Westport, Connecticut: Greenwood Press.

———.1990. Three Different Approaches to Institutional Economics. *Journal of Economic Issues* 24 (2): 361-369.

Instituto Nacional de Estadística, Geografía e Informática (INEGI). 1985. *Estadísticas Históricas de Mexico*, Vol. I. Mexico City: INEGI, SEP, INAH.

Lindblom, Charles E. 1980. *The Policy-making Process*. 2nd edition. Englewood Cliffs, New Jersey: Prentice-Hall, Inc.

Marti, Judith E. 1990. Subsistence and the State: Municipal Government Policies and Urban Markets in Developing Nations, The Case of Mexico City and Guadalajara, 1877-1910. Ph.D dissertation, Department of Anthropology, University of California, Los Angeles. Ann Arbor, Michigan: University Microfilms.

Meyer, Michael C. and William L. Sherman. 1979. *The Course of Mexican History*. New York: Oxford University Press.

Muriá, José Maria, ed. 1981. *Historia de Jalisco: de la Primera Republica Centralista a la Consolidación del Porfiriato*, Vol. III. Guadalajara, Jal.:

Gobierno del Estado de Jalisco, Secretaria General de Gobierno, Unidad Editorial.

Simon, Herbert A. 1978. Rationality as Process and as Product of Thought. *American Economic Review* 68 (May): 1-16.

Vanderwood, Paul J. 1981. *Disorder and Progress: Bandits, Police, and Mexican Development.* Lincoln: University of Nebraska Press.

Williamson, Oliver E. 1981. The Economics of Organization: The Transaction Cost Approach. *American Journal of Sociology* 87(3): 548-577.

Notes

1. This paper is based on archival research conducted in 1985-1988 in Mexico City and Guadalajara with the aid of a UCLA Mexus Research Award. It was written with release time under the California State University, Northridge Affirmative Action Faculty Development Program. I wish to thank James Acheson for his valuable insights and thoughtful criticisms. I would also like to thank the students from my Economic Anthropology and graduate seminar in Cultural Anthropology classes for their helpful comments. I am also very appreciative to my research assistants in the field, Maestra Celina G. Becerra, Maestro Alejandro Solís, Sra. Ana Elena Magís.

9

An Agency Model of the State: Contributions and Limitations of Institutional Economics

Mark Moberg

In recent decades, anthropologists have increasingly situated local cultural change in national and global contexts. Efforts to link localities to larger processes have entailed considerable attention to history, world markets, national economies, and, to a lesser extent, state policy. While political economy approaches illuminate the effects of national and global capital accumulation on precapitalist economies, such developments have not been accompanied by comparable advances in analyses of the modern state.[1] The relative neglect of the contemporary state by economic anthropologists is paradoxical, given its critical role in local cultural change. In all but a few remaining regions of the world, states administer local populations as staple and export crop producers, tax and tribute payers, and willing or involuntary constituents. In promulgating and enforcing laws, the state establishes an institutional framework and property rights that govern economic behavior. Understanding the determinants of state policy in these spheres is thus essential to analyzing how communities are affected by processes beyond their borders.

This article will outline a model of the state as a decision-making entity whose policies toward its subjects are calculated to sustain its hegemony. In contrast to models in political economy, an agency framework does not view the state as a monolithic agent of elite classes or a guarantor of prevailing modes of capital accumulation. Rather, the state acts on its own behalf, at times with a large degree of autonomy from class interests. This model owes much to the choice theoretic perspective associated with some institutional economists, but also diverges from it in significant ways. It will be argued that the state acts to maximize not revenue, as some neoclassical theorists contend (North 1981, 1990), but political control. This imperative in turn leads it to enact policies that often promote economic growth in certain sectors to the detriment of others. The approach to be developed here will also examine why certain constituents, not all of whom are elites, are more critical to the state than others.

The Nature of the State

The earliest of several political economy approaches to the state was outlined in the *Communist Manifesto*, where Marx and Engels described the state as "a committee for managing the common affairs of the whole bourgeoisie" (1977a, 223). While Marx initially considered the state an instrument of elite political and economic domination, his later writings departed from this view. Elsewhere, he recognized the heterogeneous nature of the bourgeoisie that competed for control of governments, permitting the state a measure of independence from any single set of class interests (Marx 1977c, 317). Finally, in *Capital*, Marx viewed the state as an institution that ameliorated capitalist crises with reforms that occasionally benefited the working class (1977b, 611).

Marx's evolving views of the state underlie competing "instrumentalist" and "structuralist" orientations in modern political economy, each recognizing differing degrees of state autonomy from class interests. Instrumentalist views assert that the state generally acts on behalf of a "ruling class...which owns and controls the means of production and which is able...to use the state as its instrument for the domination of society" (Miliband 1969, 22). Instrumentalists do not claim that members of dominant classes themselves occupy positions of state power. Rather, theorists such as Miliband (1983), Mills (1956), and Domhoff (1983) assert that close personal, business, and political relationships exist between economic elites and state authorities. These relationships translate into policies that favor the interests of dominant classes over other sectors of society.

Structuralists reject the view of the state as an instrument acting directly on behalf of a ruling class. Poulantzas (1978), for example, asserts that the state manages social crises to secure the reproduction of capitalism, which may involve policies contrary to the short term interests of dominant classes. The state's provision of welfare measures to the unemployed is understood in these terms. Such measures may be bitterly opposed by employers who help pay for them through taxes or employer contributions. Structuralists contend that dominant classes are too heterogeneous to act in a cohesive fashion or to recognize their self-interest in reforms that diminish resistance by dominated classes. The function of societal reproduction thus devolves to the state, which obtains a measure of autonomy from the interests of any one fraction of the capitalist class.

Among a variety of alternative models, contractual views of the state long predate either of these political economy approaches. Contractual models owe their origins to classical political theory and later development to Hobbes and the Enlightenment social philosophers (Haas 1982). The premise of such approaches is that an implicit "social contract" underlies the relationship between the state and its constituents. Contract theory holds that most members of society accept the state's claim of sovereignty in exchange for services that it alone can provide with its centralized bureaucracy, monopoly on the use of force, or ability to create economies of scale.

In anthropology, contractual assumptions are often implicated in theories of state formation, but enter less often into analyses of modern states. It has been argued that pristine states originated, and derived their legitimacy, from their role in organizing redistribution (Service 1975), providing defense (Cohen 1978), and allocating water rights (Wittfogel 1957).[2] Contractual models are also favored by neoclassical economists, who view the state-society relationship as a variety of exchange (cf. North 1981, 22). In neoclassical economics, the prescribed role of the state is to provide essential services and infrastructure that cannot be generated through market mechanisms. The state constructs roads and improves harbors, for example, since the benefits of such projects cannot easily be privately appropriated. Because the function of the state is to enforce property rights and facilitate exchange, neoclassical variants of contract theory in some ways approximate structural Marxist theories, which view the state as a guarantor of the capitalist mode of production.

Finally, pluralist models of the state have enjoyed some currency in disciplines such as economics and political science, but are largely unrepresented in anthropology. Pluralist theories view industrialized society as a heterogeneous entity comprised of diverse, interdependent occupational and status groups (Vincent 1987, 189). These groups articulate particularistic interests and pressure the state for policy rewards. As the outcome of these group pressures, public policy thus becomes the final balance struck between these exclusive interests; it is "the equilibrium reached in this struggle at any given moment" (Latham 1965, 36). While policy favors the coalitions that dominate the state at any one time, pluralists assume that all groups theoretically enjoy equal access to the state apparatus. Hence, the state formulates policy that favors capital on some issues, labor on others, and ethnic minorities on still others.

Discussion and Critique

Because most anthropological analyses of the contemporary state derive from political economy,[3] this discussion specifically addresses instrumentalist and structuralist theories. The logical and empirical problems noted with political economy approaches to the state may be extended to contract and pluralist models as well. The foregoing models all analyze critical aspects of the state-society relationship, yet they also share a common deficiency. Existing state theories generally neglect the motives of personnel who occupy positions of state power, resulting in an inability to explain policy formation and outcomes.

Instrumentalist views have been widely criticized on empirical grounds. Even in societies in which much of the population lacks suffrage or elementary civil rights, states do not consistently rule in favor of economic elites. The "bureaucratic authoritarian" (Cardoso 1979) regimes that emerged in South America since the early 1960s provide prime illustrations of the independence of state policy from narrow class interests (cf. Bamat 1977, Collier 1979). In seizing power from elected governments, military dictatorships in such countries as Brazil (1964), Peru (1968), Chile (1973), and Argentina (1976) all excluded members of their national bourgeoisies from decision-making roles (Ames 1987, 236). Military regimes commonly rationalize their seizure of power and suspension of democratic rights as a means of suppressing civil strife that had reached crisis levels under the previous elected governments. Such regimes typically view partisan politics of any kind as an impediment to national development and modernization (Collier 1979, 27). After overthrowing the elected Allende government in 1973, the Chilean military crushed leftist parties, unions, and peasant associations. Then, in an unwelcome surprise to some elites that had initially invited the coup, the military disbanded right wing and centrist parties as well (Cardoso 1979, 46). Such measures were necessary, the military claimed, to enable it to impose harsh deflationary policies "in the national interest" without organized opposition.

In adapting instrumentalist assumptions to Third World states, dependency theorists claim that policies of bureaucratic authoritarian regimes reflect the unique class structure of peripheral societies (Evans 1979, Cardoso 1979). National bourgeoisies are excluded from policy-making because the actual clients of military governments are believed to be the more politically powerful allies and representatives of international capital (O'Donnell 1977, 62). Hence, while Chilean-owned firms were devastated by the Pinochet government's creation of an open economy, foreign capital found the new investment climate highly congenial due to its absence of tariffs and unrestricted profit repatriation. The dependency revision of instrumentalist state theory is not as easily borne out, however, by the policies of other authoritarian states. Military dictatorships have pursued a wide range of economic strategies, each having different beneficiaries. The Chilean military opened the economy to foreign capital, but such was not the case for the Brazilian military, which promoted national industrialization behind high tariff barriers, or the Argentine military, which early on abandoned the economic shock treatment mandated by the monetarist "Chicago Boys" in Chile (Ames 1987, 237).

The Velasco government installed in the Peruvian military coup of 1968 is even more incongruent with instrumentalist approaches. Like the Nasser regime in Egypt, the Peruvian military attempted to implement a "revolution from above" that challenged the control of both domestic and foreign private capital over the national economy (Trimberger 1978). Both regimes engaged in large-scale nationalizations, concentrating industry, banking, communication, and transportation under the direct control of the state (Ibid., 164). Undertaking land reforms to ameliorate rural poverty and promote agricultural modernization, the Velasco and Nasser governments also expropriated properties from landed oligarchs and redistributed them to landless laborers and former tenants. These reformist policies by no means imply that the state had been captured by peasants and workers, and therefore represented their interests. Both regimes sought autonomy from demands of the poor, creating co-optative "mass organizations" that channeled protest away from the state. Trimberger demonstrates that the pace and scale of nationalization were set exclusively by the Egyptian and Peruvian militaries and their technocratic advisors, rather than the ostensible beneficiaries of such policies (Ibid., 164).

Given their recognition of relative state autonomy from capitalist interests, structuralist views are less vulnerable to empirical refutation than instrumentalist theories. Here the central difficulty is instead a logical one. Structuralist models succumb to the often-mentioned logical impasses of functionalism; namely, teleology and lack of falsifiability. In excluding the goals of state personnel from analysis, structuralists imbue the institution itself with goals but provide it with no means of enacting them. Thus, the "state serves the function of atomizing the working class...[and] the function of guaranteeing the long-run interests of the capitalist class as a whole" (Gold et al. 1975, 37). While these roles would no doubt complement the reproduction of capitalism, structuralists do not demonstrate how the state fulfills them. Like their theoretical counterparts in structural functionalism, structuralist assumptions are also immune to empirical challenge, since "every action of the state may be explained in terms of the state's postulated purpose to promote social cohesion for the greater good of the capitalist social order" (Foley and Yambert 1989, 45).

Notwithstanding their teleology, some structuralist assumptions about the state may be empirically tested. A central proposition of such models is that the state acts on behalf of the capitalist class as a whole, which fails to recognize its common interests. Because reform policies are usually opposed by fractions of or even all of the capitalist class, structuralists do not consider dominant class attitudes toward the government as empirically relevant. If the state intervened on behalf of capitalism in general, however, it should promote policies that facilitate the accumulation of capital. Among these would be private property rights and institutions designed to minimize transaction costs, which include the cost of measuring the value of what is produced and exchanged as well as the costs of protecting rights and enforcing agreements (North 1990, 27).

Where the outcome of an exchange is uncertain, either because property rights are insecure or contracts are unenforceable, firms are often unable to realize gains from trade. Neoclassical economists assert that contemporary states have more often imposed "inefficient"[4] policies than institutions that maximize societal output (North 1981). The former include monopolies in either private or public sectors of the economy, price controls, tariff restrictions, subsidies, and confiscatory taxes. Similarly, the costs of transactions are increasing in the capitalist world (North 1984, 7) due in part to the problems of measurement and enforcement arising with an increasingly complex division of labor. Because these trends have accompanied expanding state involvement in the economy, it is difficult to sustain the structuralist argument that the state's ultimate function is to facilitate capital accumulation. Whether the state imposes policies favoring capital (as in tariffs that render foreign products uncompetitive) or labor (as in minimum wage laws), its actions are more often chosen to obtain the support or mitigate the opposition of diverse, organized constituencies, rather than to efficiently manage the economy.[5]

North (1981) identifies two sets of constraints on the economic institutions imposed by states. A competitive constraint limits the capacity of a regime to treat all of its constituents with impunity. When state policies adversely affect valued constituents, the resulting disaffection often leads to the removal of regimes. To preserve their hold on power, governments grant favorable treatment to such groups, often with little regard to the effects of such policies on the overall economy. Further, property rights that maximize societal output may compromise the income-generating ability of governments, a phenomenon that imposes a transaction cost constraint on the state. The transaction costs entailed in monitoring output and collecting taxes from many small units of production are typically far greater than those for a monopoly. Consequently, regimes often find it easier to regulate and tax monopolies in some sectors rather than promoting competition that would entail greater transaction costs in tax collection (North 1981, 28).

The model of the state described in institutional economics converges with and augments approaches in sociology, history, and political science that regard the state as a social actor in its own right (Skocpol 1979; Nordlinger 1981; Bates 1981, 1983; Evans et al. 1985; Hintzen 1989). Institutional economics suggests that some constituents present greater political "opportunity costs" to the state than other segments of the population (North 1990, 48). This means that the political costs of foregoing their support are prohibitive for those controlling power. As a result, rulers must formulate policies that reward such clients or at a minimum do not alienate them. Yet institutional economics does not elucidate the source of these differing opportunity costs. As in regimes that promote "revolutions from above," it is clear that economic elites are not inevitably among these valued constituents.

In other areas as well, the conception of the state entailed in institutional approaches remains problematic. North's model of the state posits a "wealth- or utility-maximizing ruler" (1981, 23) whose actions are constrained by competition with other prospective leaders and the degree of political pluralism in a society. In accounting for the actions of those who control the state, it is implausible to ascribe a wealth-maximizing motive in most cases, nor is it satisfactory to invoke the neoclassical panacea of "utility" for exceptions. As will be indicated in the following section, the ideology of a regime cannot be considered incidental to its actions.

Extant models of the state are beset by numerous contradictions in its character: the state is alternately seen as coercive or integrative, pluralist or class-dominated, and contractual or exploitative (Haas 1982). These issues are unresolvable under the existing terms of the debate, for any state is demonstrably all of these things. While examining its institutional nature, such models neglect the agency of those who control state institutions. Far from being external to analysis of the state, the motives of those who exercise control over it should be a central focus of state theory. Regardless of their differing ideologies, class background and alliances, and degree of sincerity or cynicism, ruling groups have a common interest. Once in control of power, most wish to retain it, and they use the apparatus and resources of the state to do so.

The Regime as Social Actor

The recognition that officeholders seek to perpetuate their control of the state is both axiomatic to the citizens of most states and of considerable antiquity in political theory (see Service 1975, 22-23). One of the more pointed, if pessimistic, assertions of this position was offered in 1915 by Robert Michels as the "Iron Law of Oligarchy": "It is extremely probable that a social group which had secured control of the instruments of collective power would do all that was possible to retain that control" (1958, 401).

Michels' observations were prompted by the tendency of leaders in European socialist and communist parties to entrench themselves in leadership positions, despite their ostensible commitment to revolutionary democracy. It is apparent from electoral politics in the United States and elsewhere that the actions of state leaders, regardless of their ideological inclination, are often compelled by a similar desire to retain power. Curiously, state theorists rarely acknowledge this point, and those who do overlook its full implications.[6] The self-interest of powerholders is a major factor determining public policy, the local effects of which may go unexamined by investigators who dismiss the possibility of an autonomous state.

Political scientists often consider states with competitive electoral institutions as politically "weak" in that executives, representative bodies, and bureaucracies cannot disregard concerted public opinion and lobbying pressure (Nettl 1968). Because public concerns typically center on economic conditions, elected governments in the developed nations often manipulate the economy to insure expansionary conditions at the time of elections. A political business cycle (Tufte 1978) results from macroeconomic strategies designed to increase personal income and reduce unemployment around the time of elections, after which these policies may be reversed.

Many Third World states are comparatively "strong" in that regimes are authoritarian or face noncompetitive or co-opted opposition parties. Under such conditions state leaders theoretically have a good deal of autonomy from the demands of civil society (Evans et al. 1985, 351). Due to prevailing patterns of capital accumulation based on low wages and their vulnerable position in the world economy, governments in underdeveloped nations are also limited in their ability to implement expansionary consumption policies.

Yet these conditions do not imply that politicians retain control of Third World states with greater ease than leaders in weak states. To the extent that leaders in the Third World face electoral opposition, they are constrained in ways similar to western elected officials. Despite the absence of effective opposition parties, officeholders by no means retain a secure hold on power. Without broad support from sectors of civil society and the military, heads of state throughout the Third World face a constant threat of removal from office. Consequently, many activities of governing are devoted to recruiting allies, strengthening bases of support, and neutralizing adversaries.

Regardless of whether their leaders attain power through elections or coups, Third World states often approximate a "patrimonial" form, as the term has been used to describe Brazil (Roett 1972) and Mexico (Grindle 1977, 1986). Leaders of patrimonial states extensively utilize a "spoils" bureaucracy "to reward friends, to co-opt potential and actual political opponents, to satisfy local and regional allies, and to deal with newly emerging social groups in order to build support for the system" (Roett 1972, 29). In Brazil and Mexico, federal bureaucracies have become by far the fastest-growing employment sectors as the processes of reward and co-optation bring much of the population into direct dependence on the state for a livelihood. In addition to generating employment, the patrimonial state often acts in an symbolically benevolent fashion by instituting labor reforms and social welfare programs (Ibid., 43). Such measures are usually provided in the absence of organized public demand for them; indeed, to the extent that independent political organizations exist among the poor, they are repressed or co-opted. This suggests that the goal of policy in patrimonial states is to secure a base of support for the state while limiting policy inputs to an elite group of leaders and technocrats.

The recognition that political leaders have a common interest in retaining power does not imply that power is their sole motivation. Leaders' "substantive preferences," or what they desire from the use of power, vary from the promotion of class, ethnic, and regional interests, to a perception of the "national interest" as a whole, and the less altruistic goals of personal power or enrichment. Politicians' public statements combine both substantive preferences and strategies intended to build coalitions. Because statements of policy and ideology are in part based on calculations of the potential support they will generate, Ames (1987, 4) notes that leaders' substantive preferences are essentially unknowable to others. What is measurable, however, is the relationship between state policy and public support for governments. Here, Ames (1987) finds that Latin American governments of differing ideological orientations have used public expenditures in similar ways to mobilize support and to allay the threat of military coups. In this century, nearly all Latin American countries have witnessed a growth of public sector employment far exceeding the rate of population growth. This is because successive regimes reward critical supporters with jobs while keeping the appointees of previous administrations on government payrolls to avoid alienating them (Ames 1987, 11-12).

While patrimonial states typically rely upon combinations of patronage and pork barrel projects to reward supporters and co-opt adversaries, the actual strategies selected vary significantly between constituencies. Scott (1972) notes that mobilizing rural votes is a less costly strategy than recruiting urban support. Where rural class structures are based upon patron-client relationships, parties need only obtain the support of a landlord or other patron to procure the votes of his clients as well. Landless laborers and tenants are "locked-in" to support their patron's party by virtue of their dependence (Scott 1972, 99). Because rural voters are often clustered in village settings, parties can also obtain substantial support by putting in place collective and highly visible inducements, such as schools, roads, and health centers (Ibid., 138). Urban political strategies tend to be more particularistic, favoring patronage employment for both supporters and co-opted opponents. In part because of higher living standards in cities and the number of jobs that must be provided to supporters, patronage strategies impose substantial costs for parties that employ them.

Unlike conspicuously strategic allocations of public sector jobs and pork barrel projects, economic reform and development policies are usually interpreted in structural terms. Political economists cite the limited agrarian reforms undertaken by many Latin American governments in the 1960's as evidence for the mediating role of the state in economic and political crises. Structuralists argue that many Latin American regimes of the time were faced with rural mass movements that threatened capitalist class relations in agriculture. Forced to defuse such political challenges, many governments reluctantly implemented land reform measures designed to ameliorate rural poverty (De Janvry 1981, 199). On closer analysis, however, reformist policies may be better seen in terms of the imperatives of electoral strategy and regime survival, for reforms have usually been implemented independently of political crisis. As Grindle demonstrates, agrarian reform legislation and land distribution to peasants during the 1960's were promoted by central governments "in the absence of significant pressure from the peasants themselves and in the face of considerable opposition from landed interests" (1986, 142).

In part, such actions reflect political pressure from the United States, whose leaders feared a spread of revolutionary movements throughout the region in the wake of the Cuban revolution. Even before the Alliance for Progress encouraged Latin American governments to undertake mild reforms, however, many governments had already begun land distributions to peasants (Ibid.). In the previous two decades, urban-based political parties had "discovered" the peasantry as a newly enfranchised electoral base that could help bring them to power. Aspiring centrist politicians in Venezuela, Peru, and Chile by 1960 all endorsed agrarian reform in their political platforms, which called for "social justice for the rural and urban masses" (Grindle 1986, 142). The extent to which such statements reflect substantive preferences is unknown, but they were effective in mobilizing peasant political support critical to the electoral success of the Betancourt, Belaunde, and Frei regimes.

Throughout the region agrarian reform coerced landed oligarchs into agricultural modernization while creating a dependent clientele of rural voters. The main beneficiaries of agrarian reform policies were neither rural elites nor peasants, but the state and the political parties that controlled it (Ibid., 133). That reform policies originate primarily as political measures is suggested by their notable absence where rural residents are not critical constituents of ruling political parties. Relying upon the political support of urban middle- and working-class blacks, the People's National Congress party of Guyana de-emphasized agricultural development once in power. Because most of the farming population is made up of East Indians who were mobilized by the opposition People's Progressive Party, agricultural development would only benefit opponents of the regime (Hintzen 1989, 176). While such skewed development priorities contributed to endemic economic stagnation in Guyana, they accounted, together with varying levels of repression, for the PNC's tenacious hold on power for nearly three decades (Ibid.).

Political Survival and Economic Development

The agency model of the state presented here addresses a central issue in institutional economics; that is, how institutions affect economic processes and decision-making. The leaders of states in both the industrialized and Third Worlds often find that their strategies for political survival come at the cost of economic growth. Theoretically, politicians' need to procure resources for redistribution would create an imperative for growth, some of which can then be captured by the state as revenue. In actuality, the manner in which patronage is allocated for political support usually impairs economic development. Throughout Africa, for example, marketing boards exist ostensibly to promote agricultural modernization, but have instead become patronage tools at the disposal of governments, which allocate loans and aid "to the most loyal farmers, not to the most efficient" (Scott 1972, 129). Similarly, the nationalization of primary sectors of the economy is often irresistible to state rulers, in part because such industries then become sources of patronage employment. These priorities were foremost in the decision of the government of Guyana to nationalize foreign companies in the 1970's (Hintzen 1989, 185). Even when state industries are well-managed, as a political strategy nationalization often proves to be self-defeating. Besides incurring the destabilizing retaliation of powerful foreign interests, nationalization unwittingly turns the government into a major employer with economic interests at variance with political survival. Writing of Ghana's experience with nationalization, Scott notes that "[t]he socialization of the economy meant that many demands for higher wages or crop prices--demands that previously would have been directed at private-sector firms--were now transformed into direct confrontations with the government...[S]uch disputes unavoidably involve a direct challenge to the ruling party" (1972, 130).

While institutional economists have recognized that policies such as patronage, subsidies, tariffs, and nationalization frequently impede economic growth (North 1984, 15), less often asked is why Third World states resort to such strategies in place of the "efficient" institutions that economists prescribe for development. The record of states in the underdeveloped world that have introduced such institutions provides a ready answer: free markets may promote economic growth, but at considerable political cost. As many governments undertaking structural adjustment programs at the behest of international creditors have discovered, the removal of public subsidies, slashing of patronage workforces, and privatization of state industries have proven extremely unpopular with the poor and middle classes who depend on such programs. In recent years, the decline in living standards following structural adjustment programs have provoked rioting in such disparate locales as Jamaica, Venezuela, Egypt, Nigeria, and Costa Rica (Hayter and Watson 1985; Edelman 1990; Moberg 1992). It is no coincidence, then, that governments wishing to remain in power find themselves compelled to either substantially modify free market policies or to become more repressive. Between 1975 and 1985, Chile realized record economic growth as a result of free market reforms. To weather the societal dislocations of such policies, however, the Pinochet regime resorted to some of the most draconian political repression recorded in the region. For states lacking either coercive mechanisms or hubris on so grand a scale, the alternative path to staying in power entails precisely those institutions economists condemn as "inefficient."

Governments in the developed world rely less on such institutions for their survival and more on ensuring general economic well-being, although, as in the U.S.A., entitlements and pork barrel are still strategically targetted at critical constituencies. A primary difference between patrimonial regimes in the Third World and elected governments in developed nations relates to the ability of the latter to ensure economic growth that is relatively equitable. Political economists note that this has been a feature of western capitalism only since the emergence of extensive social welfare programs and workforce unionization during the 1930s (Amin 1976). In contrast, economic growth in the Third World is based upon low cost labor and export-oriented manufacturing, which precludes the more equitable forms of development found in Europe and the United States (De Janvry 1981, 32-37). While maintaining prevailing patterns of capital accumulation based on a low wage economy may be critical to regimes that rely upon the support of economic elites, it does little to pacify an impoverished majority. Hence, patrimonial regimes rely upon direct subsidies to the poor (in the form of patronage and pork barrel) to obtain needed political support. For their part, governments in the developed nations can better obtain support by maintaining relatively equitable patterns of economic growth, combined with with judicious use of public resources for highly valued constituencies.

In addition to explicating these dilemmas of economic development, an agency model of the state can inform anthropological analyses of political and economic change at the local level. Elsewhere (see Moberg 1991), I have shown how factional conflict in Belizean villages results from political processes at work in the national arena. In Belize, as elsewhere, the value of rural constituents to aspiring politicians determines the kind of treatment they receive in state policy. Regardless of the ideologies they articulate, political parties seeking control of the state must first obtain the support of valued ethnic groups, classes, or localities. Communities valuable to political parties become the beneficiaries of public resources distributed in the form of patronage, "pork," and favors. In such communities, competition for party-based patronage has led to a divisive factionalism cross-cutting lines of kinship, class, and ethnicity. Conversely, villages that provide insignificant rewards to politicians or that have been conceded to the opposition are overlooked as parties decide how to allocate their scarce resources. Analyzing political processes at the local level thus requires some attention to how the state crafts its policies toward rural constituents.

The agency model presented here addresses the question of why states neglect or repress some consituents while indulging others. With its recognition that constituents are associated with varying opportunity costs to the rulers of the state, institutional economics illuminates these dimensions of state decision-making. Yet it is also limited in its capacity to identify the content of those decisions. Politicians are motivated to seize or retain state power, but power is also a means to enacting longer-term substantive preferences. These preferences are in part a reflection of the class, ethnic, or regional identities of those holding state power. Here instrumentalist approaches in political economy critically supplement decision-making approaches. Trimberger, for example, notes that regimes that institute "revolutions from above" are associated with class structures in which members of the military and bureaucracy are excluded from economic elites (1978, 4). Among the contributions of such approaches has been a sociology of ruling groups, which suggests why state policy favors some constituents over others.

Finally, an agency approach begins to resolve a seemingly intractable debate in the anthropology of the state. It has been seen here that states govern both through coercion and consent, and they may reward many groups in society or a few particularistic interests. Such policies are not derived from the nature of state institutions, as previous theories of the state suggest, but from the motives of those who control them. A model of the state as a social actor in its own right can better elucidate its actions toward communities that form the traditional subjects of anthropology.

Acknowledgements

I thank various members of the Society for Economic Anthropology for their comments when I presented an earlier version of this paper at the 1992 SEA meetings. I am especially grateful to James Acheson for his close reading of the paper and his helpful suggestions for revision and editing.

References

Ames, B. 1987. *Political Survival: Politicians and Public Policy in Latin America.* Berkeley: University of California Press.

Amin, S. 1976. *Unequal Development.* New York: Monthly Review Press.

Bamat, T. 1977. Relative State Autonomy and Capitalism in Brazil and Peru. *Insurgent Sociologist* 7: 74-84.

Bates, R. 1981. *Markets and States in Tropical Africa: The Political Basis of Agricultural Policies*. Berkeley: University of California Press.

———.1983. *Essays on the Political Economy of Rural Africa*. Cambridge University Press: Cambridge.

Cardoso, F. 1979. On the Characterization of Authoritarian Regimes in Latin America. In D. Collier, ed., *The New Authoritarianism in Latin America*. Princeton, NJ: Princeton University Press.

Caro, R. 1982. *The Years of Lyndon Johnson: The Path to Power*. New York: Knopf.

Cohen, R. 1978. State Foundations: A Controlled Comparison. In R. Cohen and E. Service, eds., *Origins of the State*. Philadelphia: Institute for the Study of Human Issues.

Collier, D. 1979. Overview of the Bureaucratic-Authoritarian Model. In D. Collier, ed., *The New Authoritarianism in Latin America*. Princeton, NJ: Princeton University Press.

De Janvry, A. 1981. *The Agrarian Question and Reformism in Latin America*. Baltimore: Johns Hopkins University Press.

Domhoff, G. W. 1983. *Who Rules America Now?* New York: Simon and Schuster.

Edelman, M. 1990. When They Took the Muni: Political Culture and Anti-Austerity Protest in Rural Northwestern Costa Rica. *American Ethnologist* 17: 736-757.

Evans, P. 1979. *Dependent Development: The Alliance of Multinational, State, and Local Capital in Brazil*. Princeton, NJ: Princeton University Press.

Evans, P., D. Rueschemeyer, and T. Skocpol. 1985. On the Road Toward a More Adequate Understanding of the State. In P. Evans, D. Rueschemeyer and T. Skocpol, eds., *Bringing the State Back In*. Cambridge: Cambridge University Press.

Foley, M. and K. Yambert. 1989. Anthropology and Theories of the State. In, B. Orlove, M. Foley, and T. Love, eds., *State, Capital and Rural Society*. Boulder, CO: Westview.

Gold, D., C. Lo, and E. Wright. 1975. Recent Developments in Marxist Theories of the Capitalist State. *Monthly Review* 27: 29-43.

Grindle, M. 1977. *Bureaucrats, Politicians, and Peasants in Mexico*. Berkeley: University of California Press.

———.1986. *State and Countryside: Development Policy and Agrarian Politics in Latin America*. Baltimore: Johns Hopkins University Press.

Haas, J. 1982. *The Evolution of the Prehistoric State*. New York: Columbia University Press.

Hayter, T.and C. Watson. 1985. *Aid: Rhetoric and Reality*. London: Pluto Press.

Hintzen, P. 1989. *The Costs of Regime Survival: Racial Mobilization, Elite Domination, and Control of the State in Guyana and Trinindad*. Cambridge: Cambridge University Press.

Latham, E. 1965. *The Group Basis to Politics*. New York: Cornell University Press.

Marx, K. and F. Engels. 1977a [1848]. The Communist Manifesto. In D. McLellan, ed., *Karl Marx: Selected Writings*. Oxford: Oxford University Press.

Marx, K. 1977b [1867]. *Capital: A Critique of Political Economy V. 1*. New York: Vintage.

———.1977c [1851]. The Eighteenth Brumaire of Louis Bonaparte. In D. McLellan ed., *Karl Marx: Selected Writings*. Oxford: Oxford University Press.

Michels, R. 1958 [1915]. *Political Parties*. Glencoe: The Free Press.

Miliband, R. 1969. *The State in Capitalist Society.* New York: Basic Books.

———.1983. State Power and Class Interests. *New Left Review* 138: 57-68.

Mills, C. W. 1956. *The Power Elite.* New York: Oxford University Press.

Moberg, M. 1991. Citrus and the State: Factions and Class Formation in Rural Belize. *American Ethnologist* 18: 215-233.

———.1992. Structural Adjustment and Rural Development: Inferences from a Belizean Village. *Journal of Developing Areas* 27: 1-20.

Nettl, J. P. 1968. The State as a Conceptual Variable. *World Politics* 20: 559-592.

Nordlinger, E. 1981. *On the Autonomy of the Democratic State.* Cambridge, MA: Harvard University Press.

North, D.C. 1981. *Structure and Change in Economic History.* New York: Norton.

———.1984. Transaction Costs, Institutions, and Economic History. Zeitschrift für die gesamte Staatswissenschaft 140: 7-17.

———.1990. *Institutions, Institutional Change, and Economic Performance.* Cambridge: Cambridge University Press.

O'Donnell, G. 1977. Corporatism and the Questions of the State. In J. Malloy, ed., *Authoritarianism and Corporatism in Latin America.* Pittsburgh: University of Pittsburgh Press.

Orlove, B., M. Foley, and T. Love. 1989. *State, Capital, and Rural Society: Anthropological Perspectives on Political Economy in Mexico and the Andes.* Boulder: Westview Press.

Poulantzas, N. 1978. *State, Power, Socialism.* London: New Left Books.

Roett, R. 1972. *Brazil: Politics in a Patrimonial Society.* Boston: Allyn and Bacon.

Scott, J. 1972. *Comparative Political Corruption.* Englewood Cliffs, New Jersey: Prentice-Hall.

Service, E. 1975. *Origins of the State and Civilization.* New York: Norton.

Skocpol, T. 1979. *States and Social Revolutions.* Cambridge: Cambridge University Press.

Trimberger, E. 1978. *Revolution from Above: Military Bureaucrats and Development in Japan, Turkey, Egypt, and Peru.* New Brunswick: Transaction.

Tufte, E. 1978. *Political Control of the Economy.* Princeton, NJ: Princeton University Press.

Vincent, A. 1987. *Theories of the State.* Oxford: Basil Blackwell.

Weingast, B. and W. Marshall. 1988. The Industrial Organization of Congress; or, Why Legislatures, Like Firms, Are Not Organized as Markets. *Journal of Political Economy* 96: 132-163.

Wittfogel, K. 1957. *Oriental Despotism.* New Haven: Yale University Press.

Notes

1. The "state" is defined variously in the social sciences, a fact that has contributed to some confusion when disciplinary boundaries are crossed. This article conceives of the state as "the discrete complex of social instititions that operate together to govern a particular, highly evolved society" (Haas 1982, 2). Others may consider this to be a more appropriate definition of "government" or "regime"; my goal here is not to entertain such semantic arguments but to generate a framework that accounts for specific policies implemented by state authorities.

2. Wittfogel's "hydraulic hypothesis" asserts that ruling groups provide essential managerial skills on behalf of society. His work differs from most contract theories in its claim that state leaders are not selfless managers, but use their control of irrigation to become self-aggrandizing despots (1957, 126).

3. See, for example, the essays collected in the edited volume by Orlove et al. (1989), all of which adopt a political economy approach to state policy in Latin America.

4. The term "inefficient" is used here as it appears in the neoclassical literature. For neoclassical economists, efficiency denotes behavior that results in maximization of output (North 1981, 7). The term should be used advisedly given that such "externalities" of maximizing behavior as environmental destruction, poverty, and imperialism are usually unrecognized in neoclassical theory.

5. The ways in which constituencies are rewarded has been of major interest in pluralist theory. Legislatures such as the U.S. Congress serve such a large number of interests that members must trade votes on legislation to secure passage of bills rewarding their constituents. This in turn requires officeholders to develop legislative institutions that enforce such vote trading agreements (Weingast and Marshall 1988).

6. Miliband recognizes that politicians are motivated in part by self-interest, but asserts that their ambitions are realized by serving dominant class interests (1983, 62-64). Lyndon Johnson is cited as the archetype of a politician who craved "power in its most naked form, for power not to improve the lives of others, but to manipulate and dominate them, to bend them to his will" (Caro 1982,: xix). The full implications of this example are overlooked in Miliband's discussion. Johnson's political ascent was achieved with the support of elites, but his ambitions also yielded populist positions intended to consolidate his support with the electorate. That the Voting Rights Act of 1965 empowered formerly disenfranchised minorities seems beyond dispute. Whether dictated by his principles (of which he was alleged to have none) or ambitious pragmatism, Johnson's vigorous support of the Act altered the institutions and politics of modern America.

10

The Commercialization of the Guatemalan Economy, 1871-1944: Political and Military Dimensions

Paul V. McDowell

Introduction

The quincentennial of Columbus' encounter with the Americas also marks the continued development of a global production system, an economic institution writ worldwide (Rothstein and Blim 1992). Guatemala's integration within the system is manifested in the recent proliferation of garment *maquiladoras* in the country, increasing from 6 operations employing some 2,000 workers in 1984 to 250 factories employing more than 50,000 workers in 1992 (Petersen 1992, 1). Yet how individual countries have come to be annexed to this world system remains an underresearched question. This paper examines a critical period of this transition for Guatemala, the liberal era initiated under the *reforma* of Justo Rufino Barrios during the 1870s and early 1880s and ending with the ambitious economic development programs under Jorge Ubico during the 1930s and early 1940s.

During this period, these rulers attempted to link Guatemala to the world economy by undertaking new strategies and developing a new set of institutions. Their attempt at development essentially failed. Despite a desire to modernize the country and develop economically, the path they chose was one taken by innumerable developing countries. It resulted in a set of institutions that allowed little incentive for growth and resulted in poor economic performance. It also led to the consolidation of power of a small elite and displacement of Indians from their land.

The key to liberal strategy was to develop the coffee industry; ample land and large inputs of labor were needed to realize that aim. Corporate Indian communities, which had under the conservatives exercised control over much of the country's land suitable for coffee, and the bulk of the country's labor, were inimical to both these objectives. Hence, tenure laws were changed to foster private ownership and discourage communalism. Forced labor laws were enacted to ensure a quota system by community, enforce debt peonage, and, later, to outlaw vagrancy. A national system of militias was fostered to ensure the enforcement of these laws, and this was soon backed by an efficient telegraph network, albeit also by a less-than-reliable road system.

Then, at the turn of the century, a vertically integrated agroexport system was installed in Guatemala in the form of the United Fruit Company (UFCO). This company derived huge land, right-of-way, and tax concessions from the governments in power between 1901 and 1944. From plantation to railway to dock facilities to the Great White Fleet, the United Fruit Company consolidated its assets into one continuous operation. President Ubico's wide-ranging reforms and projects in the 1930's, from a centralized governmental and military apparatus to an all-weather road system and multimodal telecommunications network, behaved as if they were but extensions of the United Fruit Company banana-exporting machine. Under President Ubico, too, the military further strengthened its control throughout the country, and incentives were introduced to minimize administrative corruption. These policies, combined with increased foreign (especially U.S.) investment, brought about the commercialization of the Guatemalan economy and its integration into the world system. Nevertheless, they also resulted in dependency, an inefficient set of institutions, and economic stagnation. It has brought devastation to the Indian people, who comprise more than half the population of Guatemala.

Not unlike other countries throughout Latin America, Guatemala took a path of development that differed considerably from the so-called Asian Tigers--Singapore, Taiwan, Hong Kong, Malaysia--whose rapid industrialization and diversified, integrated development have proven legendary in the past two decades (Gereffi 1989, 92-104; Lüders 1991, 1-14). In retrospect, the irony is that this path was taken in the name of liberalism by an elite who thought they would model themselves on the developed countries of the world.

This paper explores in detail the various strategies that the rulers of Guatemala used to link their economy to the world market. As will be shown, much of what occurred can be explained in terms of findings set forth within the school of institutional economics (North 1990; Coase 1937, 1960; Williamson 1975).

A Liberal Design of the Americas

Today, a visitor cannot help but be struck by the extent to which middle- and upper-class Latin Americans imitate *norteamericanos* in everything from Coca Cola to music styles to supermarkets. This is nothing new. During the nineteenth century, liberal elites throughout Latin America saw as their model of economic development the countries of the North Atlantic: the United States, Great Britain, and France. All these countries had spawned a remarkable technology, which, in turn, facilitated their development. Roads, canals, railroads all solidified their national unity and fostered their economic and industrial development (Burns 1980, 7-9).

Thus, the new elites in Latin America came to believe that "progress" involved re-creating their nations as closely as possible to their North Atlantic counterparts, from infrastructure to Parisian fashions. Inevitably, the economic system the elites associated with progress was capitalism. Yet, as Burns points out, while progress "might have materially improved the lot of some elites," it "plunged Latin America into deeper dependency." Indeed, one might say that most Latin Americans were worse of at the end of the nineteenth century than they were at the beginning (1980, 7-11).

This outcome can be linked to a threefold liberal economic strategy. First, an infrastructure and industries similar to that in the North Atlantic states were to be developed: roads, telecommunications, steel. All these projects required large infusions of capital. Second, the way to attract capital involved fostering relations with foreigners who could and would invest. Some entrepreneurs might be induced to settle in Latin America. Others might be encouraged to finance the countries' projects. Still others might import the countries' coffee, or tin ore, or bananas. Indeed, foreigners were not unwilling to invest. North Atlantic investors had been looking abroad for lucrative investments, and Latin America, with its natural resources, was indeed attractive. By 1914, North Americans had invested $8.5 billion in Latin America, and the British had put over 20 percent of their overseas investment there (Burns 1980, 7-8).

Meanwhile, immigrant entrepreneurs were committing as much of their land as possible into sugarcane, coffee, indigo, cacao--any crop that would yield a satisfactory profit from abroad (Burns 1980, 10). Not only did the liberal Latin American elite imitate their North Atlantic counterparts, then, they also tied their country's fates to them.

Third, this elite issued orders to mobilize land and labor for their newly found god, capital--and not without conflict with their people. Among the indigenous peoples, especially, land had been a sacred trust inherited from time immemorial. Now, through privatization decrees, this land would pass from community or peasant to an entrepreneurial elite. This elite would withhold the land from subsistence, whether for reasons of speculative investment or of forcing a reluctant peasantry into the work force. This land was to be used to cultivate crops that could be of little or no use locally, but would sell profitably in distant markets. Those agrarians unwilling to sell their property might be removed by force. However achieved, land alienation became an inevitable accompaniment of liberal "progress." Labor was similarly forced, by decree, by taxation, or by sheer necessity, into the market economy (Burns 1980, 11-13).

Baseline to Commercialization: Guatemala before Barrios

Guatemala, and Central America as a whole, differed from this pattern only in detail. The Spanish Conquest of Central America, as elsewhere, laid the groundwork for a dependent economy. There had been strong promises of mineral wealth in Central America. To create labor reservoirs for the mines and haciendas, dispersed Indians were relocated into consolidated villages known as *congregaciones* (300 in Guatemala alone by 1600). Semiautonomous civil and religious governments were installed, and the towns laid out in a Spanish-style grid, each with a central plaza containing church and town hall (Lovell 1985, 89-104; Lutz and Lovell 1990, 41).

Promises of mineral wealth proved disappointing. Spanish entrepreneurs sought their wealth elsewhere, followed by colonial administrators and clergy. In time, many Indian communities became isolated to a greater or lesser degree. Some of the Indian peasants returned to the mountain hamlets from which they came. They had "nurtured a strong, cultural resistance to the European invaders centuries by reverting, in the course of the seventeenth and eighteenth centuries, to many of their former ways," that is, in the form of a "creative blend of the elements of European culture that the Indians had accepted" as well as those from pre-Columbian culture that they had maintained (Lovell 1985, 84). Specifically, the religious and civil offices created under the Spanish regime came to be merged into the hierarchical complexes extensively described in the anthropological literature (Wolf 1959, 216-219; McDowell 1974, 1979, 1980; Cancian 1967; and numerous others). Saints became facades for indigenous spirits. Community control was exercised over land and individual wealth; exclusionary mechanisms arose, ranging from distinctive clothing design and dialects to prescribed village endogamy (Wolf 1957; 1959, 226-228).

In 1823, following independence, the five republics banded together in an attempt to form a United Provinces of Central America under a common government, and to develop a commercial economy within the union. Political rivalries, combined with a rudimentary technology, poor roads and communication, and, especially, the absence of exportable cash crops or manufactures led to the dissolution of the union. Under the conservative leadership of Rafael Carrera, the Guatemalans secured independence for their republic. The citizenry of the other republics similarly declared independence; the union was dissolved by 1840.

Carrera's adherence to a conservative design, characterized by a landed elite, clerical domination, and paternalism toward the Indian population is well known. He fostered a regional economy, assigned education and social service functions to clergy, and left Indian villages intact with their communal land. It is less widely known that Carrera was not opposed to trade and commerce. When coffee was introduced into the country in the 1840s, the Carrera government, in cooperation with the preindependence Consulado de Comercio, a semiprivate merchants' guild, promoted the crop. In that decade, coffee seedlings were distributed, pamphlets containing instructions for cultivation were disseminated, and an agricultural school founded with coffee agriculture as its main curriculum (Woodward 1966, 48-54). By 1870, coffee replaced indigo and cochineal dyes as the leading export (Woodward 1985, 150).

Carrera's strategy, however, was one of slow transition from a subsistence to a commercial economy. Change, he believed, should not be imposed upon an unwilling peasant population but be "sold" to them (Burns 1980, 98-99). It was also conservative policy to encourage Indian communities to plant coffee, in contrast to liberal policy, which preferred that plantations grow the crop (Woodward 1990, 68). Additionally, conservatives, ever suspicious of foreigners, stressed independent control over this transition. Except under circumstances of extreme duress (such as British incursions during that time), the Carrera government deemphasized foreign investment, free trade, and immigrant colonization as development strategies. Justo Rufino Barrios, his liberal successor, would embrace these very strategies (Smith 1990a, 1990b, 82; Woodward 1985, 156-7).

Another legacy of Carrera's policies was the relative autonomy of Indian communities; this policy amounted not so much to protection of the Indian population from entrepreneurial ladinos, as neglect. The church, too, lacked resources to minister to them very often, leaving the Indian communities largely on their own (McCreery 1990, 101). This freedom often meant that Indians would fight among themselves, usually over land. McCreery cites as illustration the land disputes between Santa Catarina Ixtahuacán and its neighbors, and shows how this community eventually split into two warring villages (McCreery 1990, 101-104). "Not only could state authorities not bring this situation under control," he adds, "they commonly had little or no idea of what was going on"--despite maintaining a military presence in Santa Catarina (Smith 1990b, 104).

Early Transition: Barrios and his Successors

Carrera died in 1865, and his successor, Vicente Cerna, was overthrown in 1871 by liberal forces led by Carlos García Granados and Justo Rufino Barrios. Barrios, who assumed the presidency in 1873, set the framework for a transition to a commercialized economy and laws to reinforce it. His strategy matched those of liberal regimes throughout nineteenth-century Latin America, and his successors maintained this design.

The Agroexport Sector

The twin exports that hooked the Guatemalan economy into the global economy were coffee and bananas, and they did so in different ways. Coffee attracted foreign immigrants, mostly Germans, who, with their own connections and credit facilities, produced the lion's share of the crop in Guatemala. Bananas involved a foreign firm that came to control not only the external marketing of that crop, but also the country's railway and port facilities.

Contrary to common belief, Barrios and his associates were not unmindful of the risks of monoculture, and they did try to promote several agroexports; besides coffee and bananas, the products included sugar, cotton, chicle, cacao, rubber, timber, wheat, and sarsapharilla, as well as cattle. The country participated in several trade shows abroad. In 1884, for example, at an exhibition in New Orleans, they displayed some 1,000 varieties of crops. Although some of these products were indeed successful on the domestic market--cattle and wheat, for example--coffee outperformed them all as a successful agricultural export and so became the mainstay of Guatemala's exports (Woodward 1985, 157-158).

Thus it fell upon Barrios to promote the cultivation and sale of coffee, and he relied extensively upon foreign participation. His most successful venture came in attracting several enclaves of German planters to the Verapaz regions, but it also set the pattern of Guatemala's historical dependence on foreign capital, expertise, and marketing arrangements. Between 1880 and 1900, about 150 Germans settled in that region (Falcon 1970, 27). By 1913, although German planters owned only 170 coffee farms as compared to the 1,657 controlled by Guatemalans, they produced two-thirds of the country's total crop. The German planters ran autonomous operations, borrowed from German banks, owned their own transport facilities, and fully integrated their marketing and distribution networks into a seamless web (Handy 1984, 66).

Other foreigners played similar roles in processing coffee, and, through contacts and assistance of their consuls, they opened new markets in Europe and North America--entirely out of Guatemalan hands. In 1913, Germany became the leading importer of Guatemalan coffee at 432,329 *quintales* (100 pounds), followed by the United States (211,886 *quintales)*, and the United Kingdom (106,666) (Woodward 1985, 158); this pattern continued with minor changes into the 1920s and 1930s (Grieb 1979, 146-147).

One can say, at least, that the Guatemalan coffee trade involved a multiplicity of investors and foreign markets. In contrast, the banana trade was dominated by one investor, the United Fruit Company, from one country, the United States. The company had started small: its forerunner began in 1878 as an adjunct to a railroad project in Costa Rica. The banana trade grew exponentially, so that by 1899, the United Fruit Company was formed and soon moved into other Central American countries, building railroads and port facilities in an enclave pattern. By 1912, it was operating a fleet of steamships, the fabled Great White Fleet, between Central American ports and New Orleans, and, through its subsidiary, the International Railways of Central America (IRCA), it had built, or otherwise secured ownership of, a railroad network throughout the isthmus (Woodward 1985, 178-179).

United Fruit began its Guatemalan operations in 1901, and its agreement, through its IRCA subsidiary, to complete a railroad from Puerto Barrios on the Caribbean coast to Guatemala City set a Faustian model for all later agreements. This first agreement entailed generous concessions by the government of land, monopoly rights on rail transport, long-term exemption from taxes, and investment bonds, which the government itself would raise. To these concessions, later governments would add low export taxes (1.97 percent in 1928 as compared to 8.7 percent for coffee exporters), and freedom of the company from government inspection of its records (Woodward 1985, 178-179). Control over transportation and land, minimum taxes, freedom from rival competition--all these minimized the transaction costs which concern all vertically integrated firms (North 1990, 28-33, 67).

The benefits from United Fruit's activity were undeniable, but so were the disadvantages. Wages were generous, higher than those in plantations along the Pacific, but the high prices charged by company stores absorbed these wages--and working conditions were worse on United Fruit than on Pacific plantations. Contract growers, lacking other buyers, received little for their crops (a maximum of $20 per acre). Rate discrimination for non-United Fruit Company freight was standard practice. IRCA charged $.026 per ton per mile for coffee going through United Fruit's facilities in Puerto Barrios, but it charged $.097 per ton per mile for shipping coffee to Puerto San José on the Pacific coast (Handy 1984, 82-85).

The monopoly expanded. By the 1930s, through its subsidiary lands, transportation system, and company stores, United Fruit controlled an estimated 40 percent of the country's economy (Handy 1984, 80-82). This pattern was set for other economic sectors in Guatemala. The U.S. War Board forced the regime of Enrique Estrada Cabrera (1898-1920) to sell Empresa Eléctrica, a German-owned enterprise, to the U.S.-owned Electric Bond and Share Company for a fraction of its value (Handy 1984, 87). An attempt by his successor, Carlos Herrera, to cancel this deal contributed to the latter's ouster in 1921 (Handy 1984, 88). The Swedish Match Company imposed as a condition of its 2.5 million dollar loan, floated also in 1930, a monopoly of the Guatemalan market for its matches, regarded locally as inferior. (One of the major accomplishments of the Ubico regime was to pay off the loan in ten years.) (Grieb 1979, 179).

Land and Labor Reforms

As cash crops assumed major importance in the country, the Barrios regime was quick to recognize the need to mobilize land and labor into the commercial sector. The inaccessibility of land for coffee cultivation during the conservative era, whether because Indian communities refused to sell or lease such land or because of unclear titles, had been a sore point among coffee growers before the 1871 revolution; thousands of acres of cultivable land therefore sat useless (McCreery 1990, 105).

Barrios acted swiftly to rectify this state of affairs. Ecclesiastical lands were seized in 1873. Then *decreto* 170, enacted in 1877, abolished the land tenure system known as the *censo enfitéutico*, by which communal land had been rented to residents at low rates. This law provided for individual purchase of such lands.

Authorities differ on the interpretation of the law, whether it amounted to outright abolition of all communal lands or merely of a specific rental arrangement. Handy claims that the decree "required that all village communal land be sold," stipulating the conditions under which the transfer was to be made (1984, 68). According to McCreery, however, the Guatemalan Liberals "did not 'abolish' or 'outlaw' communal property," unlike the outright abolition of *ejidos* in El Salvador. If anything, the *reforma* maintained communal lands in part because indigenous communities produced most of Guatemala's food, and they served as "suppliers and reproducers of seasonal labor for the coffee estates." The would-be possessor had to apply individually for title and carry out procedures more or less in cooperation with the village. (1990, 106-107).

Nor is there general agreement whether all Indian communities were initially affected by the *decreto*. Some researchers contend that all Indian communities faced loss of land from the very beginning, and even before the decree: Samalá in 1873, Momostenango in 1874 (Handy 1984, 68; Carmack 1979,248). Others argue that only communities located in or near coffee-growing areas were affected at first (Perez-Brignoli 1989, 84; McCreery 1990, 106-107); McCreery goes so far as to say that the massive takeover of lands by coffee *fincas* involved only a small portion of the Indian population in the western highland region (1990, 106-107). Whatever the initial effect, in any event, it is known that communal lands gave way to private property in the long term, with the attendant effects of that change.

Land loss might be sustantial; the *decreto* often fostered land invasions. For example, in 1905, San Antonio Ilotenango lost 225 hectares of land to five ladinos from the nearby *municipio* of El Quiche, who had in 1892 denounced the area as "vacant" for lack of a registered title. Through other denunciations, particularly by residents of the neighboring *municipio* of Chiquimula, San Antonio had lost by 1905 a total area of 6,386, cutting the area of the municipio to almost half its former size (Falla 1970, 283-284).

Barrios was hardly unaware that Indian peasants did not willingly work on coffee plantations; the heat of a tropical climate, diseases such as malaria, and low wages were the primary disincentives. Barrios enacted, under *decreto* 177, the provisions of forced labor. Debt peonage was legalized, and workers were categorized according to resident, indebted, or nonindebted laborers. Labor quotas, imposed under colonial rule, were again assigned to villages under the *mandamiento.* Extralegal practices were tolerated as well: Labor contractors "captured" laborers through monetary advances to be worked off. Planters often sought title over village land as a device to control workers, and so create *fincas de mozos*, or "farms that yield workers"; villagers' access to land was then contingent upon their working on the plantations (McCreery 1990, 107). Although the *mandamiento* was abolished in 1894, a fugitive law passed the same year continued to guarantee an adequate labor supply (McClintock 1985, 9; Woodward 1985, 174).

Enforcing the Reforma: Military and Police

Prior to Barrios's regime, there was barely a military force (McClintock 1985, 10). Only with the coffee boom did Barrios and his associates undertake to replace the rag-tag militias under Carrera with a professional army and police force. In 1873, a military academy was organized for officer training, and military codes providing for reorganization were enacted in 1878 and 1892 (McClintock 1985, 10). In rural areas, Barrios and his successors established and maintained militias in key towns and regions, rewarding their services in various ways, including land grants (McCreery 1990, 242). The military budget skyrocketed: from $67,323 in 1870 to $307,832 in 1890. Other government expenditures were similarly increased (McCreery 1990, 104-105).

The effectiveness of the system of militias was reflected in the decline in the number of revolts listed in the records of one court, from 24 cases in the 1860s to zero in the 1880s (McCreery 1990, 108-109). An incident arising from labor recruitment abuses in San Juan Ixcoy illustrates the militia's effectiveness. One night, on July 17, 1898, having endured several years of such abuses, a group of Indians set fire to a building that housed labor agents, who had been sleeping, and cut them down as they fled. Potential ladino witnesses were also murdered. Militia contingents from nearby Solomá and Chiantla hunted down the perpetrators, killed an unknown number, and sent 60 to stand trial in Huehuetenango, the departmental (provincial) capital (McCreery 1988, 242; 1990, 111). Revolts in Momostenango (Carmack 1979, 264-265) and Cantel (Valladares Rubio 1962, 439; McDowell 1974, 1) were also violently suppressed.

In the years following Barrios's rule, although the military and police were beset with problems, the national government tightened its grip over the country and developed prototypes of a secret police to reinforce the military.

The Estrada Cabrera regime (1898-1920) subordinated the army and militia to "a vast and shadowy secret police apparatus" at the service of the president alone, and extended the network of military commands in each of the 23 departments (provinces), with 215 local command posts around the country (McClintock 1985, 11-13). A National Police was formed in 1925; a special subdivision, the judicial police (*judiciales*), was made up of detectives who performed political police functions. The *judiciales* have since formed the core of the country's death squads (McClintock 1985, 12-13, 53-54).

Infrastructural Supports

Improvements in communication systems, and, to some extent, transportation infrastructure contributed to the country's military strength. Telegraph networks proved crucial to military control over the country. In 1873, the first telegraph line was built between Guatemala City and Amatitlán, and by 1879, lines were extended to the major towns and military posts throughout the Indian highland region (Barreda 1960, 238-244). Both local military and political chiefs could now keep abreast of developments in their jurisdictions and report on "anything unusual" to the hierarchy up to the president. Telegraph operators "worked late into the night" sending reports and receiving official orders, circulars, and labor requisitions" (McCreery 1990, 110-111). Telephones, introduced in 1893, were installed in 20 departmental capitals by 1895 (Barreda 1960, 87-88). The telecommunications network was thus an additional factor in minimizing problems of enforcement of land and labor laws.

In transportation, railroads were crucial to the developing coffee economy, but were slow in coming. The first project was not initiated before 1877--and in any case connected the capital city only with the coffee-growing regions and the country's ports; none was constructed in the highlands during the early Liberal period (Barreda 1960, 89-90). Roads, despite continuous commitment of labor, did not provide ready access to the highlands. They were cart tracks at best, subjected to washouts every rainy season, and they had to be continuously maintained. There were regions not accessible by road at all, and others could be reached only on foot or by muleback (Grieb 1979, 127).

Late Transition: The Ubico Regime

If Barrios initiated the liberal economic strategy for Guatemala, it was his godson and the son of his interior minister who brought this strategy to maturity. With the ascension of Jorge Ubico Castañeda to the presidency on February 14, 1931, came the implementation of an ambitious program, ranging from development and diversification of the country's domestic and export crops to a road building project unprecedented in history. An efficient but ruthless administrative and military apparatus was installed. Thousands of functionaries lost their jobs for minor mistakes; hundreds lost their lives for more serious errors (Handy 1984, 95-96). So thorough was Ubico's administration and police that not one letter was said to enter the country unread by his censors (McClintock 1985, 85).

Domestic Agriculture and Agroexports

Among the problems Ubico inherited was an agricultural sector so underdeveloped that basic crops such as corn and beans had to be imported. This situation, he sought to reverse. A landowner himself, he urged other *latifundistas* to turn their fallow expanses into productive cropland. For *minifundistas*, he attempted to bring their products into the national market through a system of roads (described below; Grieb 1979, 152-153). His efforts paid off. Domestic production increased, dependence on imports was reduced or eliminated, and the country actually began to export some of these staples. Maize was the prominent example. In the period 1928-1929, the country had produced 2,049,544 *quintales* and imported 401,372 *quintales*; by the period 1941-1942, the amount produced increased sevenfold to 14,931,722 *quintales* and the country became a corn exporter. Similar changes occurred for most of the other domestic crops: beans, rice, yucca, cacao, sugar, and potatoes (Grieb 1979, 152-162).

Despite the increased productivity and diversification of domestic agriculture under Ubico, the reliance of Guatemala upon foreign capital, markets, and manufactures continued to increase. Furthermore, Guatemala came to rely increasingly on the United States for these necessities. The market for coffee was one example of this dependence. Up to the 1930s, the primary markets for Guatemalan coffee were European, particularly German and British. The imminence of another war in Europe, combined with the efforts of promoters to tap a large potential of the North American market for a coffee thought superior to the cheaper Brazilian varieties, led to a shift in coffee exports from Europe to the United States. By 1936, exports to the United States surpassed those to Germany (49.37 percent compared to 24.81 percent). With the outbreak of World War II, Guatemala lost its German and other European markets, and the United States virtually became the sole purchaser

(Grieb 1979, 147-148). Through a United States-Guatemala agreement reached by the end of the 1940s, a U.S. monopsony was established for both coffee and bananas. Although both crops were allowed into the United States duty-free, Guatemala was compelled to abandon its European (including British) markets (Handy 1984, 94).

Bananas, the second export, increased in importance; the ratio of income from bananas to that from coffee climbed from 1 to 9 in 1930, to 1 to 3½ in 1932, where it remained for the rest of the 1930s (Grieb 1979, 148, 183). In other ways, the heavy dependence of the Guatemalan Faust on its corporate Mephistopheles was all too evident, a fact Ubico himself recognized. According to a 1931 advertisement of *Nuestro Diario* the government's newspaper, United Fruit employed 4500 Guatemalans, spent $120,400 on Guatemalan products for its enterprises, paid $264,250 to the Guatemalan government, and spent a total of $5,116,000 within the republic. By 1941, United Fruit increased its payroll to 14,135 persons. According to an estimate by the U.S. Embassy, the number of jobs indirectly related to the company's activities was 25,000. IRCA, United Fruit's subsidiary, employed 3,800 persons in 1931 (Grieb 1979, 183-184).

Not unpredictably, Mephistopheles collected his due. In its negotiations with the Ubico government, United Fruit, which had lost much of its cultivable land to sigatoka, a soil disease destructive to banana trees, asked that it be released from a prior contract to expand facilities in the Pacific port of San Jose. The company had sweetened the pot by urging the Guatemalan government to support Ubico for a second term in 1936. The Caudillo had little choice. Facing the prospect of losing an important source of export earnings, not to mention a liquidity crisis that year, Ubico agreed to release United Fruit from its obligation to renovate the Pacific port (Grieb 1979, 184-185; Barry 1987, 70-71).

Although Ubico promoted other exports, they did not assume the importance of coffee and bananas during his regime. Chicle became a steady third crop, reaching $1 million in value by 1945, and quinine yielded further (temporary) revenue during to World War II, but other crops, such as henequen and rubber, failed (Grieb 1979, 150-152). Dependency upon American capital, markets, and, later, military domination, came to be a fact of life in Guatemala.

Land and Labor Laws

Labor inputs increased in importance for the developing commercial sector, and the continued reluctance of Indians to work in the Pacific lowlands mandated forced labor policies. Thus, Ubico promulgated the Vagrancy Law in 1934. All citizens, not only Indian *peones*, were under the legal obligation to work. Any person not having a trade or profession was obliged to work for others for 100 or 150 days per year, depending upon landownership status and, among landowners, type of crop farmed. The government's preference for commercial to subsistence crops was reflected in the lesser legal minimum land requirement for such export-oriented cash crops as coffee, sugarcane, and tobacco (three *manzanas*; this minimum also applied to corn grown in hot regions, where two crops annually could be harvested) than the minimum legal land requirement for such subsistence or domestically oriented crops as corn, wheat, potatoes, or vegetables (four *manzanas*). Noncompliants were "offered" any available job, with incarceration (and forced labor) as the alternative (Jones 1940, 162-163, Grieb 1979, 38-39). At the same time, provisions were made to eliminate debt peonage, and all such debts were canceled by 1936. Now that the peon was no longer tied to a single landowner through debt, he was free to choose his employer; hence one effect was an increase in wages. For this reason, coupled with the debt cancellations, the Vagrancy Law proved popular among rural Indian workers (Grieb 1979, 38-40).

Apart from a modest distribution of government-owned lands located in remote areas, no significant changes in land tenure were enacted under Ubico. Still, the effects of land tenure laws decreed under Barrios now ramified throughout the Indian communities of the highlands. Ethnographers of this period report that land was in private hands, much of it monopolized by ladinos. An interesting exception is that of the Chorti regions (especially Jocotán Pueblo in Chiquimula, Eastern Guatemala), as observed from 1931 to 1933; there, land was still communally owned, with individual usufruct rights (Wisdom 1940, 276-278). Elsewhere, private land tenure is reported as dominant among virtually all communities studied during the 1920s and 1930s. Among the ethnographers of the time, Wagley provided (for Santiago Chimaltenango; known locally as Chimbal) the most detailed description of private land tenure, its conversion from the communal form, the extreme differentiation of landownership, and the heavy dependence of Indians on wage labor in the coffee plantations of the Pacific piedmont (1957, 63-76, 84-102; see also Watanabe 1990, 185-190; 1992, for an update on Chimbal; Bunzel 1952, 16-25 for Chichicastenango; Tax 1953, with an update by Hinshaw

1975, for Panajachel; LaFarge 1947, with an update by Davis 1970, for Santa Eulalia). As the population increased and land became ever scarcer, the Vagrancy Law became redundant; repealed in the 1944 revolution, it was not reinstated in the 1954 counterrevolution.

Nevertheless, there were important local variations. Some communities were wiped out, particularly those near coffee planations, as already shown above; their citizens either became resident *colonos* or were forced to leave (McCreery 1990, 106-107; Perez-Brignoli 1989, 84). Others survived, though with loss of much land. As shown above, San Antonio Ilotenango lost half its land to both ladino and Indian neighbors, mainly because of the provisions under *decreto* 170 (Falla 1978, 283-284). Many others, like Chimbal, were fortunate enough to be distant from coffee plantation regions and survived relatively intact. For Chimbal, Watanabe argues that the changes "coincided more closely with local circumstances than with national law," and goes on to specify three phases in this transition: (1) petitioning for a municipal title in 1879--as a defense against encroachment by neighboring *municipios* in 1891; (2) "freezing" by 1910 of individual usufruct rights over land into a fixed pattern of landholding, a product of increasing population; and (3) widespread registration of land title by 1937 (Watanabe 1990, 170).

Administrative and Military Apparatus

An ambitious program of economic development and foreign trade demanded, in Ubico's eyes, an efficient administration free of corruption, one backed by a ruthless police force. Discovering a depleted treasury from previous administrations--the national treasury contained exactly Q27.00 when he assumed office--Ubico's first acts were to review the account books, to interrogate all officials over any discrepancy, and to arrest those whom he judged responsible for any irregularity: "They were fortunate to escape the firing squad." These measures did much to stop these leakages of the treasury. (Grieb 1979, 33).

Ubico's quest for centralization was obsessive. For his ministries, he only chose associates who shared his views, particularly the ruthless General Roderico Anzueto for the National Police. Even then, the president met with him daily, to maintain personal control of all police operations by reviewing lists of prisoners and investigations. As for the National Assembly, according to a Costa Rican envoy, any disagreement with Ubico would have prompted him "to throw the Assembly out." That it was unnecessary showed that it "was never foolhardy enough to disagree with the Caudillo." He delegated even minor tasks, such as the details of roadbuilding projects, with the greatest reluctance. He often made inspection tours of rural communities, dispensing justice, checking on his officials, and granting small favors to local residents. The Vagrancy Law was intended in part to wrest control of the labor force from the *finqueros* (Grieb 1979, 23-25, 35-40).

The administrative apparatus Ubico set up reflected this distrust. He increased the power of the *jefe político*, or governor, of each of the 23 departments. In 1935, he replaced the elective mayor of every *municipio* with appointed *intendentes,* although he allowed the election of other local officials to continue (Jones 1940, 310-311). Ubico sought to professionalize the Guatemalan army. He reorganized the military academy, appointed an American army officer as its head, and rendered merit the sole criterion for graduation--much to the consternation of senior officers, who had relied on personal connections for the advancement of their sons. Ubico ordered the army to "render assistance" to civil authorities in rural areas; his success was such that a U.S. military intelligence officer wrote, "Since General Ubico took office the death penalty has been enforced against highway robbers. It has had a most salutary effect upon the lawlessly inclined element" (McClintock 1985, 14). Militarization impinged on civilian life; civil servants, including telegraphers, radio operators, and postal workers were given military rank, and subject to military law. One route to the Indian "ladinization" program was through military service (Grieb 1979, 47).

Over the long term, the army declined, partly because of a top-heavy retinue of officers assigned trivial functions, and partly because of high turnover of its conscripts (McClintock 1985, 18-19; Grieb 1979, 45-47). By 1941, a U.S. intelligence report characterized the state of decrepitude of the army as one with "an octogenarian, illiterate Secretary of War and a preponderance of hopeless incompetents on its active list of 67 general officers" (McClintock 1985, 18-19).

Thus, the job of maintaining Guatemala's security system fell upon the National Police. As early as 1932, this organization had a force of 800 personnel in the capital, with an additional 600 distributed among the 23 departments under the command of the *jefes políticos.* The treasury police, comprising 400 more men, patrolled the rural areas, mainly halting clandestine liquor distribution (McClintock 1985, 17). The importance of the National Police may be gauged from a budget allocation of Q6,000 for March and April 1935, to cover the costs of secret expenditures of this organization. It was a large sum for a country this size, and other funds may have been available as required (McClintock 1985, 18). The ruthlessness of its chief, Roderico

Anzueto, was reflected in his responsibility for "much of the torture and the excesses that characterized the police and the prisons." Although Ubico had few qualms about such methods, Anzueto was said to have carried out his orders with such zeal that he exceeded directives (Grieb 1979, 28-29, 34). The effectiveness of the National Police is apparent from a U.S. intelligence report: "Since early in 1932, the attempted communist outbreak was nipped in the bud, and the ringleaders tried and shot, there has been a complete absence of communist activity in Guatemala" (McClintock 1985, 18).

Infrastructural Supports

Yet the Ubico era is remembered as much for its road system as for its ruthlessness embodied in the National Police. Railroads served only plantation areas; only one railroad to the highlands was built, and it was a "colossal and expensive failure" (Grieb 1979, 179). Roads everywhere required continual maintenance. So poor was the transportation network that, according to one story, German *finqueros* in the Verapaces sent shirts overseas to Hamburg rather than the capital city to be laundered (Grieb 1979, 127; Adams 1970, 180).

Constrained financially and lacking much earth-moving equipment, Ubico used human labor power and local materials to build and extend the roads. Roads involving simple construction techniques were laid out. As financing became available, they were widened and paved, and wooden bridges were eventually replaced with stone structures or, rarely, with steel and concrete spans (Grieb 1979, 128-130).

All citizens were subject to the *vialidad*, a road tax of two *quetzals* per year or two weeks of labor; most rural workers had to choose the latter. Yet this arrangement was not without rural support. The roads made it easier for villagers to visit regional markets or their neighbors, and often they initiated requests for thoroughfares to run through their village, or at least spurs to the main highway. Such arrangements entailed their added "contribution" to the project, usually in additional free labor; the government provided the planning, technical assistance, and materials not locally available. *Finqueros* benefiting from a particular stretch of highway similarly "donated" additional labor. According to the Ministry of Agriculture, only one-fifth of the unskilled labor involved in road construction was salaried (Grieb 1979, 130-133).

Initially, roads were built in the most densely populated regions of Guatemala, particularly the Indian-dominated northwestern central highlands and the eastern portion. One road system was built connecting Quezaltenango to the coffee-growing region surrounding Retalhuleu, with one trunk going on to the Pacific port of Champirico, and another to the Mexican border town of Tapachula, then back to Quezaltenango through San Marcos to form a loop. Another trunk connected Quezaltenango through the highland core to Guatemala City. An artery was then built from San Cristóbal Totonicapán to the northern center of Hueheutenango, and roads were extended west and east from there. The highlands system was completed by 1938. The eastern extension from the capital city to Puerto Barrios, however, was not completed during Ubico's tenure, nor was the northern route to the Petén (Grieb 1979, 133-134).

Although the road system was Ubico's major achievement, other infrastructural systems were introduced. National and international air connections were put in place during the 1930s, a canal was built linking Pacific plantations to the port of San Jose, and the railway system was extended to previously unserviced plantation areas (Grieb 1979, 138-140). The telegraph, telephone, and postal systems, largely developed by Ubico's regime, were centralized into a single department. Transmission lines and offices were also expanded, so that by 1940, only two departments had fewer than five telegraph offices; all sizable towns of the country had one (Grieb 1979, 170-171). Thus the benefits of infrastructure, not to mention control, were evident even in remote hamlets (Grieb 1979, 171-172).

Conclusion: Toward Global Integration

The liberal economic strategy, then, which began with Barrios' promotion of cash crops and external commerce, culminated under Ubico with a fully established export-led economy, one whose networks extended well into the Indian hinterland. Laws were passed governing land and labor, and they were enforced by a relatively wide-ranging army and national police force. Thus, 1871 to 1944 were crucial years in integrating the entire population into a commercialized economy which, in turn, would be linked into a global one.

This study raises several issues for future research. Much ethnohistorical research remains to examine the trajectory of land tenure conversion from communal to private. We need to establish tighter linkages between changes in the national, and indeed international, economic and political systems and those of the locality and region. A reformulation of Steward's levels-of-integration model may well be in order; Wolfe's (1977) notion of a supranational level of production may represent such a first step. To allow for a temporal dimension, LaFarge's (1940) sequence-of-culture model applied to the Mayan peoples could perhaps be reformulated to accommodate supralocal levels of integration as well.

Another conceptual framework that is likely to yield considerable insight into the direction the elite took during these critical years is institutional economics. Defining institutions as the rules of the game of any society, or part thereof (including the economy), North argues that their major role is to "reduce uncertainty by establishing a stable (but not necessarily efficient) structure to human interaction" (1990, 1, 6). Reduction of uncertainty does appear to inform Barrios' strategy to ensure adequate land and labor for coffee cultivation. As shown above, coffee was the surest agroexport among a host of uncertain alternatives--from cotton to sugarcane. An uncertain land and labor supply could be assured only by the twin *decretos*: privatization of land; forced mobilization of labor. Other devices served to reduce uncertainty of access: the *fincas de mozo* employed provisions from both *decretos*, as demonstrated. The factorylike arrangement between the elite and UFCO, created by the necessity of getting a perishable crop to market quickly, further served this strategy.

But uncertainty-reduction strategies for the elite meant heightened uncertainty for peasants and rural proletarians alike--in the form of land deprivation and onerous working conditions. One could, then, conceptualize not one but two institutional economic strategies: the elite's who saw their road to wealth through a burgeoning economy heavily involved in international trade; and the peasantry's whose well-being rested in land, self-employment, and household production oriented toward subsistence. The one could occur only at the expense of the other, conflict was inevitable, and the outcome favored the more powerful.

Revolts, then, were not unexpected, and it is no surprise that Barrios and his successors sought to professionalize the national army, to post garrisons throughout the country, and to bolster control through rewards (land), telegraph networks, and roads. The results were apparent in the lower frequency of local conflicts during Barrios' rule as compared to Carrera's, and in their swift suppression (such as the 1898 San Juan Ixcoy uprising) when they occurred. The reduction of administrative corruption combined with improved road and telecommunications systems, accomplished under Ubico, vastly enhanced the control function of liberal economic strategy. In establishing control over the country's land and labor, then, the liberal oligarchy ensured the prerequisites of a stable internal state.

Paradoxically, however, these strategies did not guarantee a high-performing economy in the country's future. For, as North also points out, once a certain path is set, the process become self-reinforcing through increasing returns to scale (1990, 94-95). Particularly in Third World countries, conditions favor redistributive rather than productive activity, create monopolies rather than competitive conditions, and therefore generate efficiencies in the redistributive rather than in the productive spheres (1990, 9). Following Coase (1937, 1960) and Williamson (1975), North adds that such circumstances drive transaction costs through the roof, a condition favorable only to highly integrated operations (1990, 61-67, 77).

This point is amply illustrated by United Fruit Company, which intensified the trend created by an earlier agroexport, coffee. It did so with a vertically integrated operation, which alone could have handled the high transaction costs in banana production, transportation, and marketing, force government and society alike to accept its terms, and still turn a profit. At the same time, it intensified even further Guatemala's dependence on external profits; for UFCO to withdraw its operations was an effective threat, indeed a bargaining chip during the 1936 renewal negotiations. But the cost was dear; it limited diversification of the agricultural sector, and the industrial sector never developed past processing plants and processing industries--in contrast with the Asian Tigers mentioned at the beginning of this paper.

Nor did the impoverished state of the Indian population prove beneficial in the long term, even for the elite. The loss of land by the many robbed the country of a yeomanry that might have formed the backbone of a viable economy, not unlike Costa Rica's (Woodward 1985, 107, 213-214). As Smith argues, the Indian population had shown strong signs of entrepreneurship in trade and even in engaging in commodity production during the cochineal boom of the early Carrera period (1990b, 82). As for labor, Indians working long hours on the plantations lacked the opportunity to enhance their education and training, or acquire skills that might have contributed to the industrialization that was evident in other small geographical areas--such as Singapore and Hong Kong. The failure of the Indian population to flourish under Barrios and his successors demonstrates yet another side of inefficiency that came with a self-reinforcing path to dependency.

These issues of institutional theory thus imply further comparative work--here at a cross-national level. As the global factory grows apace, ever greater concessions from Third World countries will be demanded from integrated operations. How some countries have managed to profit from globalization--the Asian Tigers mentioned above--while most of the others have failed to do so, or, at best, have attracted *maquiladoras*, reflects the scope of the research yet to be conducted. On this matter, the insights derived from a multiple framework, of which sociocultural levels of integration, sequence of cultures, and institutional economic theory represent three, should prove a highly useful tool for that purpose.

References

Adams, Richard N. 1970. *Crucifixion by Power: Essays on Guatemalan National Social Structure, 1944-1966.* Austin: University of Texas Press.

Barreda, Pedro F. 1960. *Geografi'a e Historia de Correos y Telecommunicacciones de Guatemala.* Guatemala City: n.p.

Barry, Tom. 1987. *Roots of Rebellion: Land and Hunger in Central America.* Boston: South End Press.

Bunzel, Ruth. 1952. *Chichicastenego: A Guatemalan Village.* Seattle: University of Washington Press.

Burns, E. Bradford. 1980. *The Poverty of Progress: Latin America in the Nineteenth Century.* Berkeley: University of California Press.

Cancian, Frank. 1967. Political and Religious Organizations. In M. Nash, ed., *Social Anthropology, Vol. 6. Handbook of Middle American Indians.* Austin: University of Texas Press.

Carmack, Robert M. 1979. *Historia Social de los Quiches. Seminario de Integraci'on Guatemalteca.* Guatemala City: Editorial José de Pineda Ibarra.

Coase, Ronald H. 1937. The Nature of the Firm. *Economica* 4: 386-405.

———.1960. The Problem of Social Cost. *Journal of Law and Economics* 3: 1-44.

Davis, Shelton. 1970. Land of our Ancestors: A Study of Land Tenure and Inheritance in the Highlands of Guatemala. Ph.D. Dissertation, Harvard University.

Falcon, Guillermo N. 1970. Erwin Paul Dieseldorff, German Entrepreneur in the Alta Verapaz of Guatemala, 1889-1937. Ph.D. Dissertation. Tulane University.

Falla, Ricardo. 1978. Quiché rebelde: Estudio de un movimiento de conversión religiosa, rebelde a las creencias tradiciones en San Antonio Ilotenango. *Colección Realidad Nuestra, Vol. 7*. Guatemala: Editorial Universitaria de Guatemala.

Gereffi, G. 1989. Development Strategies and the Global Factory. *Annals of the American Academy of Political and Social Science* 505: 92-104.

Grieb, Kenneth J. 1979. *Guatemalan Caudillo: The Regime of Jorge Ubico, Guatemala 1931-1944*. Athens: Ohio University Press.

Handy, Jim. 1984. *Gift of the Devil: A History of Guatemala*. Boston: South End Press.

Hinshaw, Robert. 1975. *Panajachel: A Guatemalan Town in Thirty-Year Perspective*. Pittsburgh: University of Pittsburgh Press.

Jones, Chester Lloyd. 1940. *Guatemala, Past and Present*. Minneapolis: University of Minnesota Press.

LaFarge, Oliver. 1940. Maya Ethnology: The Sequence of Cultures. In C. Hays, ed., *The Maya and Their Neighbors*. New York: Appleton Century.

———. 1947. *Santa Eulalia*. Chicago: University of Chicago Press.

Lovell, W. George. 1985. Co*nquest and Survival in Colonial Guatemala: A Historical Geography of the Cuchumatan Highlands*. Kingston, ON, and Montreal: McGill-Queens University Press.

Lüders, Rolf. 1991. The 1980's: Economic Revolution in Latin America, Continuing Development in Asia. *ASEAN Economic Bulletin* 8: 1-14.

Lutz, Christopher, and George Lovell. 1990. Core and Periphery in Colonial Guatemala. In C.A. Smith, ed., *Guatemalan Indians and the State, 1540-1988*. Austin: University of Texas Press.

McCreery, David. 1988. Land, Labor, and Violence in Highland Guatemala: San Juan Ixcoy, Huehuetenango, 1893-1945. *The Americas* [October]: 237-249.

———. 1990. State Power, Indigenous Communities, and Land in Nineteenth-century Guatemala, 1820-1920. In C.A. Smith, ed., *Guatemalan Indians and the State, 1540-1988*. Austin: University of Texas Press.

McClintock, Michael. 1985. *The American Connection, Vol. 2: State Terror and Popular Resistance in Guatemala*. London: Zed Press.

McDowell, Paul V. 1974. Political and Religious Change in a Guatemalan Community. Ph.D. Dissertation. The University of British Columbia.

———. 1979. Economics, Prestige, and Fiestas: Reorganization of Fiesta Systems in Mesoamerica. *Reviews in Anthropology* Spring: 175-182.

———. 1980. The Decline of the Civil-Religious Hierarchy: The Case of Cantel. *North South: Canadian Journal of Latin American Studies* 5: 17-35.

North, Douglass. 1990. *Institutions, Institutional Change and, Economic Performance*. Cambridge: Cambridge University Press.

Perez-Brignoli, Hector. 1989 [1985]. A brief history of Central America. (Trans. Sawrey, Ricardo, and Susana Stetri de Sawrey). Berkeley: University of California Press.

Petersen, Kurt. 1992. *The Maquiladora Revolution in Guatemala*. New Haven, CT: Center for International Human Rights Yale Law School.

Rothstein, Frances Abrahamer, and Michael L. Blim, ed. 1992. *Anthropology and the Global Factory: Studies of the New Industrialization in the Late Nineteenth Century*. New York: Bergin and Garvey.

Smith, Carol A., ed. 1990a. *Guatemalan Indians and the State, 1540 to 1988*. Austin: University of Texas Press.

———. 1990b. Origins of the National Question. In C.A. Smith, ed., *Guatemalan Indians and the State, 1540-1988*. Austin: University of Texas Press.

Steward, Julian. 1955. *The Theory of Culture Change*. Urbana: University of Illinois Press.

Tax, Sol. 1953. *Penny Capitalism: A Guatemalan Indian Economy*. Washington: Smithsonian Institute of Social Anthropology.

Valladares Rubio, M. 1962. *Estudios Historicos*. Guatemala City: Tipografía Nacional.

Wagley, Charles. 1957. *Santiago Chimaltenango*. Seminario de Integracíon Guatemalteca. Guatemala City: Tipografía Nacional.

Watanabe, John M. 1990. Enduring Yet Ineffable Community in the Western Periphery of Guatemala. In C.A. Smith, ed., *Guatemalan Indians and the State, 1540-1988*. Austin: University of Texas Press.

———. 1992. *Mayan Saints and Souls in a Changing World*. Austin: University of Texas Press.

Williamson, Oliver E. 1975. *Markets and Heirarchies: Analysis and Antitrust Implications*. New York: Free Press.

Wisdom, Charles. 1940. *The Chorti Indians of Guatemala*. Chicago: University of Chicago Press.

Wolf, Eric R. 1957. Closed Corporate Peasant Communities in Mesoamerica and Central Java. *Southwestern Journal of Anthropology* 13: 1-18.

———. 1959. *Sons of the Shaking Earth*. Chicago: University of Chicago Press.

Wolfe, Alvin. 1977. The Supranational Organization of Production: An Evolutionary Perspective. *Current Anthropology* 18: 615-620.

Woodward, Ralph L., Jr. 1966. *Class Privilege and Economic Development: the Consulado de Comercio of Guatemala, 1793-1871*. Chapel Hill: University of North Carolina Press.

———. 1985. *Central America: A Nation Divided, 2nd ed.*. New York: Oxford University Press.

———. 1990. Changes in the Nineteenth-Century Guatemalan State and Its Indian Policies. In C.A. Smith, ed., *Guatemalan Indians and the State, 1540-1988*. Austin: University of Texas Press.

Part IV

Case Studies: Institutions and Credit

11

Village Credit And The Reproduction of Proverty In Contemporary Rural Bangladesh

J. Allister McGregor

Introduction

Credit has been for many years a subject of considerable fascination for academic observers of agrarian developing societies, from social anthropologists such as Raymond Firth, to "new institutional" economists such as Pranab Bardhan and Joseph Stiglitz. It also has been a major focus of attention for policy makers and practitioners in developing countries. In Bangladesh, "development" is a major industry. Since its independence in 1971, huge amounts of resources, both national and international, have been devoted to the cause of "development," including credit projects and programs. Yet, all the signs are that poverty is as deeply entrenched in the society as it ever has been (Abdullah et al 1990). The question as to why this massive development effort has apparently failed to make any substantial impact on the poverty of the people of rural Bangladesh is a poignant one.

This paper is based upon fieldwork on credit in Bangladesh during the 1980s. The research was conducted both at the village level and with actors at all the levels in the policy process, and explores the relationship between development interventions and change in rural areas. In this sense, the case-study that is presented here is not specifically of a village, a community, or of a group of economic actors; rather, it is a case-study of credit as a development issue. In answer to the question above, it will be argued that we must see community institutions, the state and the "market" all as being profoundly implicated in the day to day reproduction of poverty in contemporary Bangladesh. That is, in order to understand the persistence of poverty in that country we must begin to develop a more profound understanding of the complex interplay of the institutions, social, political and economic, which comprise the society as a whole.

Credit, Economists, and Development

As in developing countries throughout the world, successive regimes in Bangladesh have regarded credit as a key element in their development strategies, and particularly in the struggle for rural development. By the mid-1970s, however, the failures of credit projects and programs were inescapable. Following the work of the neo-classical economists McKinnon (1973) and Shaw (1973) disillusionment with targeted and subsidized credit programs as a form of development intervention grew to a crescendo. These authors argued that by using the banking system to deliver subsidized development credit, governments in developing countries had induced a condition of "financial repression." The distortions which were introduced into financial markets inhibited them from making their potentially vital contribution to the development process. The detailed rejection of the role of subsidized credit programs and projects in rural development has been championed by agricultural economists such as Adams and von Pischke (see Adams and Nelson 1979, von Pischke et al 1983). The analysis advanced by these authors has been embraced by the major international development institutions and represents the basis for much current policy with respect to the banking systems of developing countries (World Bank 1989).

Over this same period, however, many economists of development, looking more from a micro-economic perspective, have become ever more intrigued by credit. The literature on interlocked markets and interlinked transactions places credit firmly at the core of many transactions in rural areas (Bardhan 1989b, Stiglitz 1986, Bhaduri 1983). The giving and receiving of credit is seen as a key element in securing other types of transactions; for example, between landowner and share-cropper, material supplier and artisan, retailer and producer. The "new institutional economics" emphasizes the significance of high transaction costs and the particular problems of imperfect information in rural developing economies. The insights which these analyses give into the ways in which interlinked contracts may represent an optimal institutional solution to the particular economic conditions confronting transactors in rural developing societies represents a refreshing and vibrant contribution to the economics of development. One weakness of this growing literature, however, is that it makes little connection with other work on agrarian developing societies. Key contributions from other perspectives such as the work of Geertz (1963), and most notably the moral economy debates between Scott (1976) and Popkin (1979), are seldom acknowledged by the new institutional economics, and yet the institution of patronage clearly is a concern that lies at the heart of much of these literatures (for a refreshing exception see Basu 1984). As with interlinked contracts, the giving and receiving of credit tends to be identified as one of the relationships which is characteristic of systems of patronage in agrarian societies (Eisenstadt and Roniger 1984). Patron-client relations have long been an area of ambiguity and controversy in the study of development (Breman 1974, Schmidt et al 1977); as a complex and deeply embedded feature of many agrarian societies they have been perceived both as a mechanism of social security and of economic and political exploitation.

The new institutional economics and the financial repression thesis both draw on the same neo-classical economic inspirations, but they now present us with two different stories about credit in developing countries. For those involved in development policy and practice this may be a source of confusion. The financial repression literature treats financial markets as it would any other type of market and eschews direct interventions with respect to credit; while the new institutional economics points to the peculiarities of financial markets in agrarian developing societies and confirms the significance of credit in the reproduction of major "economic" institutions in rural areas. There is also of course a highly emotive dimension to the credit debate which is felt perhaps especially by those working close to the issues on the ground. While the institution of patronage, in the form of interlinked contracts, may be efficient in any number of technical senses (with respect to insuring against high levels of risk, lowering the possibilities of opportunism, and securing factors of production and so on), it can still be perceived as a backward institution which appears to reproduce the kind of bondage and impoverishment which development expressly has claimed it seeks to eliminate. In this respect, and in spite of the contributions of economists of whatever persuasion, credit is still regarded by many development practitioners as important a policy instrument for the alleviation of rural poverty as it ever has been.

Despite the overarching theoretical linkage of a neo-classical frame of thought, there is a problematic gap between the observations of those economists who focus on the financial market and those concerned with institutions. Credit's centrality to interlinked contracts and to patronage suggests that there are good reasons, beyond government intervention, for the imperfections of rural financial markets. This implies that it cannot be assumed that financial markets in rural areas are going to be easily "freed-up" by the liberalization measures which are recommended by the financial repression thesis, and that it may not be quite such a simple task to reorient financial markets so that they might meet the needs of the development process and of the rural poor. At a general level, this paper suggests that there are some serious problems for contemporary economic analysis in comprehending the relationship between the "macro" and "micro" in developing countries. This can be highlighted in greater detail by a close examination of policy, which is concerned essentially with the translation of ideas and intentions between the "macro" to "micro" levels.

The Importance of Credit in Predominantly Agrarian Societies

The arguments which follow will be presented in an abstracted form, based not only on fieldwork in Bangladesh between 1984 and 1985, but on subsequent involvements with a range of government and non-governmental credit programs. However, the specific case material which is presented is drawn from intensive study in and around the village of Khotkhot. This village, of around two-hundred and twenty households, is located in Tangail District of Bangladesh. Its population is entirely Muslim and it is known in the area as a weaver's village. One hundred and thirty of its households reported weaving as their main source of income, with most of the remainder receiving their main income from agriculture, trading of one sort or another, and petty artisan activities. Although a weaving village, more than half of the households reported some direct involvement in agriculture, ranging from cultivation of small self-owned plots, to share-cropping, to day-labouring.

A prominent feature of the recent history of Khotkhot has been a struggle between two factions in the village (see McGregor 1989a). During the latter half of the 1970s and into the 1980s a group of younger men were challenging an older more established faction for formal recognition as the village leaders (*matbor*) of Khotkhot. In seeking to capture the support of the majority of villagers and to build up their hierarchies of patronage, the members of these two factions engaged in a complex manipulation of political and economic opportunities. In Khotkhot, as elsewhere in rural Bangladesh, an important aspect of factional competition has been the struggle to secure management over access to development interventions which might bring additional resources to the village. Development programs and projects which might turn out to be a source of formal credit have been particularly significant in this respect.

If we turn to consider specifically the role of credit in rural communities such as Khotkhot, one of the first and most obvious characteristics of most developing societies which must be acknowledged in our analysis is that their economies are dominated by agriculture. Recent work by Phillip Raikes on Africa (1988) and Bina Agarwal on South Asia (1990), which builds upon Amartya Sen's "entitlements" approach, highlights the importance of seasonality in our understanding of poverty and vulnerability in developing societies (see also Chambers et al 1981). These authors point out that seasonal fluctuations of income and other earnings, and therefore also of demand, pose particular problems with respect to household consumption and production. As Sen's analysis of famines suggests (1981), in the context of poverty, these fluctuations can and do seriously threaten survival.

Like any other economic unit, however, rural households in developing countries are not passive in the face of these fluctuations, but can be seen as seeking to manage their affairs in such a way as to smooth income flows over the year. In this sense, it is possible for us to analyze household behaviour as a form of "portfolio" management, although this need not lead us to ascribe conscious "portfolio" decisions to the household. Such an approach suggests that we can regard households as "investing" their resources in a diversified way, in an effort to spread risk. In Khotkhot, although a household might have been referred to as a weaving household, this should not obscure the fact that other important flows of income were generated at different times of the year from activities undertaken by all the members of the household, including the children. For a weaving household, other sources of income might include: sales of agricultural or garden produce, day-laboring, keeping of goats, chickens and ducks, mat-making, fishing and from any number of other small-scale activities.

This "portfolio" approach can be improved even further if we broaden of our definition of household resources. In conventional terms we must consider the usual economic resources of the household: its income and wealth and its human resources, including skills, but in order to fully understand household "portfolios" in developing countries we can also add categories of social and cultural resources (see Swift 1989, for a similar framework). By social and cultural resources we are referring to a combination of relationships and status.

In the category of social resources we might include relationships with influential members of the community, or with local government officials, or with powerful actors in local markets. Each of these might be considered to be of importance to a household in that from them they may secure preferential access to new resources, or enhance the value of their existing resources. For example, good connection to a local bureaucrat may give the household better information with which to secure access to a government credit scheme, while a direct relationship with a large trader may mean that the household is able to avoid the costs of having to trade its produce through smaller intermediaries.

The idea of cultural resources can be related to Bourdieu's concept of symbolic capital (1992), and refers to culturally specific forms of status within a community on social, religious or political grounds. As Bourdieu suggests, "Symbolic capital is valid even in the market, ... " (1992, 119). Status of different kinds may result in the different treatment of the household and its members by others in the community, by government officials, and in the market. For example, a small-trading household in Khotkhot with a reputation for its piety and religiosity is treated with particular respect by other market traders. The trust which is accorded to this household because of its religious reputation permits them, under some circumstances, to secure conditions of trade which are not generally available to other small trading households.

In these senses, both cultural and social resources can be seen as having value to households in their efforts to survive or advance. This approach allows us to develop an alternative perspective on credit in rural communities. A major premise of this view is that: in seasonally affected and resource scarce societies, there is necessarily a strong and persistent demand for arrangements which can increase the flexibility of transactions over time. The giving and taking of credit allows households to shift consumption between the present and the future, and the need for such arrangements is especially pronounced where there is absolute poverty. Moreover, in rural Bangladesh, in the face of uncertainty as a consequence of floods, illness, market slumps (to name but a few of the possible calamities) households may find it necessary to resort to credit arrangements at any time.

Under such conditions, we must perceive credit as more than just a good to be demanded and/or supplied at a particular point in time. Rather, it must be seen as a relationship which can constitute an important social resource for a household. While we can understand the need for credit in economic terms our analysis must go beyond that. The credit relationship is vital to the very ability of households in rural Bangladesh to reproduce themselves and, as such, it has a distinctive place in the social and cultural order of the society.

This emphasis upon the flexibility of the transaction over time brings us to a major point of departure from the conceptual framework which is central to the McKinnon and Shaw financial repression thesis. The conception of "the market" which lies at the heart of their analysis is an abstract which essentially treats transactions as single point interactions between suppliers and demanders. As such, it has fundamental limitations in understanding transactions which are open-ended relationships over time. In a discussion of "relational exchange" in a North American fishing community, Acheson notes that while price may remain important in such arrangements, "...nonpecuniary values and personal relationships intrude" (1985, 396).

While it could be argued that flexible transactions over time can be analyzed as markets for "options" and "futures," this also is inadequate if we wish to place these transactions in their wider societal context. Analyzing credit relationships as "options" and "futures" may be satisfactory if the transaction in question is the sole purpose of the relationship. However, where the relationship has other dimensions, where it is multiplex, and particularly where it is an ongoing part of the construction of a community and society, more is missed by this approach than is comprehended. As an analysis of patronage by Li Causi (1975) notes, patron-client relations within communities must be seen as consisting not just of an economic dimension, but also as fulfilling political and ideological functions. The institution of patronage is a key feature in political structures of domination in rural society and also serves as a highly effective ideological mechanism for the regulation of consensus.

The notion of credit relationships as being flexible and open-ended transactions over time, suggests that households which are in danger of falling into deprivation, or who at certain times of the year are unable to meet their investment needs, will seek to develop credit relationships as a central part of their household "portfolios." That is, they will seek to establish relationships with patrons in their communities and in their business arrangements, through which credit may be demanded in times of need and where they might reasonably expect those demands for credit to be met. In return, the credit giver may expect to receive something from the resources which his client's household has at its disposal. It is important to note, however, that there tend to be limits as to who can expect to receive credit under such systems. In Khotkhot, if a household has so few resources that it has very little to give in return to potential credit givers, such as widow households, they are usually not considered as eligible for such exchanges. These households are either given charity or nothing at all.

There is a wide range of such relationships between clients and patrons in Khotkhot. While there are relationships between households of relatively equal standing in which credit may be asked for and given, the most apparent examples are a number of poorer households which have built up very close relationships with wealthy families. Each of the exchanges is slightly different in character: some involve the clients acting as share-croppers for their patrons, others revolve around the provision of labor by the client household. This can include not only the provision of agricultural labor by the male members of the household, but also sending children to act as servants in the houses of patrons, or women to work in the homestead of the wealthier patron during the busy crop-processing periods.

Such close relationships also tend to require the client household to give support to the patron household in social and political terms. While this may simply take the form of voting it can also manifest itself in more subtle ways in village life. This can be illustrated with reference to the case of Shamsul, a landless labourer and share-cropper in the village. One afternoon a small group of labourers had gathered at the fieldworker's house and were discussing how the wealthy families in the village had become rich. After some convoluted family histories and dark hints of double-dealing the discussion increased in intensity. Shamsul angrily turned to the fieldworker and said, "How do the rich become rich? By (gesture) screwing poor people." The meeting came to an end shortly after, but the irony of this answer was recognised by many of those who had gathered. Shamsul was known in the village as a man who had steadfastly and publicly rejected precisely this kind of view from a development non-governmental organization (NGO) which had been working in the area attempting to improve the economic condition and political consciousness of landless labourer households. Shamsul is a close client of one of the leading families in the younger faction in Khotkhot. Apart from labouring and acting a strong-arm man for this household, he is also noted as a stout defender of them in village debate. In social and political terms in the village, his position in relation to this household made it impossible for him to be seen to be lending credence to the NGO view of the socio-political order of the village.

Hierarchies of patronage not only extend throughout Khotkhot, but ramify beyond it. This is particularly evident with respect to the business of weaving. Many of the weavers in Khotkhot regularly turn to the traders who supply them with yarn and other weaving materials for credit. A number of smaller traders, who both sell yarn and dye it for their customers, are based in the village itself, but the main traders are to be found at a nearby weekly market. This market is dominated by a cartel of large traders who transport yarn from the main port in Bangladesh to this market. Most of the weavers and a number of the smaller trader/dyers in Khotkhot are locked into buying from a particular trader at the weekly market because of the credit relationship. They take yarn on a credit basis, paying a small premium over the cash price, and pay off their debt when they have sold their woven products the following week.

In the senses which are described above, the credit relationship is a form of social resource, which can be regarded as a vital dimension of household "portfolios" in poor agrarian societies such as Bangladesh. For poorer households which are prone to fluctuations in their incomes, access to credit can be a necessary means of financing both production and consumption during low periods. For more wealthy households the giving of credit represents an extra and important dimension of their diversification of the investment of their resources.

This "portfolio" perspective on credit affords us some important insights into household strategies in agrarian societies and into the dynamics of the relationship between the resource rich and the resource poor. As with portfolio theory in general, investment is diversified in order to deal with risks, and generally speaking the more a household can diversify its portfolio the more stable it is likely to be (the co-variance of risk should be reduced). However, the ability to diversify a household portfolio is dependent upon the amount of resources which a household has available to invest. It is a statement of the obvious, therefore, that poor households with fewer resources tend to be more susceptible to the disruptive effects of natural, personal and social disasters which diminish the value of their resource holdings. The analytical value of this approach in the context of rural Bangladesh should not be overlooked. It suggests that poor households, which will often be landless and illiterate, will be less likely to be able to establish portfolios which will successfully smooth-out income flows in orthodox economic terms alone. Denied an autonomous means of coping with their environment, the poor have little option but to "invest" some of their scarce resources in their dependence upon patrons within the community. Thus to a poor household the "price" of a credit relationship with a more wealthy patron may involve the commitment of any of the households resources: money, labor, muscle-power, or a range of social and political loyalties. While for the rich, credit relationships are a means whereby spare resources can be invested in the poor, in order to build up economic, social and political position within communities.

Credit and Wider Market Structures

Having argued that credit plays a vital role in agrarian societies, it is important to examine the implications of this for wider market structures. One important observation from studies of informal credit in rural Bangladesh which we must deal with first, is that as much as 70 percent of informal lending is reported as being between friends, neighbours, and relations. Often these loans will be reported as being made without interest, or at least without an interest rate which can be calculated in straightforward monetary terms. However, taking this observation at face value can be misleading, since it should be recognized that the fact that a lender is cited as a friend or relative need not necessarily obscure or eradicate the political and economic dimensions of the relationship.

The socialized nature of many trading relations in Bangladesh make it quite possible for a weaver from Khotkhot for example to introduce his yarn supplier, who would be referred to as a *mohajon* (a term used to mean businessman, but which can be literally translated as boss), as a friend. Nor indeed in many situations would it be too surprising to find that the *mohajon* was a relative of some kind. This would be especially the case within the village, but this does not mean that the *mohajon* or other credit giver, who may well have given the loan free of interest, would not be accruing some benefit from giving the loan. This benefit could either be an explicit economic gain through the trading relationship, as in the case of the large traders at the weekly market, or it could simply be that it ensures that the lender may be able to call upon the borrower or even the borrower's kin to honour their "debt" by returning the favor at some stage in the future.

As studies of the social and economic organization of rural Bangladesh indicate, credit is an important nexus at which the intertwining of economic and political power is most clearly apparent (see, for example, Jansen 1986). In many situations, the control over credit interacts with and reinforces control over markets. The need for credit in rural Bangladesh, for the reasons outlined above, and the unequal distribution of resources, permits those who are able to gain control over credit to use it as a major means of inhibiting the operation of markets. The effectiveness of markets, that is simply their ability to function, can be regarded as being directly affected by tied credit relations in two ways.

Firstly, the fact that credit relations can be used to tie customers and suppliers to existing credit givers, often will make it very difficult for new traders to find enough untied custom and/or untied supply to challenge the position of existing powerful traders. This is something which Bardhan suggests when he notes that,

> ... interlocking itself may act as a barrier to entry for third parties and be a source of additional monopoly power for the dominant partner (usually the employer-creditor-landlord) in such transactions. (1989a, 1391).

In the case of weaving, in order to attempt to enter the market a new yarn trader must have a very strong resource base, not only economically, but also socially and politically. The new trader must not only be in a position to offer credit to his/her clients, and be able to bear some amount of non-repayment, but must also have sufficient social and political clout within the community to secure and maintain the loyalty of those clients.

The case of Abu Hossein, one of the small-scale yarn traders and dyers in Khotkhot, illustrates this point. His usual business involves him each week buying around eight bundles of yarn from his *mohajon* at the nearby weekly market. He transports this yarn to the village where he dyes and sells it to a small group of eight or nine regular customers. Because these are regular customers he is prepared to sell yarn to them on a credit basis, but previous experience of non-repayment has made him very wary about selling to occasional customers on credit. Occasionally Abu Hossein will agree to dye yarn which weavers have bought for themselves, but he regards this as disruptive of his own business and tries to discourage it.

When he received two government loans, Abu Hossein decided to add this capital to his own modest savings to start large-scale yarn trading. He went to Narayanganj, the wholesale center for yarn located to the south of Dhaka, and bought one bale of yarn (forty bundles). He transported this back to Khotkhot, to sell in the village and at the weekly market. However, on his return to the village he found it difficult to sell this yarn and was only able to do so to his traditional circle of customers in the village. Even in trading at this level he continued to resist requests to sell the yarn on a credit basis. His funds were limited and he also felt that he did not have sufficient strength either in the village or in the wider area to secure its repayment. Since Abu Hossein apparently was not able to present himself as a credible alternative patron, it appears that few weavers were prepared to leave their traditional suppliers to buy yarn from him. He was only able to sell at his usual pace and before he had managed to sell all of the yarn, its price had dropped at the weekly market. The outcome of his venture was that, after the costs of transport had been taken into account, he lost money in the venture. The loss was not completely disastrous for Abu Hossein and his family, but it was enough to make him realize that he did not have an adequate resource base, in either economic or socio-political terms, to do that kind of trading. Abu Hossein did not go to Narayanganj again, rather he went on doing his usual small scale trading and dyeing business. Using what capital remained he took the much safer option of mortgaging-in some land on which to cultivate winter rice.

Following a similar line to that proposed by Bhaduri (1983), the second way in which market effectiveness may be affected by tied credit, is that increases in productivity due to innovation or technological change which threaten the market control of the existing powerful actors may, if they cannot be captured, be resisted, and if possible suppressed. This, of course, inhibits the long-term dynamics of the market and is particularly relevant for development interventions which seek either directly or indirectly to change existing relationships. Even where development interventions have been perceived as offering simple and neutral, technological improvements, their potential impact on existing economic and political interests ensures that they almost always become insinuated in political and economic struggles in rural communities (McGregor 1989a). In this context the threat by a patron to cut off credit relations with a client can be a very effective form of persuasion for the client not to be involved with the innovation or new technology.

This kind of control over markets via credit has a dampening effect upon their productivity and the effects upon wider markets are inevitably interlinked to the unequal distribution of resources in rural Bangladesh. The existing unequal distribution of resources has the potential to breed further inequality, as those with greater resources are considerably better placed to capture benefits from production. As is noted above, the leap from petty trader to major trader is not a small one. It requires a large stock of resources and yet these resources are very difficult to accumulate precisely because of the nature of existing "tied" trading relationships. The terms of trade between large traders and their client suppliers and customers, enforced by the credit relationship, are often a very effective means of siphoning off small producer and small trader surpluses in economic terms. But they are also effective in maintaining poorer households in a weaker socio-political position, whereby they cannot easily accumulate the necessary social and even cultural resources to ensure their transition to becoming more significant actors within the community.

The adverse distributional effects of this market structure, of course, have a negative impact upon incentives in general in the rural economy. In exploring the relationship between credit and wider market structures we begin to grasp the complexity of "financial repression," as it might be viewed from the village. From this perspective it is not easy to imagine "markets" in the neo-classical sense, suddenly emerging to overcome the problems of the reproduction of poverty in Bangladesh. The structures of production and exchange are deeply embedded in rural society and it is likely that it will require more than the removal of subsidies and the manipulation of prices to change these significantly.

The Role of Formal Credit

As was indicated in the introduction, formal credit programs and projects have been a mainstay of rural development strategies in Bangladesh since independence. The rationale for formal credit interventions in development has been multidimensional, ranging from breaking the vicious circle of poverty, to increasing productivity under the Green Revolution, to the freeing of the peasantry from the clutches of usurious moneylenders. While most of the literature on interlinkage and interlocking focuses upon informal credit as an important element of these relationships, it is important to note that the "tying" of clients to patrons in contemporary rural Bangladesh has also been achieved through the manipulation of access to formal credit.

A distinctive feature of the participation of banks in development credit programs in rural Bangladesh has been their reluctance to establish a direct relationship with the target populations. This tendency has been especially notable in programs directed at the poorer sections of rural society. The normal way of organizing access to formal credit has been that a specialized agency or designated elected official is cast in the role of "broker" between the bank and the client. These brokerage functions have been carried out either by the staff of government agencies, or by the elected local officials.

As has been noted in an earlier paper (McGregor 1989b), bankers have a range of explanations for their preference for this "brokerage" structure of access. These hinge around the fact that local figures are more likely to know the potential customers and that it would be prohibitively costly for the banks themselves to take on the screening of the credit-worthiness of each potential borrower. However, what this structure of access actually does, is hand over the management of access to formal credit to prominent local figures, who are locked into webs of patronage. There are two important features of this arrangement which need to be distinguished. On the one hand, it ensures that banks, and bank managers in rural areas, are not required to live up to the rhetoric of formal credit policy by trying to challenge a system of patronage which depends in part on maintaining control over access to credit. On the other hand, the structure of brokerage actually allows access to formal credit to be used as a further resource to be deployed in the maintenance of networks of patronage.

In 1982, the Government of Bangladesh established a Task Force for the handloom weaving sector and it was decided that an initiative would be undertaken to resuscitate and revitalize the handloom industry. A major study of the handloom weavers argued that they were caught in a network of dependencies on suppliers and moneylenders. In the belief that these conditions served to depress the productivity of the entire sector, the government designed an integrated program to assist weavers. A major feature of this scheme was that it would provide weavers with secure and formal access to both credit and inputs. A countrywide survey was carried out by the Handloom Board and the Ministry of Textiles, during which weavers were registered for the receipt of passbooks. When taken to the designated banks by the weavers these passbooks would certify that they were eligible for loans on easy terms under the scheme.

The way in which the connection with the Handloom Board scheme was made in Khotkhot represents a good example of the integration of development schemes with the institutions of patronage and factionalism. When the two Handloom Board officials, who were to carry out the survey for the registration of weavers for passbooks, were walking along the track into the village they met a villager by the name of Mohammed Murshed Ali. With the usual sense of curiosity which is provoked when official looking men venture off the road to visit villages in Bangladesh, Murshed Ali made it his business to find out what the purpose of this visit was. When he found out that they intended to carry out a registration of weavers, Murshed Ali, himself a weaver and trader, invited them to return to his homestead to take some food. After settling the two officials into the village, Murshed Ali sent for Nurul Master, who was the leader of the younger faction which was competing with an older more established group of families for recognition as the undisputed leadership of the village. The struggle between these two factions had progressed by this time to the extent that key figures from each of the factions were recognised as being members of the village council (*salish*). The common courtesy in Khotkhot is that when officials of one sort or another enter the village then one of the better educated village leaders (*matbor*) should be called upon to talk to the officials on behalf of the village. As a loyal member of Nurul Master's faction in the village, Murshed Ali had little doubt that the most appropriate *matbor* to deal with this situation was Nurul Master.

Over the next two to three days the two officials used Nurul Master and Murshed Ali as key informants in their survey of weavers. These two acted as guides for the officials on their inspection tours around the village. Following the survey, access to Handloom Board loans amongst villagers generally was good. Nurul Master's role in the distribution of access to the Handloom Board loans in the village was pivotal. Almost by good fortune, he and members of his faction were able to gain control over the registration phase of the access process, and then were able to retain control over the later access to credit. Within the village, the management of access to this source of formal credit and particularly the arrangement of loans for many poorer weaving households did much to bolster the position of both Nurul Master himself and his faction. For Murshed Ali his chance connection on the road to the village with the Handloom Board officials improved his standing in the village and his stature within the faction.

However, not all weavers in Khotkhot received Handloom Board loans. When the Handloom Board officials were inspecting the *para* (a collection of households with a shared compound) opposite to his own, Thandu Mia had gone to speak to them. They assured him that they would be to coming to his *para* eventually, but they never did. The officials left the village without inspecting or registering any of the fifteen weavers in Thandu Mia's *para*.

When asked about this oversight, Murshed Ali said that he had not been able to accompany the Handloom Board officials on all their visits through the village, and since Thandu Mia's *para* was in the crowded centre of the village it would have been very easy for outsiders to overlook it. In an effort to resolve the matter, Murshed Ali proposed that if each of the weavers in Thandu Mia's *para* gave him a small amount of money he would make a special journey to the Handloom Board offices in Dhaka to attempt to persuade them to add the missed households to their records. The households in Thandu Mia's *para* decided against giving Murshed Ali this money, but local Handloom Board officials in Tangail told Murshed Ali that his journey to Dhaka would have been pointless anyway and that it would not be possible to put the error to right.

Since his household had not been registered, Thandu Mia could not receive a weaver's passbook and was excluded subsequently from taking a Handloom Board loan. In the factional divisions within the village, Thandu Mia's *para* had been notable for its attempts to remain detached. Although when interviewed, Thandu Mia suggested that he was broadly sympathctic to Nurul Master's faction, it was clear that the households in that *para* could not be counted on as undoubted supporters of Nurul Master. It also was apparent when households in this *para* were interviewed that there was a certain resentment of the two main factions in the village. However, their exclusion from the Handloom Board Credit Scheme forced them to consider more carefully their strategy with respect to the two factions.

This type of structure of access to development goods and services has meant that village elites in Bangladesh have been able, either directly, in their roles as locally elected officials, or indirectly, through their connections to locally based officials, to capture and manipulate access to formal credit as a patronage resource. In this sense, relations to the state itself can be regarded as an element in interlinkage. The arrangement of a loan from a bank can substitute for the giving of informal credit and be similarly used to tie clients to patrons. There is little doubt that relationships to state bureaucracies, including the public sector banks, can be viewed as an important resource in household portfolios. The brokerage structure of access to formal credit has ensured that development funds have become part of the wider pool of resources which patrons are able to use to secure their positions in the hierarchy of rural society. The arrangements which have been established for the implementation of formal credit policy have been both shaped by the structures of rural society, and contribute to the reproduction of those structures. To borrow some terminology from the policy analysis literature, this is the "context" in which policies, such as financial liberalization, must be enacted (Grindle 1980). By understanding village patrons as one layer in a hierarchy of patronage, upon which the legitimacy of the state in Bangladesh is ultimately founded (McGregor 1989b), one again grasps the magnitude of difficulty in intervening to affect rural credit relations.

The Economic and the Social in New Institutional Economics

In building up this picture of "financial repression" from the village the paper has sought to capture some of the complexity which surrounds the issue of credit in rural Bangladesh. Taking a portfolio perspective on household strategies, it has been argued that resources, in a broad sense, are invested in ways which not only have economic but also social and political significance. From the perspective of traditional, orthodox, western economics, it might appear that the financial system is wracked by irrational decisions about the extension of credit and by the non-productive use of loans. This, however, would be to underestimate the extent to which socio-political stability affects the economic performance of households in rural areas. It is a sign of good management that the spare resources which households accumulate are used to reinforce the socio-economic position of the household. Even using scarce resources for a marriage, viewed as a set of new relationships which may in turn secure preferential access to a local bureaucrat, a market trader, or a new patron, can be seen to be a sensible strategy. In the face of seasonality, poverty and uncertainty, households in rural Bangladesh know that if they are to survive, and even to advance economically, they must be able to invoke reciprocity and call upon "friends, neighbours, or relations" to honour their "debts" or to meet their obligations when the need arises.

When we consider "financial repression" from below, we end up with a picture of the financial system that is considerably at odds with the view proposed by McKinnon, Shaw and others. This suggests that the liberalization policy prescriptions which arises out of their analysis are almost certainly inadequate. While there may be some important insights to be taken from the work of these authors, their analysis is critically undermined by significant gaps in their understanding of the developing economies and societies they are discussing. These gaps in understanding are filled, or are covered over by assumptions and inappropriate recourse to models and abstracts developed in the industrialized North. In particular, and unforgivably given that these authors are analyzing policy issues, there is little understanding of the organizations and institutions which constitute the financial systems which they are discussing and which are responsible for the implementation of the policies which are the subject of analysis. The analysis also shows little understanding of the nature and structure of markets and economic activity which are the context in which the policies they attack have been operating and into which the policies they advocate are being inserted.

This question of policy relevance is also one that is significant for the new institutional economists. While they emphasise that their intention is to focus upon transactions which are primarily economic (see Bardhan 1980), they nevertheless are focusing upon relationships in which a distinction between the economic and the social is profoundly difficult to maintain. In Bardhan's recent overview of approaches in the new institutional economics, the old institutionalist literature, such as, one assumes, the work of Gunnar Myrdal in South Asia, is described as being intellectually lazy (Bardhan 1989b, 3). The laziness and descriptiveness of the old institutionalists is set in opposition to the rigorousness of the new. However, if laziness involves the recognition that you can only translate so much of complex relationships which are continually being renegotiated, into static mathematical relationships, then perhaps the lazy old institutionalists were not as far off-track as Bardhan suggests.

As the paper has sought to illustrate, while the economic functions of credit and the institution of patronage are important, these cannot be isolated from their social, political and ideological dimensions. Nor can these other functions be seen simply as subordinate to the economic. Patron-client relations, or interlinked contracts, are an important feature of the structure of rural Bangladeshi society, but it is the ways in which they are profoundly integrated with other elements of that society's structure that provides us with a key to understanding the continued reproduction of poverty in contemporary Bangladesh.

While the study of development has been fascinated by change, it is important also that we understand why situations such as that in Bangladesh appear not to change. As is argued here, it is not that there is no change in response to development interventions, for example, but that fundamental aspects of the society interact and the pressures to maintain the existing distribution of social, economic and political power are strong.

Having come so close to carefully examining actual institutions in agrarian developing societies, it is frustrating to find the new institutional economists caught in seeking to maintain the distinction between "the economic" and "the social." A particular difficulty with the study of credit in developing societies is that it is also an important policy issue. As such, there are connections between academic understanding of these issues and the formulation of development interventions in countries such as Bangladesh. One could argue, that for purely analytical purposes it is worthwhile separating the economic from the social in the study of interlinkage and interlocking. However, we must consider how realistic the kinds of recommendations that arise out of such analysis are likely to be when translated to policy circles. Perhaps this is what Bardhan is aware of when he warns his fellow collaborators in the new-institutionalist adventure that,

> If the reformist zealot erred in ignoring the micro foundations of institutions, we in turn should be careful that our theories of principal-agent games and moral hazard do not cover up basic, often ugly, power relations in the phenomena we are studying. (Bardhan 1989b, 238)

In some senses the new institutional economics is close to internalizing a debate which has a long history in the study of developing societies. At its root this debate between economics and social anthropology can be caricatured by two questions about our construction of understanding: to what extent should we model what we see, or to what extent should we allow our models to tell us what it is that we are seeing? Previous forays into this area have often been abandoned more through exhaustion than through the achievement of satisfactory conclusions. However, the fact that these questions keep resurfacing is evidence of their continued relevance. With respect to the future development of the new institutional economics one can only hope that the disciplinary nature of their core discipline, does not stop them from making themselves more aware of other literatures on these issues and from participating in such debates.

References

Abdullah, A. et al. 1990. Poverty in Bangladesh. *Special Issue Bangladesh Development Studies* 18(3).

Acheson, J.M. 1985. The Maine Lobster Market: Between Market and Hierarchy. *Journal of Law, Economics and Organization* 1(2): 385-398.

Adams, D.W. & Nelson, G.O. 1979. Rural Financial Markets in the Development of Bangladesh. In *Problems and Issues of Agricultural Credit and Rural Finance*. Dacca: Bangladesh Bank.

Agarwal, B. 1990. Social Security and the Family: Coping with Seasonality and Calamity in Rural India. *Journal of Peasant Studies* 17(3): 341-412.

Bardhan, P.K. 1980. Interlocking Factor Markets and Agrarian Development: A Review of Issues. *Oxford Economic Papers* Vol 32(1).

Bardhan, P. 1989a. The New Institutional Economics and Development Theory: A Brief Critical Assessment. *World Development* 17(9): 1389-1395.

———.1989b. *The Economics of Agrarian Institutions*. Oxford: Clarendon Press.

Basu, K. 1984. *The Less Developed Economy: A Critique of Contemporary Theory*. London: Blackwell.

Bhaduri, A. 1983. *The Economic Structure of Backward Agriculture.* Cambridge: Academic Press.

Bourdieu, P. 1992. *The Logic of Practice Polity*. London.

Breman, J. 1974. *Patronage and Exploitation: Changing Agrarian Relations in South Gujarat*. London: University of California.

Chambers, R. Longhurst, R. & Pacey, A., eds. 1981. *Seasonal Dimensions to Rural Poverty*. London: Frances Pinter.

Eisenstadt, S.N. & Roniger, L. 1984. *Patrons, Clients and Friends: Interpersonal Relations and the Structure of Trust in Society*. London; Cambridge University Press.

Firth, R. & Yamey, B.S., eds. 1964. *Capital, Savings and Credit in Peasant Societies*. London: Allen & Unwin.

Geertz, C. 1963. *Peddlers and Princes*. London: University of Chicago.

Grindle, M.S. ed. 1980. *Politics and Policy Implementation in the Third World.* New Jersey: Princeton University Press.

Jansen, E. 1986. *Competition for Scarce Resources*. London: Norwegian University Press.

Li Causi, L. 1975. Anthropology and Ideology: The Case of 'Patronage' in Mediterranean Societies. *Critique of Anthropology* 4(5): 90-109.

McGregor, J.A. 1989a. Boro Gafur and Choto Gafur: Development Interventions and Indigenous Institutions. *Journal of Social Studies* (Dhaka) (43): 39-51.

———.1989b. Towards a Better Understanding of Credit in Rural Development. *Journal of International Development* 1(4):467-486.

McKinnon, R.I. 1973. *Money and Capital in Economic Development.* Washington: Brookings Institute.

von Pischke, J.D. et al, eds. 1983. *Rural Financial Markets in Developing Countries*. Baltimore: John Hopkins University Press.

Popkin, S. 1979. *The Rational Peasant: The Political Economy of Rural Society in Viet Nam*. London: University of California Press.

Raikes, P. 1988. *Modernising Hunger*. London: CIIR/James Currey/ Heinemann.

Schmidt, S.W. Scott, J.C. Lande, C. & Guasti, L., eds. 1977. *Friends, Followers and Factions: A Reader in Political Clientelism*. London: University of California.

Scott, J.C. 1976. *The Moral Economy of the Peasant*. London: Yale University Press.

Sen, A.K. 1981. *Poverty and Famines*. Oxford: Clarendon Press.

Shaw, E.S. 1973. *Financial Deepening in Economic Development*. London: Oxford University Press.

Stiglitz, J.E. 1986. The New Development Economics. *World Development* (14): 257-265.

Swift, J. 1989. Why are Rural Poor People Vulnerable to Famine? *IDS Bulletin* 20(2): 8-15.

World Bank. 1989. *World Development Report: Financial Systems and Development.* London: Oxford University Press.

12

Time And Money In The Western Sahel: A Clash Of Cultures In Gambian Rural Finance

Parker Shipton

When Benjamin Franklin wrote, "Remember that time is money," in his "Advice to a Young Tradesman" in 1748, he revealed starkly a cultural assumption common to northern Europe and North America.[1] He continued, "Remember that credit is money..." and "Money can beget money," summing up a way of thinking that Max Weber, a century and a half later, would call a hallmark of the Protestant ethic. It is conventional in northern countries to conceive of interest charges on loans in terms of rates per unit of time, and to distinguish fair moneylending from usury in terms of such rates. So embedded is this way of thinking that savings banks advertise six percent interest, for instance, without needing to add that this is an annualized rate. Both borrower and lender take it for granted that the rate of interest to be paid will depend on the time elapsed between loan and repayment, or between deposit and withdrawal. They assume, moreover, that the base interest rate is linear--six percent after one year, 12 percent after two; nothing could be more natural. It is the rate, not the ratio of interest to principal, or just the amount finally paid, that determines whether the interest charge is fair.

Why might the young tradesman have forgotten that time is money? Does anyone think differently? Evidence from research in rural areas of The Gambia suggests that some in West Africa do.[2] Among farmers and traders there, calculation of interest as "rates" per unit of time is only one of a range of conventional modes of thought about it, and certainly not the most common. Whether this mode or some other applies may depend on the borrowers' and lenders' identities, their relatedness, their familiarity, their circumstances, and the forms the loan and repayment take, among other things.

The argument is not that rural Gambians cannot conceive of interest in terms of a linear rate, or that they never entertain such thoughts. Many can and do.[3] Nor, conversely, could one sensibly argue that American or English bank customers pay no attention to the absolute amounts they gain or lose as interest, or to the ratios between principal and interest when they finally withdraw their savings or repay their loans. The findings suggest, rather, that the tendencies and the preferences of time-money construction can differ between one culture and another. These are not differences of mental capability, but of idiom and convention. British-based national moneylending laws in force in The Gambia are based on assumptions that are fundamentally different from the rules of Islamic law and custom that pervade the countryside. The differences are far more complex than "interest versus no interest;" and the overlaps of European, Middle Eastern, and African cultural codes leave much room for local debate and uncertainty about what is correct behavior in rural finance. The personal and contextual dimension renders meaningless a conventional notion of "market interest rates." In The Gambia a financial market--the persons and transactions involved in borrowing and lending money or related commodities--is segmented or fragmented, and even the concept of a "market" fits rural Sahelian financial systems only up to a point.

Nor can a simple concept like reducing "transaction costs," as discussed elsewhere in this volume and as used in a broader literature on institutional economics, adequately capture the reasoning behind rural Gambians' individual or collective decisions about entrustments and obligations. Transactions have benefits as well as costs, and both of these can take many forms and flavors. Where relationships are multi-stranded, and economy itself only one of many dimensions a tie between humans may embody (others being political, religious, psychological, or even aesthetic, for instance), the concepts of costs and benefits themselves can seem reductionist and straightjacketing. It is not that they cannot be applied, for here as anywhere, these concepts and the concept of "institutions" may indeed help in analyzing financial and other economic risks and rewards. But west Sahelian social ties, sometimes convoluted and long-standing, often have many dimensions at once. Here distinct cultural traditions are in play simultaneously, as in the Gambian case where European, Arab-Islamic, and indigenous West African understandings of propriety and profitability, or of censure and sin, intermingle without really melting together. Here the language of "institutions" and "transaction costs and benefits" can no more fully describe the motives and meanings in the relationships concerned than can a black and white picture do justice to the brilliant silkwear in a Gambian marketplace or Friday mosque.[4]

Gambian Rural Society and Economy

The Gambia, a former British colony and officially English-speaking, is surrounded by Senegal (a former French colony and officially French-speaking) except for a short coastline on the western side. Essentially a narrow strip of land on both sides of the winding lower Gambia River, the country was affected by trade with Britain beginning in the late sixteenth century, and heavy slaving up to the abolition in 1874. The country has a long and complex history of trade over long and short distances. The Gambia was hotly contested by European imperial powers during the early part of its British colonial rule (and intermittent company jurisdiction in the early years) from 1588 to its independence in 1965. Today, in a different way, a lively cross-border commerce of persons and things, legal and illegal, qualifies The Gambia's separate identity.

Ethnically, The Gambia has a rich mixture (in decreasing order of size) of Mandinko, Fula (subgroup of Fulani or Peul), Wolof, Jola (also spelled Diola), Serahuli (or Serakhole, elsewhere commonly called Soninke), and other ethnic groups including Mauritanian Moorish and (now only urban) Lebanese trading minorities. Because several of these groups are also represented in Senegal and other neighboring countries, The Gambia shows in some ways a cross-section of a larger region of the western end of Africa. Within the country, ethnic group distributions do not correspond closely to national administrative units (which, largest to smallest, are divisions, districts, and villages). Rural Gambians live in nucleated villages with fields surrounding them. Many of the villages are multi-ethnic, though some have ethnically more homogeneous neighborhoods within them. Nearly all villages in the country are connected by some sort of road to The Gambia's two main highways. Each village has a headman and usually a woman who heads a women's or senior women's association. Nearly all the country's ethnic groups are strongly patrilineal in most respects, and village endogamy (in-marriage) is common though not universal. Broad age grades correspond with village associations and voluntary groups (*kafo or kafoo* groups, in Mandinka). Most Gambian ethnic groups are also notable for endogamous castes and subcastes (e.g. "freeborn" or *alkalo*, headman, or farmer; craftsperson [metalworker, woodworker, or leatherworker]; *griot* [oral historian, musician, or praise-singer], and dependent or "slave"). While these statuses structure rural marriage choices and some other social and economic relations, they do not necessarily correspond closely with individuals' actual occupations or basic livelihoods.

The country's population, enumerated at 751,000 people (1985), about 80 percent of them now rural at any time, lived at an average density of about 172 per square mile in a total land area of 4,361 square miles (somewhat smaller than Connecticut). Rural land shortage is just now becoming a concern as farmers grow their coarse grains (millet, sorghum, maize), their groundnuts, sometimes their rice, and other crops with new tools including ox-ploughs; as livestock grazing challenges the country's sparse woodlands; and as soil quality, never high, deteriorates. The country relies on a single rainy season, usually from June to October, and on seasonal migrant laborers ("strange farmers") from Senegal, Mali, and Guinea.

By conventional economic standards, including per capita gross domestic product (GDP), The Gambia is one of the poorest countries in Africa and one of the dozen poorest in the world.[5] This remains so despite a dramatic economic reform program in the 1980s, a liberalization and structural adjustment program designed and implemented by the Ministry of Finance, the International Monetary Fund (IMF), and the World Bank, that is generally considered to have stimulated trade and at least some kinds of investment.[6] The country remains heavily dependent on its main agricultural export crop, groundnuts, on fish, and on its entrepot trade for its foreign exchange; and it imports rice, some as foreign aid, to supplement its own production of that rural staple and of millet and maize and other crops.[7]

These conditions of long exposure to travel and trade, a rich mixture of religious and linguistic influences, and secularly deteriorating material and economic environments characterize all the largest ethnic groups of The Gambia and southern Senegal. Their shared circumstances and frequent comingling can allow some kinds of guarded general statements about rural Gambians, but in many of these the Jola peoples would require separate treatment because of their rather unique settlement patterns and agricultural economy, with its relatively heavy emphasis on wet rice growing, and because of strong resistance to Islamic and Mandinka influence in the histories of many Jola communities.[8] Exceptional, too, are the people living on irrigation schemes like the Jahally-Pachar project, whose somewhat steadier (if inadequate) incomes give their annual economic cycle a different profile. Most of the description to follow refers more specifically to dryland farming people among the largest three groups, the Mandinko, Fula, and Wolof.[9]

Formal Financial Institutions and Their Relevance

Rural institutional finance in The Gambia revolves around the groundnut trade, reflecting the main foreign interests in Gambian farming.[10] Several large international and domestic trading firms operate in the capital Banjul, and (decreasingly in recent years) in the countryside.[11] Over the past two decades, state-controlled producer cooperatives for input supply and marketing, under the Banjul-based Gambia Co-operatives Union (GCU), have practically displaced them in the groundnut trade and related lending to farmers, becoming ubiquitous in the countryside with up to eighty-six primary-level societies ("seccos") in the late 1980s. These units cover areas not based on any indigenous social entities, being larger than villages but smaller than districts. Repayment rates are poor, by world standards, and the co-operatives have consistently run at a deficit at government expense.

The expansion of the cooperatives has been an issue hotly debated by foreign aid agents, many of whom now consider their workings corrupt and inefficient; the World Bank and IMF have recently been trying to "reliberalize" the country's groundnut trade by policy measures and stricter financial controls on the co-ops, resulting in the recent closure or merging of about a third of the primary societies. The co-operatives were instructed in 1987-88 to charge an annual interest rate of 26 percent for farm input loans issued in cash or kind. Their rates have sometimes been positive and sometimes negative in real terms, but never high enough to keep the cooperatives solvent.[12] The rates are lower than private traders normally offer, though few farmers know the official figure, and many doubt the honesty of the weighers and clerks (as with the private groundnut traders). Some men borrow from the cooperatives and relend to their wives or foreign migrant share tenants; and some add their own interest charges, even for their wives. Farmers are ambivalent about the cooperatives: although they mistrust them they nonetheless feel dependent on them. Banks are almost insignificant in rural areas. They include two international commercial banks, the British-run Standard Bank and the Meridian Bank (which bought the government-owned Gambia Commercial and Development Bank, GCDB, in 1991-2), and the post office savings bank. All the institutions have interest policies based on annual rates, until lately regulated by the Central Bank of The Gambia: in 1987, 22 percent to 29 percent for bank loans; 15 percent for commercial bank savings and 15 percent for post office savings.[13] Few farmers, and almost none of the women, know these rates. To most rural Gambians, these institutions remain rather exotic, and most, particularly the banks, are not fully trusted. Outside Banjul and nearby Serrekunda and Bakao, commercial bank branches were found, by the time of research, in only two towns, Farafeni and Basse. Few farmers without major off-farm incomes use the formal banking system, as discussed later.[14]

Quickly entering the picture by the late 1980s, with a well-established local foundation of good will, were several foreign-based private voluntary organizations, including Action Aid, Catholic Relief Services, Freedom from Hunger Campaign, and Save the Children. All have lately tried to turn away from "relief" toward "development" efforts, especially promoting small enterprises. Most are experimenting with credit and, to a lesser extent, savings. The indigenously run but foreign-sponsored Gambia Women's Finance Company has tried to organize banking facilities for women, as have a few other small indigenous and foreign groups. The expertise of the banks in money management and the public goodwill and trust of the private voluntary organizations have yet to be allied. Until they are, rural Gambians will prefer to organize their own systems of saving and credit. What are they?

How Rural Gambians Save

Gambians save most of their wealth in non-monetary forms, a point foreigners are apt to misunderstand.[15] Much of it they keep in the forms of livestock (large stock are particularly important for men), and gold earrings and other jewelry that smiths can expand with new metal (particularly important for women). These are forms the sexes use to safeguard their wealth from each other's daily demands, among other things. Savings also take the forms of stored crops, farm machinery, household furniture, radios, and other goods likely to be resold in rural villages. The main saving strategy of rural Gambians is to remove wealth from the form of liquid cash, and the game is to remove it from the constant claims of relatives and neighbors without appearing selfish. Gambians prefer to save in animals--cattle, donkeys and horses for men, and sheep and goats for both men and women--partly because they breed.[16] Time is livestock, perhaps more than it is money; and the *Qur'an* (or Koran) does not forbid this kind of "interest."

Stored crops and seeds are an important form of saving, but not an ideal one, from the saver's perspective, since their divisibility makes them subject to demands for charity and loans from family granaries. Hence the locked crop stores in many villages, to which only one or two village leaders hold the keys. Farmers who sell food crops tend to do so just after harvest. They recognize that withholding crop sales until the scarce season, when prices rise, can yield them more cash. But few feel they can afford to wait, and needy relatives' demands make it hard to sell food in the scarce season rather than sharing it. A few of the best-off farmers speculate in foods, buying neighbors' crops and selling them back similar foods later in the season at higher prices.[17]

To the extent that cash is saved, it is saved mainly by "informal" means within villages. These are many. One of the oldest means is burial, which, with paper money, cuts out risks of loss in house fires as well as those of theft. For saving at home, one of the simplest ways is the wooden *kondem* ("condemned") box (or *kondaneh,* from the French *condamnée*), which rural people paid five or six *dalasis* in 1987-8 (6.9 Gambian *dalasis* = $1 U.S. then) for a carpenter to construct, with a small slot. The box must be broken to be opened, rather like an American piggy-bank.[18] Some use locked suitcases or trunks.

Another widely-used strategy is the money-keeper.[19] Some rural Gambians (about 34 percent in the twelve months preceding my 1987 survey) had given money to other villagers (7 percent), often trusted relatives or solvent shopkeepers, to hold for them. Sums deposited ranged from 25 to 2,000 *dalasis*; but over 80 percent of the deposits were below 500. Some 95 percent of the deposits were for periods of less than one year; most were for no longer than three months. Interest payments or service charges are unheard of in this money-keeping, and the saver often expects to receive back the same notes or coins left off.

A related way of saving, for wage earners, is to ask employers to withhold wages over short times to let them accumulate. Gambian share contractors, too, prefer arrangements in which they receive their main compensation seasonally rather than at shorter intervals (see Robertson 1987, 221).

Village women's and men's groups are being increasingly recognized, both by insiders and outsiders, as valuable for raising capital. Some women, in towns and increasingly in the rural villages, form rotating savings and credit associations (or ROSCAS, also known along the West African coast as *osusu* or *esusu* groups, from the Yoruba, or as *tontines*, from the French) to mobilize savings for personal or household purchases.[20] In each of a series of regularly scheduled meetings, all members contribute a fixed amount and one takes home the lot. Each member takes a turn until the cycle is completed; whereupon it may or may not start again. Among the many advantages of this system to members is that it allows them to save without appearing antisocial.[21] Another advantage is that the groups keep the money circulating in a community.

All these local savings mechanisms in The Gambia are interest free. Indeed, when inflation (12.5 percent in 1987-88) is taken into account, nearly all represent negative real interest.[22] Gambians are thus willing to pay to remove their cash from their own individual hands: evidence of an illiquidity preference if such thinking is to be reduced to "preferences." The many Gambians who use these boxes want their money accessible in emergencies, but not just grabbable from day to day. Time erodes money, and it erodes it most quickly in one's own pocket.

Problems with Banking

Obviously, the large majority of Gambians who save their cash at home or with money-keepers forego the interest they might earn in banks or other financial institutions (lately 15 percent). A 1975-6 survey of rural Gambian villages found that only two percent of 94 informants had bank savings (Dunsmore et al. 1976, 307). In my 1987 survey, three percent of 138 male and female informants stated they had deposits in commercial banks, and three percent more in post office savings. Only one of 69 women interviewed had either kind of account. Branch bank information confirmed that most farmer depositors held amounts below about 250 *dalasis*, that very few of them were women, and that almost no farmers borrow from banks.[23]

When asked about their reasons for not using banks, farmers in the villages surveyed cited several: distance, inconvenient banking hours, minimum deposit rules, difficult paperwork, and distrust of clerks.[24] Some cited with bitterness their losses in the collapse of the Agricultural Development Bank in the early 1980s. A few, including Mauritanian shopkeepers, stated that they avoided banks because of Islamic prohibitions on charging interest, but since some of these merchants do charge interest in informal lending, this answer should probably not be taken at face value.

Though few use banks now, most farmers interviewed liked the idea that small branch banks should be established, or mobile banks tried or retried, in their areas.[25] A problem in The Gambia, as in some other countries dependent on rainfed agriculture, concerns the seasonal covariance of incomes. A savings bank has stronger financial incentives to stay open or make the rounds in the "trade season," when farmers have significant sums to deposit, than during the rest of the year, when farmers are more interested in withdrawals. But inaccessibility has clearly been a major barrier to institutional savings. Here, "time is money" acquires another meaning. Whether in the "trade season," when farmers would be most likely to deposit, or in the hungry season that is also the busy weeding season, when they would be most likely to withdraw, time is valuable. The time required to obtain identification photos, to travel to the banks, to wait for them to open, to queue, and to wait for countersignatures all carries transaction costs for rural people living far away from banks.

Sources of "Informal" Credit

Gambians do not share the Euro-American concept of "loan" as a single idea covering all types of exchanges for delayed compensation.[26] In the Mandinka language, for instance, there is a sharp division between *furo*, to make a helping loan of, say, tools or clothes, to be returned in a few days; and, on the other hand, *ndontoro*, to make a business loan, normally longer-term and carrying an interest charge. Whether 20 percent, 40 percent, or 80 percent of the rural economy takes the form of "loans" depends on how one asks the questions, and in how many different ways.

The Easiest Loans: Kin and Friends

It is to relatives that farmers or small businesspeople tend to turn first when they wish to borrow. Reasons for the preferences may variously include the lenders' proximity and persuadability, the unlikelihood of interest charges, and the chances of leniency in the event of nonrepayment. Kin lend all kinds of goods and services, including foods, cash, labor, and farm inputs; and the smallest and biggest debts in life are likely to be incurred between relatives. Extended family members sometimes sell their livestock to lend large amounts of money--thousands of *dalasis*--to a promising young man to send him abroad for schooling, work, or both, as an investment in his future remittances and contacts.

Marriage entails some of the largest savings and debts that rural Gambians accumulate in their lives. Bridewealth payments from the groom's to the bride's family are commonly made on the "installment plan," often taking a decade or more to complete.[27] A bride's family is likely to have saved for many years for earrings and other jewelry to give her upon her marriage.

Loans between nonrelatives also involve an enormous variety of goods and services, on widely varying repayment schedules, but rural cash loans, in the late 1980s, only seldom rose above a few hundred *dalasis* in value. Between unrelated borrowers and lenders, small interest charges may be made--often about five to ten percent over six months--though these arrangements too vary greatly.

Loan seekers lacking kin ties to invoke usually lean on village ties and other kinds of social commonality, notably age-grade and age-set, caste, ethnicity, and school ties from government or local Qur'anic schools.[28] Among friends and neighbors, and among kin, no guarantees or collateral are used to secure loans--confidence usually relies on the threat of refusing future loans or the possibility of involving mutual acquaintances as third parties--and debts may be cancelled upon crop failures.

In The Gambia, land, labor, livestock, and farm implements are all directly exchangeable for each other at local levels by an infinity of ad hoc, unnamed, and individually tailored arrangements, many of which take the form of short-term loans and counterloans. Most often, these occur between close neighbors, who may also be close kin. But agricultural exchange partnerships also occur between seasonal migrants and their hosts, often unrelated; land and lodging are given in exchange for labor, the details varying according to farmers' and migrants' circumstances.[29]

Harder Bargains: Local Shopkeepers and Other Merchants

It is usually only in the absence of other kin, friends, or neighbors with disposable assets that farmers or other rural people will turn to unrelated merchants (in Mandinka, *juloo*; in Pulaar and Wolof, *julaba*) for loans. Their terms are stiffer. Interest charges are much more likely to be imposed, and will probably be higher. The forms of the loan and repayment are likely to be more strictly specified, repayment periods may be shorter, and a defaulter might be prosecuted. But traders' possession of liquid capital makes them an important source of credit for rural people throughout the country.

While the major lending merchants in the villages and small towns are usually shopkeepers, many small-scale and seasonal traders, most of them at least part-time farmers, also lend from their houses without special shops. The Gambia does not have an institution of specialized rural moneylenders or moneylender-landlords comparable to those found in parts of southern Asia.[30]

In addition to money, shopkeepers and other merchants commonly lend household goods like rice, sugar, coarse grains, cooking oil, and some durables. They may lend groundnut or other seeds, but almost never fertilizers or farm implements. Merchant loans vary in duration from a few hours to a year, or occasionally longer. The largest loans these lenders offer are expected to be repaid at the time of the main groundnut harvest around December or January.

In choosing a merchant for a loan, the farmer will usually rely, again, on depth of acquaintance and ties of ethnicity, village coresidence, age-set, and similar ties. The roughly 1,000 Mauritanians and the eastern Gambian Serahuli and increasingly the Fula as well have established reputations as rural merchants.[31] But shopkeepers appear at least as often to come from the majority groups of their villages or towns as from minorities. Many Gambians have clear preferences on the ethnic groups from whose members they might borrow.

Relations between members of a local majority and minority traders are ambivalent and complex. Farmers depend heavily on the latter for capital and goods in times of need, but at the same time they resent the traders' wealth and what they may perceive as insularity. The common Mandinka term for a small-scale trader or for a loan, *juloo*, also means rope, and Gambians speak of having debts tied around their necks with well-understood connotations of slavery. Particularly resented are Mauritanian traders, who repatriate profits from their sales and loans and return periodically to their home country, and who do not normally intermarry with Gambians.[32] Gambian institutions do not normally give Mauritanian traders financial or other assistance. The hostility behind the violent 1989 popular expulsions of Arabic-speaking Mauritanian traders from Senegal (and the reported temporary emigrations, less important, of some from The Gambia) reveal the ethnic and class tensions underlying daily trade relations in the villages. The Mauritanian migrants' families rely on their remittances for a part of their livelihood in their more desolate Saharan country.

It appears to be poorer villagers who must borrow most commonly from local or immigrant shopkeepers, and lending is liveliest after poor harvests. Richer farmers rely more on their own means, on kin or neighborly lenders, or on institutions to which they have privileged access. Of course, merchants' high interest charges can impoverish their borrowers in a vicious circle.[33] And they lend their clients not only staples, but also fancier consumer goods.

Village and town merchants lend to farmers only on the basis of personal acquaintance, on request of a trusted go-between, or on the strength of kinship and friendship ties that will be invokable for recovery, as ties sometimes are between residents of neighboring villages. Loans may be issued without written agreements, though literate merchants do keep records of loans issued. To lend relatively large amounts to near-strangers, the lenders may insist on witnesses or written agreements. Collateral or loan guarantees are not normally taken. Instead lenders rely heavily on informal social sanctions; they can dishonor their borrowers and damage their informal local "credit rating" by pursuing them visibly. In cases of obvious hardship, as when the borrower's pledged crop fails, merchants and other local lenders normally defer collection until the following harvest season, with or without charging further accrued interest.

When personal and social pressures fail, merchant creditors frequently resort to local legal authorities to back up their claims. Debt cases are among the most common kinds of cases arising in civil law, and the courts usually favor creditors, but they do not knowingly uphold substantial interest charges. Lenders who charge interest and who wish to sue defaulters in court must weigh the risk of being exposed and stigmatized as usurers.

Default rates on merchants' loans are always hard to gauge, but some lenders suggest that about 10 percent of their loans are ultimately unrecoverable. In local lending, whether between merchants and villagers, or between friends or kin, loans not repaid after two or three years are normally left as dead. This is, incidentally, what the *Qur'an* instructs lenders to do--a point that may bear also on institutional lenders.[34]

Private Groundnut Traders as Lenders

Private groundnut traders compete with the state-controlled cooperatives in lending to farmers and marketing their groundnuts. The largest are based in Banjul and deal through agents in market towns. The private traders' share of the groundnut market has fallen from 84 percent in 1962-63 to 19 percent in 1985-86, and most of the largest have abandoned the commodity because of the expansion of the cooperatives, though international funders and the government have lately tried to reverse the trend by cutting special allowances and discounts favoring the cooperatives.[35] A balanced system of public and private lenders in competition with each other has so far remained elusive.

Seasonal migrant share-tenants from neighboring countries finance groundnut inputs by borrowing indirectly, through their land patrons, from the cooperatives or private traders as they can; and the patrons pass on interest charges, perhaps at times adding their own.

Small Business Credit

Merchants lend cash and merchandise to other merchants, sometimes on very short terms, and this kind of credit, often following kinship ties, is how most small rural businesses in The Gambia appear to get started. On a larger scale, wholesalers and retailers in the provincial towns also borrow rice, sugar, and other merchandise from large Banjul wholesalers, sometimes indirectly through these large merchants' rural agents. Confidence built on long-term acquaintance and customer loyalty, if not also on kinship, is essential in these arrangements. The interest charges that urban wholesalers demand from provincial traders, often about five to ten percent over six months, are much lower than those the latter charge their rural borrowers in turn, perhaps because the risks of default are smaller.[36]

Institutional credit has been far less important than informal credit in the establishment of small businesses. The government does have an agency to help arrange bank loans for small businesses, however, and private voluntary organizations are now entering the enterprise development field in The Gambia as elsewhere.[37]

Interest Charges in Informal Credit

To foreign observers, the rates of interest that private rural lenders in West Africa charge often appear extortionate, and those found in The Gambia are no exception. Gambian merchants and other rural lenders commonly charge interest of 50 to 150 percent over six to eight months, but rates vary enormously outside this range.[38] The wide variation may result in part from the secrecy surrounding interest charges. Not only is it common for researchers to receive inaccurate reports, but there are also uncertainties and disagreements in the rural population itself as to what rates are conventional.

Before judging the appropriateness or fairness of the seemingly high charges, many factors must be taken into account: (1) *Inflation.* A loan at five percent interest in a year of ten percent inflation is a loan with a negative real rate of interest. (2) *The likelihood of default.* A lender who lends at 20 percent interest to borrowers whose probability of default is ten percent can count on only an eight percent nominal profit. High interest may be considered in part a risk premium. (3) *The opportunity cost of capital.* Are there more profitable uses, like shop re-stocking, to which the lender might alternatively put the resources? (4) "*Administration costs*" (if any) and "overhead," and the bothers associated. How much time and money will the lender spend pursuing borrowers in arrears, or checking produce received as repayments? (5) *Seasonality.* A sack of groundnuts lent as seed during planting time or as food during the hungry season is worth more in the rural community, in terms of either use value or exchange value, than a sack of equal weight in January just after harvest.

The last seasonal dimension is particularly important in The Gambia, where most rural economic activity involving money revolves around the one annual groundnut harvest, and where, six months later, both food and money to buy it are everywhere short. To borrow in the scarce season and repay the same amount at harvest time is not considered an equitable deal. It would be rather as if a desert traveler said to a companion, "Lend me a glass of water now, and I'll give you one back when we get to the river." In the western Sahel, poverty, wealth, and fair lending are all seasonally defined.

Not Just a Financial System

This discussion of rural lenders has suggested that their lending terms depend on the social distance between them and their borrowers, and on a variety of other circumstantial factors. The secretive nature of informal borrowing and lending in The Gambia, and the variability of the terms on which it occurs--in interest charges, repayment schedules, and other terms--mean that rural credit cannot easily be described as a "market" in the conventional sense of the word, with free information and readily identifiable prices based on supply and demand. Nor can the terms of lending, even at rates over 100 percent per annum, be summarily labeled fair or unfair.

In the following sections we examine some international influences on informal rural credit, considering first the role of Islamic law and then the role of colonially imposed British law. The relation of time and money in interest charges appears in these pages as a focal point of cultural clashes and misunderstandings.

Some of the differences stem from literacy. Gambian and many other local African traditions have historically differed from some of the great traditions of Islam, on the one hand, and from European financial custom on the other, in that loan contracts have been oral, not written. Their enforcement has often depended on multiple witnesses, and thus on continued good community relations and citizenship, since a borrower or lender who misbehaves may find that his or her witnesses have evaporated, or have permuted their stories over time. The renegotiability of oral contracts allows some flexibility to accommodate changing personal or family circumstances. Written contracts change the rules. Witnesses become less necessary, and so do the good behavior and favors or payments once needed to keep or gain their support.[39]

Rules are still invoked and manipulated, however, and after several centuries of Islamic and colonial influence, borrowers or lenders have several sets of rules by which to operate. The codes of behavior differ most profoundly in the underlying ideas about interest--especially with regard to the varying distinctions between fair lending and usury.

Islam and Rural Financial Custom

Islam in Gambian Economic Life

Some 85 to 95 percent of Gambians now participate at least nominally in Islam, which, since its appearance in the country in the fourteenth or fifteenth century, has waxed and waned in influence, affecting not just religious belief but culture and economy more broadly.[40] The *Qadiri* and *Tijani* strains of Islam found locally also touch large parts of several neighboring countries, including Senegal. Most Gambians and seasonal immigrants combine Islamic with local religious and social practice and belief.[41] But Muslims in The Gambia, as elsewhere, like to conceive of their religion as influencing all aspects of life, rather than as being confined to particular times, places, or activities. Scriptural and oral Islamic teaching has something to say about trading, saving, spending, sharing, borrowing, lending, and investing; and many aspects of these activities are encoded in the *shari'a*, the sacred Law of Islam embodying ethical rules. Law, economics, and religion are so deeply intertwined in Islamic life that they cannot be understood separately: the sacred and secular merge.

Nearly every Gambian village has one or more Muslim *imams* (mosque and prayer leaders), who may serve at times as moral counselors on practical matters and as redistributive nodes of tithes and charities. Many also have *marabouts*--a blanket term covering various kinds of holy men and mystics, who may also be Qur'anic teachers, legal experts, diviners, healers, magicians, and combinations of these--who differently combine Islamic and local religious traditions.[42] So *marabouts* are major players in local economic affairs, though the Gambian ones tend not to be organized into politically powerful brotherhoods like some Senegalese ones. Gambians tend to practice almsgiving (*zakāt in Arabic*, *jako* in Mandinka), fasting, and feasting and ceremony as prescribed by the *Qur'an* and scriptural exegesis, sometimes with their own modifications. Arab countries have financed aid projects providing many Gambian villages with wells, mosques, and other constructions. Local branches of pan-African and pan-Arab educational and social institutions provide scholarships for study abroad and help organize pilgrimages to Mecca. Islam influences local financial matters profoundly across the country. So does the Arabic language, taught along with Islam in local *Qur'an* schools. Probably more rural Gambians can read and write Arabic than English or their own tongues. Written records of loan transactions, where they exist, are as likely to be kept in Arabic as in English. It is in Arabic that some of the most important concepts in financial life are expressed.

Interest and Usury in Islamic Law

Some Gambian practices and concepts concerning interest charges differ radically from those familiar to many foreign financiers, and the failure of outsiders to take into account these differences is a frequent source of misunderstanding. Rural credit and savings in The Gambia cannot be understood without noting a few basic tenets of Islamic law and custom. As noted above, the vast majority of Gambians are at least nominally Muslims, and Qur'anic interpretations have profoundly influenced both financial systems and the legal systems that enforce them.

The *Qur'an* explicitly forbids usury, repeatedly promising damnation for those who practice it (though it condones profitable trade). Noteworthy among others are these verses of Part III, Sura II, "The Cow."[43]

> Verses 275-6: Those who swallow [charge] usury cannot rise up save as he ariseth whom the devil has prostrated by (his) touch. That is because they say: Trade is just like usury: whereas Allah permitteth trade and forbiddeth usury...As for him who [refraineth and] returneth [to usury] -- Such are rightful owners of the Fire. They will abideth therein. Allah hath blighted usury...
>
> Verse 282: O Ye who believe! When ye contract a debt for a fixed term, record it in writing. Let a scribe record it in writing between you in (terms of) equity. (Pickthall translation).

Elsewhere the Sura of "The Cow" states:

> It shall be no offence for you to seek the bounty of your Lord by trading... Those that live on usury shall rise up before Allah like men whom Satan has demented by his touch; for they claim that usury is like trading. But Allah has permitted trading and forbidden usury. (Dawood translation, 344, 354.)

Memorized from the *Qur'an* in the elementary local religious instruction of which children in almost every village partake, the lessons are reinforced, explicated, and elaborated for the small minority who continue to higher training, in written and oral exegesis.

Like other Muslims from West Africa to Indonesia, Gambians refer to usury by the Arabic term *ribā*, meaning unjustified enrichment, or consumption at the expense of others for no good reason.[44] Many consider *ribā* a sin second only to murder.[45] "Dirty money" from *ribā* (in Mandinka, *kodi jawo*, bad money, or *haaramoo,* forbidden or ill-gotten gains) may not be used for pilgrimages to Mecca, for charities or religious feasts, for funerals, or for other holy expenditures.[46] Nor does *ribā* refer only to money; interest-bearing loans in kind are also sinful. These rewards are dangerous. "Eating" or consuming the rewards of usury will give the lender a swollen belly, as one young Fula man explained his understanding of it, and ultimately vultures will pull out the lender's intestines.[47]

To many Gambian Muslims who interpret holy scripture strictly, the prohibition refers to any charges that could be considered interest. To others, usury simply means any interest charges they deem unfairly high. The key term that recurs in the scriptures is "doubling." There is much debate in The Gambia about whether the prohibition is absolute or leaves scope for lesser charges. Many Gambians will say that even one percent profit earned by loan interest is more sinful than 100 percent earned by trade.[48] For many others, however, the ideal and real practice seem to differ; lending at interest goes on all the time.

Interest Rates and Ratios: When Time Is Money and When Not

What interest charges are accepted? A crucial point is that the *Qur'an* discusses usury in terms of the relation between the amount lent and the amount repaid, but not in terms of the amount of time elapsing between the loan and repayment.[49] This means that even if a low rate of interest is charged per month or year, it can eventually add up to an absolute amount that is considered usurious. What matters to rural Gambians is not so much the rate of interest per unit of time as the ratio of interest to principal. As a district chief explained it, his court might find a loan at ten percent interest over a year acceptable, but it would never consider a loan at ten percent annual interest over ten years acceptable, because that would be doubling. Moreover, he said, even a loan at two percent annual interest over fifty years would be unacceptable, for this too would be doubling.[50]

From this principle follow several others fundamental to Gambian financial custom. One is that the duration of loans is usually kept as short as possible, for the lender's sake if not also for the borrower's.[51] Loans of cash, seeds, food, or other consumer goods are rarely if ever issued for periods exceeding one year, and most are lent for not longer than seven months. For small household goods, as noted previously, loans of only a few days are common.

Preferences for short-term lending seem to militate against local credit sales of large, nondivisible goods, including animal-drawn and engine-driven farm machinery. These goods are simply not available to farmers to purchase by installment or other credit arrangements, except occasionally from the cooperatives. Farmers certainly perceive this as a gap to be filled. Development planners may see it this way too, but they should also realize that medium-term or long-term loans accruing high absolute interest will cause resentments which might lead to deliberate nonrepayment.

In informal lending in rural Gambia, interest is not necessarily assumed to accrue at a constant rate, month by month, as it does in a European bank account. Instead, charges are geared to the agricultural cycle. A lender who lends one sack of rice to an impoverished farmer early in June, at the start of the hungry season, demanding two in return at the December harvest time (in defiance of Qur'anic law), will also lend one sack for two to another borrower who needs a sack in September, even though the two borrowers are expected to repay at the same time. When asked about such cases, farmers insist that the lender is following the same policy for both. So a three-month loan often carries the same actual interest charge as the six-month loan (one sack, or 100 percent interest). If time is money, it sometimes comes only in large denominations.

Gambian farmers, then, do not always think of interest in terms of annualized rates. They repay seasonal loans at harvest time if they are willing and able to do so; otherwise they wait until the subsequent harvest. They are thus more accustomed to thinking of loan durations in terms of six or eighteen month periods than in terms of twelve-month periods. After the end of a harvest season, interest on an unrepaid loan may be expected to jump to its double on the expectation that it will not be repaid until the following year's harvest. It accrues stepwise, jumping year by year.

But at least as often, no further interest will be charged after the first year. The lender simply agrees to defer collecting the principal and the initial interest until the following harvest, then collects the same sum. The interest-time function turns flatly horizontal. Rural groundnut seed lenders charging 100 percent on six-month loans sometimes demand further accrued interest after the harvest season; others do not. Shopkeepers sometimes sell items like cigarettes on credit for 100 percent interest within the month (as for buyers who may have monthly salaries or remittances). But these loans do not simply keep piling up interest if unpaid. It makes little sense to think of them in terms of a 1,200 percent annual rate, and no one does.

As these various patterns suggest, linear time is not taken for granted in loan arrangements. Rather, there are at least several modes or idioms, temporal or atemporal, linear or non-linear, for constructing agreements. Which will be chosen is negotiable, if not at the time of the deal, then in renegotiation later. In rural Gambia, time is an optative element.

This variable conception makes sense in communities where many have no major sources of cash besides annual rainfed agriculture, but where some farmers or families do have remittances, salaries, and trading incomes throughout the year. Time seems in some way to be a bracketable or detachable part of rural Gambian interest calculations, included for rates or excluded for ratios, and negotiated into or out of contracts. Flexibility is the essence of the system, and interest and usury are context-specific.

Is the time dimension becoming more deeply entrenched or more prominent in local thought about usury? This is hard to determine. Statutory law and cooperative society practice have been based heavily on the linear-time principle, and in the past two decades farmers in nearly every Gambian village have dealt with the cooperatives. Evidence from other parts of West and East Africa suggests that "informal" land pledging agreements have newly begun to incorporate time deadlines, becoming foreclosable mortgages, in crowded rural areas where competition for land has grown severe. In The Gambia, too, secular changes may be occurring in financial thinking, such that deals are being more closely linked to linear notions of time. Snapshotlike field investigation cannot track such changes well, and more longitudinal study is needed.[52]

How Lenders Conceal Interest Charges: The Commodity Switch and Other Strategies

Another practice that results from the Qur'anic prohibition of usury is that in lending for any but the shortest periods, lenders seek ways of making profits from lending without appearing to charge interest. To their borrowers and to outsiders, they may seem to be concealing or disguising interest charges. Several conventionalized dodges are found in The Gambia. These are known by the Arabic term *ḥilā* (pl. *ḥiyal*), meaning "legal device" or "evasion."[53] One way, used when written records of loans are kept, is a method one might call "double entry bookkeeping" with a new meaning: to record a loan agreement by entering only the doubled amount to be repaid, but not the amount actually lent. Lenders' books, and local court records examined on debt cases, do not mention interest charges, though of course these are standard practice in reality. Some of the strategies involve semantics: a fee for a loan is more acceptable when it is considered a gift or a service charge.

Other elaborations involve reclassifying loans as sales and resales. A wishes to lend B money, and B wishes to borrow it. A "sells" B a sack of sugar with delayed payment, and re-purchases the sack of sugar immediately, for cash, at half price. Thus B receives cash immediately, and returns its double later. The loan is disguised as two sales, and the sack of sugar need never move from the lender's shelf.

A common way of concealing loan profits is by insisting that a loan in one form be repaid in another. Loans issued in cash in June are frequently collected in groundnuts upon the December harvest, even if the borrower could easily have sold the groundnuts elsewhere for cash first to repay in cash, and even if the lender will only then sell the groundnuts to a third party for cash.[54] Even though both borrower and lender usually know well the cash values of the things borrowed and lent, the switch in the form of payments makes accusations of usury less likely. The changes in values of the two items over the course of the loan, and the fact that these changes are not fully predictable at the time the agreement is made, further obfuscate the lender's profit. All are aware that the lender is making a profit, but no one may be sure how much.

The switching practice in turn leads to interesting patterns of interest charging or profit taking in credit. In loans in which the forms of payment are switched, interest rates are usually much higher than in loans where they are not. Thus, while a 300 percent interest charge in a seasonal cash loan repaid in cash is virtually unheard of, it is common practice for shopkeepers to lend in cash 25 percent of the expected value of a bag of groundnuts, demanding the payment of a full bag upon harvest. In monetary terms, this would of course be calculated as a charge of principal plus 300 percent interest. Interest rates in cash-for-cash loans or groundnut-for-groundnut loans seldom rise above 100 percent, and in many cases are much lower. Borrowers usually know all this, of course, and they perceive that it is in their interest to make agreements to repay in the same form as they borrow. But since most credit is demand-led, lenders can generally dictate the terms and succeed in effecting a switch.

Two general conclusions follow from these observations. One is that credit analysts working in The Gambia should not assume that the same interest rates acceptable in short-term loans will also be acceptable in long-term loans. As time elapses, interest accruing at a constant rate may rise to an unacceptable ratio (of interest to principal). Accordingly, rates of interest applied to smaller scale loans may be locally considered unreasonable in larger scale loans. The second conclusion is that financiers in The Gambia should not simply record, generalize about, or set interest rates without considering both the forms in which loans are issued and the forms in which they are collected. In this area, conventional European or American modes of economic analysis may not be applicable.

Loan Forgiveness Custom: A Safety Net for Borrowers

Although rural Gambians do not always calculate interest as though time were linear and inexorable, rules and conventions about loan forgiveness in fact prevent interest from accumulating *ad infinitum* as time passes. If two or three years elapse without a repayment on a seasonal loan, the lender is usually expected to forgive the loan. (He or she will of course be wary of lending to the same borrower again.) As Gambians know, The *Qur'an* counsels lenders to give needy debters extra time, or better, to forgive their debts.[55] Villagers expect the same of governmental and other institutional lenders.[56]

Further Differentials

Some rural Gambians state that loans issued in cash should carry higher interest than loans issued in kind, other things being equal.[57] Why cash loans should be more expensive is not clear. One reason might be the opportunity cost of capital for lenders: they can use money in more ways than seednuts, for instance, and seednuts take time to sell for cash. Another reason might be that the value of cash is easier to assess than the value of groundnuts, which can vary in size or quality; and therefore a cash loan is more likely to be judged usurious. Might it also be that a kind of "spiritual risk premium" is being added into the interest charge in cash loans?

The size of loan may make a difference as well. Whether coming from kin or neighbors, relatives, or merchants, the smallest loans are often expected to be given free of interest or profit. As the quantities or values of loans rise, so may the rates of interest charged. One group of farmers indicated hypothetically that while they might expect a seasonal loan of D10 to be issued interest free, they would expect D100 to be issued at five percent interest, D1,000 (a rare loan) at ten percent and D10,000 (rarer still) at twenty percent--between the same borrower and lender, over the same period. But since the persons engaging in small and large transactions are likely to be different, these distinctions may not hold in the aggregate, and there are signs that the reverse may in fact be the case when different lenders' and borrowers' transactions are compared.[58]

The differences between the lending and borrowing habits of indigenous Gambian ethnic groups have not been thoroughly studied--this is a field ripe for further research--but there is evidence of substantial variation. Puetz and von Braun (1988, 18) have found that Wolofs charged an average of 58 percent higher interest on loans than other Gambian ethnic groups. Others have observed that village or town lenders appear to give more generous terms to wealthier borrowers and those who have saleable property (livestock, machinery) than to poorer borrowers or those who do not.[59]

Summary of Gambian Interest Practices

Informal interest charges in The Gambia depend on many things, in addition to strictly economic determinants. These include the presence and closeness of kinship and friendship ties, and the ethnic identities of the borrower and lender. They also include the duration, amount, and time of year of the loan, the solvency of the borrower, the nature of the commodity borrowed, and its relation to the one returned. Time and money are not necessarily understood as linked in linear function, and the notion of "rates" per unit of time appears artificial and alien to Gambians in many contexts. The complex calculations and negotiations involved in Gambian interest charges are not all easily amenable to conventional western economic analysis.

Some Implications for Financial Institutions

Gambian farmers have seen everything, from free hand-outs and loans with negative real interest to interest charges of several hundred percent. In this sense, at least, there is some latitude for policy experimentation. These farmers' understandings of interest charges are so complex, however, and so deeply embedded in religion and culture that institutional lenders are advised to design and redesign their policies sensitively, carefully watching pilot projects and listening with open minds.

Does institutional finance need to conform to all Islamic proscriptions of usury? Some Gambians say not if the institutions are public, as in a co-operative, since the public supposedly benefits from the interest charged its members. Others reason, too, that the law of the land governs banking and financial institutions, that the public has a sacred duty to abide by the law of the land, and that this duty can be just as important as other sacred duties. But a privately held enterprise is thought guilty of *ribā* in charging interest for someone's personal profit when that profit will not be shared with family or community. Some Gambian rural traders claim they do not save in banks because doing so would be charging interest. This claim should not always be taken at face value--they often have other reasons too--but the idea is always present in decisions and debate.

Although the *Qur'an* explicitly forbids charging high interest, it does not explicitly forbid paying it. Rural Gambians debate whether such borrowers are also sinners. A Mandinko *marabout* in Lower River Division explained that borrowing at interest to feed one's family is not sinful, but doing so for strictly personal or unnecessary purposes is. Although an institution charging high interest may be resented and perhaps thought sinful, religious beliefs may not necessarily diminish the demand for its credit. No evidence is available on this point.

Of course, Islamic banks in other parts of the Muslim world have their own *ḥiyal* or legal devices for evading Qur'anic prohibitions on interest. These cannot be examined in detail here, but they usually label such payments "profit" or "profit-sharing" instead of interest; this is more convincing if they declare them at the end of a year or a lending term rather than at the beginning. Provisions for risk sharing between borrowers and lenders may be incorporated to avoid Qur'anic prohibitions of unilateral risk.

It was noted earlier that Gambians expect loan forgiveness, from institutional as from informal lenders, in cases of need and delayed repayment. Here the issues are not just religious or economic. Institutional credit is political. Just as dispensing loans can win voters or supporters, forgiving loans maintains loyalties. It is to the advantage of politicians that loan forgiveness by institutions not be too routinized--that is, that there be leeway for discretion about clemency because of drought, or the amount of time elapsed and interest accrued. Politicians try to arrange that announcements of new loan programs or forgivenesses be associated with their own names (and that they occur in election years). Patronage systems reinforce the Islamic-inspired safety net of forgiveness for borrowers, but they may desynchronize the timing of forgiveness from periods of peak need.

We turn now away from the subject of Islamic law to the other major international legal influence on Gambian financial customs: the legacy of the British Empire from which the Gambian nation gained independence three decades ago.

National Moneylending Law: The Imperial Legacy and the "Per Annum" Rule

Gambian statutory law prohibits usury under specific terms, copied with little modification from European law. The relevant law is written with reference only to money: it is the Moneylenders Act. The wording of the act refers to money loans but nowhere specifies whether the act applies to loans in kind, or to cash loans collected in other commodities.[60] The law is thus technically irrelevant, or only ambiguously relevant, to much rural lending in The Gambia.

The Moneylenders Act, with its deeply embedded assumptions about what constitutes interest and usury, has a centuries-long pedigree exotic to Africa.[61] Its immediate basis was the Money-Lenders Act of 1900 in the United Kingdom, redrafted and amended in 1927 to the effect that transactions would normally be considered unfairly harsh at interest rates above 48 percent per year. The figure was copied straight into Gambian law. It developed in the form of the Moneylenders Ordinance of 1934, which required the registration of moneylenders, and the Moneylenders Act of 1955 (Cap. 126), revised under the Revised Edition of the Laws Act of 1965. This was the law still in force and being distributed in pamphlet form by the Government Printer in Banjul in 1988.[62]

The law defines a moneylender as "any person who lends money at interest or who lends a sum of money in consideration of a larger sum being repaid" (Cap. 126, sec. 4), and it requires him or her to be licensed. It does not acknowledge that most of the moneylending in The Gambia is done by nonspecialist moneylenders. The law refers to "interest" as permissible under certain circumstances. In this respect, it differs sharply from Qur'anic teaching, which never explicitly condones interest but instead prohibits "usury" (*ribā*), variously interpretable to allow some charges resembling interest. The law makes it clear that interest is to be calculated as an annual rate per unit of time, rather than simply as a ratio of principal to interest. Implicit is the assumption of linearity in the relation of time to money.

The Moneylenders Act of The Gambia states (Cap. 126, sec. 13, para. 1):

> The interest which may be charged on loans, whether by a moneylender or by any person other than a moneylender shall not exceed the respective rates specified hereunder -
>
> (a) On loans secured by a charge on any freehold property [or government bonds or other specified forms of collateral] simple interest not exceeding the rate of fifteen per centum per annum for the first five hundred pounds or part thereof

and not exceeding the rate of twelve-and-a-half per centum per annum on any amount in excess of five hundred pounds;

(b) on loans secured by a second charge... [2.5 percent higher than in (a)];

(c) on unsecured loans simple interest not exceeding the rate of forty-eight per centum per annum.

The "per centum per annum" clauses force lenders to record interest, and courts to assess fairness, in terms of time elapsed. Later sections make doubly sure (Cap. 126, sec. 16, para. 2, as follows; see also sect. 21):

> Where the interest charged on a loan of money is not expressed in terms of a rate per centum per annum the rate of interest per centum per annum charged on the loan shall be calculated according to schedule A [which shows how to divide years into months, weeks, and days]... or schedule B to this Act [which gives the algebraic formula for calculating interest, by months elapsed].[63]

Significantly, the British-based laws still in force in The Gambia include nothing like a statute of limitations: they mention no period of time after which the amount of the accrued interest becomes unfair, and no period after which a loan or any of its interest must be forgiven.[64] Nothing in the law limits the ratio of interest to principal. According to the letter of the law, then, an unrepaid loan may legally continue accruing interest indefinitely. What the *Qur'an* condemns as "doubling and quadrupling" is quite legal under the British-based system, provided the rate is gradual enough and enough time elapses. This is a key difference between British law and local conventions based on Islamic and indigenous law and custom.

By the 48 percent per annum rule, many of the seasonal loans that Gambian farmers contract with each other and with shopkeepers are illegal. A six-month loan at 100 percent interest--about the most common arrangement--carries more than four times the legally allowable interest if calculated on an annualized basis.[65] Interest charges on many of the shorter-term loans, for instance larger traders' loans to smaller traders for stocking up, appear ridiculously high when annualized: they may come to well over 1,000 percent. Annualization, and laws based upon this kind of calculation, thus become meaningless. Of course, since loans not issued in cash may not be deemed subject to the Moneylenders Act, the law is only of limited relevance anyway.

Other Areas of Fit and Misfit in the Moneylenders Act

The Moneylenders Act's breakdown of interest rates, in terms of security offered, tacitly takes into account lenders' needs to pass on the risks of unsecured lending to borrowers as an interest premium. Seen in a more critical way, it allows them to extract higher rates of profit from poorer borrowers, who are unlikely to have collateral to offer. Fair or unfair, the direction of the difference fits Gambian local practice.

There are, however, significant areas of misfit. Allowable formats for repayment schedules are also set out in English, but not in the Arabic that many Gambians learn to write in *Qur'an* school or in any other local language. Strangely, although the Moneylenders Act specifies allowable interest in terms of rates, thus accommodating loans of any amount (with only one minor differential for amounts above or below £500),[66] it specifies the fines in terms of a fixed (presumably maximum) amount:

> Any person who loans money at a rate of interest higher than that authorized by this Act shall be guilty of an offence and shall be liable, on summary conviction, to a fine of fifty pounds in respect of each such loan. (Cap. 126, sec. 14, para. 1)

The law discriminates against smaller lenders. A loan of £10 or £1,000 could incur the same £50 fine. The lender who lent £1,000 in £10 amounts would risk 100 times the fines of the lender who lent a single £1,000 loan. Lenders are of course likely to try to pass such risks or costs on to the borrowers as premiums on interest. This section of the law thus disfavors not just small lenders, but also small borrowers. Gambian law includes provisions whose enforcement would block some *ḥiyal* (legal evasions), but not others. The law prohibits direct or indirect payment of interest in advance by deduction from the principal sum borrowed or otherwise (Cap. 126, sec. 15, para. 1). It prohibits "negotiation fees" (sec. 17), bonuses, fines, and expenses that might be levied as surrogate interest charges (sec. 13, para. 3). But, as noted earlier, the act does not address the commodity-switch device--for instance, cash loans repaid in groundnuts, one of the most important devices in local lending practice.

Loans with pledged property are subject to the Pawnbrokers Act of 1905, revised 1965 (Cap. 136) and still being issued from Banjul in 1988.[67] This law also lists maximum profits on loans or debts allowable, in terms of rates, calculated by monthly and fortnightly intervals, for instance: "On a loan of above forty shillings - for every month or part of a month for every sum of two shillings and sixpence or fraction of a sum of two shillings and sixpence . . . one halfpenny" (Cap. 136, sec. 12, item B). Here again, profits may legally continue to rise indefinitely, as long as they rise slowly enough. What matters according to this act, like the Moneylenders Act, is not the amount of interest finally paid, nor its ratio to principle, but only the relation between time and money.

Implications for Policies and Projects

The differences in assumptions underlying Islamic law about usury and the more secular European rules are not just philosophical or religious. They also influence real behavior and thus resource flows. Project and program designers interested in issuing or recovering loans in the western Sahel, or in mobilizing savings there, should pay attention to both these sets of rules, as well as to local customs on which they are superimposed. The following are some practical implications about local and international finance in The Gambia, and they are likely to apply elsewhere in the western Sahel.

1. There is much latitude for experimentation in financial program design. Rural Gambians have seen most everything, including interest charges ranging from negative figures to several hundred percent (or several thousand if annualized). They have also seen other Gambians devise complex ways of dodging rules and laws, including sacred laws.

2. Official attempts to regulate interest charges made by local lenders are likely to fail. Government policy can, however, influence the kinds and numbers of urban-based merchants who trade in particular commodities in the countryside, and who lend in connection with them.

3. More emphasis should be placed on saving, to balance the heavy and rather unconstructive emphasis on credit, in policies and projects. Although they save mainly in non-monetary forms, rural Gambians would like more, and more convenient, ways of saving cash. The *kondem* boxes, the money-keepers, the requests for delayed wage payments, and the rotating savings and credit associations all suggest an illiquidity preference and a possible demand for accessible saving deposit channels. If institutional interest rates on loans are to be raised, as is happening now, interest rates on savings should be raised as well.

4. Financial institutions are publicly considered subject to Islamic rules concerning interest, but those rules are more tolerant of some kinds of financial institutions than others, and the public has ways of rationalizing counterventions.

5. Rural Gambians often conceive of interest in terms of ratios rather than rates. The idiom of annualized rates, so familiar in the West as to be taken for granted, is not second-nature, or even necessarily acceptable, to Gambians. They do not necessarily conceive of time as linear. It is detachable, optative, and not taken for granted in interest calculations. Time is, however, taken into account in debt forgiveness.

6. One should not assume that the same interest rates acceptable for short-term loans will be acceptable for longer-term loans. It is easier to collect shorter term than longer term credit. This is probably even more true in Islamic societies like The Gambia than in other poor countries. Institutional lenders may be able to charge higher interest than they are accustomed to charging if they keep their loans short enough.

7. Cultural pressures favor smaller loans. Gaps are therefore left in large-scale, long-term lending. Large-scale investments like milling or threshing machines are likely to be impracticable to finance with credit, and unlikely to be replaced by local initiative except by unusually solvent traders or businesspeople. Such gaps may be hard to fill with institutional credit at anything like market rates and may instead require hire-purchase arrangements, grants, subsidies, or other arrangements.

8. Financiers should not simply record, generalize about, or set interest rates without considering both the forms in which loans are issued and the forms in which they are collected. Conventional European or American modes of economic analysis may not neatly apply.

9. Some institutional lenders to farmers may want to experiment with options of interest scheduling other than linear rates. Interest charges that accrue stepwise each year in the trade season might more closely reflect the realities of rainfed farming cash flows for some purposes.

10. Lenders should be prepared to forgive loans that go more than two or three years without repayment. Letting interest accrue *ad infinitum* is

not considered ethical in The Gambia. This is a further reason for caution when considering large-scale loans--for instance for heavy machinery.

11. Depreciation funds for replacing goods like farm machinery by regular deposits within the year are likely to be considered unnatural. They are based on a conception of a linear time-money relationship that is not second nature to rural Gambians.

12. Mortgage systems, not at present widespread in rural Gambia, are likely to prove inappropriate and possibly quite dangerous there, particularly where they might involve land or animals as collateral.[68] Interest charges and foreclosures are likely to be disputed.

Conclusion: Financial Customs Across Cultures

Indigenous and superimposed foreign understandings of time, money, and the relationship between them have left rural Gambians with a range of practices to choose among, to manipulate, and to debate. If these financial systems are to be understood as markets, they are certainly not unified or discrete ones. Kinship, friendship, neighborhood, and ethnicity are intimately concerned, and tangible and intangible reciprocities mix with profiteering as strategies of individual and group livelihood. Religion is also inseparable from economy, to the point of influencing whether repaying a loan in the same commodity or a different one changes the interest charge, and to the point of ensuring some secrecy in local financial dealings. Interest charges not only fluctuate but also vary simultaneously. The concept of markets is only half appropriate to describe a many-sided and partly covert financial life like this. Nor can one assume a universally shared understanding about how to distinguish fair from unfair lending once a market is identified. The distinction between interest rates and interest ratios is fundamental. Both tools--one overused by foreign financiers in West Africa, the other underused--are needed to understand financial thought in rural Gambia.

National moneylending laws, based on the concept of interest rates, are not widely heeded in the countryside. There is no reason why they should be. Their stipulations appear tailored to a different culture and have been arbitrarily applied to this West African setting. More appealing to locals by far is the sacred Quranic law, one far more widely known, even though its meaning may be debated. That local court records do not show interest payments that have obviously been made shows much more attention is paid to the Arab-based than the European-based code: not just high interest but all interest is concealed from the government in informal lending. But Gambian financial custom is equally remote from the letter of Qur'anic law in that, as elsewhere in the Muslim world, interest is being charged and only thinly veiled between borrowers and lenders.

The Gambia has two legal codes, then, based more on exogenous ideals than on actual practice. Hence the wide latitude for borrowers and lenders to arrange their own deals on their own terms. This rural and peripheral area of West Africa, accustomed to centuries of competing alien powers and philosophies, is in a sense ironically cosmopolitan in its outlook and its tolerance.

Probably similar cultural clashes and overlays concerning time and money, and focusing on interest and usury, are widespread in Africa--as widespread as the *Qur'an* in the northern half of the continent, and the Bible in the southern half; as widespread as the legacy of colonial rule and the widening reach of international institutional finance. Would an African sage advise a young tradesman not to forget that time is money? Probably not without knowing whom that novice was to deal with. That is the difference.

References

Ardener, Shirley. 1964. The Comparative Study of Rotating Credit Associations. *Journal of the Royal Anthropological Institute* 94(2): 201-29.

Ba, Cheikh. 1986. *Les Peul du Sénégal*. Dakar: Nouvelles Editions Africaines.

Barrett, Hazel. 1988. *The Marketing of Foodstuffs in the Gambia, 1400-1800: A Geographical Analysis*. Aldershot, U.K.: Avebury, Gower.

Christensen, Garry. 1988. *Rural Credit Markets in Burkina Faso: Structure and Performance.* Department of Agricultural Economics, Cornell University. Typescript.

Clark, R.H. 1987. *A Study of Agricultural Credit Operations of the Cooperative Movement in the Gambia.* Report to the United Nations International Labor Office, Co-operative Development Project. Geneva: ILO.

Colvin, Lucie, Cheick Ba, Boubacar Barry, Jacques Faye, Alice Hamer, Moussa Soumah, and Fatou Sow. 1981. *The Uprooted of The Western Sahel: Migrants' Quest for Cash in the Senegambia.* New York: Praeger.

Cuevas, Carlos. 1989. *Rural Household Finance in the Kindia and Nzerekore Regions of Guinea.* Report to the World Council of Credit Unions. Economics and Sociology Occasional Paper no. 1576. Department of Agricultural Economics and Rural Sociology, Ohio State University, Columbus.

David, Philippe. 1980. *Les navétanes: histoire des migrants saisonniers de l'arachide en sénégambie des origines à nos jours.* Dakar: Les Nouvelles Editions Africaines.

Derman, William, Frank Casey, Sarah Lynch, Cynthia Moore, and Charles Steedman. 1985. *Rural Development in the Gambia River Basin.* Ann Arbor: Center for Research on Economic Development, University of Michigan.

Diop, Abdoulaye-Bara. 1981. *La société Wolof: tradition et changement.* Paris: Karthala.

———.1985. *La famille Wolof.* Paris: Karthala.

Dunsmore, J.R., A. Blair Rains, G.D.N. Lowe, D.J. Moffatt, I.P. Anderson, and J.B. Williams. 1976. *The Agricultural Development of The Gambia: An Agricultural, Environmental, and Socio-Economic Analysis.* Land Resource Study no. 22. Surbiton, England: Land Resources Division, Ministry of Overseas Development.

Dupire, Marguérite. 1970. *Organisation sociale des Peul: étude d'ethnographié comparée.* Paris: Librairie Plon.

Franklin, Benjamin. 1958 [1748]. Advice to a Young Tradesman. In Russel B. Nye, ed., *Autobiography and Other Writings.* Boston: Houghton Mifflin.

Gambia. 1966. *Moneylenders Act. Laws of The Gambia.* Bathurst: Government Printer.

———.1986. *Population and Housing Census, 1983, Provisional Report.* Banjul: Central Statistics Department.

Gambia Produce Marketing Board (GPMB). Annual Reports.

Gambia Rural Development Programme. 1978. Crop and Farm Development. Banjul: Gambia Rural Development Project.

Gamble, David. 1955. *Economic Conditions of Two Mandinka Villages: Kerewan and Keneba.* London: Research Department, Colonial Office.

Geertz, Clifford. 1962. The Rotating Credit Association: A Middle Rung in Development. *Economic Development and Cultural Change* 1(3): 241-63.

Graham, Douglas H., Richard L. Meyer, and Carlos E. Cuevas, eds. 1993. *Financial Markets in The Gambia, 1981-91.* Report to the USAID Mission, Banjul, The Gambia.

Graham, Douglas H., Carlos E. Cuevas, and Kifle Negash. n.d. *Rural Finance in Niger.* Report to the U.S. Agency for International Development.

Hammsa, Sonia. 1984. *Informal Financial Circuits in West Africa.* Washington, D.C.: Office of Housing and Urban Programs, U.S. Agency for International Development.

Haswell, Margaret R. 1975. *The Nature of Poverty: A Case-History of the First Quarter-Century after World War II.* New York: St. Martin's Press.

Hill, Polly. 1982. *Dry Grain Farming Families: Hausaland (Nigeria) and Karnataka (India) Compared.* Cambridge: Cambridge University Press.

Hodge, Carleton T., ed. 1971. *Papers on the Manding.* Bloomington: Indiana University, Research Center for the Language Sciences. The Hague: Mouton.

Hopkins, Nicholas S. 1971. Mandinka Social Organization. In Carleton T. Hodge, ed., *Papers on the Manding.* Bloomington: Indiana University, Research Center for the Language Sciences; The Hague: Mouton.

Hugo, Victor. 1862. *Les Miserables.* New York: C. Lassalle.

Jones, Christine W. 1986. *The Domestic Groundnut Marketing System in The Gambia.* Report to the Ministry of Finance and Trade, The Gambia.

Kargbo, Alimami M. 1983. An Economic Analysis of Rice Production Systems and Production Organization of Rice Farmers in The Gambia. Ph.D. diss., Michigan State University.

Khan, M.S.A. 1929. Mohammedan Laws against Usury and How They are Evaded. *Journal of Comparative Law,* pp.: 233-44.

The Koran. N.J. Dawood, trans. 3d rev. ed. 1968. Harmondsworth: Penguin.

Linares de Sapir, Olga. 1970. Agriculture and Diola Society. In Peter F.M. McLoughlin, ed., *African Food Production Systems*, pp. 195-22. Baltimore: Johns Hopkins University Press.

Linares, Olga. 1992. *Power, Prayer and Production: The Jola of Casamance, Senegal.* Cambridge: Cambridge University Press.

Marx, Karl. 1906[1867]. *Capital.* Chicago: Charles H. Kerr.

McPherson, Malcolm F., and Steven C. Radelet. 1991. Economic Reform in The Gambia: Policies, Politics, Foreign Aid, and Luck. In Dwight H. Perkins and Michael Roemer, eds., *Reforming Economic Systems in Developing Countries,* pp. 115-136. Cambridge, Massachusetts: Harvard University Press.

Moore, Sally Falk. 1986. *Social Facts and Fabrications: "Customary" Law on Kilimanjaro, 1880-1980.* Cambridge: Cambridge University Press.

Nelson, Benjamin N. 1949. *The Idea of Usury.* Princeton: Princeton University Press.

Pélissier, Paul. 1966. *Les paysans du sénégal: les civilisations agraires du Cayor à la Casamance.* St.-Yrieux: Imprimerie Fabrègue, for the Centre National de la Recherche Scientifique.

Puetz, Detlev, and Joachim von Braun. 1991. *Parallel Markets and the Rural Poor in a West African Setting*. In Michael Roemer and Christine Jones, eds., *Markets in Developing Countries: Parallel, Fragmented and Black.* pp. 29-43. San Francisco: ICS Press.

The Qur'an. Published as Marmaduke Pickthall, trans. 1971. *The Meaning of the Glorious Qur'an.* Beirut: Dar al-Kitab Allubnani.

Ramamurthy, G.V. 1986. *Agricultural Credit Policy and Structure: The Gambia.* Report to the United Nations Food and Agriculture Organization, Technical Co-operation Program.

Robertson, A.F. 1987. *The Dynamics of Productive Relationships: African Share Contracts in Comparative Perspective.* Cambridge: Cambridge University Press.

Rodinson, Maxime. 1966. *Islam and Capitalism.* Brian Pearce, trans. London: Allen Lane.

Schacht, Joseph 1964. *An Introduction to Islamic Law*. Oxford: Clarendon Press.

Schaffer, Matt, and Christine Cooper. 1980. *Mandinko: The Ethnography of a West African Holy Land.* New York: Holt, Rinehart and Winston.

Shipton, Parker. 1989. *Bitter Money: Cultural Economy and Some African Meanings of Forbidden Commodities.* American Ethnological Society Monograph 1. Washington, D.C.: American Anthropological Association.

———.1990. *African Famines and Food Security: Anthropological Perpectives.* Annual Review of Anthropology. Palo Alto, Calif.: Annual Reviews.

———.1992a. The Rope and the Box: Group Savings in The Gambia. In Dale W. Adams and D.A. Fitchett, eds., *Informal Finance in Low-Income Countries*, pp. 25-41. Boulder, Colo.: Westview.

———.1992b. Debts and Trespasses: Land, Mortgages, and the Ancestors in Western Kenya. *Africa* 62(3): 357-88.

———.Forthcoming. How Gambians Save: Culture and Economic Strategy at an Ethnic Crossroads. In Jane Guyer, ed., *Money Matters: Instability, Values, and Social Payments in the Modern History of West African Communities.* Portsmouth, NH: Heinemann.

Snyder, Francis G. 1981. *Capitalism and Legal Change: An African Transformation.* New York: Academic Press.

Swindell, Kenneth. 1978. Family Farms and Migrant Labor: The Strange Farmers of the Gambia. *Canadian Journal of African Studies* 12: 3-19.

———.1981. *The Strange Farmers of The Gambia: A Study in the Redistribution of Population.* Centre for Development Studies, University College of Swansea, Monograph Series no. 15. Norwich: Geo Books.

Tapsoba, Edouard K. 1982. Crédit agricole et crédit informel dans la région orientale de haute-volta: analyse economique, performance institutionelle et implications en matière de politique de développement agricole. MSU International Development Working Paper no. 2. East Lansing: Department of Agricultural Economics, Michigan State University.

Tuck, Laura. 1983. Formal and Informal Financial Markets in Rural Senegal. Report to the U.S. Agency for International Development.

United Nations Development Programme. 1991. *Human Development Report.* New York: Oxford University Press.

Von Pischke, J.D. 1991. *Finance at the Frontier.* Washington, D.C.: The World Bank.

Von Pischke, J.D., Dale W. Adams, and Gordon Donald. 1983. *Rural Financial Markets in Developing Countries: Their Use and Abuse.* Baltimore: Johns Hopkins University Press.

Walker, Patricia. 1987. Savings Mobilization and Development: The Potential for Mobilizing Rural Savings in Senegal Under the New Agricultural Policy. Banque Centrale des Etats de l'Afrique de l'Ouest, Agence de Dakar.

Weber, Max. 1958 [1904]. *The Protestant Ethic and the Spirit of Capitalism.* Talcott Parsons, trans. New York: Charles Scribner's Sons.

Weil, Peter M. 1971. Political Structure and Process among the Gambia Mandinka: The Village Parapolitical System. In Carleton T. Hodge, ed., *Papers on the Manding.* Bloomington: Indiana University, Research Center for the Language Sciences; The Hague: Mouton.

Wellington, Martin W. 1955. Aspects of Moneylending in Northern Sudan. *Middle East Journal* 9: 139-46. Republished by Development Digest (July 1980): 71-8.

World Bank. 1985. *The Gambia: Financial Sector Review.* Washington, D.C.

Yusuf, Ahmed. 1975. Capital Formation and Management among the Muslim Hausa Traders of Kano, Nigeria. *Africa* 45(2): 167-182.

Notes

This chapter is reprinted with permission, from *Markets in Developing Countries: Parallel, Fragmented, and Black.* Michael Roemer and Christine Jones, eds., (San Francisco, Calif.: ICS Press, 1991), with some changes. Research was sponsored by the Harvard Economic and Financial Policy Analysis project in the Ministry of Finance and Trade, The Gambia, funded by the Agency for International Development. Special thanks go to my hosts and my research assistants in The Gambia, including C. Baldeh, E. Baldeh, A. Jallow, A. Jammeh, F. Janneh, C. Jones, F. Khan, J. Newlands, M. Sanyang, A. Sillah, M. Trawally, Y. Dem, and their families. For advice and other help I am grateful to D. Cole, C. Cuevas, C. Elias, B. Gilman, T. Herlehy, J. Ito-Adler, M. McPherson, S. Potok, D. Puetz, S. Radelet, M. Robinson, M. Roemer, L. Sanneh, J. Shipton, B. Sidibe, P. Steele, J. Von Pischke, and K. Yost, and not least, to this volume's Editor, J. Acheson. All opinions expressed, however, are my own.

1. "We reckon hours and minutes to be dollars and cents," wrote T. C. Haliburton (1796-1865) in *The Clockmaker.* "Take away time is money, and what is left of England?" wrote Victor Hugo in 1862 in *Les Miserables.* Weber's 1904 classic, *The Protestant Ethic and the Spirit of Individualism,* was far from the first study to trace links between religious and economic ethics, but fused them most compellingly. Marx's *Capital* criticized as "commodity fetishism" the assumption that "money begets money" (part 1, chapter 1, section 4).

2. Research in The Gambia was conducted mainly in April and May, 1987 and from July to October 1988. A revisit in 1992 for work on another topic allowed some further observation. In addition to participant-observation and open-ended interviews, structured surveys were conducted with equal numbers of men and women informants, totalling about 138 in the first visit and 186 in the second, each visited repeatedly, in five randomly chosen villages among Foni Berefet District (Western Division) Niani District (MacCarthy Island Division), and Wuli District (Upper River Division). Working with experienced local assistants chosen for their previous ties and rapport in the particular villages, I stayed mainly in two of the villages and benefited from close contact with several key informants and friends as well as from acquaintance with the broader field of respondents.

3. Formal and informal schooling, however, have prepared few rural Gambians for the arithmetic involved in calculating interest as rates. Those who can manage the math may be able to take advantage of neighbors who cannot, in dealings among themselves or with financial institutions.

4. In this article the term "institution" is used in both its senses, according to context: as a named organization of people or as a set of rules, customs, and conventions that guide recurrent behavior. A criticism to be made about some of the institutional economics (in the second sense) of the 1980s and early 90s has been that it tended to seek, in loose descriptions of "institutions," a single term for all useful and recurring human interactions, and in transaction costs, a single answer for all questions about why they exist. When costs and transactions are defined as broadly as institutions are, the thinking soon begins to seem tautologous, as if, by answering all questions, one might really be answering none.

5. In 1991 the U.N. Development Programme listed The Gambia as second from the bottom (159th out of 160), ahead of only Sierra Leone, in the Human Development Index (a combined measure of life expectancy at birth, adult literacy, mean years of schooling, educational attainment, real GDP per capita, and adjusted real GDP [UNDP 1991: 121]). For 1987-88, the Gambian Ministry of Finance and Trade estimated the gross domestic product at 1,257.8 million dalasis (or 479.3 million at 1976-77 prices).

6. McPherson and Radelet (1991) describe the economic reform program and some of its effects.

7. Barrett (1988) summarizes the production and marketing of Gambian foods in historical and geographical perspective. Dunsmore et al. (1976) and Derman et al. (1988) also analyse the country's agriculture with multidisciplinary approaches. Kargbo (1983) details the workings of the rice economy within the picture.

8. Linares (1992) offers a nuanced description of Jola intervillage variations in ecological and religious life.

9. I hope on another occasion to describe more fully some differences observed between the economic cultures of these groups as they bear on entrustment and obligation.

10. A body of recent economic surveys variously comparing the roles of formal and informal financial systems in particular West African countries includes Christensen (1988), Cuevas (1989), Graham et al. (n.d.), Hammsa (1984), Puetz and von Braun (1987), Tapsoba (1982), Tuck (1983), and Walker (1987). Most emphasize quantitative dimensions. Comparing the findings from the different countries is a task ahead, but a delicate one, given the different research methods and translations used.

11. See Haswell (1975) for detailed descriptions of the rural operations of the trading firms and their agents.

12. The Ministry of Finance and Trade calculated the inflation rate of the *dalasi* as 45.9 percent in 1986-87 (an unusually high rate resulting from the floating of the currency that year) and 12.5 percent in 1987-88.

13. At the time of research the government was in the process of de-regulating the interest rates of banks and other institutions. The trends up to 1992 are discussed in Graham et al. (1993).

14. In 1986, 48 percent of The Gambia's money supply was reported to be outside of the banking system (Ramamurthy 1986, 25). See also World Bank (1985).

15. For more detailed treatments of the topics discussed in this and the next section, see Shipton (1992a, forthcoming). For a few of the many ethnographic descriptions of other facets of community life in Gambian and related Senegalese societies, see Diop (1985), Gamble (1955), Hodge (1971), Hopkins (1971), Weil (1971), Haswell (1975), and Schaffer and Cooper (1980), on the Mandinko; Dupire (1970) and Ba (1986) on the Fulani including the Fula; Diop (1981) on the Wolof; and Snyder (1981) and Linares (1970, 1992) on the Jola. Pélissier's study (1966), though now dated, remains the most comprehensive summary on the peoples of the region.

16. Farmers give several reasons for preferring to save their wealth in stock, in addition to the subtler considerations of gender noted above. These include the fact that animals breed, the advantages of milk and manure production, the usefulness of animal traction, the ceremonial values of animals, and the prestige and other satisfactions of having herds. See also Shipton (1990).

17. This process is also discussed elsewhere (Shipton 1990).

18. I have also noted similar break-open boxes in use for domestic cash saving in Kenya.

19. For comparisons see Tuck (1983, 66), on Senegal; Graham et al. (1987, chapter 4, 18-21), on Niger; and Cuevas (1989, 9), on the Kindia and Nzerekore regions of Guinea.

20. Rotating savings and credit associations are also known by many other names, including *tondas* (Spanish), merry-go-rounds, or in The Gambia, *compin* ("company") groups. In Cameroon, where the Bamileke and other groups have some of the best-established practices of rotating savings and credit associations in Africa, these are called *ndjangi.* Though most Gambian and African groups are women's groups, Gambian men sometimes also belong to them, and some salaried men, for instance in the Gambian army, are known to form them.

21. See Geertz (1962), Ardener (1964), and Shipton (1992a) for more detailed discussions of rotating savings and credit associations.

22. The exception is a participant in a ROSCA whose turn falls early in the cycle. She or he benefits from inflation by repaying later small amounts totaling the amount borrowed.

23. In May 1987 the Basse branch of the GCDB (one of only two branches of the bank outside the greater Banjul area) reported that 49 percent of its 858 savings depositors had less than 250 *dalasis* in their accounts (that is, less than the value of one sheep). Interviews with bank staff suggested that most of the roughly 100 farmers (people whose primary source of income is farming) saving at the bank were among those with less than 250 *dalasis.* Only an estimated 10-15 percent of the 858 depositors were women. Only about five farmers were currently borrowing from the branch.

24. Particular choices for answers were not prompted in my surveys. Von Pischke (1983) concisely summarizes poor rural peoples' incentives and disincentives to save in financial institutions. His *Finance at the Frontier* (1990) expands on some of these ideas and suggests a balance between savings and credit.

25. The Agricultural Development Bank had tried mobile banks in the early 1980s, but it was unable to sustain them before it failed.

26. A loan or credit may be defined in English as any transfer of goods or services from one party to another, or to any of its members, for a delayed compensation in the same or another form, with or without interest.

27. Currently Mandinka, Jola and Manjago cash bridewealth payments appear often to amount to less than 500 *dalasis*; but Wolof bridewealths often appear to be around 1,000 *dalasis*, and Fula bridewealths frequently exceed 2,000 *dalasis* in rural Gambian villages. Families of particularly well-educated or well-connected women may demand much higher bridewealth. In addition to these transfers, grooms and their families are usually expected to provide cattle or other livestock and other food for the weddings, and grooms to give their new wives goods like beds, boxes of clothing, pots and pans, radios and tape recorders, watches, and sometimes animals and jewelry as they set up house.

28. Cuevas found in two regions of Guinea that about 90 percent of a sample of 250 people arranged their main informal financial loans in their own villages (1989, 8).

29. See Robertson (1987) and sources cited therein for a study of African share contracting, including a chapter on The Gambia and Senegal. See also Swindell (1978 and 1981), David (1980), and Colvin et al. (1981) on these two countries.

30. Christensen (1988, 68) similarly comments on the absence of professional moneylenders in Burkina Faso. See Wellington (1955), and Yusuf (1975) on moneylenders elsewhere south of the Sahara. Von Pischke (1991) discusses high-interest moneylending more generally from economic perspectives.

31. Lebanese and Ako merchants have until now more or less confined their direct operations to the Banjul area, though some may have agents in the smaller towns.

32. Most of the larger-scale traders in The Gambia are men. Among Mauritanians a particularly high proportion are male: in The Gambia, Mauritanian men outnumber Mauritanian women by over three to one (Population and Housing Census, *Provisional Report* 1983, 30). See also Haswell (1975, 188-9) on relations between traders or lenders and the rest of the rural public.

33. A main theme of Haswell (1975, 65-66 and passim).

34. The Sura of "The Cow" Sura II, Part III, of the *Qur'an* reads, "And if the debtor is in straitened circumstances, then (let there be) postponement to (the time of) ease; and that ye remit the debt as almsgiving would be better for you if ye did but know" (Pickthall translation, verse 280).

35. See GPMB Annual Report, 1971-72 and Jones (1986, 15); Clark (1987, table 1) gives yearly figures from 1974-75 to 1985-86. Haswell (1975) describes some changes in groundnut marketing and credit patterns up to the mid-1970s. Private groundnut traders finance crop purchases by borrowing from the commercial banks if they can, or by mortgaging urban land or other property; others purchase from farmers on credit. Gambian farmers have always had opportunities to sell their groundnuts informally in Senegal, but this trade seems seldom to involve credit.

36. Urban merchants are said to charge substantially higher interest for foreign merchants borrowing for cross-border trade, perhaps because the risks of lending are high.

37. The main government organ assisting small businesses is the Indigenous Business Advisory Service (IBAS), of the Ministry of Economic Planning and Development. Most of its clients are based in the cities and larger towns.

38. Dunsmore et al. noted moneylending rates varying between 50 percent and 150 percent (1976, 310). Haswell noted that a wealthy compound head who lent money in Genieri village charged rates between 49 percent and 157 percent over eight months in 1973-74 (1976, 186). Reports collected for the present study in 1987 suggest that these figures do still represent the most common range for seasonal loans--the figure of 100 percent being the most commonly recorded--but that the rates may vary between 0 and over 1,000 percent, if calculated in monetary values and on an annual basis. As one might expect, shorter-term loans reach the highest rates when calculated on an annual basis.

39. Moore (1986) discusses at greater length such historical changes in East African contract law and practice.

40. Although western church-based aid organizations like Catholic Relief Services are active in the countryside, Christian religious influence remains much smaller than Islamic. Here again, some of the Jola groups of southwestern Gambia would be exceptional.

41. Some of the indigenous aspects of religious belief and practice include ancestral spirits, local celebration scheduling, and some forms of witchcraft and sorcery, house magic, and worn amulets.

42. In Mandinka, imam is *alimaamo*, and the French term *marabout* is translated *mooroo*. These are permutations of Arabic terms.

43. Of course, translations from classical Arabic lose some of their poetry and rhetorical force, and Gambians sometimes debate whether the *Qur'an* in any other language than Arabic is really the *Qur'an*. Those who know Arabic usually say, predictably, that it is not; those who do not sometimes argue, as one upper river Fula put it, that "Allah understands all languages; it's people who make it hard for themselves."

44. See Schacht (1964, 12, 145-48) for a general treatment of *ribā* in Islamic law.

45. Some consider *ribā* ironically to be a kind of debt that the lender acquires to the borrower, for which the borrower may or may not forgive him or her on the judgment day.

46. The sura of "The Cow" states: "Believers, give in alms of the wealth you have lawfully earned" (*The Koran*, Dawood translation, 354). "Lawfully" is taken in The Gambia and elsewhere to exclude wealth earned as *ribā*, usury.

47. For comparable findings in other African traditions (Christian and local), in which specific prohibitions on earning are linked with specific prohibitions on spending, see Shipton (1989). For a detailed historical treatment of concepts of usury in Judeo-Christian traditions, see Nelson (1949).

48. Gambians say trade profits become sinful, however, when a seller raises them expressly to take advantage of a particular buyer known to be in difficulty.

49. Part IV, Sura III, "The family of 'Imran'", Verse 130: "O Ye who Believe! Devour not usury, doubling and quadrupling (the sum lent)... and ward off from (yourself) the Fire prepared for disbelievers" (Pickthall trans.). See also Part VI, Sura IV, "Women", Verses 160, 161. Though it does not explicitly say how long it takes for interest to accrue to the double, the Qur'an does tell believers, "So do not fail to put your debts in writing, be they small or big, together with the date of payment" (*The Koran:* "The Cow," Dawood trans., 355). The emphasis on the date here suggests recognition that interest may accrue, in one way or another, as time progresses.

50. Any loan arrangement involving "double profit" is likely to meet with disapproval in The Gambia. In the case of crop loans, the idea of "doubling" itself has a double meaning. As a district chief explained it, Allah gives humans profit from seeds sown, by multiplying them for harvest. If humans then lend these at interest to obtain further profits from each other, they are seeking double profit, and thus committing a sin (in Mandinka, *junubo*). Muslims are taught that only divinity should be able to make rewards multiply. The *Qur'an* repeatedly states that the charitable will collect back on the day of judgment. "He that gives his wealth for the cause of Allah is like a grain of corn which brings forth seven ears, each bearing a hundred grains" (*The Koran*, Sura of "The Cow", Dawood translation, 353). "That which you seek to increase by usury

will not be blessed by Allah, but the alms you give for His sake shall be repaid to you many times over" (*The Koran*, Sura of "The Greeks", verse 39, Dawood trans., 191).

51. There are, of course, other reasons for lenders to keep loans short, such as the opportunity cost of capital and the possibility of borrowers' moving away.

52. Haswell's research on Genieri village in The Gambia, conducted over twenty-five years, is one of Africa's best examples of longitudinal research. She has not dealt conclusively, however, with the questions raised here about perceptions of time in interest and usury.

53. For surveys of *ḥiyal*, legal devices, in other Islamic countries, see Khan (1929), Schacht (1964 chapter 11 and pp. 208-ll, and the bibliography on p. 242), and Rodinson (1974, 36ff). In The Gambia, borrowers and lenders may not believe that divinity can be fooled; but many say they are more comfortable following the *ḥiyal* strategies regardless. Schacht's classic work discusses sympathetically the relation between theory and practice in Islamic contract law.

54. The *ḥiyal* principle helps explain, I think, why Haswell observed in Genieri village that "loans were not always made in cash but frequently in food grains payable in cash or groundnuts" (1975, 188).

55. Gambians likewise speak of Allah as merciful and forgiving, and they supplicate this quality. Muslims use many of the same terms to discuss forgiveness between humans as they use to discuss divine forgiveness of humans, just as Christians supplicate their divinity to "forgive us our debts as we forgive our debtors" in the Lord's Prayer.

56. Compare this finding on courts among the Chagga of Tanzania in the 1940s and 1950s: "it seems that where the claim was promptly brought to the court, before a large debt piled up, the court was more likely to allow a high rate [of interest]" (Moore 1986, 188).

57. The findings of Puetz and Von Braun (1988, 18), on MacCarthy Island Division, agree with my own on this point: "food loans are lower [in interest] than other loans, all other factors held constant."

58. Puetz and von Braun found in central Gambia that "the higher the loan amount the lower the interest" (1988, 18). Hill notes, in her study of Hausaland in Nigeria and Karnataka in India, that "as a general rule, bigger creditors charge lower interest rates" (1982, 215).

59. Haswell (1975, 186) and Dunsmore et al. (1976, 310), and I have found the same differential in our studies in The Gambia, but Puetz and von Braun report no such difference discernable in theirs (1988, 18), leaving the general finding open to question. Hill (1982, 215) found the differential in Hausaland, Nigeria, as have others elsewhere in West Africa.

60. The nearest other law that might apply is the Pawnbrokers Act.

61. For a thorough treatment of medieval European doctrines concerning usury see Nelson (1949). Moneylending laws have appeared and disappeared in England since at least the sixteenth century. Henry VIII's statute of 1541 forbade interest over ten percent per year. In subsequent reigns over 170 years, usury law was scrapped and reinstated at rates that varied from eight percent to five percent. By 1867 usury laws had been reabandoned.

62. Though the Gambian legal code was issued two years after internal self-government had been achieved and in the year of independence, it is unabashedly British, printed in London, and listing amounts in pounds, not dalasis, which became the national currency in 1971. It still lists the capital city as Bathhurst, not Banjul as renamed in 1973.

63. The formula given in Schedule B of the Moneylenders Act for calculating an interest rate, per cent per annum, is

$$\frac{100 \times I \times 24}{(N + I) \times P \times L}$$

where I = total interest payable, N = number of instalments, P = principal, and L = number of calendar months in the intervals between instalments. The sense is unclear.

64. The law stipulates, however, that moneylenders may not wait more than a year after an (unspecified) "cause of action" to start legal proceedings to recover money or security (Cap. 126, sect. 30).

65. Annual interest of 48 percent after two calendar years remains just short of the "doubling" that the *Qur'an* expressly forbids. Since most rural loans are contracted during the hungry season and repaid during the harvest and trade season anyway, the difference between 48 percent and 50 percent is not of great importance.

66. The sums mentioned in this paragraph are Gambian pounds. From 1843 to 1913 The Gambia participated in the United Kingdom's monetary system. From 1913 to May 13, 1964, the Gambian currency was the West African pound. From then until July 1, 1971, it was the Gambian pound, divided into 20 shillings, or 240 pence. The

Gambian pound replaced the West African pound at par. On July 1, 1971, the nation replaced the Gambian pound with the *dalasi*, at the rate of 1 *dalasi* = 4.00 Gambian shillings = 0.48 U.S. dollars. The Gambian *dalasi* is divided into 100 *butut*.

67. Tellingly, the Pawnbrokers Act still in force requires the pawnbroker to exhibit, in large letters over his outer door, "his Christian name" and other names (Cap. 136, sec. 10, item 1b), even though the person is twenty times more likely to be a Muslim than a Christian.

68. A land titling program and bank mortgage lending have lately been attempted in the Kombo districts of The Gambia; the outcome has not yet been systematically studied. Shipton (1992b) describes the outcome of a northern-style land mortgage system in western Kenya, briefly comparing its unhappy outcome to those of other similar attempts elsewhere in tropical Africa. One of the many reasons why the idea does not fit is that where farmers live surrounded by kin, as they do in the densely settled patrilineal societies of western Kenya, relatives of persons dispossessed can make it difficult for others to take over their land.

Part V

Theoretical Issues Concerning Institutional Economics

13

"But Where on Earth Has Mamadou Hidden His Production Function?" French Africanist Rural Economics and Institutionalism

Jean-Philippe Colin & Bruno Losch[1]

In the last twenty years social scientists in the English-speaking world have become increasingly interested in the effect of institutions on economic performance. Similar interests have arisen among French researchers. French rural economists working in Africa have developed an original approach to this subject. Although there has been no interaction between French Africanist rural economists (FAREs[2]) and American and English institutionalists,[3] they share common methodological ground and certain similarities in their work which should not be overlooked. In this paper, we will describe the work of French Africanist rural economics (FARE), and assume that the reader is familiar with American institutionalism.[4] With fortune, this essay will stimulate communication between the two groups of social scientists.

In the first part of this text we will put forward the characteristics of the works of French Africanist rural economists.[5] In the second part, we will outline the underlying paradigm to which these works can be most often related. We will show that like American institutionalists, the FAREs are heterodox in relation to the dominant trend in economics. Their heterodoxy may be seen in their research agenda, in their methodological choices and in the contents and form of their published papers. Hence the title of this paper--the reluctance of the FAREs to use econometric tools and mathematical models partly explains why they do not publish in mainstream academic journals. The FAREs' approach is based on:

- a broad conception of economics--economic agents are situated in their social, cultural, historical and political environment;
- the use of inductive methods, starting from real situations and case studies;
- a holistic and dynamic approach, integrating the facts studied into the overall picture, and integrating spatial and temporal scales;
- the rejection of any postulated rationality, i.e. the rationality of peasant behavior is a question of empirical research, not of postulate.

Genesis of French Africanist Rural Economics

French Africanist rural economists focus on the effects of institutions on production. Their main objective is to understand peasant practices[6] and strategies in the light of the management of natural resources, access to the factors of production, and the relations between production and distribution. They also emphasize the way production units function and their relations with the economic and institutional environment, particularly the state and the development agencies. They do not base their analyses on the neoclassical model, the aim of which is to explain prices and markets.

FAREs may include in their research an economic component which is marginal, dominant or exclusive. The work of FAREs is thus characterized by plural approaches corresponding to different methodological and conceptual frameworks which in turn are linked to the history of the research institutions and their mandates.

The Intellectual Roots

FARE is part of the melting pot of French research in social sciences, which is characterized by a humanist tradition (expressed by Universities, the *Collège de France*, the *Ecole Pratique des Hautes Etudes* or the *Ecole des Annales*) and influenced by Marxist thought between the years 1950 and 1970. It is also a product of colonial history, which gave rise to a wide range of research on tropical zones. It therefore might be described as the fertilization of the French intellectual tradition by the African field of study. This fertilization has been enriched by the dynamic processes of decolonization and then by cooperation and development aid policies.

There is also a clear common ground with the French (or French-speaking) school of development which was set up just after World War II. While the dominant economic school reasoned in terms of growth and accumulation models, French-speaking economists stressed the socio-cultural environment, historic processes, institutions and power relationships (Hugon 1991). This intellectual movement gave rise to various schools of thought which are united only in their opposition to mainstream economic theory. The 'social' and globalizing approaches developed by the school of *Economie et Humanisme* (L.J. Lebret), the contributions to the structuralist current (F. Perroux) and the radical critics of the school of dependency (S. Amin, G. de Bernis, etc.) are representative of these schools.

In such a context, the work of FAREs has been designed to untangle and reconstruct the complex reality of African agricultural economies, in a cognitive or operational perspective according to their institutional origin.

Institutions

To understand FARE it is necessary to recognize that it evolved within bureaucratic institutions and is marked by their histories, especially if one recalls with Bourdieu et al. that it can't "be useful to treat epistemological professions of faith as professional ideologies which, in the last analysis, aim to justify less the science than the researcher, less the real practice than the limits imposed on that practice by the position and the past of the researcher" (1983, 99).

The colonial period led to the establishment by the French State of agricultural administrative departments and agronomic and basic research institutions supporting development. Thus the State has maintained or set up specialized research institutes and has founded or favored the emergence of institutions supporting development. Their coordination and funding are basically carried out by the Ministrie of Cooperation & Development and the Ministry of Research & Technology, both of which supervise the research institutes. The *Caisse Centrale de Coopération Economique* (CCCE), a specialized financing institution, successor of the *Caisse Centrale de la France d'Outre Mer*, also intervenes in this process. It is important to note that there is a relative absence of private sources of financing such as the foundations which play a key role in financing American research.

1. *The Research Institutions*: The originality of French institutions specializing in the tropical zone in comparison with other national research bodies is the result of several characteristics:

- the concentration on research activity: researchers are *full-time* researchers;
- the perennial nature of research: researchers usually have tenure; the programming of activities relies on an annual budget provided all or in part by the Authorities, but which is managed by the institutions. This situation allows long-term fieldwork to be financed;
- the researchers are sent to developing countries for long term assignments, in order to conduct research programs *in situ*;
- the existence of several disciplines within one institution facilitates contacts between researchers belonging to different disciplines.[7] This contact may be fostered by the creation of interdisciplinary departments or research units.

The specialized research institutions either have a general or a sector-based vocation. Among those intervening in the rural studies field, particular mention may be made of ORSTOM and CIRAD.

ORSTOM (*Institut Français de Recherche Scientifique pour le Développement en Coopération*),[8] undertakes research in fields as diverse as health sciences, plant sciences, social sciences, etc. There are about 1,500 researchers and engineers, 200 of whom belong to social sciences. Research is carried out with cognitive or applied aims.

CIRAD (*Centre International de Recherche Agronomique pour le Développement*), was set up in 1984, incorporating different research institutes of tropical agronomy.[9] Most of its work is not in the social sciences. What social science work it does is increasingly oriented towards understanding the social and cultural factors influencing the adoption of technological innovations. Today out of one thousand researchers, however, only five percent are engaged in social science endeavors.[10]

Research teams of other institutions, working mainly in France, are also developing programs linked to developing countries. Apart from specialized university laboratories, special mention may be made of the EHESS, the INRA and the CNRS,[11] which contribute largely to the Africanist social sciences field.

2. *The Operational Structures*: The operational structures include the technical departments of certain administrations. Among these, one must mention the Cooperation department of INSEE which plays an important part in the publication of research results and methods,[12] as well as the publications department of the Ministry of Cooperation and Development, which has provided considerable support for research publications.[13]

The operational structures also include different consulting organizations (*bureaux d'études*) which for a long time have been the mainspring of the operational side of development. These organizations are either of para-public origin like SEDES,[14] or of private or associative origin (like IRAM[15]), but they intervene above all in public contracts and financing. Their action has recently been complemented by certain non-governmental organizations and independent experts.

The *bureaux d'études* have their own permanent staffs who bring with them considerable experience and expertise. They send staffs for long term technical assistance of foreign governments or on shorter-term assignments. They are engaged in regional socio-economic studies, economic planning, and the elaboration, follow-up and evaluation of rural development projects.

SEDES may be considered as the model of these consultancy organizations. In addition to making notable contributions relating to fields of knowledge,[16] it has produced methodological works which have become classics. One can mention its contribution to information collection techniques in the rural milieu and above all its role in the formalization and the promotion of the so-called 'effects method,' both of which lie behind the French approach to economic evaluation of projects.[17]

Diversity and Convergence in FARE Research

There is a great deal of diversity in FARE research. Although there are many institutions working in the field of Africanist rural economics, each institution carries out a certain brand of research. The following major factors account for this:

- the mandate of the institution: cognitive research, problem-solving research, or direct intervention related to development;
- the field of activity: agronomic research, research in various disciplinary fields, economic or socio-economic studies;
- the training of researchers and experts: Due to the the French system of education[18] there is a dominance of engineering degrees (agronomists,

economists, statistitians) in the field of operational research and a majority of university degrees for more fundamental research.

the mode of financing: What distinguishes some of the mentioned research institutions (like ORSTOM) is that they are financed almost completely by the State, with few constraints in the definition of research programs themes, localization and length. Institutions which are only partly financed by the State (like CIRAD) or institutions which do not receive grants, are much less free when it comes to the innovation of programs.

We can, however, single out two dominant frameworks of analysis which reflect the distinction between research with a cognitive orientation and operational research aiming to support the decisions of public or private decision-makers. The final objectives of the work indeed determine the choice of methods, the themes studied and the concepts applied.

Problem-Solving Research

Two major branches of problem-solving research may be distinguished: work relating to economic evaluation of development projects, and agro-economic studies of agricultural systems.

The application of the concepts and methods of the French school of economic evaluation in the African rural milieu has resulted in the accumulation of a great deal of knowledge and the improvement of means of analysis. The concept of agricultural production subsectors and the 'effects method' have allowed the consideration of both the economic and social aspects of production. Economic evaluation has involved identifying direct or indirect value added by projects and has required above all recognition of the various economic agents and their characteristics. It has also led to identifying different flows (circulation of products and by-products, circulation and redistribution of incomes) in order to be able to set up subsector economic accounts. This procedure has led in particular to the enrichment and formulation of fieldwork methods in rural areas. It has also given rise to many detailed case studies which have broadened the the base of available references.

The framework of agro-economic approaches, undertaken mostly by agronomists, is that of agricultural development without reference to an academic disciplinary field. The economic part of the work is generally limited to borrowing a few concepts and methods.[19] The reference to agro-economics (frequent in France over the past fifteen years) may be interpreted as a means for agronomists to explore empirically the field of social sciences in order to gain a better understanding of peasants' behavior. Agro-economic approaches are behind a variety of research projects, ranging from simple techno-economic analysis of production costs, to historic studies of access to and implementation of production factors through the analysis of the dynamics of production and agrarian systems. The dominant theme of the work remains that of technical changes and response to innovation.

Research With a Cognitive Orientation

This research focuses on the linkage between the behavior of economic actors and the dynamics of economic systems. Some studies emphasize historic processes and institutional change such as monetarization of exchanges, transformation of land ownership systems, disruption of production relationships, economic and social conditions and effects of the introduction of technical or organizational innovations. Other studies are primarily concerned with the behavior and strategies of producers in a more micro-economic perspective and on a shorter time scale.[20] These studies are concerned with topics such as crop choices, conditions of access to and the implementation of production factors, anti-risk strategies, or accumulation patterns.

The natures of these two types of cognitive studies are not fundamentally different. A distinction may be seen, however, in the emphasis placed on the behavior of economic actors versus the dynamics of economic systems. In the first group of studies, the behavior of economic actors is always seen in the context of networks of constraints and opportunities defined by the social, economic, institutional and natural environment. In the second, the dynamic-structural analyses are always founded on observations on the local scale.

Although problem-solving research and cognitive-oriented research represent two different approaches to FARE research, there are ways in which the two approaches converge. Not only do problem-solving research and cognitive-oriented research share African rural economies and their environment as their object of analysis; they have common sources of funding (principally the French State) and common methods. The AMIRA[21] group was founded in 1975 to promote interdisciplinary and interinstitutional research and scientific debates between experts, consultants, researchers and teachers, and to improve research methods in African rural studies. Before it was dissolved in 1989, this group helped to consolidate a common system of references and made substantial methodological and theoretical contributions.

Unfortunately these contributions have generally been available only to members of the AMIRA network.

The FARE research community is characterized by personalized relationships (with the dynamics of informal networks) and inter-institutional mobility.[22] This environment encourages the sharing of a corpus of references both in methodological and practical fields.[23]

Exploring a Heterodox Rural Economics

In this second part we will present an outline of the main characteristics of the research themes, methodological foundations and theoretical bases for FAREs' work, concentrating mostly on cognitive oriented research.[24] We will also clarify the place occupied in the research process by fieldwork, which distinguishes FARE studies from much economic research. We will also present what we see as major convergence points between FARE and the 'old' American institutionalism.

Major Features of Research Themes

Certain common features of FAREs' studies may be discerned from the themes of their research. FARE studies may be characterized as follows:

- They are carried out at the local or regional level.
- They are not restricted to the analysis of resources allocation but give considerable attention to the social conditions of access to resources. The economic calculation in terms of production costs and factor valuation is also systematically situated in the institutional context which gives it its meaning. The economic calculation is not in itself the purpose of the research but is used to explain peasant practices and economic dynamics, which also parallel other factors. This orientation explains the fact that in the literature quoted in the bibliography, there is no trace of the traditional writings of economists, such as papers aiming to verify a relation between factors of productivity and the size of smallholdings on the basis of statistical data collected on a large scale, or those seeking to determine the price-elasticity of supply of any given agricultural product.[25]
- The analysis includes a historical and spatial dimension which brings to light the present conditions of access to resources and the ambient economic system.

- The processes of economic differentiation are stressed. African rural society is considered as neither stable nor homogeneous. Recognition of this heterogeneity is key to understanding the diversity of peasant practices, even on the local level.

Some fields of research have been particularly studied by FAREs: the analysis of development projects, the economy of transition from a subsistence to a market economy, the dynamics of the peasant plantation economy, the intensification of production systems, the relationships between local economic systems and kinship, religion or migratory phenomena.

These themes are approached in particular through the analysis of land tenure systems, social relations of production, intrafamily relations of production and accumulation, conditions of the introduction and diffusion of technical innovations, and relations forged between peasants and development corporations.

The research carried out by FAREs ultimately deals as much with institutional change as with the allocation of production factors. However, this allocation is studied on a very different scale (the local one) and uses very different information collection techniques and analytical tools from those generally used by orthodox economists.

Methodological and Theoretical Features of the FAREs' Production[26]

An Inclusive Conception of Economics

Like the institutionalists, the FAREs refer--usually implicitly--to a substantive conception of economics, understood as a discipline studying not only the production / distribution / consumption processes in their man - object dimensions, but also the social relations involved in these processes. This conception means going beyond the neoclassical perspective centered on resource allocation processes through maximization behavior to open up 'black boxes' considered by the neoclassicists as outside the economic field.[27] The determinants of economic phenomena (i.e. those considered as economic by the mainstream) can thus be identified in a field more expansive than the one usually explored by economists.

Partial Theories and Practitioner's Knowledge

Starting from empirical questions, the FAREs try to provide an outline to make intelligible a specific localized reality (the titles of the publications are explicit in this respect). This perspective tends to expand the connection with established theoretical bodies and with a 'hard' disciplinary approach. In terms of scientific production, the final aim is not to propose a general theory or to embellish an existing theoretical edifice, but to provide explanatory models which are valid locally, i.e. partial (as opposed to general) theories. To build up these locally valid models, it is necessary to immerse oneself in this local reality, to gain a many-sided perception of rural society, and to accumulate knowledge which is specific to that society. The FAREs are therefore in agreement with an institutionalist like Ramstad, when he writes "one needs a theory capable of saying a great deal about a few cases, rather than very little about all cases. (...) to develop 'practitioner's knowledge,' that is, knowledge directed to the understanding and control of the specific case. This is in sharp contrast to the formalist's preoccupations with the development of knowledge applicable to aggregates even if it is of limited applicability to individual cases" (1986, 1075).

In fact, the pattern model of explanation--considered as the typical institutionalist mode of explanation (Wilber and Harrison 1978, Ramstad 1986)--describes quite well the kind of procedure followed by most FAREs. The first step is the socialization of the researcher, allowing him to remain close to the system, grasping its norms and categories, observing recurrent themes (such as socio-economic or technical practices, etc.). The next step is to formulate tentative hypotheses about parts of the system and to try to capture the linkages between themes which contribute to the system's uniqueness. The interpretations are based on a wide variety of data (case studies, survey data, and personal observation).[28] The last step is to construct a model of the system by linking validated hypotheses or themes in a network or pattern.[29]

Immediate Induction But Not Hyperempiricism

The (non-mathematical) models built up by FAREs are not the result of hypothetico-deductive procedures, but refer to a process of immediate induction[30] which enables one to connect facts to produce a sequence which creates meaning (Couty 1984). However, these facts are not given; they do not speak for themselves. They are constructed on the basis of previous questioning or at the very least on the basis of a conceptual framework itself making up an implicit theoretical framework. Resorting to an inductive approach does not therefore mean a hyperempiricist methodology.[31]

Ad Hoc Concepts

The concern to stay close to the concrete situations studied often leads to conceptual construction or redefinition (for example, the identification of economic units).[32] This flexibility, which is shared by the institutionalists, is necessary when one wishes to define situations rather than to fit them into an existing theoretical body taken as an obligatory framework--whether it be neoclassical or Marxist.

Theoretical Eclecticism

One rarely finds in FAREs' work coherent and exclusive references to an existing theoretical paradigm. The dominant trend is a rejection of both neoclassical and Marxist paradigms. This rejection does not preclude borrowing from those theories, however. From one an interest in resources allocation and economic calculation may be retained, and from the other a dynamic perspective, the consideration of reproduction, of power relations and conflicts of interests.[33]

The place that Marxist thought gives to historic and structural determinism and to conflict as the sole driving force of history is fundamentally questioned by FAREs. More practically, the generality of the concepts proposed (like that of production mode) reduces their relevance when takes into account the diversity of peasant practices at the local level (Olivier de Sardan 1985).

The rejection of neoclassical theory is today widely accepted in professional circles--thus one can understand that it is rarely mentioned explicitly. In fact, neoclassical theory is now less often criticized than it is ignored,[34] but most FAREs implicitly agree with the criticisms that the "old" institutionalists address to the dominant paradigm[35] when they call into question its formalism, its non-historical approach, its indifference toward social structures and the dynamics of human interrelations, its conception of a balanced world of harmonious complementary interests joined together in a neutral market, and its omission of power relationships.

In fact, neoclassical theory considers as exogenous and therefore eliminates from the field of investigation those problems with which FAREs' research is concerned, such as the condition of access to productive resources, the rationality of actors's behavior, the institutional context, the concrete mechanisms of exchange, or technical change.

Limited Interest in Mathematical Models and Econometric Analysis

This standpoint is generally justified by the classic problem (which is particularly acute in the African context) of the quality of initial data, by clear reticence towards mathematical modeling of qualitative information, dynamic processes and risk factors. However, this does not imply a refusal of quantification[36] or a sterile opposition between the quantitative and the qualitative.[37] Although it is nowadays considered fashionable to revile descriptive studies, the importance of description (of situations, facts, practices) in FAREs' studies should be stressed. Description is not an end in itself; it may reveal the facts necessary to understand a previously unexplained phenomenon or may suggest new, more relevant questions which help one to avoid falling into the reductionist traps of certain models.

Methodological Interactionism

Between individualism and methodological holism, the majority of the FAREs seem to lean towards interactionism, defined as the simultaneous consideration of individuals and structures (Mingat et al. 1985). Research tends therefore to reconcile the tension between two poles--the individual as a member of a social group, relatively constrained by the relations between groups and the individual as an economic actor who has a freedom of action which is materialized by a strategy and a behavioral logic that cannot be reduced to his belonging to a particular social group. The degree of social determination of behavior remains an empirical question--an object of study--and not a postulate. This interactionism does not exclude a holistic approach to observation, considering this term to mean that the understanding of an element of the system studied necessitates an overview of the system.

In Situ Research

In the African context, information is available in limited quantities and is of doubtful quality--especially those statistical series which are the delight of econometricians. The possible use of such data is limited by a desire for rigor, making necessary the collection of information during research. Even when reliable statistics are available, collecting first hand information is nonetheless indispensable because the type of studies carried out cannot be simply reduced to figures and realized on the basis of pre-existing works.

What distinguishes FAREs as economists, however, is less the collection of first hand information--nowadays a common practice in rural economics--than the fact that data collection is delegated only partially or not at all, in the tradition of anthropological works.[38] As Couty stresses (1991, 4), "in social sciences, experience requires personal sincere and long term involvement in the historicity and singularity of the situation under study. Without this we are threatened by empty mathematical formalization or by verbiage." In most cases, long assignments in the country under study are possible due to the institutional characteristics of French research (especially for researchers from ORSTOM and CIRAD). The length of extended stays in the field is rarely less than three years.[39]

This tradition of information gathering is not without epistemological implications. The nearness of the 'realities'[40] of the field in all their complexity makes one sensitive to the interrelations between the economic, technical and sociological dimensions of the research problems. Awareness of local circumstances is an excellent antidote against the reductive oversimplification of grand theories which contribute little to the understanding of peasant practices in a specific environment. This tradition also allows one to not succumb to what A. Hirschman calls the syndrome of the economist on an assignment: "(the) habit of giving peremptory opinions and prescriptions while invoking economic principles and remedies of universal values (...) after having barely got to know the 'patient'" (1984, 76). Finally, the usual sequence... definition of the problem / formulation of hypotheses / choice of operational concepts / information collection / analysis, can give way to an iterative process leading to a reorientation of the problem under study, or a redefinition of the concepts chosen; in short, it can lead to a more flexible and less pre-established research practice.

The FAREs thus do not follow Heady (1952) when he qualifies information collection as simple routine; this phase is conversely seen by FAREs as an extremely important component of the research process,[41] justifying an on-site time investment of the researcher, even if he already has his PhD. Thus the emphasis of FAREs on methodological concepts and observation techniques can be explained. In this vein, the AMIRA network has produced and published documents on as varied topics as the comparison of aleatory and non-aleatory sampling, the connection between the qualitative and the quantitative, the complementarity of statistical survey and monographic studies, the definition of economic units, and the problem of scale of analysis. This critical reflection on concepts and information collection techniques is considered fundamental in order to guarantee a minimum degree of rigor in research efforts.[42]

The eclecticism of the FAREs is not limited to the realm of theory; the information collection techniques they use are many and are borrowed from both anthropologists and geographers: participant observation, informal interviews, kinship and biographic descriptions, one-shot questionnaires (demographic and agricultural censuses, thematic questionnaires), follow-up questionnaires with a variable frequency (recording effective labor requirements per hectare, work time per individual, expenditures, consumption), yields and area measurements, or cartography, etc.

When all is said and done, the heretical FAREs' practice of economics--when compared with norms of the theory--does not constitute an apology for woolliness. Is this not a decisive way of contributing to the understanding of the reality, when one goes beyond the magic of equations to wonder--on the basis of the researcher's direct knowledge of the studied situation--about the objects observed (or rather, constructed) and on the methods of observation?

Economics or Socio-Economics?

Given the approach that FAREs have chosen and the object of their studies, they contribute, as do researchers from other disciplines, to what Couty (1985) qualifies as historic and spatialized socio-economics, a scientific field made up of the combination of two fields of studies, systems of production and production relationships. We think of historic and spatialized socio-economics less as a new discipline, as Couty suggests, but as a field of research practice bringing closer anthropologists, economists, geographers and some agronomists.[43]

There are a number of interests which socio-economic studies share. Their general object of study (African rural societies, peasant practices) and their desire for empiric analyses entrenched in the locality and depth of time of phenomena are two such shared interests. Also an awareness of the limits of a strictly disciplinary approach, emphasis on the importance of fieldwork, and similar investigation techniques are recognizable in the work of FAREs. It is sometimes difficult to give a disciplinary label to certain publications, just as it is difficult to distinguish between the economist and the anthropologist in the *Norfolk Bar* in Nairobi described by C. Gladwin (1989)... the meeting-points in our case being the *Bar Bozo* in Mopti or *La Canne à sucre* in Abidjan.

Can FARE's contribution to socio-economics be classified under the heading of economics? We tend to answer positively for two reasons:

First of all because we think that it is epistemologically unfounded to give a normative definition of economics--here we follow Schumpeter when he reminds us that "the frontiers of the sciences are incessantly shifting; there is no point in trying to define them either by subject or method" (1986, 10).[44] After all, cleavages between disciplines are often less deep than paradigmatic splits. If it were possible to calibrate thought, an economist and a sociologist referring to the same paradigm (neo-classical for example) would be closer than two economists or two sociologists referring to different paradigms.

Secondly, while FAREs contribute an economic perspective to socio-economics,[45] explanations are found outside the realm of orthodox economics and concepts and methods of investigation are borrowed from other disciplines. Perceiving the economy as an 'open system' (Grunberg 1978), the economist will consider kinship relations as unavoidable in the understanding of the implementation of household labor input decisions; this will not, however, turn him into an anthropologist.

It is clear that such a conception of economics does not correspond to the neoclassical norms, nor to the representation that other social sciences often have of economics, where it is reduced to an accounting systems builder and to the technical analysis of costs and markets.

Should the socio-economic approach--whether it be understood as a discipline or as a contribution of economics to a research field--be limited to problem-solving research as A. Etzioni (1988) has suggested? According to Etzioni, 'explaining the world' would proceed from a selective and disciplinary construction of the object of research, whereas the political decision-maker has to act on the world such as it is, beyond the frontiers of disciplines. We agree with this last point but to us it is questionable whether the interest of socio-economics has to be reduced in this fashion. It is precisely because 'hard' disciplinary approaches proved to be insufficient to 'explain' the African rural world that socio-economics is so dynamic in French research. Far from being limited as an instrument in the service of political decision-makers, the socio-economic approach seems to us a desirable way to gain the real knowledge of the African rural world which is necessary for efficient action.

Limits of FAREs' Works

In addition to recognizing the heterodox conception of economics of FARE we also consider it important to recognize that FARE has certain weaknesses, some of which may also be shared with the "old" institutionalism.

We just pointed out that research was often limited to what should be its first phase (construction of a conjectural model on the basis of immediate induction).

The risk of the one-man band, or of uncontrolled borrowing is increased when the researcher succumbs to the temptation of going beyond his discipline without having sufficient knowledge of the other disciplines explored and without making explicit the methodological coherence of this encroachment.[46] Looking for explanatory tools in another discipline is not devoid of risks--it is sufficient to recall the pseudo-anthropological explanations in terms of traditionalism put forward by certain agronomists or economists in their efforts to analyze response to technical change.

From a theoretical point of view, it seems to us that the rejection of the neoclassical paradigm--which is often an ideological rejection--would gain from being argued and modulated. The fact that this paradigm is not efficient as an exclusive conceptual framework in the FARE research field does not mean that it should be forgotten.[47] This rejection should center on the pretension of neoclassical theory to explain everything[48] and not on its capacity to provide a coherent set of hypotheses or partial explanations. We are thinking here in particular of the neoclassical theory of production and above all of the perspectives developed by the new institutional economics. In other words, one should explain the theoretical eclectism practiced in order to avoid sinking into the same normative shortcomings as mainstream economics.

In the same light, the fact that econometric tools are not always appropriate for the type of questions handled by FAREs should not lead to their unconditional rejection. Here again, the problem is not to exclude *a priori* certain research orientations or analytical tools, but to promote synergy between disparate but complementary approaches. We consider that econometric studies are useful, indeed indispensable, if they are well done, i.e. if they are critically adapted to their object and realized on the basis of reasonably reliable data. As this reliability is to be appreciated in relation to the object of study, the purism shown by many FAREs regarding data quality seems to us often to be excessive and may, in some cases, lead to a decreasing margin of productivity in the research effort.

The weak support given to development by FAREs' studies--which are said to be more critical than constructive--has sometimes been criticized.[49] We believe that although this criticism is not unfounded, it should be reformulated.

Let us note first that the criticism cannot be accepted if the relevance of cognitive research is acknowledged and if the limits of problem-solving research are recognized. Is it necessary to recall that the activist pleas justifying this kind of research often result in self-interested pieces of rhetoric, designed to convince backers to finance the research? One must avoid 'pragmatic totalitarianism,' a form of intellectual and institutional totalitarianism which leads to the opinion that research which does not lead directly to action if of no interest whatsoever.

Secondly, the problem in our view is less one of gaining the knowledge on peasant behaviors and more generally African rural societies which is a prerequisite for development management than it is the transfer of this knowledge within the sphere of decision-makers. The diffusion of results is often less than perfect. Due to style, size and time-limits the products of research may not be easily accessible and the desired audience of decision-makers may not themselves be accessible. In other words, there is first and foremost a problem of communication and of presentation of results.

Finally, one should stress the effective use of FARE works by the French government in its cooperative programs with African countries even when the studies did not display a finalized aim in terms of action. By this we are not referring to the use of concrete localized empirical results, but to the recognition of the logic of peasant practices, of agricultural production organization, and so forth. Consequently, a major contribution of FARE will have been to modify the perception, at least in France, of African economies.

Conclusion

The main contribution of FARE is not of a disciplinary nature but is concerned with the knowledge of the economic systems of the peasant societies of Africa and with the production of suitable methodologies for information collection in rural Africa. Its contribution to economics can be interpreted in terms which are principally critical regarding orthodox economics (definition of economic units, rationality of the actors).

Generally speaking, FARE's methodological position might belong more to the French intellectual tradition earlier mentioned than to the African context of FARE research. One only has to read the work of M. Blanc and Ph. Lacombe (1990) or of M. Petit (1982, 1986) concerning French rural economics to realize the closeness (even though institutional links are virtually non-existent) which would lead many FAREs to associate themselves with this statement of Petit : "In the old economics debate between the wish to build a 'hard' science that is as rigorous as possible but at the expense of necessarily simplifying abstractions, and the concern to take into account the social and political dimensions of the phenomena under study, I lean very much towards the second attitude. (...) To explain is sometimes to shed light on conflicts which are sometimes hidden. In that sense, our role becomes one of social criticism (...)" (1986, 53).

We believe that in the theoretical and methodological foundations of the research carried out by FARE, we have brought to light many common points with the "old" institutionalism as we perceive it: a similar research agenda, a substantive conception of economics, a pattern model of explanation, the production of 'partial' theories, a theoretical eclectism, the development of a practitioner's knowledge, the development of *ad hoc* concepts, the importance given to description, a critical perspective toward the neoclassical paradigm, a comon neglect of mathematical modelization and of the econometric tool, and the importance alloted to fieldwork.

A better knowledge of institutionalism and an attempt to formalize with greater detail French Africanist rural economics may well lead to as many points of divergence (such as the institutionalists' pragmatic philosophy and their great interest in the value problem discussion) as their are of convergence. However, the establishment of a shared criticism of the neoclassical paradigm as the only recognized framework for economic research seems to us a plea in favor of the development of transatlantic scientific exchanges between heterodox economists and economic anthropologists, especially in these times of revival of an ideology aiming to institute the Market as the sole regulator of economic and social life.

References

Ancey, Gérard. 1975. *Niveaux de décision et fonctions objectifs en milieu rural africain.* Note AMIRA 3. Paris: INSEE.

Badouin, Robert. 1987. L'analyse économique du système productif en agriculture. *Cahiers des Sciences Humaines* 23(3-4): 357-375.

Blanc, Michel, and Philippe Lacombe. 1990. Rural Economics in France. In Philip Lowe and Maryvonne Bodiguel, eds. Pp. 144-164. *Rural Studies in Britain and France.* London: Belhaven Press.

Blaug, Marc. 1982. *La méthodologie économique.* Paris: Economica.

Boudon, Raymond. 1984. *La place du désordre.* Paris: PUF.

Bourdieu, Pierre, Jean-Claude Chamboredon, and Jean-Claude Passeron. 1983. (first edition 1968) *Le métier de sociologue.* Paris: Mouton.

Caldwell, Bruce. 1985. *Beyond Positivism, Economic Methodology in the Twentieth Century.* London: George Allen and Unwin.

Chervel, Marc, and Michel Le Gall. 1976. Manuel d'évaluation économique des projets. *La méthode des effets.* Paris: Ministère de la coopération.

Couty, Philippe. 1984. La vérité doit être construite. *Cahiers des Sciences Humaines* 20(1): 5-15.

———.1985. Information, méthodes d'investigation et décision en milieu rural africain. Handout lecture notes, DESS Développement 1985-86. ORSTOM/Université de Paris-X Nanterre.

———.1991 Editorial. *Chroniques du Sud* 4: 3-5. Paris: ORSTOM. Couty, Philippe, and Gérard Winter. 1983. *Qualitatif et quantitatif. Deux modes d'investigation complémentaires. Réflexions à partir des recherches de l'ORSTOM en milieu rural africain.* Note AMIRA 43. Paris:INSEE.

Dugger, William. 1979. Methodological Differences Between Institutional and Neoclassical Economics. *Journal of Economic Issues* 13(4):899-909.

———.1990 The New Institutionalism: New But Not Institutionalist. *Journal of Economic Issues* 24(2): 423-431.

Etzioni, Amitai. 1988. *The Moral Dimension. Toward a New Economics.* New York: The Free Press.

Freud, Claude. 1988. *Quelle coopération? Un bilan de l'aide au développement.* Paris: Karthala.

Gastellu, Jean-Marc. 1980. Mais où sont donc ces unités économiques que nos amis cherchent tant en Afrique? *Cahiers ORSTOM,* Série Sciences Humaines 18(1-2): 3-11.

Gladwin, Christina. 1989. On the Division of Labor Between Economics and Economic Anthropology. In Stuart Plattner, ed. *Economic Anthropology.* Stanford: Stanford University Press.

Gruchy, Allan G. 1987. *The Reconstruction of Economics. An Analysis of the Fundamentals of Institutional Economics.* New York: Greenwood Press.

———.1990. Three Different Approaches to Institutional Economics: An Evaluation. *Journal of Economic Issues* 24(2): 361-369.

Grunberg, Emile. 1978. "Complexity" and "Open Systems" in Economic Discourse. *Journal of Economic Issues* 12(3): 541-560.

Heady, Earl O. 1952. *Economics of Agricultural Production and Resource Use.* New York: Prenctice-Hall.

Hirschman, Albert. 1984. *L'Economie comme science morale et politique.* Paris: Gallimard-Le Seuil.

Hodgson, Geoffrey. 1988. *Economics and Institutions, A Manifesto for a Modern Institutional Economics.* Philadelphia: University of Pennsylvania Press.

———.1991. *Institutional Economics: Surveying the 'Old' and the 'New.'* Paper presented at the 4th symposium of Charles Gide Association for the Study of Economic Thought, Marseille, September 19 and 20.

Hugon, Philippe. 1991a. a L'économie du développement, le temps et l'histoire. *Revue Economique* 42(2): 339-364.

———.1991b, La pensée française en économie du développement. *Revue d'Economie Politique* 2: 171-230.

Klein, Philip A. 1990. Institutionalism as a School - A Reconsideration. *Journal of Economic Issues* 24(2): 381-388.

Mayhew, Anne. 1987. The Beginnings of Institutionalism. *Journal of Economic Issues* 21(3): 971-998.

Mayhew, Anne, and Terry Neale. 1991. The Implicit Theory and Method of the Old (and Real) American Institutionalists. Paper presented at the 4th symposium of Charles Gide Association for the Study of Economic Thought, Marseille. September 19 and 20.

McCloskey, Donald. 1983. The Rhetoric of Economics. *Journal of Economic Literature* 21: 481-517.

Milleville, Pierre. 1987. Recherches sur les pratiques des agriculteurs. *Cahiers de la Recherche-De'veloppement* 16: 3-7.

Mingat Alain, Pierre Salmon, and Alain Wolfesperger. 1985. *Méthodologie économique.* Paris: PUF.

Myrdal, Gunnar. 1978. Institutional Economics. *Journal of Economic Issues* 12(4): 771-783.

North, Douglass. 1990. *Institutions, Institutional Change and Economic Performance.* Cambridge: Cambridge University Press.

Olivier de Sardan, Jean-Pierre. 1985. *Sciences sociales africanistes et faits de développement.* In Pierre, Boiral, Jean-Fran çois Lanteri, and Jean-Pierre Olivier de Sardan, eds. Pp. 27-43. *Paysans, experts et chercheurs en Afrique Noire. Sciences sociales et développement rural.* Paris: CIFACE-Karthala.

Parsons, Kenneth H. 1949. The Logical Foundations of Economic Research. *Journal of Farm Economics* 31(4): 656-686.

Perlman, Mark. 1991. Understanding the "Old" American Institutionalism. Paper presented at the 4th symposium of Charles Gide Association for the Study of Economic Thought, Marseille, September 19 and 20.

Petit, Michel. 1982. Is There a French School of Agricultural Economics? *Journal of Agricultural Economics* 33(3): 325-337.

———.1986 L'état et le statut de l'économie rurale. *Economie Rurale* 172: 49-54.

Petrie, Hugh G. 1976. Do You See What I See? The Epistemology of Interdisciplinary Inquiry. *Journal of Aesthetic Education* 10(1): 29-43.

Ramstad, Yngve. 1986. A Pragmatist's Quest for Holistic Knowledge: The Scientific Method of John R. Commons. *Journal of Economic Issues* 20(4): 1067-1105.

Samuels, Warren, ed. 1979. *The Economy as a System of Power. I. Corporate Systems*. New Brunswick: Transaction Books.

———.1988. *Institutional Economics* (3 Vol.). Hants: Edward Elgar.

Samuels, Warren. 1984. Institutional Economics. *Journal of Economic Education* 15(3): 211-216.

———.1987. Institutional Economics. In *The New Palgrave Dictionary of Economics*, Vol. 2. Pp. 864-866. New York: Macmillan.

Schmid, Allan. 1987. *Property, Power, & Public Choice. An Inquiry into Law and Economics.* New York: Praeger.

Schumpeter, Joseph. 1986. (first 1954) *History of Economic Analysis*. New York: Oxford University Press.

Stevens, Robert, and Cathy Jabara. 1988. *Agricultural Development Principles. Economic Theory and Empirical Evidences.* Baltimore and London: The John Hopkins University Press.

Tool, Marc, ed. 1988. *Evolutionary Economics.* Foundations of Institutional Thought. Vol. 1. Armonk: M.E. Sharpe.

Wilber, Charles, and Robert Harrison. 1978. The Methodological Basis of Institutional Economics: Pattern Model, Storytelling, and Holism. *Journal of Economic Issues* 7(1): 61-89.

Williamson, Oliver. 1985. *The Economic Institutions of Capitalism.* New York: The Free Press.

Bibliographical Sources Related to FAREs' Studies (apart from the references already quoted)

These non exhaustive references rarely take into account unpublished literature (by far the majority of the papers written by FAREs) and quote mainly books. They do not include the sometimes related studies of researchers from other disciplines (geographers, anthropologists and sociologists).

Fieldworks

Ancey, Gérard, Jean Chevassu, and Jean Michotte. 1974. *L'économie de l'espace rural de la région de Bouaké*. Paris: ORSTOM.

Ancey, Gérard. 1983. *Monnaie et structures d'exploitations en pays Mossi, Haute Volta.* Paris: ORSTOM.

Anonymous, ed. 1977. *Essais sur la reproduction de formations sociales dominées (Cameroun, Côte d'Ivoire, Haute-Volta, Sénégal, Madagascar, Polynésie)*. Paris: ORSTOM.

———.1978. *Maîtrise de l'espace agraire et développement en Afrique Tropicale.* Logique paysanne et rationalité technique. Proceedings of the Ouagadougou Symposium, December 4-8, 1978. Paris: ORSTOM.

———.1983. *Le développement: idéologies et pratiques.* Paris: ORSTOM.

———.1987. *Etat, Développement, Paysans.* Proceedings of the Vth Rural Economics Seminar, September 16-20, 1985. Montpellier: CIRAD.

———.1987. Systèmes de production agricole en Afrique tropicale. *Cahiers des Sciences Humaines* 23(3-4) (special issue).

———.1988. Systèmes de production agricole en Afrique tropicale. *Cahiers des Sciences Humaines* 24(1) (special issue).

———.1990. *Dynamique des systèmes agraires. La dimension économique.* Paris: ORSTOM.

———.1990. *Economie des filières en régions chaudes. Formation des prix et échanges agricoles.* Proceedings of the Xth Rural Economics Seminar, September 11-15, 1989. Montpellier: CIRAD.

Bonnefond, Philippe. 1980. L'étude de la force de travail en milieu rural africain. *Cahiers ORSTOM,* Série Sciences Humaines 17(1-2): 117-123.

Boutillier, JeanLouis. 1960. *Bongouanou, Côte d'Ivoire. Etude socio-économique d'une subdivision.* Paris: Berger-Levrault.

Charmes, Jacques. 1976. Evolution des modes de faire-valoir et transformation des structures sociales dans la région de l'Anony (Nord-Ouest du lac Alaotra, Madagascar). *Cahiers ORSTOM,* Série Sciences Humaines 13(4):367-382.

Colin, Jean-Philippe, and Bruno Losch. "Touche pas à mon planteur." Réflexion sur les "encadrements" paysans en Côte d'Ivoire. *Politique Africaine* 40:83-99.

Colin, Jean-Philippe. 1990. *La mutation d'une économie de plantation en basse Côte d'Ivoire.* Paris: ORSTOM.

Copans, Jean, Philippe Couty, Jean Roch, and Guy Rocheteau. 1972. *Maintenance sociale et changement économique au Sénégal.* Paris: ORSTOM.

Delaunay, Daniel. 1984. *De la captivité à l'exil. Histoire et geographie des migrations paysannes dans la Moyenne Vallée du Fleuve Sénégal.* Paris: ORSTOM.

Dupire, Marguerite, and Jean-Louis Boutillier. 1958. *Le pays Adioukrou et sa palmeraie.* Paris: L'Homme d'Outre-Mer N°4.

Gastellu, Jean-Marc. 1981. *L'égalitarisme économique des Serer du Sénégal.* Paris: ORSTOM.

———.1986. *Une économie du trésor : les grands planteurs du Moronou.* Paris: ORSTOM.

Leplaideur, Alain. 1984. *Les paysans du Centre-Sud Cameroun. Montpellier:* CIRAD.

Le Roy, Xavier. 1983. *L'introduction des cultures de rapport dans l'agriculture vivrière sénoufo.* Paris: ORSTOM.

Losch, Bruno, Jean-Louis Fusillier, and Pierre Dupraz. 1991. *Stratégies des producteurs en zone caféière et cacaoyère du Cameroun. Quelles adaptations à la crise?* Montpellier: CIRAD.

Minvielle, Jean-Paul. 1985. *Paysans migrants du Fouta Toro.* Paris: ORSTOM.

Robineau, Claude. 1971. *Evolution économique et sociale en Afrique centrale. L'exemple de Souanké (République Populaire du Congo).* Paris: ORSTOM.

Robineau, Claude, ed. 1992. *Les terrains du développement. Approche pluridisciplinaire des économies du Sud.* Paris: ORSTOM.

Ruf, François. 1982. Les règles du jeu sur le foncier et la force de travail dans l'ascension économique et la stratification sociale des planteurs de Côte d'Ivoire. *Economie Rurale* 147-148: 111-119.

———.1988. *Stratification sociale en économie de plantation ivoirienne* (8 vol.). Montpellier: CIRAD.

Weber, Jacques. 1977. Structures agraires et évolution des milieux ruraux : le cas de la région cacaoyère du Centre-Sud Cameroun. *Cahiers ORSTOM,* Série Sciences Humaines 14(2): 113-139.

Weigel, Jean-Yves. 1982. *Migration et production domestique des Soninké du Sénégal.* Paris: ORSTOM.

Syntheses, Methodological Production

Agel, Christian, Jean-Michel Danel, Henri Raymond, Jean-Yves Rouchy, and Jean-Michel Yung 1981. *Guide des enquêtes statistiques pourle suivi des opérations dedéveloppement rural.* Paris: Ministère de la coopération.

Ancey, Gérard. 1975. *Les notions d'activités et d'actifs à l'intérieur d'une exploitation agricole.* Note AMIRA 11. Paris: INSEE.

———.1984. *Enquêtes rurales en Afrique sur échantillons restreints.* Note AMIRA 45. Paris: INSEE.

Anonymous, ed. *1983 Etat des travaux sur les indicateurs de transition.* Paris: AFIRD.

———.1985. *Approche anthropologique et recherche économique à l'ORSTOM.* Paris: ORSTOM.

———.1986. *Les unités d'observation.* Note AMIRA 49. Paris: INSEE.

Aubertin, Catherine, Robert Cabanes, Jean-Pierre Chauveau, Philippe Couty, Guy Pontié, and Claude Robineau. 1982. Où il est dit que le développement est un objet historique. *Tiers-Monde* 23(90):297-344.

Badouin, Robert. 1971. *Economie rurale.* Paris: Armand Colin.

———.1985. *Le développement agricole en Afrique tropicale.* Paris: Cujas.

Benoit-Cattin, Michel, and Jacques Faye. 1982. *L'exploitation agricole familiale en Afrique Soudano-sahélienne.* Paris: PUF.

Boiral, Pierre, Jean-François Lanteri, Jean-Pierre Olivier de Sardan, eds. 1985. *Paysans, experts et chercheurs en Afrique noire. Sciences sociales et développement rural.* Paris: CIFACE-Karthala.

Bosc, Pierre-Marie, Peter Calkins, Jean-Michel Yung. 1992. *Développement et recherche agricole dans les pays sahéliens et soudaniens d'Afrique.* Montpellier: CIRAD.

Boutillier, Jean-Louis. 1968. L'enquête d'ethnologie économique. In *Ethnologie générale.* Jean Poirier, ed. Pp. 214-256. Paris: Gallimard.

Couty, Philippe. 1979. *Des éléments aux systèmes. Réflexions sur les procédés de généralisation dans les enquêtes niveaux de vie en Afrique.* Note AMIRA 28. Paris: INSEE.

———.1987. La production agricole en Afrique sub-saharienne: manières de voir et façons d'agir. *Cahiers des Sciences Humaines* 23(3-4): 391-408.

———.1990. Vingt-cinq de recherche sur les agricultures africaines (Cahiers ORSTOM, série Sciences Humaines, 1963-1987). *Cahiers des Sciences Humaines* 26(3): 343-363.

Couty, Philippe, and Antoinette Hallaire. 1980. *De la carte aux systèmes. 20 ans d'études agraires au sud du Sahara* (ORSTOM 1960-1980). Note AMIRA 29. Paris: INSEE.

Couty, Philippe, Antoinette Hallaire, André Lericollais, Guy Pontié, Claude Robineau. 1984. Terroirs, ethnies et régions. Recherches de l'ORSTOM en milieu rural africain. *Cahiers ORSTOM, Série Sciences Humaines* 20(1): 25-28.

Dubois, Jean-Louis. 1989. *Réfléchir pour mesurer. Innovations méthodologiques pour la collecte et l'analyse d'informations statistiques.* Note AMIRA 57. Paris: INSEE.

Duruflé, Gilles, Raoul Fabre, and Jean-Michel Yung. 1988. *Les effets sociaux et économiques des projets de développement rural.* Paris: Ministère de la Coopération.

Legotien, Hélène. 1971. *Sur les structures internes et externes de l'économie agricole traditionnelle africaine.* Paris: SEDES.

Malassis, Louis. 1973. *Agriculture et processus de développement.* Paris: UNESCO.

Mercoiret, Marie-Rose, et al. 1989. *Les interventions en milieu rural. Principes et approche méthodologique.* Paris: Minitère de la Coopération.

Robineau, Claude. 1983. A la recherche des unités économiques. Trois approches : Comores, Congo, Tahiti. *Cahiers ORSTOM, Série Sciences Humaines* 19(1): 119-135.

———.1987. L'anthropologie économique. In *Images des Sciences de l'Homme, supplément au Courrier du CNRS* 67: 37-39.

Thénevin, Pierre. 1978. *L'investigation en milieu rural et la pratique du développement. Cadre d'intégration et approche systémique.* Note AMIRA 18. Paris: INSEE.

———.1983. *Pour un système d'enquêtes légères.* Paris: AMIRA-INSEE (mimeo).

Young, Jean-Michel, and Pierre-Marie Bosc. 1992. *Le développement agricole au Sahel (5 volumes).* Montpellier: CIRAD.

Journals publishing FAREs' articles

Cahiers d'Etudes Africaines, Cahiers des Sciences Humaines, Cahiers de la Recherche-De'veloppement, Politique Africaine, Tiers-Monde.

Notes

1. Respectively economists at ORSTOM (*Institut Français de Recherche Scientifique pour le Développement en Coopération*) & at CIRAD (*Centre International de Recherche Agronomique pour le Développement*). We would like to thank our colleagues for their comments and criticisms. We assume responsability for the imperfections of this paper and for the positions presented in the document, which in no way involve our institutions.

2. FAREs will designate French Africanist rural *economists*. The use of this acronym for reasons of facility of presentation will doubtless displease many of our colleagues who are so reticent about being classified. May they forgive us for this liberty of choosing an acronym which is by no means intended to be a lasting or definitive one.

3. We do not refer here to the new institutional economics (a development of the neoclassical theory, see for example Williamson, 1985, or North, 1990) but to Veblen's or Commons's heirs (as the contributors to the *Journal of Economic Issues*).

4. See for example Dugger (1979 and 1990), Gruchy (1987 and 1990), Hodgson (1988 and 1991), Klein (1990), Mayhew (1987), Mayhew and Neale (1991), Myrdal (1978), Perlman (1991), Ramstad (1986), Samuels (1979, 1984, 1987, 1988), Schmid (1987), Tool (1988), Wilber and Harrison (1978).

5. For references regarding FAREs' publications, see the bibliographical orientations. We have to clarify that this paper has been written more in the spirit of an essay rather than of a survey. We do not claim to be exhaustive in our attempt to reproduce an

original approach in relation to a research field made up of the economics of agricultural production in Africa. In this it only completes the small number of other synthetic approaches on which it has drawn (see in particular Ph. Couty's work).

6. Including both social and techno-economic practices. The qualifying adjective 'peasant' is used here for convenience; it does not correspond to a position in relation to the debates about the farmers' theoretical status.

7. Contacts and exchanges are real; however, carrying out truly interdisciplinary programs has proved to be more delicate.

8. Originally *Office de la Recherche Scientifique Coloniale*, set up in 1943, then *Office de la Recherche Scientifique et Technique d'Outre Mer* (the acronym ORSTOM has been kept after the ultimate change of denomination).

9. These research institutes either came out of professional groups, the oldest of which were founded before World War II (1936 for the IFC--*Institut Français du Caoutchouc* --afterwards called IRCA), or out of colonial agricultural departments (like IRAT--*Institut de Recherches en Agronomie Tropicale*--founded in 1960 at the time of independences in Africa).

10. If one includes the agro-economists, i.e. agronomists using methods and concepts drawn in part from economics (see infra).

11. *Ecole des Hautes Etudes en Sciences Sociales*, *Institut National de la Recherche Agronomique* and *Centre National de la Recherche Scientifique*.

12. The INSEE (*Institut National de la Statistique et des Etudes Economiques*) periodically publishes through its Cooperation department a liaison report with a collection of articles (*Stateco*) and a bibliographical report. It undertook the permanent secretarial tasks of the AMIRA group (see *infra*).

13. See in particular the collection "Méthodologie de la planification".

14. The SEDES (*Société d'Etudes pour le Développement Economique et Social*), founded in 1958, is an offshoot of the public *Caisse des Dépots et Consignations*. Its founding corresponds to the French government's wish to have operational structures to help set up administrations and development projects in the newly-independent former colonies.

15. *Institut de Recherches Appliquées et de Méthodes.*

16. In this respect, the regional socio-economic studies carried out on behalf of the Ministry of Economic Planning of the Côte d'Ivoire in the sixties are particularly revealing. Unfortunately this type of study is normally not published and is of difficult access.

17. This method (see Chervel & Le Gall, 1976) can mainly be set against the 'shadow-prices method' developed by the World Bank.

18. Characterized by the duality of the universities on one hand, and the *Grandes Ecoles* (mainly engineering schools) on the other hand.

19. On this point it may be compared with the original Farm Management research in the U.S.

20. These last studies can also have an operational aim, when public decision-makers are willing to take them into consideration.

21. *Amélioration des Méthodes d'Investigation en Milieux Informels et Ruraux d'Afrique, Asie et Amérique Latine* (Improvement of Investigation Methods in Informal & Rural Milieu in Africa, Asia and Latin America). It is not insignificant to note the development of the thematic and geographical fields of the group which originally dealt only with rural Africa. This development bears witness to the role of Africanist rural research in methods and concepts of French development experts.

22. Between research organizations, cooperation administrations & research institutions.

23. The work on economic evaluation of rural development projects, ordered between 1981 and 1986 by Evaluation unit of the Ministry of Cooperation & Development is a good illustration of the mobilization of this professional community (see Freud, 1988).

24. While at the same time stressing the proximity of numerous studies dealing with economic evaluation or developments of the agro-economic approach.

25. Such works do exist, but they are carried out by university economists who do not consider themselves as ruralists; see for example the publications of the CERDI of the University of Clermont-Ferrand, or of the Delta group (Departments of theoretical and applied economics of the *Ecole Normale Supérieure*, *Centre National de la Recherche Scientifique*, etc.).

26. This presentation is an attempt at reconstruction; in the writings of the FAREs, what is theoretically and methodologically implicit generally contrasts with the importance

of developments devoted to conceptual framework and to information collection techniques.

27. At least before the contributions of the new institutional economics.

28. Unfortunately, as is correctly pointed out by Wilber and Harrison (op. cit., p. 76), "this technique of contextual validation can never produce the rigorous certainty espoused by logical positivists; it can only indicate varying degrees of plausibility."

29. If one considers in Popper's perspective that the scientific nature of research work comes from the testing of a conjectural model for a refutation purpose, one is reduced to qualifying the majority of the FARE's production as belonging to the pre-scientific stage of a research procedure. But is it necessary to recall the limits of a normative methodology (Caldwell 1985, Hodgson 1988) and the proportion of rhetoric found in a large number of economic works with scientific pretention (McCloskey 1983)?

30. Which Blaug (1982) calls adduction.

31. At least for the majority of researchers.

32. See Ancey (1975) or Gastellu (1980).

33. The Marxist influence has come above all from the French neo-Marxist economic anthropology during the sixties and the seventies (works of Godelier, Meillassoux, Rey, Terray).

34. In our view, the weakness of FARE's epistemological production can be explained by the lack of domination of the neoclassical stream and therefore the lack of necessity to justify an heterodox economic orientation (the American institutionalists adopt a very different position).

35. See references in note 4.

36. The FAREs make abundant use of statistical methods, such as those developed by the French school of data analysis (i.e. factorial analysis of correspondences).

37. See AMIRA's work (in particular Couty & Winter, 1983).

38. People tend to forget the originality that the choice of 'setting up in the village,' which was done during pioneering studies carried out just after World War II by researchers like Boutillier, Couty or Robineau, represented for economists.

39. Experts from the *bureaux d'études* are subjected to more time constraints.

40. The quotation marks are there to remind us that these realities are not given, that they have to be constructed from a paradigmatic framework.

41. In this way they are in agreement with an institutionalist like K. Parsons who, as early as 1949, stressed that the data collection constitutes an integral part of research--and one of the most difficult ones.

42. "Given that one can ask anything of anyone and that anyone is almost always willing enough to reply at least any old thing to any old question, the questioner who, without a theory of the questionnaire, does not question the specific meaning of his questions, may too easily find a guarantee of the realism of his questions in the reality of the replies that are given" Bourdieu et al. (1983, 62).

43. In their analyses of the logic of technical practices (see Milleville 1987).

44. Boudon means nothing else when he writes "I believe it is an error when people sometimes try--rather like a geographer--to cut continents out of the real world which would be placed under the authority of the sociologist, the economist or the demographer. Of course, each one of these disciplines deals preferentially with one or another type of phenomena. But the frontiers separating them are more apt to be found at the level of certain trains of thought" (1984, 52).

45. i.e. generally recognized as such by the scientific community, as for example resources allocation and product distribution.

46. "(...) cross-fertilization might easily result in cross-sterilization," stressed Schumpeter several decades ago (op. cit., 27).

47. Notwithstanding, the analyses put forward by the FARE sometimes tend to reintroduce implicitly elements of the neoclassical model; the interpretation of an extensive agricultural production logic as a brake on certain forms of technical change could, for example, be rewritten in 'orthodox' terms.

48. Expressed by the authors of a recent textbook: "(...) these neoclassical economic tools, if used in the right way, enable an understanding of how traditional agricultural systems work. And thus no special, or different, economic theory is required to explain the economics of agricultural systems in developing nations" (Stevens and Jabara 1988, 84). As for us, we remain convinced that the subtle handling of isoquant and isocost lines remains largely insufficient for such a purpose.

49. We are not referring here to the studies done by experts from the *bureaux d'études*, whose job is precisely to provide support for decision-making in economic policies or to set up and evaluate projects.

14

Inside the Economic Institution: Modelling Household Budget Structures[1]

Richard Wilk

Introduction

Several years ago I led an interdisciplinary seminar on household economics at Indiana University. Our goal was to develop taxonomies and models of household budgetary systems, so we could explore some of the underlying causes of household economic diversity. For weeks we waded through ethnographic accounts of domestic life in exotic cultures--particularly from Africa where the best research has been done, struggling with ways to describe an enormous variety of structures, roles and practices. One afternoon, exhausted by an attempt to describe the structure of power and control over grain in a household in Cameroon, we decided to find something we could agree on for a change. What could be easier than the household budgets of American college professors? Two incomes at most; regular and measurable expenses; limited kinship complexity and few outside obligations; and annual accounting for the IRS. We went around the room and each described how we managed money decisions, accounts and bills in our own households. I cannot overstate the disbelief and shock around the table as each household economy was described. The eight of us had eight completely different systems. There were even eight ways of managing checking and savings accounts. Some couples had a single joint account, some had a joint account and individual accounts, some had only individual accounts. Some households paid all bills from a single fund, others divided up particular expenses into different areas of responsibility. Even people living alone managed their money differently from each other! And composite households formed through second and third marriages generated an almost unbelievable diversity of arrangements. Each one seemed to follow alien ideas about gender, authority and fairness. And each of us thought that the way our own household worked was normal!

To decide who really was normal, the following week we each interviewed two other people about household budgeting. The resulting sample of 24 households yielded 15 distinct systems of routine money management. For the rest of the semester we abandoned Africa and just tried to understand those 15 varieties. I would like to report a stellar success, but our enterprise ran aground on the very same rocks which sank our African work. Though we had a lot of theories, controversies and ideas, we simply had no vocabulary to describe household budgeting systems--no taxonomy, no definitions, not even a clear idea of how to go about building them. This absence of common tools and vocabulary means that every ethnographic account works in a relative vacuum, attacking the problem anew; the eyes rediscover the nose every morning.

The lack of tools for description and comparison is crippling for cross-cultural comparisons of household systems; it is equally damaging to understanding the range of variation within a single society, including our own. This paper makes some suggestions for putting this project on firmer ground. In doing so we should also ask why anthropology has built comparative typologies for every possible aspect of human culture except the art of household management. (I suggest some answers in another paper [Wilk 1989b]).

Research Issues: Emerging Common Problems

Scholars interested in domestic life in a number of different disciplines seem to be converging on some common approaches and ideas. Though the different disciplines have separate research traditions and objectives, Becker's version of the New Home Economics has spurred a common reaction. People now recognize that the household has an internal political economy, and is not always a discrete social and economic unit with a normative role structure and a neat developmental cycle (e.g. Lamphere 1974, Isvan 1991, Wilk and Netting 1984, Fapohunda and Todaro 1988, Wallman 1984, Whitehead 1981, Sabean

1990, and papers in Harris 1979, Young et al. 1981, Agarwal 1988, Oppong 1983, Medick and Sabean 1984, Moock 1986, Wilk 1989a, Dwyer and Bruce 1988, and Roberts and Wortzel 1984 among others).

Perhaps the best term for the emerging consensus is that used by Gail Wilson (1991 drawing on Sen [1984]): the "cooperative conflict" model. The term implies that domestic life cannot be decomposed into autonomous bargaining individuals, nor aggregated into placid collectivities. Such an approach accepts that issues of power and inequality are ever lurking beneath the even most pacific domestic settings and shared ideologies.[2]

The idea of cooperative conflict complements a growing sophistication about household structure, the ambiguity of boundaries and social distinctions and the interplay of pragmatic action with ideology and values (discussed in Wilk 1989c, 1991a). It is a sophisticated alternative to static formalist approaches that relate household behavior solely to stocks of economic or social capital and variation in external opportunity sets, as well as to substantivist references to culture, norms and values.

It is perhaps easier to see that households are complex "contested terrains" (Kevane 1992) when the object is a polygynous West African household, where there is overt bargaining, and a complex partition of property, rights and duties. Our seminar's experience of discovery raises the question of why and how this complexity is so much less obvious in Euroamerican industrialized societies.[3]

Obvious or not, there is also an increasing consensus that understanding the internal political economy of households is an important practical problem. Practitioners in several fields find their efforts vexed by the unpredictable ways that households respond to incentives, allocate resources and make their decisions. Demographers initially argued over whether fertility decision making was a matter for the individual, the family, or cultural values. But research found that matters were not so simple--it was not one or the other. A new generation of anthropologically informed researchers now understand that fertility decisions are contested, complex and nonlinear and that they lie at the center of household politics (e.g. Isvan 1991, Fapohunda and Todaro 1988, Mathews 1987, Nardi 1983). Fertility is neither completely internal or external, instrumental or moral. And most interesting in the context of this paper, fertility rates have now been linked to the economic and political structure of households (Caldwell 1990).

There are remarkably similar themes emerging in the study of nutrition and diet. By the early 1980s a lot of research in the Third World found that growth in household income was not translated into improved diet for all household members. And the amount of labor household members contributed to farm production was not always reflected in their shares of the proceeds (e.g. Schrijvers 1988, Van Esterik 1985, Guyer 1986, papers in Sharman et al. 1991). Inequity became an important issue, household allocation a problem of fundamental importance.[4]

Similar developments took place in the study of farming systems, where the disjunction between studies of household production and consumption has begun to break down (Poats et al. 1989). Anthropologists working on labor allocation and agricultural change, mostly in Africa, have given numerous accounts of complex household systems with long and short term exchanges among members, different kinds of property and pooling arrangements, and areas of acknowledged and contested control (e.g. Oppong 1983, Moock 1986, Wilk 1989a, Dwyer and Bruce 1989). Yet this knowledge remains unsystematic; anthropologists seem almost pathologically uncomfortable with household budget typologies and classifications.

Consumer research has perhaps made the most progress in developing typologies of internal household structure, growing from an initial need to target decision makers for advertising (see Davis 1976, Bonfield et al. 1984, Ferber 1973, Ferber and Lee 1974, Spiro 1983). Taking the decision event as a point of departure, most of this work is stuck in a Eurocentric mold, concerned with the roles of husbands and wives in simple nuclear families. Various resource-based or normative theories of marital power (e.g. Blood and Wolfe 1960, Heer 1963, Rodman 1972, Davis 1976) are used with typologies that typically have four poles:

husband dominated
wife dominated
joint
autonomous (specialized)

Cross cultural work by consumer researchers exposes the obvious weakness of the typology and the thin self-reported survey data that it is used upon (Hempel 1974, O'Connor et al. 1983, Green et al. 1983, cf. Wilson 1991). It is usually not clear what is being compared. A more interesting recent effort by Foster and Olshavsky (1989, 667) looks at other dimensions of decision making than dominance (Figure 14.1). They allow for a parallel structure in which two or more people work independently on the same decision, a hierarchical one where unresolved problems go up to another level, rings of specialists, and stars of specialists with a coordinator at the center. Consumer research on types and patterns of conflict and negotiation within households has produced some more interesting typologies, though limited to the

Euroamerican setting. Figure 14.2 shows a chart (from Bonfield et al. 1984, 253) that scales individual assertive goals on one axis and accomodative goals on the other, producing a range of outcomes. Tactics have been categorized in various ways (e.g. Spiro 1983, Park 1982), with the list in Figure 14.3 being one of the more complete (Bonfield et al. 1984, 256). A similar typology for types of power might include such things as veto power, bargaining power, the power to define possible options, and the power to delegate to or force decisions on others.

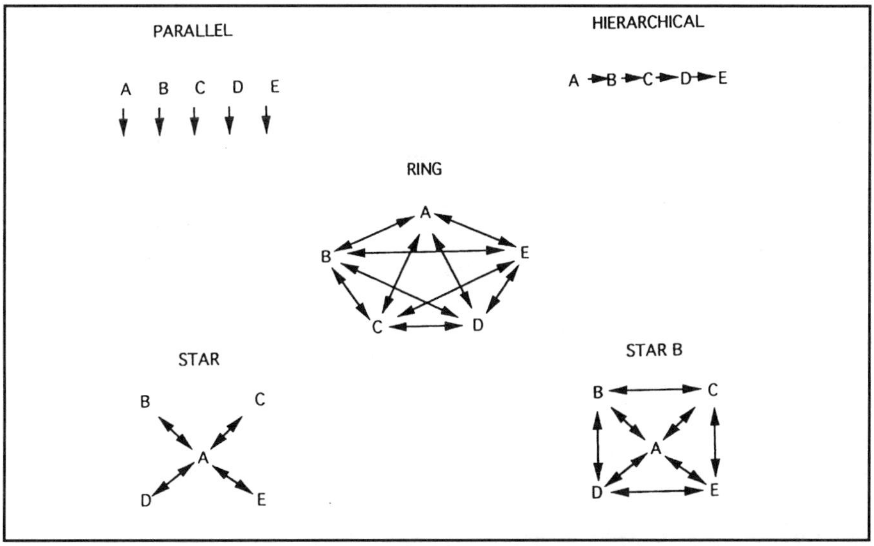

Figure 14.1: Structures Of Household Decision Making (after Foster & Olshavsky 1989:667)

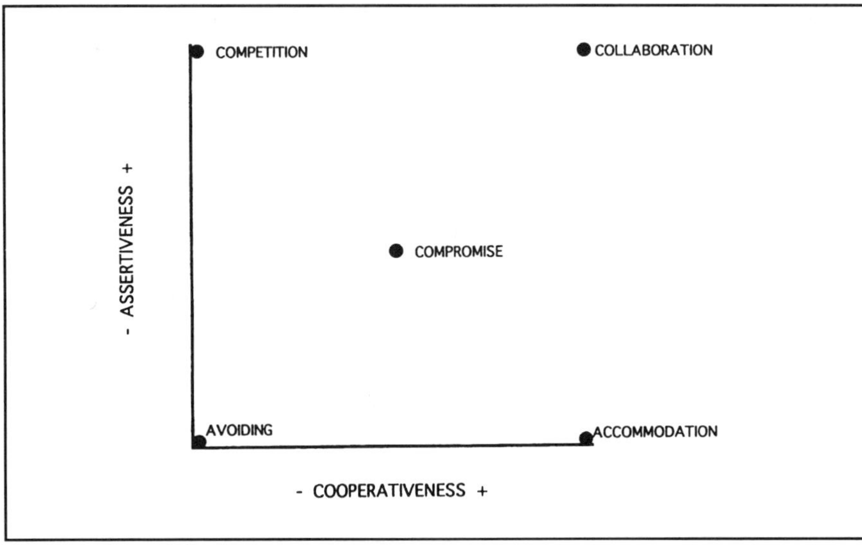

Figure 14.2: A Model Of Conflict Behavior (after Bonfield et al. 1984, 253)

1. Reason: Use of facts to support development of a logical argument.
2. Coalition: Mobilization of other members of the household.
3. Ingratiation: Use of impression management, flattery and goodwill creation.
4. Bargaining: Negotiation through exchange of benefits or favors.
5. Assertativeness: Use of a direct forceful approach; demands.
6. Higher Authority: Gaining support of higher level household members.
7. Sanctions: Use of derived rewards and punishments or threats of them.

Figure 14.3: Tactics In Household Negotiations (from Bonfield et al. 1984, 251)

In all of these areas, important empirical work is being done, crucial insights are accumulating. A stronger case can be made for understanding the household economy every day. But the evidence is accumulating in a haphazard way; there is no center of debate. We have a better idea of what the household is not, some indications of the crucial dimensions of variability, and a growing number of case studies. But the cases often speak right past each other. Partly this is because household studies are pursued by specialists in different disciplines with different vocabularies, interests and journals.[5]

What Does This Have to Do With Institutional Economics?

I would argue that most of the research I have discussed so far is seeking, in various ways, to independently reinvent institutional economics (as described in North 1990). They begin with the assumption that the household is an economically functional arrangement for its members, and seek to make sense out of the institutional arrangements of the household as a means of simplifying decision making, and reducing the costs of information. In our seminar, much of the variation we discovered bore directly on issues of specialization to minimize transaction costs. Much of the theory we were scavenging from different fields paralleled institutional economics, especially implicit contract theory--which argues that high transaction costs are the major enforcement of long term domestic agreements (see England and Farkas 1986). There is substantial agreement between North's approach, and implicit contract theory that within the household information and enforcement costs are low, partially because the costs of leaving the household are high.[6] This is because household interaction entails a lot of relationship-specific investment--for example learning about a spouse's personality and tastes--that is not transferable to another relationship (North 1990, 73, England and Farkas 1986, 23). There are also high search costs for new relationships, often because of ascribed kinship, age or gender roles.

Both sets of theory ultimately seek to understand the dialectic between pragmatic action and institutional form, accepting that institutions are adaptive, but imperfectly so. But to date applications of these methods have tended to be overly functional, and have tended to mask issues of inequality, power, exploitation and discord. It is clear that many households do not function well by any economic or social measure. The question then becomes, can institutional economics make sense of these disfunctional situations too? I believe it can, especially if we follow North's lead in writing culturally specific historical narratives of institutional evolution (cf. Donham 1990, Wilk 1991b).

The major problem remains--understanding why there is such a huge variety of household economic structures around the world, even within a single society. There is no substitute here for a comparative effort that must rest on an enlightened taxonomy--one that is measuring the kind of variation that is important to institutional economic analysis. Elsewhere I have argued that existing typologies of the household are useless for understanding household economics because they focus on household membership, genealogy and morphology, rather than the economic and practical relationships that exist between members (Wilk and Netting 1984, Wilk 1989b).

To give a brief example, let us look at the superb study of English households by Pahl (1989). Structurally--in terms of membership and kinship--the households fit a single neat developmental model, regardless of class, income and location. Labor schedules and task allocation within the household also varied within a narrow range. But Pahl found huge variability in the way money and property was managed, the way budgets and spending were allocated, and power and authority were exercised. In some households male earners gave their wives their entire wage, and got back an allowance. In others men kept the whole wage and gave their wives a housekeeping allowance. Some couples put wages into joint bank accounts, but exercised different degrees of control over it. Some couples kept their own separate accounts, and negotiated on which expenditures were to be paid from which accounts.

Pahl's careful ethnography of budgeting is confounded by an effort to sort households into types ("wife management," "shared management," etc.) that mix different dimensions of variability together. For example the four household budget types include such dimensions as who earns the wage, where it is kept, who has what rights to it, and who accounts for it. Such composite types are specific to this particular social setting and have no real comparative utility.

Rethinking the Problem

The basic issue here is how the household manages money and property. There are many ways to divide or classify the flows of funds in the household budget, and sometimes the flow stops and instead we have reservoirs--pools or funds that accumulate money and property.

It is tempting to start with folk concepts in classifying the parts of the domestic economy, using local terms that can be glossed as "budgets" or "funds." Two examples of how such "folk mapping" can be accomplished are given in Figures 14.4 and 14.5. The first, by Grey (1979) uses folk categories

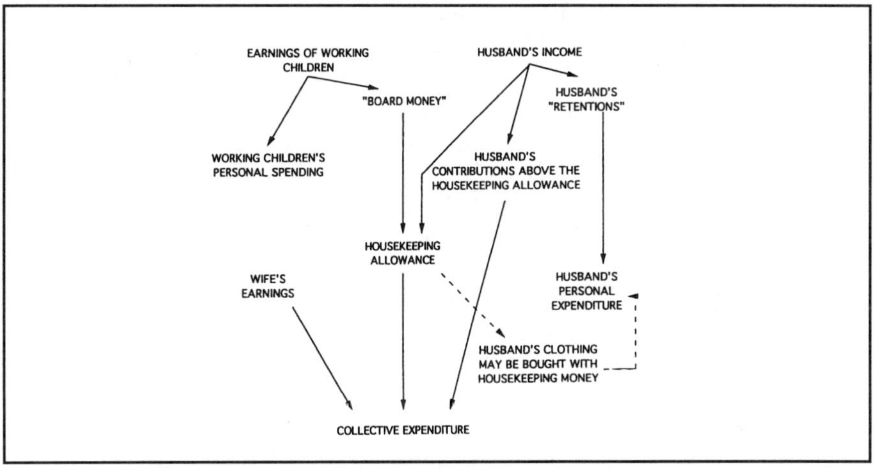

Figure 14.4: The Structure Of An English Housekeeping System (after Grey 1979:190)

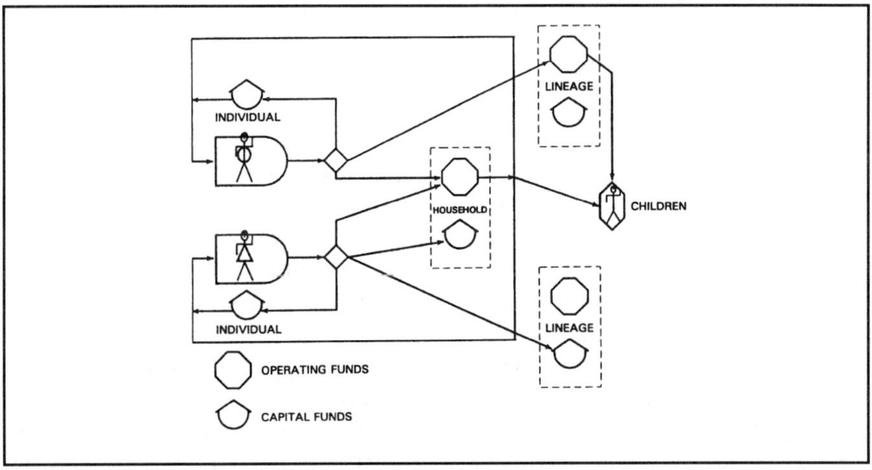

Figure 14.5: Flows to Different Kinds of Funds in Ashanti Marriages

such as "board money" to label funds, and arrows to show flows of income between them in a working class English household. The second from my own work (Wilk 1989b, 37) shows flows and funds in an Ashanti marriage, distinguishing both operating funds and longer-term capital funds that belong to individuals, household and the respective lineages of both spouses.

Rogers and Dant use the *destinations* of expenditures to organize a typology of household funds (1988, cited in Magrabi et al. 1991, 12). They divide the household's spending into Rent, Subsistence funds (for physical necessities), Replacement funds (for cultural necessities), Ceremonial funds (for social necessities), and Personal funds. As a way of cross-culturally comparing expenditures, this seems initially attractive. But it runs aground on the problem of distinguishing physical from social and cultural needs in a universally valid manner. There is a great deal of cross-cultural variation in the definition of social necessities, and there may be no consensus within the culture or even within a single household on what is a household social necessity and what is a personal discretion.

Using expenditures and funds as basic building blocks creates some other immediate problems--for example not all households have budgets, and not all households accumulate money in funds. Some households may act as no more than conduits, taking a flow from a set of sources, and diverting or combining them to pay expenditures that are fixed or regularly periodic. Other households may have stocks of money and property that provide irregular income that does not belong to any single individual. "Income" and "funds" embody too many assumptions from a fully capitalist monetary economy. A comparative taxonomy cannot build particularistic assumptions into its fundamental categories.[7]

There is another fundamental problem with categorizing the ownership of income, funds, or expenditures. It is tempting to start by dividing them into "individual" or "group." This inevitably leads to eliminating the essential dynamism of the household economy. What makes household budgets dynamic and changeable is not so much their structural properties (i.e. number of funds, sources of funds or kinds of expenditure), as it is the variable degrees of access and control that household members have to the flows, funds and expenditures. In other words, what most often changes is not the number of bank accounts or checkbooks, but who controls those accounts and checks. Ownership is too complex and crucial to be treated in this way. To elaborate further, the easiest thing would be to accept that some kinds of funds are personal property, while others are group property. But in reality, most "individual" property is subject to constraint and claim by other group members within defined limits. My own checkbook may be my own, but that doesn't mean I can buy anything I want with it. Conversely, what often seems to be group property is usually subject to individual obligations and claims.

It is possible for a teenager to give all her income to her parents' household fund, but that does not mean that she loses all claim to it, or to things that are bought with it. In some sense it remains encumbered.

We need to recognize degrees of ownership and control as the normal state of affairs, and absolute possession by individuals or group as a special case. We cannot begin with the assumption that a person 'owns' their earnings and freely donates them to others. A typology must recognize that the definition of the individual as an independent economic actor is culturally determined. The linkages between people and things cannot be assumed at the start.

Where then, should we start? For three years I have been working to translate household economics into the symbols of systems dynamics, as implemented in the Stella simulation program for the Macintosh computer (Richmond et al. 1987). While I still have not constructed a satisfactory working model of a household economic system, there are some important insights to be gained from the effort.

The basic building blocks of a simulation model are *flows* and *stocks* of material and nonmaterial items, and *converters* that measure or regulate flows. Stella links them together in familiar systems models which are built graphically instead of mathematically.[8] But what should constitute a stock in a household? This is the question I want to pursue in the rest of this paper.

Stocks and Flows in Household Systems

Pooling--the creation of stocks--has been identified by some as the single most important function of the household unit (Selby et al. 1990). Wallerstein (1984 and Friedman 1984) even defines the household as an income-pooling unit that combines wages and homework to reproduce labor for capitalist industry (1984). But Wallerstein, like Sahlins, is a primordialist who believes that household relations are undifferentiated--in other words that all household property is common property. One of the major advances in household studies in the last ten years has been the belated recognition that numerous kinds of property exist within the household, and some households have no common property.

But simply distinguishing households that have common property from those that don't is far too crude a set of distinctions. Clearly, the kinds of funds and stocks within the household are crucial variables. First are types of funds defined in terms of their periodicity and control.

An *obligated* fund is one set up for a purpose that predates the accumulation. It is preallocated by social agreement, and a contribution to it is therefore no longer subject to negotiation about purpose. Decision-making is limited to timing of expenditure. Obligated funds may be linked to particular sources of income, as when all money from selling eggs goes towards the childrens' school clothes. Some forms of obligated funds should properly be called *reservoirs*--they only accumulate because of different periodicities of income and expenditure. Some resource will be kept in the household temporarily, but will be gone by the time the next income arrives.

A *personal* fund is obligated not by its destination, but by reference to the person or people who control it. There is no overt restriction on purpose, only on who has a right to influence its disbursement. Again the fund may be tied to a source--everything from selling wood belongs to the son who carries it to market. Or a portion of group production may be divided and allocated to one or more personal funds. It may be worthwhile to divide the category of personal funds into those held by individuals and those held jointly by two or more (less than the whole household).

A *general* fund is unobligated and unallocated. It remains available, under group or individual management, for a number of uses in the future. Some general funds may be allocated to particular obligations or people in the future, or they may be transformed and consumed within the group. For non-consumables in a general fund, there may be a complex division of management and use rights. For capital in a general fund destinations may be obligated for rents, interest or other income. There may also be rules for individuals to borrow from a general fund or use it as security. Distinguishing these three kinds of funds makes different schemes of household budget management more intelligible and distinct. Gudeman and Rivera's model of the 'house schema' economy of Colombian peasants can be seen as a system of sequentially overflowing obligated funds (1990, 119, cf. Wilk 1989b Figure 3.2). As each one fills to a predetermined level, excess passes to the next obligation, with the total surplus reallocated back to a general fund. Presumably some overflow is also apportioned to personal funds after cash sales.

Figure 14.6 shows a Kekchi Maya household, in which all three kinds of funds exist. There is some question about the degree to which womens' individual cash gained from selling eggs, chickens and handicrafts should be seen as personal or obligated. Most of their money is spent on improving the family's diet, on their own clothing and on childrens' school supplies that men refuse to pay from the general fund. Perhaps the best solution is to define these funds as *contested* in some cases, an outcome which serves to define the domains of institutional conflict in this setting.

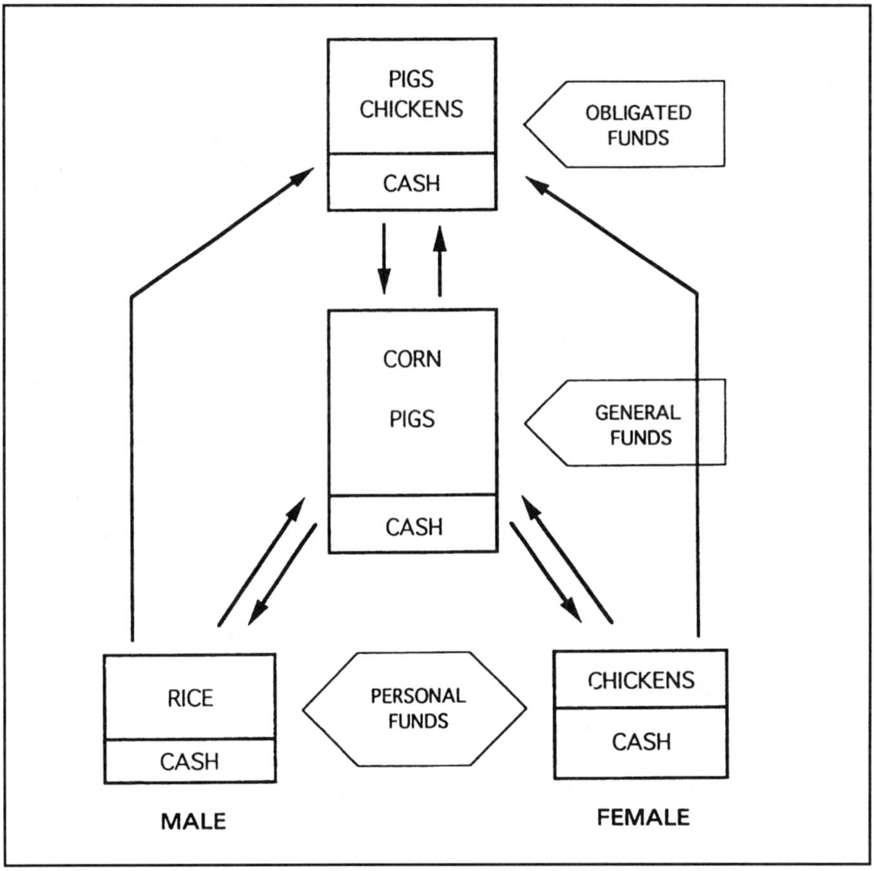

Figure 14.6: Different Kinds of Funds in a Kekchi Household

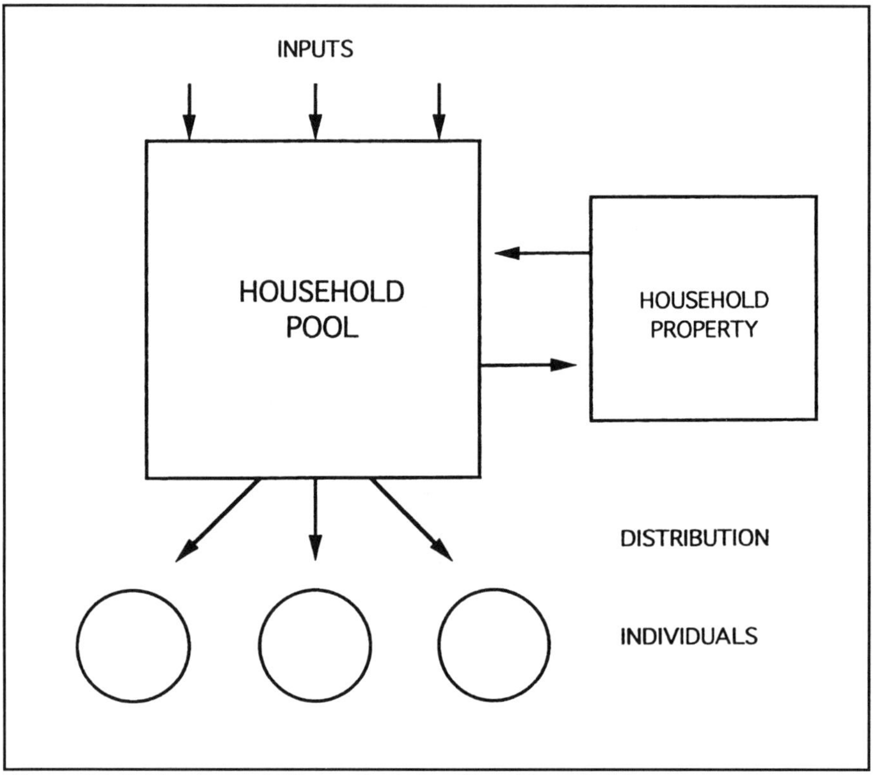

Figure 14.7: Funds And Flows In A Pooling Household

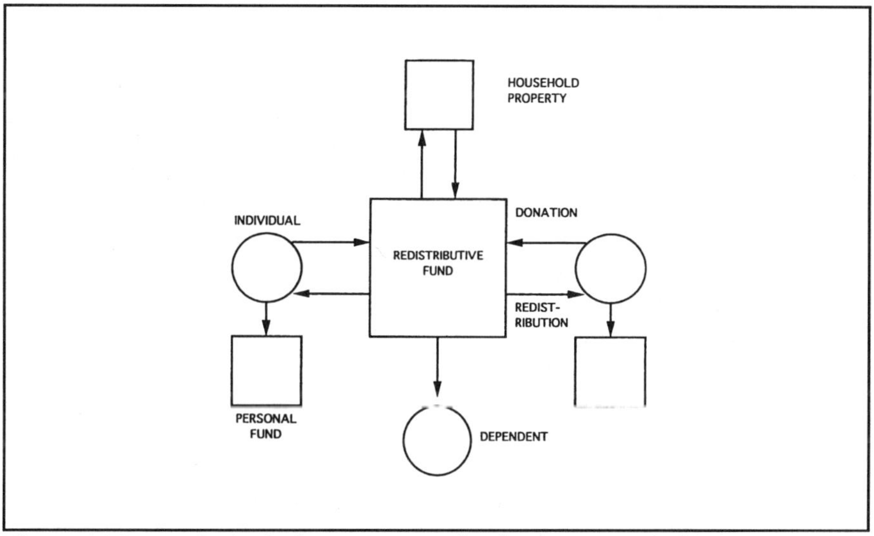

Figure 14.8: Funds And Flows In A Redistributive Household

Using this typology of funds, we can begin to build more meaningful categories of household systems. I have three major types to propose here, as a basis for further work, and to help understand how households of different kinds work as economic institutions.The first option may properly be called *pooling* (Figure 14.7). All products, income and stocks belong to the household, and the task of the household is essentially allocative. The common corporate enterprise has property rights superior to any individual. Household members derive their access to property by right of their participation and role in the household--not by reference to external sources of income or affiliation with other groups (though power within the household over allocation can certainly be influenced by externalities). Household resources can flow to individuals, but this is not redistribution or exchange; it is simply *distribution.* Household resources can also be allocated to corporate household purposes--investment, consumption, display or ceremony.

How does this institutional framework influence economic performance and management? Information and management costs are high--decision making, even if vested in a single authority, is time consuming and consensual. But in a society of such units, the opportunity costs of leaving the household are also high; there are few niches for individual actors. Members are highly invested in knowledge of each other's skills and abilities. Even if someone departing can take a share of household property with them to a new household, their productive efficiency will decline. Social and moral sanctions outside the household are liable to be formidable obstacles to departure.

If at least some kinds of income and property are acknowledged to originate from the efforts of at least some individuals, other kinds of household arrangement are possible; there are now at least three options. Individuals can place all or part of their income or production into a common fund, or they can set up personal funds, or they can do both.

If personal income is pooled in a common fund, we properly have an economy that can be called *redistributive* (Figure 14.8). Now each producing individual is in a situation of bargaining, but not on the basis of exchange or reciprocity (see Bell 1987). Instead of reciprocity, another kind of balance is sought, one that is longer-term and multi-stranded. Balance consists not in the relationship between what each person gives and what they receive, but in the relationship between what one person gives and receives, and what the others give and receive. This is a crucial difference between redistribution and exchange.

A redistributive household economy can have lower information and management costs, depending crucially on the structure of authority and decision making in the household. If redistributive decisions are made by one or two people with the knowledge and consent of the rest, allocation can be very efficient. The benefits of participation are likely to be high; as Sahlins found on Moala, this kind of household structure allows a high degree of specialization and both temporal and spatial dispersion of household activities (1957). Yet enforcement costs are also likely to be high, because of the clear opportunities for free riding on the household fund, for shirking and for cheating by holding back portions of individual production.

Recognizable subtypes within redistributive household economies include those where the amount each member receives from the common fund is *fixed* (sometimes called an allowance or share system), and where the amount can be *negotiated.* Clearly there is a trade off here between flexibility and management costs; the issue of fairness is not so clear. Fixed allowances or shares can both protect and exploit (and in a particular case both interpretations may be possible).

If household members do not contribute to a common fund, but instead make measured contributions to obligated funds, or to each others' personal funds, we can speak of a *reciprocal* household (Figure 14.9). We would expect to find explicit reckoning of balances on relatively short terms, overt agreements about spheres of responsibility and a lack of central authority or decision making.

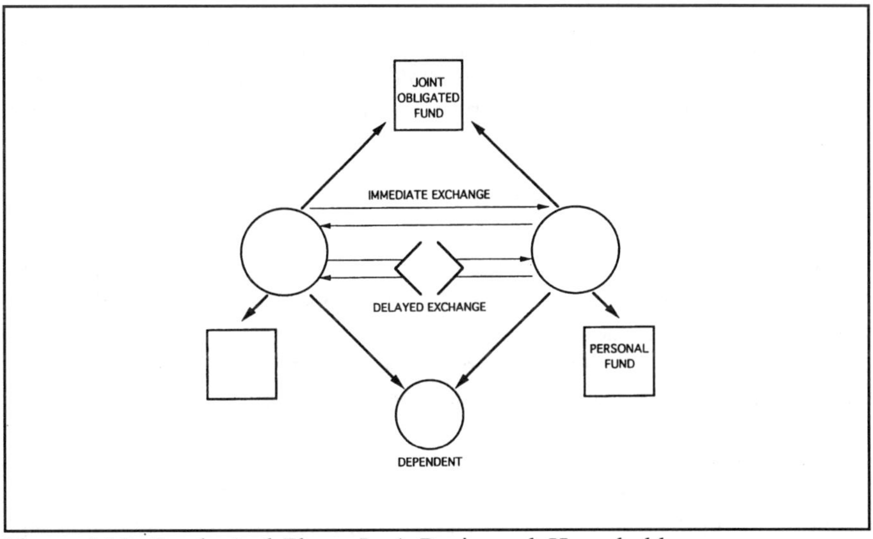

Figure 14.9: Funds And Flows In A Reciprocal Household

Just because there is reciprocity and the appearance of exchange in such a household does not mean that there is balance, equity or equality among the members. As most of us well know from personal experience, bargains between household members are not like those in a marketplace. There is a constant mixture of long and short term returns, and both costs and benefits are hard to reckon, especially when measurable and immeasurable, material and nonmaterial all enter the exchange (see Wilk 1989c for an example). While overt reckoning of loans, debts and balances is found in some reciprocal households (especially where divorce is easily obtainable; for good examples see Sabean 1990, Abu 1983, Jones 1986), more often balance is a covert issue. As in the Kula, raising the balance of a single exchange can call an entire relationship into question.

As institutions, reciprocal households have high transaction costs and high enforcement costs. Parties to exchange must know a great deal about each other. The long term stability of the implicit contracts depend on the economic environment--which determines what benefits will accrue from task specialization and how much "social insurance" is needed. It also depends on the opportunity costs of leaving the relationship and establishing a new one, costs that are also determined externally. It is tempting to depict the reciprocal household as the most flexible and adaptable of the three types, but it may not be so. In many settings a redistributive system would be better capable of redeploying labor or capital to take advantage of new economic opportunities (for example the Mexican urban households discussed by Selby et al. 1990). It might be better to say that reciprocal households offer *individuals* greater flexibility as actors.

Discussion

I don't have a momentary hope that real households are going to fall neatly into these categories. Every household represents some mixture, and every society has a wide range of mixtures. But at least we can now describe the mixtures, and begin to relate them to their environments and trace their histories. At the very least, I find I can now wade through the floodwaters of ethnography and begin to find my way (until lately I felt more as though I were drowning).

These types also detour around the black cloud of confusion that gathers whenever people try to apply Sahlins' typologies of reciprocity and redistribution to the household (see Hess and Bell 1992). I have appropriated (perhaps foolishly) his familiar terms from *Stone Age Economics* (1972), but I have given them more precise definitions.

Perhaps this typology can also help in rethinking some crucial problems about the appropriate kinds of theory to apply to what happens within the household. For the last 20 years we have been arguing about whether or not microeconomics is appropriate for domestic life, if the household is a moral economy, or perhaps a political economy. The question of what tools are empirically useful has been thoroughly mixed up with issues of human nature, free will and epistemology (Wilk 1991a).

Instead, consider the possibility that different kinds of analysis are appropriate and useful in each kind of household. The pooling household may properly be modeled as a moral economy, where members have largely internalized the institutional form as part of the natural order. A redistributive household has many of the elements of a political economy--one where positions of power and authority are the objects of contest, negotiation and dispute, not economic relations or flows themselves. A political ethos of fairness or order is more salient than any economic ideology. Finally, a reciprocal household is best understood using the tools of microeconomics, which presume that individuals have some autonomy to make bargains with ultimately material goals. Only in a reciprocal household can we have some confidence that our etic categories of exchange, cost and benefit have any emic validity and consistent effect on behavior.

And this is the last point I would like to make: that 50 years of economic anthropology have taught us that both emic and etic categories make a difference, and neither can stand alone. In the household the need to combine formal analytical tools with an ethnographic understanding of emic categories and logic is undeniable. I hope these typological efforts will further that project instead of providing yet another barrier.

References

Abu, K. 1983. The Separateness of Spouses: Conjugal Resources in an Ashanti Town. In C. Oppong, ed., *Female and Male in West Africa*. George Allen and Unwin: London.

Agarwal, Bina, ed. 1988. *Structures of Patriarchy: The State, the Community and the Household.* London: Zed Books.

Bell, Duran. 1987. Production and Distribution within Hierarchically Structured Cooperative Groups. *Journal of the Steward Anthropological Society* 16: 96-124.

Blood, R.O. Jr. and D.M. Wolfe. 1960. *Hubands and Wives*. The Free Press: New York.

Bonfield, E., Kaufman, C., and S. Hernandez. 1984. Household Decisionmaking: Units of Analysis and Decision Processes. In M. Roberts and L. Wortzel, eds., *Marketing to the Changing Household.* Cambridge, Mass.: Ballinger.

Bryant, W. Keith. 1990. *The Economic Organization of the Household.* Cambridge: Cambridge University Press.

Caldwell, John. 1990. High Fertility in Sub-Saharan Africa. *Scientific American* 262(5): 118-128.

Davis, Harry. 1976. Decision Making within the Household. *Journal of Consumer Research* 2: 241-260.

Donham, Donald. 1990. *History, Power, Ideology: Central Issues in Marxism and Anthropology.* Cambridge: Cambridge University Press.

Dwyer, Daisy and Judith Bruce, eds. 1988. *A Home Divided: Women and Income in the Third World.* Stanford: Stanford University Press.

England, Paula and George Farkas. 1986. *Households, Employment, and Gender.* New York: Aldine.

Fapohunda, Eleanor and Michael Todaro. 1988. Family Structure, Implicit Contracts, and the Demand for Children in Southern Nigeria. *Population and Development Review* 14: 571-595.

Ferber, Robert and Lucy Lee. 1974. Husband-Wife Influence in Family Purchasing Behavior. *Journal of Consumer Research* 1: 43-50.

Ferber, Robert. 1973. Family Decision Making and Economic Behavior: A Review. In E. Sheldon, ed., *Family Economic Behavior: Problems and Prospects.* Lippincott: Philadelphia.

Folbre, Nancy. 1988. The Black Four of Hearts: Toward a New Paradigm of Household Economics. In Daisy Dwyer and Judith Bruce, eds., *A Home Divided: Women and Income in the Third World.* Stanford: Stanford University Press.

Foster, Irene and Richard Olshavsky. 1989. An Exploratory Study of Family Decision Making Using a New Taxonomy of Family Role Structure. *Advances in Consumer Research* 16: 665-670.

Friedman, Kathie. 1984. Households as Income-Pooling Units. In J. Smith, I. Wallerstein and H. Evers, eds., *Households and the World Economy.* Sage Publications: Beverley Hills.

Green, Robert, J. Leonardi, J. Chandon, I. Cunningham, B. Verhage and A. Strazzieri. 1983. Societal Development and Family Purchasing Roles: A Cross National Study. *Journal of Consumer Research* 9: 436-442.

Grey, Anne. 1979. The Working Class Family as an Economic Unit. In Chris Harris, ed., *The Sociology of the Family: New Directions for Britain.* University of Keele: Sociological Review Monograph 28.

Gudeman, Stephen and Alberto Rivera. 1990. *Conversations in Colombia: The Domestic Economy in Life and Text.* Cambridge: Cambridge University Press.

Guyer, Jane. 1986. Intra-Household Processes and Farming Systems Research: Perspectives from Anthropology. In J. Moock, ed., *Understanding Africa's Rural Households and Farming Systems.* Boulder: Westview Press.

Harris, Chris, ed. 1979. *The Sociology of the Family: New Directions for Great Britain.* University of Keele: Sociological Review. Monograph 28.

Heer, David. 1963. The Measurement and Bases of Family Power: An Overview. *Marriage and Family Living* 25: 133-139.

Hempel, D.J. 1974. Family Buying Decisions: A Cross Cultural Perspective. *Journal of Marketing Research* 11: 295-302.

Hertz, Rosanna. 1986. *More Equal Than Others: Men and Women in Dual-Career Marriages.* Berkeley: University of California Press.

Hess, James and Duran Bell. 1992. A Comment on Lambek's "Exchange, Time and Person in Mayotte." *American Anthropologist* 94: 166-167.

Isvan, Nilufer. 1991. Productive and Reproductive Decisions in Turkey: The Role of Domestic Bargaining. *Journal of Marriage and the Family* 53: 1057-1070.

Jones, C. W. 1986. Intra-Household Bargaining in Response to the Introduction of New Crops: A Case Study from North Cameroon. In J. Moock, ed., *Understanding Africa's Rural Households and Farming Systems.* Boulder: Westview Press.

Lamphere, Louise. 1974. Strategies, Cooperation, and Conflict Among Women in Domestic Groups. In M. Rosaldo and L. Lamphere, eds., *Women, Culture & Society.* Stanford University Press: Stanford.

Magrabi, Frances, Young Chung, Sanghee Cha and Se-Jeong Yang. 1991. *The Economics of Household Consumption.* New York: Praeger.

Mathews, Holly. 1987. Predicting Decision Outcomes: Have We Put the Cart before the Horse in Anthropological Studies of Decision-Making? *Human Organization* 46: 54-61.

Medick, Hans and David Sabean, eds. 1984. *Interest and Emotion: Essays on the Study of Family and Kinship.* Cambridge: Cambridge University Press.

Millman, Marcia. 1991. *Warm Hearts and Cold Cash: The Intimate Dynamics of Families and Money.* New York: Free Press.

Moock, J., ed. 1986. *Understanding Africa's Rural Households and Farming Systems.* Boulder: Westview Press.

Nardi, Bonnie. 1983. Goals in Reproductive Decision Making. *American Ethnologist* 10(4): 697-714.

Netting, Robert. 1989. Smallholders, Householders, Freeholders: Why the Family Farm Works Well Worldwide. In R. Wilk, ed., *The Household Economy: Reconsidering The Domestic Mode of Production.* Boulder: Westview Press.

North, Douglass. 1990. *Institutions, Institutional Change and Economic Performance.* Cambridge: Cambridge University Press.

O'Connor, P. J., G. L. Sullivan and D.A. Pogorzelski. 1983. Cross Cultural Family Purchasing Decisions: A Literature Review. *Advances in Consumer Research* 10:59-64.

Oppong, C., ed. 1983. *Female and Male in West Africa.* George Allen and Unwin: London.

Pahl, Jan. 1989. *Money and Marriage.* New York: St. Martin's Press.

Park, C. 1982. Joint Decisions in Home Purchasing: A Muddling-Through Process. *Journal of Consumer Research* 9: 151-162.

Poats, Susan, Hilary Feldstein and Dianne Rocheleau. 1989. Gender and Intra/Inter-Household Analysis in On-Farm Research and Experimentation. In R. Wilk, ed., *The Household Economy: Reconsidering the Domestic Mode of Production.* Boulder: Westview Press.

Richmond, Barry, Steve Patterson and Peter Vescuso. 1987. *An Academic User's Guide to Stella.* Lyme, MA: High Performance Systems.

Roberts, Mary and Lawrence Wortzel, eds. 1984. *Marketing to the Changing Household.* Cambridge, Mass.: Ballinger.

Rogers, S.D. and R. P. Dant. 1988. Societal Antecedents of Contemporary American Resource Allocation. Paper presented at the annual meeting of the American Marketing Associetion.

Rodman, Hyman. 1972. Marital Power and the Theory of Resources in a Cross Cultural Context. *Journal of Comparative Family Studies* 1: 50-67.

Sabean, David. 1990. *Property, Production and Family in Neckarhausen.* Cambridge: Cambridge University Press.

Sahlins, Marshall. 1957. Land Use and the Extended Family in Moala, Fiji. *American Anthropologist* 59: 449-462.

———.1972. *Stone Age Economics.* Aldine: Chicago.

Schrijvers, Joke. 1988. Blueprint for Undernourishment: The Mahaweli River Development Scheme in Sri Lanka. In Bina Agarwall, ed., *Structures of Patriarchy: The State, The Community and the Household.* London: Zed Books.

Selby, Henry, Arthur Murphy and Stephen Lorenzen. 1990. *The Mexican Urban Household: Organizing for Self-Defense.* Austin: University of Texas Press.

Sen, Amartya 1984. *Resources, Value and Development.* Oxford: Basil Blackwell.

Sharman, Anne, Janet Theophano, Karen Curtis and Ellen Messer, eds. 1991. *Diet and Domestic Life in Society*. Philadelphia: Temple University Press.

Singh, Inderjit, Lyn Squire and John Strauss, eds. 1986. *Agricultural Household Models: Extensions, Application and Policy*. Baltimore: Johns Hopkins University Press.

Spiro, Rosann. 1983. Persuasion in Family Decision-Making. *Journal of Consumer Research* 9: 393-402.

Van Esterik, P. 1985. Intra-Family Food Distribution: Its Relevance for Maternal and Child Nutrition. In *Determinants of Young Child Feeding and Their Implications for Nutritional Surveillance*. Ithaca, New York: Cornell International Nutrition Monograph Series, Number 14.

Wallerstein, Immanuel. 1984. Household Structures and Labor-Force Formation in the Capitalist World-Economy. In J. Smith, I. Wallerstein and H. Evers, eds., *Households and the World Economy*. Beverley Hills: Sage.

Wallman, Sandra. 1984. *Eight London Households*. London: Tavistock.

Whitehead, Ann. 1981. 'I'm Hungry, Mum': The Politics of Domestic Budgeting. In K. Young, C. Wolkowitz and R. McCullagh, eds., *Of Marriage and Market: Women's Subordination In International; Perspective*. London: CSE Books.

Wilk, Richard, ed. 1989a. *The Household Economy: Reconsidering the Domestic Mode of Production*. Boulder: Westview Press.

———.1989b. Decision Making and Resource Flows Within the Household: Beyond the Black Box. In R. Wilk, ed., *The Household Economy: Reconsidering the Domestic Mode of Production*. Boulder: Westview Press.

———.1989c. Houses as Consumer Goods: The Kekchi of Belize. In Ben Orlove and Henry Rutz, eds., *The Political Economy of Consumption*. University Press of America.

———.1991a. Altruism and Self Interest: Building a Theory of Household Behavior. Presented at a conference "Family/Household Behavior--Consumption and Production Perspectives," Irvine, California, March 28-30.

———.1991b. *Household Ecology*. Tucson: University of Arizona Press.

Wilk, Richard and Robert M. Netting. 1984. Households: Changing Form and Function. In R. Netting, R. Wilk and E. Arnould, eds., *Households: Comparative and Historical Studies of the Domestic Group*. Berkeley: University of California Press.

Wilson, Gail. 1991. Thoughts on the Cooperative Conflict Model. *IDS Bulletin* 22(1): 31-36.

Young, K., C. Wolkowitz and R. McCullagh, eds. 1981. *Of Marriage and Market: Women's Subordination in International Perspective*. London: CSE Books.

Notes

1. This paper grew from the collaborative efforts of a seminar on household economics held in 1989, sponsored by the Multidisciplinary Ventures Fund of Indiana University. Major contributors in the seminar included Robert Netting, Laurel Cornell, David Altig, Holly Yanker, and Jeff Cohen. Others who have helped me along in thinking these issues through include Stephen Miller, Susan Greenhalgh and Richard Olshavsky. I also thank Michael Jackson for a crucial push when I was stuck, and Anne Pyburn for constant inspiration. Several comments from the audience at the SEA meetings were helpful in making this revision, but only I am responsible for the final form of the argument.

2. I should note that while some economists are moving towards accepting conflict within the household, many continue to produce elaborate and complex household models of production and consumption that assume the household is a single unit, whose members' needs and resources can be summed. Then optimal allocations are calculated--there is no conflict, culture or gender involved--except in the generation of utilities. For examples see Bryant (1990), Singh et al. (1986), and portions of Magrabi et al. (1991), and an elegant refutation by Folbre (1988).

3. It is interesting that the whole terrain of decision making in American households did not arise as a topic of academic discourse until large numbers of middle class households had problems with earnings and housework in the 1970s and 1980s.

Though the allocation of time, money and housework are a legitimate academic subject now, a surprising amount of reseach is still impressionistic and ethnocentric (e.g. Hertz 1986, Millman 1991).

4. Some particularly intriguing parallel ideas appear in British research that shows how different kinds of taxation have unequal impacts on male and female domains of the household economy (Wilson 1991, Pahl 1989).

5. In this respect I see the bibliography of this paper as one of its main achievements; just identifying a common literature of which the participants are usually unaware is part of a solution to the problem.

6. Netting (1989) makes an intriguing argument that households are uniquely effective agricultural production units just because they minimize information and enforcment costs, compared with capitalist businesses and socialist collectives.

7. This is by no means an attack on particularistic ethnographies of the folk economy. Careful elucidation of the metaphorical construction of emic economic categories is vital to understanding the decision making process, as demonstrated by Gudeman and Rivera (1990).

8. There are some potentially powerful uses for simulation in institutional economics. The main problem is that in its present form Stella forces the researcher to specify the institutional linkages in advance and then explore the performance of the system given different inputs. There is no provision for the institutional framework itself to change. The researcher has to model a number of possible institutions, and then look at how each one performs in a particular environment. This is time-consuming, even on a Macintosh.

15

Reevaluating Economic Rationality: Individuals, Information and Institutions

Barry H. Michie

Since the demise of the formalist-substantivist debate in the 1970s, discussion of theoretical issues such as economic rationality has been dead in economic anthropology. My intention is not to exhume the exquisite corpse of that debate although the discussion will of necessity touch upon perhaps still sensitive points. My purpose, rather, is to reexamine the notion of rationality in light of recent thought and debate within economics, much of it coming from Europe, where controversy appears far from dead. The primary objectives here are to examine: (1) the evolution of thought about rationality and its relation to economics in the U.S. within the intellectual and political context of the past forty years, (2) what relation this evolution has had with anthropology, other social sciences generally and on the new institutional economics, (3) consider the portents for a truly institutionally oriented mainstream economics in the U.S. and its challenge to economic anthropology.

One expects critiques of instrumental rationality, particularly that based on methodological individualism, from institutional and normative economists (e.g. Heap 1989; Hodgson 1988). But more significantly, critiques are emerging from that bastion of methodological individualism, positive economics and econometrics as well (e.g. Pesaran 1988). Problems encountered in positive economics range from poor predictive capacity of econometric models, epistemological problems of how economic knowledge on which agents make decisions is generated and acquired to questions of whether facts stand independently of theory. Questions asked center on whether or not there is a 'true' economy 'out there' apart from human will, manipulation and thought, and whose principles and behavior are reflected in invariant human nature and behavior. A parallel question is whether or not economic behavior results from variable expectations shaped by a given institutional context itself affected by theory.

If anthropologists hear echoes of the formalist-substantivist debate, the effect is totally serendipitous as the impetus for the discussion stems mainly from macro-level prescriptive and policy concerns for industrial market systems. By way of contrast, the anthropological debate centered on how to conceptualize and analyze 'things economic' across the full range of societies within our purview and was essentially micro-economic in nature--the production, exchange and consumption behavior of individuals and larger corporate units.[1]

The formalist-substantivist debate, however, often centered on the instrumental conceptualization of rationality (e.g. Burling 1962; LeClair 1962; Schneider 1974) contained within Lord Robbins' (1932) formal definition of economics as the study of the allocation of scarce means to alternative ends. Associated with this definition are the concepts of preferences, utility maximization and economizing, markets and sovereign economic agents acquiring knowledge and pursuing their individual ends. The substantive side, simplified, stressed economics as an instituted process best understood in terms of variable institutional contexts and wider processes in which societies materially provision themselves. This was but one skirmish in the larger debate as to whether neo-classical liberal-utilitarian economic principles and theory are universally applicable or are artifacts of western capitalist market economies and at best represent but one competing theoretical set for examining the manner in which societies organize their economic life.

Unfortunately, this theoretical debate simply petered out, people went their separate ways and the debate is barely a passing footnote in the literature.

I long ago concluded that much of the formalist-substantivist debate produced more heat than light and was conducted as a zero sum game. With hindsight, the two can be resolved in great part if one distinguishes several entwined meanings of rationality--instrumental, procedural and normative--in both their formal and substantive aspects.

Simply put, if one distinguishes abstract *formal* logico-deductive principles of thought from actual *substantive* processes, structures and behavior, form from content, and most importantly sees their connectedness but not define the former as any specific case of the latter, e.g. materially maximizing Homo Economicus, we can go a long way to resolving many issues. Thus formal rationality--in whatever sense above--is singular and can encompass infinite numbers of substantive rationalities.[2]

In a formal sense, instrumental rationality refers solely to combining and putting resources to work to attain some end--the means-ends relationship that is subject to calculations of efficiency. Procedural rationality deals with the organization of means--institutions and working rules governing how resources are combined toward some end and constrain behavior into consistent and predictable patterns. Normative rationality deals with ends: the conscious evaluative and selective process that determines what is worthy, moral and desireable to do, achieve, obtain, be and become. Logically, procedural and normative rationality inform each other and both inform instrumental rationality--although these relations are not necessarily finely meshed and without contradiction.

Substantive systems, however, cannot be reduced to nor explained solely in terms of rationality, which essentially proceeds from the human mind and will. While allowing one to discover systematic and functional relationships and their internal logic, the problem arises of explaining substantive differences between behaviors and systems that in principle are more or less equally rational. The ontology of substantive systems requires more than the human mind, and requires a material dimension whereby substantive systems arise from peoples' willed and unwilled, conscious and unconscious interaction with each other and, through production, with their bio-physical environment (Cook 1973, 1974; Godelier 1972, Part III, & 1986).

To elaborate, instrumental rationality is that aspect of conscious and willed human behavior that in John Commons notion of "futurity" anticipates, plans and combines resources to bring about some future state or utility (1934, 619-620). Instrumental rationality can be universally found in or, at least, imputed to human behavior and is a useful but very limited tool for analyzing people's conscious and purposeful--but not all--behavior[3] and forms of organization including that which may be distinguished as 'economic'. But as means and ends by themselves can be anything and everything, instrumental rationality is applicable to any and all types of activity. Thus, if instrumental rationality is equated with economic rationality, then everything becomes economic in principle with no separate substantive domain of life demarcated, except by fiat or custom, as economic in fact.

Given this indeterminacy, instrumental rationality is incapable of accounting for differences between individuals, groups and societies. Analysis based on this concept may have predictive value within (but not across) units of analysis provided behavior is consistent over time. The problem is, in part, explaining how particular ends, preferences or utilities are established and acted upon instead of others. This is the central problem of variability and divergence that exists at all levels. In Commons words, "individuals are not mechanical uniformities of desire ..., they are highly variable personalities" (1934, 74). This problem can only be approached by incorporating and giving an active role to the social and cultural content of institutions through which people learn and act in society. This realization is not particularly new nor confined to anthropology. John Commons recognized this long ago with his notion that individuals do not stand *de novo* as isolated individuals in a state of nature but are, rather, shaped by the institutions in, by and for which they live and that exist prior to and after them; that they in large part act by learned habit, custom and the mandatory compulsions of their institutions (1934, 701-702).

The question, then, is why the role of institutions is such a difficult one to recognize and encorporate within mainstream economics which, despite institutionalists old or new, is dominated by individualistic positive economics.

The Rise And Hegemony Of Positive Economics

The period of the formalist-substantivist debate marks the ascendancy and hegemony of positive economics in the West. This is particularly the case for the United States where liberal-utilitarian social and economic thought has been historically dominant in contrast to much of Europe where it is but one of a number of contending schools of thought (see Colin and Losch, this volume).[4] Following Kuhn (1962), one must acknowledge the effects of the wider intellectual and political environment within which this occurs, that amplifies and gives support to the particular instrumental version of rationality found in this school of thought (Green 1979, 1984; Hodgson 1988, 16, 48).

Two things are salient here. First is the cold war whose dynamic partakes of a struggle between social and individualist conceptions of human beings and society which often hinges on the notion of freedom (e.g. Friedman 1962). Second, the U.S. becomes increasingly involved in economic development assistance programs to non-European, non-industrial societies. On both dimensions, patronage and recognition from governmental and other institutions support this school's ability to define the problem, approach and agenda, and to control resources and ignore any contrary points of view.

Accordingly, policies and resources of western governments and international agencies are marshalled to promote and support western market ideas and forms of organization throughout the world. As this effort develops, any appreciative or action oriented concern with distribution and equity, social control over productive resources, any necessary relationship between economic and socio-cultural structures and any limitation of individuals' freedom to produce, exchange and accumulate is gradually rejected in favor of focusing on markets and growth of aggregate commodity production.

This is particularly clear with regard to activist governmental intervention in land relations and institutions as one traces the thrust of U.S. involvement in economic development and reform over the past forty-five years. This shift can be traced from the Post World War II efforts in Taiwan, Japan and Korea through the experience in South Vietnam, the Green Revolution in South Asia and reaches its apogee in the free market development assistance policies of the U.S. in the last decade.[5]

The basic theoretical underpinnings of this gradual change derive from classic liberal-utilitarian thought whose modern version holds that the only requisites of an economy are information, material resources, technology, capital, market institutions, competition and the removal of any constraints impeding their free flow, operation and individuals' access to them in their pursuit of individual utility and self interest. Furthermore, social utility--or what is best for society as a whole--is consonant with allowing individuals to pursue and maximize their own ends, the social equilibrium being nothing more or less than the aggregation, or in economics terms the composite, of all individuals' actions and interactions (Hodgson 1988). It is also an idealist conception that holds that there is a natural order with universal principles governing human nature and human affairs best approximated by free market capitalism and competitive liberal democracy[6]--in Theodore Lowi's terms, an automatic economy guided by the unseen hand and an automatic society that operates best through popular sovereignty without other human regulation or institutional interference (Lowi 1969, 13-28).

The Early Rationality Debate In Economics

Significantly, at the outset of this evolution of thought and policy, the rationality issue is at the fore of debate in development economics in the 1950s. This debate centers on whether production and exchange behavior in so-called 'traditional' societies and, in particular, their agrarian economies are bound and operate by social custom or follow and are amenable to analysis based on universal principles of neo-classical economics (e.g. Boeke 1953; Higgins 1959).

From my perspective this is a particularly sterile formulation of the problem as it does not squarely address conceptual and operational problems of rationality at all. Its outcome, however, has major consequences for the subsequent course and application of economic theory in the U.S. For U.S. development economics, particularly, it leads to the view that since all people are rational they are essentially the same--without having to address the question of how and why they are obviously different--and dismisses the relevancy of variable socio-cultural and institutional factors. This is a legacy with which we still suffer. The observation must be made that answers are only as good as the questions posed.

Positive economics gains the upper hand in this debate with the 1964 publication of Theodore Schultz' *Transforming Traditional Agriculture* which becomes *the* authoritative reference for agricultural development programs and policy emanating from U.S. and many western international agencies. Significantly, this work is based largely on three case studies. Two are anthropological, the only instances I have found of anthropology's use as an authoritative reference in U.S. international agricultural economics literature. This is not surprising as their manner of use bolsters the positive economics paradigm and negates any further anthropological relevancy.

The message Schultz presents is the 'poor but efficient' farmer. 'Traditional' farmers have low yields and are poor not because of their culture but due to the poverty of their opportunity structure that results in an equilibrium at a low level of productivity. They are, however, efficient organizers and economizers of limited resources, maximize individual utility, are positively responsive to economic opportunity presented in the marketplace and only lack opportunity. "Once there are investment opportunities and efficient incentives, farmers will turn sand into gold" (1964, 5).

Significantly, *Transforming Traditional Agriculture* is a major theoretical departure from Schultz's earlier work on U.S. agriculture that demonstrates (and at times bemoans) U.S. farmers' production non-responsiveness to market demand, relative inefficiency compared to the industrial sector, and variability in allocative efficiency and productivity across regions and socio-economic groupings (e.g. Schultz 1945, 12-13; 1950, 49-63).[7] In this work, however, Schultz makes a very selective use of passages from Sol Tax's *Penny Capitalism* (1963) and David Hopper's unpublished anthropology and agricultural economics dissertation (1957) on the economic organization and production behavior of Indian farmers. In both cases he blatantly misrepresents authors' evidence, statements and conclusions that are contrary to his thesis. Similarly, his other major case is Raj Krishna's unpublished dissertation (1961) of Indian cotton farmers' positive response to market price, ignoring similar studies showing a range of responses, including negative and none, for other commodities (see Adams 1986).

The implications of Schultz's thesis are several. First, all people everywhere are just as economically rational as farmers in Iowa.[8] Second, policy and program prescription does not have to take into account the complexities of variable socio/cultural institutions and structures. Only technology, information, markets, prices and the formal institutions through which they operate matter. They will be the solvent for any obstacle or distortion social or cultural factors may throw in the way. Third, U.S. development economics, in line with positive economics, becomes insulated from other social sciences--with the exception of psychology, as we shall see below.

Anthropology, in particular, becomes superfluous for formulating or understanding economic problems or finding solutions. Schultz's misuse of anthropology to make his case is a classic example of Schumpeter's warning about cross disciplinary borrowing in which "cross-fertilization might easily result in cross-sterilization" (1986, 27) (see Colin and Losch, this volume). This is subsequently reflected in U.S. development economics thought and literature where anthropology, sociology and geography are seen as at most contributing to the removal of social/cultural obstacles in technology transfer (e.g. Ruttan 1975, 171), a position with which many non-economist social scientists have concurred.[9] This manner of formulating problems and approaches is also clearly reflected in USAID project design, couched in terms of identifying and removing constraints--bureaucratic, infrastructural, social, etc.--that would impede project recipients from adopting proffered benefits assumed consonant with their best self and material interests.

With Schultz's book, development and agricultural economics thus comes into line with positive economics which is gaining the upper hand over normative and institutional schools of thought. With the issue 'settled', economic rationality becomes a given--about which questions elicit either patronizing smiles or angry sharp retorts that such questions imply that people are stupid or irrational.

Instrumental Rationality And The Positive Position

Now, what is the particular version of rationality found in positive economics and shared generally with neo-classical thought? First, again, it is an idealist conception that sees a natural order in the universe governed by laws and principles operating prior to human action and unalterable by human intervention. Furthermore, these laws and principles correspond to a universal human nature.

Second, it is based on methodological individualism that sees individuals as the fundamental unit of analysis and from whose psyches and endogenously derived preferences all decisions, behavior and forms of organization flow. Social patterns, culture, and institutions, at most, are the aggregation (or composite) of innumerable sovereign individuals exercising free choice on the basis of personal preferences. Most importantly, there is no feedback onto the individual, separately or collectively, from institutions, culture or theory that might variably influence or shape who or what individuals are and do.

The import of this position is the denial of any social or cultural definition of human beings, that their thoughts, values, preferences, dispositions and predispositions may be shaped, influenced or reoriented by their socio-cultural and, most importantly, political milieu.[10] Thus in positive economics, theory does not shape or alter individual or aggregate economic behavior, rather it reflects behavior and is driven by facts the same way biological theory supposedly is driven by the behavior of plants and animals unaffected by biologists' theorizing about them.

Third, it is instrumental in that it focuses on how individuals (agents) relate means to ends. Sovereign individuals have endogenously derived preferences (utilities or ends) that they rank, toward which they allocate scarce means at their disposal and maximize in some optimal way. Significantly, the concept is incapable of specifying any particular ends toward which maximizing behavior is oriented. Furthermore, it does not explain how particular substantive ends are established except arising endogenously and freely from individuals' psyches and preferences. In the words of Hollis and Nell's critique of economic man, "(w)e do not know what he wants. But we do know that, whatever it is, he will maximize ruthlessly to get it" (1975, 54).

The beauty of the instrumental version is its applicability to every type of human behavior if one can determine the utility pursued, a problematic area to which the discussion will return. Gary Becker, for instance, has applied it to politics, crime, marriage, families, fertility and racial discrimination--however with individual or societal material well-being the utility assumed (Becker 1976). I have even come across a study of undergraduate dating behavior examined in terms of markets, costs-benefits and material and non-material utility maximization which found companionship the salient utility pursued--a refreshing case of love winning out over money (Bloch 1990).

If, then, utility can be anything arising from sovereign individuals' freedom of choice, the problem becomes one of explaining and predicting behavior and patterns. Logically, loafing in the shade is just as rational as toiling in the sun if prompted by different utility functions. On *a priori* methodological grounds, one cannot predict how individuals, groups or societies in fact will behave other than they will be maximizing something. Thus, its operationalization as maximizing material and pecuniary ends only is done at worst by convention and at best on shaky methodological grounds. In defense of this position, positive and neo-classical economics usually refer to Adam Smith's oft-cited passage concerning the propensity of humans to truck and barter which rests on self-evident assumptions of human nature.[11] Violating its own theory, neo-classical and positive economics gives birth to vulgar economic man.

Fourth, the application of instrumental rationality to commodity production and exchange (particularly where there are integrated factor and product markets), and assuming monetary profit as the individual utility maximized, focuses on how individuals obtain knowledge about market conditions and adjust their production, exchange and consumption behavior according to market price signals.

Instrumental rationality, with monetary profit the utility assumed, is the behavioral assumption central to Milton Friedman's empiricist and pragmatic brand of positive economics. In Friedman's methodology, mathematical equations, models and the economic rationality assumption are justified not for their realistic correspondence to how economic actors actually calculate and organize their economic affairs. Rather, as long as economic actors behave 'as if' they do correspond and models accurately predict how actors and an economy will behave, the assumption and models are pragmatically valid. The test of a model is its empirical predictability, with theory and model building driven by empirical economic fact (1953).[12]

The Dilemma Of Rational Expectations In Positive Economics

Within econometrics there is a field of enquiry centered on the rational expectations hypothesis devoted to the longitudinal study of expectations--how economic actors form expectations about economic events and what relationship this has to the actual operations of the 'true' economy in which they participate.[13] Thus the problem rests on information acquisition, learning and how expectations are formed, the answers to which are useful for predicting aggregate economic behavior.

The rational expectations hypothesis originated within neo-classical economics from a debate between Keynesian and monetarist economists over governmental expenditures to stimulate employment demand. According to the monetarist (Chicago school) position, such intervention has no long term net effect on the employment equilibrium (or any other equilibrium) because government taxation and expenditure are simply allocations of resources that would have taken place otherwise in the private sector. Accordingly, government expenditures--especially deficit ones--are inflationary, temporarily lower the real wage rate below its natural equilibrium and produce a short term rise in employment. However, economic agents (employers and employees) understand the 'true economy,' base their decisions to allocate their own and hired labor accordingly and ultimately short circuit such distortions. The employment equilibrium reasserts itself at original levels with the only net effect inflated prices (Nell 1984, 13-14).

The central argument of the rational expectations hypothesis consists of two parts: (1) a 'true economy' operating according to universal laws and principles, and (2) economic actors who understand, perhaps only intuitively, the operations of this economy and out of rational self interest adjust their allocative decisions according to probability projections of economic outcomes.

Applied to a range of substantive issues, the rational expectations hypothesis examines the relationship between (1) the probability distribution of economic actors' own 'subjective' beliefs concerning the operation of the economy currently or in the future and (2), the actual or 'objective' probability distribution of events in the 'true' economy. A 'strong' version of this hypothesis posits there will be no discrepancy between the two (after Muth 1961), ostensibly because economically rational actors search out necessary information and learn the operations of the 'true' economy on which to base their decisions.

Now we come to the crux of the problem. Everything is fine in the mind of the positive economist as long as models can be built that predict what will happen. The problem is, however, that things are not working out the way they should. Fundamental problems have been encountered in fitting econometric models incorporating the rational expectations hypothesis to substantive situations they purport to explain and predict.

In the course of a recent methodological assessment and critique of the rational expectations hypothesis, *The Limits to Rational Expectations*, M. Pesaran literally pushes the positivist paradigm to the limits, peers over into the abyss of methodological problems and discrepancies but having neither a parachute or bridge can only retreat back into the paradigm. He notes the following.

The hypothesis appears to work well in models analyzing current expectations formation, despite a number of unexplained "degenerate" cases (1987, 4, 77).[14] However with regard to future expectations he finds the hypothesis does not work well, although he finds no fault with the basic rationality assumption and the notion that theory is driven by fact. First, the correspondence between subjective and objective probability distributions cannot be demonstrated outside long-term economic stability. Second, if one cannot depend on the 'as if' assumption, it must be demonstrated that actors actually know or are capable of learning the 'true' model of the economy (1987, 2). This raises troubling epistemological questions of how knowledge is acquired, which is couched in terms of individual learning processes and ignores the socio-institutional milieu. Third, when information is costly and uncertainty high, actors may rely on *a priori* beliefs or not find it worthwhile to learn the 'true' model even if it were in fact possible to do so. This raises the problem of heterogenous information (and presumably different behaviors) and/or self-fulfilling prophesies based on beliefs different from the 'true' economy. However, "even an apparently irrational behavior, when adhered to collectively, can produce *limiting* outcomes that are rational" (1987, 46-48). Fourth, under uncertainty and costly information, trade will not necessarily eliminate discrepancies between subjective belief (and presumably agents behavior) and the 'true' economic model nor reveal all profitable opportunities. Individuals may become trapped in a "vicious circle of ignorance" (1987, 271).

If Pesaran truly believes the latter two are possible, one wonders what empirical facts create the model of the 'true' economy other than hypothetico-deductive principles of what is supposed to happen. Taken together, one also wonders about the predictability of economic agents, individually or in aggregate, and how the 'true' economy operates.

Pesaran, however, is unfazed and maintains faith that all these special cases and problematic features can be mathematically modeled and reconciled within the paradigm. This he attempts by constructing a new model based on his "augmented adaptive-learning expectations formation hypothesis" which he applies to expectations about inflation in UK industries. He finds his results unclear, though encouraging, and concludes that more research into the learning process is needed combined with exploring models based on non-linear equations (1987, 245-272).[15]

The Problem Of Information And Psychology

The problem of information in positive economics is couched in terms of how sovereign individuals, unaffected by socio-economic experience and theory, come to know how the 'true economy' operates and how they gather, evaluate and make decisions on information from the marketplace. The problem becomes, as in Pesaran's case, a conundrum when discrepancies are found between actual behavior and what should happen according to the principles of that 'true economy.'

This has been handled in neo-classical economics in a number of ways. The concepts of risk and uncertainty are familiar examples from development economics (e.g. Wharton 1971) and, with the addition of institutional parameters, in economic anthropology (e.g. Cancian 1972; Ortiz 1973).

Most attention has centered on problems posed by the limited capacity of the human mind to comprehend and process the vast amounts of information required to obtain perfect knowledge of current and future economic conditions and markets. Kenneth Boulding's devastatingly witty critique of rational decision making and his second revised law of economics is one example (Boulding, 1956, 86-87). Herbert Simon's concepts of bounded rationality and satisficing, derived on the same grounds, is another (e.g. Simon 1967). Interestingly, both are seen as maintaining the basic model of economic man who makes rational decisions but on a limited and comprehendible set of possibilities (e.g. Hodgson 1988, 79). Simon, however, discusses non-material maximization (e.g. being a shopkeeper, with "psychic income") in his discussion of retail businesses. This is a crack in the economic man model which unfortunately has not been explored fully within orthodox economics, perhaps because it contains innumerable complexities for measurement, explanation and prediction of outcomes.

A more fundamental problem with information exists, however, with how economic actors acquire their individual 'subjective' models of how the economy and world operates, how preferences are formed and how information on which to base decisions is evaluated by economic actors. This is Pesaran's problem of learning. The positive position's explicit assertion that economic theory is neutral to the facts and that preferences are endogenously determined rules out institutional or cultural factors. Positive economics' fall back position is to psychology, assumed to provide support for the methodological individualist notion of universal processes and predilections of the human mind, ie. human nature.

Hodgson thoroughly critiques this variety of 'psychologism' in his *Economics and Institutions* (1988). He argues that contrary to orthodox economic belief, modern psychology has a strong social element with innumerable experimental results demonstrating the effects of things such as social position, power relations and deference to others on perception and behavior. Similarly, social psychology explores the anthropologically familiar domains of enculturation and socialization. Furthermore, cognitive theory includes multiple levels of consciousness that excludes the notion of the invariant consciously calculating and deliberative mind (1988, 61, 106-111). "This flies in the face of the widespread assumption in economics that we are (sovereign) masters and mistresses of our fate" (1988, 107). He further argues that orthodox economists' retreat to psychology in defense of methodological individualism is simply a ploy to deflect the issue away from socio-political and historical considerations as psychology is not considered seriously in any event (1988, 61).

Furthermore, if preferences are endogenously determined by individuals, even in their collectivity, a contradiction arises for explaining the differences in substantive ends pursued and forms of organization cross culturally. This is not so apparent if one is comparing just industrial societies, but once the full range of different societal types are considered, as in anthropology, the problem comes to the fore. If psychology is the ultimate refuge, one would have to posit different mentalities and psychic structures *sui generis* for different types of societies which violates the assumption of universals and borders on racism, a problem further compounded when one takes into consideration change.

If, then, an ally cannot be found in psychology and things are not turning out as they should, the problem lies with the basic formulation of the problem. One must reach out to the social and cultural factors and the institutional nexus within which individuals operate.

The New Institutional Economics

The new institutional economics is in part successful in its attempts to bring an institutional focus to economic discussion. It is, however, built upon many of the same assumptions of neo-classical economics in general and positive economics in particular. Although, arguing that things like markets are human and not natural creations and thus subject to change, theory is built on individual behavior with exchange as the central feature of economic behavior and systems (e.g. North 1990, 5; Williamson 1975, 20).

In its fundamentals, the new institutional economics is an extension and elaboration on risk, uncertainty and bounded rationality in models of decision behavior. The main focus is on the role of institutions in transactions. The intellectual roots of the approach are several. Knight finds uncertainty and risk a central problem to the neo-classical assumptions of perfect knowledge and markets. He argues that business institutions and forms of organization--such as partnerships, insurance, corporations, diversification, etc.--are methods of reducing uncertainty (Knight 1921, 233-265). Commons can be read as making much the same point; however he stresses the infinite variability of individual motivations, with institutions arising from an evolutionary rationalizing process that justifies the "customs" of currently dominant groups in society. Institutions are historical, changing and are "working rules for future collective action in control of individual action" (Commons 1934, 680-684). Simon's work stresses the limits of the human mind as the need for institutions; "it is only because individual human beings are limited in knowledge, forsight, skill and time that organizations are useful instruments for the achievement of human purpose" (Simon 1957, 199). Out of this are abstracted the ideas that where information affecting decisions about the future --and thus transactions--are costly, institutions matter (Coase 1937 and 1960; North 1990, 12; Williamson 1975, 20-40). What appears common to the new institutionalists is the notion that institutions are basically mutually agreed upon instrumentalities for individuals to achieve their individual ends. These arise from individuals interacting and transacting who find a need for rules governing these activities. Furthermore, given limited human capacity to comprehend complexity they are substitutes or shortcuts for information that routinize, stabilize and make more predictable the outcomes of individual decision making. This notion is not unlike the one found in the Austrian school of economics, that institutions are the unintended outcomes of the pursuit of individual interests (see: Menger 1963).

At the base, however, remains the notion of methodological individualism in which the invariant maximizing individual stands *sui generis* with material ends the utility maximized. As a consequence the wider problem the new institutionalists share with traditional neo-classical thought is eloquently stated by North.

> The central puzzle of human history is to account for the widely divergent paths of historical change. How have societies diverged? What accounts for their widely disparate performance characteristics? This divergence is even more perplexing in terms of standard neo-classical and international trade theory,

> which implies that over time economies ... would gradually converge (North 1990, 5).

North attempts to answer this with the notion of imperfect markets characterized by fragmentary information; transaction costs are significant and thus institutions matter. This produces a situation in which "subjective models of actors modified both by very imperfect feedback and by ideology .. shape the path" (1990, 95). In other words, divergence is due to the imperfectability of the market caused by costly information systems. The corollary, following neo-classical thought, is that if information and transactions are cost free, then everyone would be the same and institutions, being unnecessary, would not matter.[16] I find this a most perplexing exposition of the role of institutions in economic and social life.

To the contrary, institutions matter in a number of ways, not just because they reduce transaction costs for maximizing individuals. What is missing, and in line with Commons (Ibid), is the active and interdependent role institutions have on individuals and their behavior, that humans are social and cultural beings as well as individuals. Institutions are things that in and of themselves provide identity, place, meaning, order and purpose to human life and do not spring from individuals in isolate. Furthermore, institutions are things that individuals commit themselves to follow and perpetuate as worthy in and of themselves.

To understand this relationship it becomes necessary to explore the various senses of rationality and not just the instrumental version that predominates in the new institutional approach.

Multiple Senses Of Rationality

In *Rationality in Economics* (1989), Heap critiques, modifies and substantially expands the rationality concept. His main concern is public policy and he takes explicit issue with the instrumental version of rationality, the notion that economic systems are automatic and the empiricist stance that economic theory is neutral to the facts. For instance with rational expectations, he dares to cross the line Pesaran delineates but from which he pulls back.

> (J)ust consider the logic of the rational expectations argument. We form expectations using theory and these expectations affect our actions, the upshot of which become the 'facts' we observe (1989, 2).

For instance, if all or most economic actors form expectations informed by Keynesian theory, outcomes will be different than if the same economic actors follow monetarist thought.

Heap delineates and discusses three different senses of rationality found in social science: (1) the familiar instrumental variety which deals with action relating means to ends, (2), procedural--the organization and consistency of rules of conduct centering on means, and (3) expressive (what I call normative) --self-conscious reflection on making sense of the world, what is worthy of pursuit, what is of value and what is not and contains a moral component--those aspects of thought that centers on ends. The types of explanation and prescription associated with each are diagramed below.

Rationality Type	Explanation Type	Form of Prescription
Instrumental	Intentional	Consequential
Procedural	Functional	Rights Based
Expressive	True Interest	

* Based on Heap's diagram (1989, 3 & 209).

Heap's basic argument is that while instrumental rationality, based on peoples' intentions, can be a powerful explanatory concept, it has to rely on institutional and informational props that cannot be explained in instrumental terms (1989, 7, 66-69). Thus economics requires the incorporation of the other two. This informational problem is recognized by Pesaran (1987, Ch. 3) in terms of how actors obtain *a priori* knowledge of the operations of the 'true' economy. But Pesaran leaves this an unexplored question, perhaps because he would have to admit to institutional and cultural dimensions (i.e. exogenous to individuals) to economic behavior.

The point is that models based on the instrumental version have never been able to explain or specify what utilities people pursue, other than arising from preferences or by fiat, and has never been able to explain differences in utility functions. As Godelier pointed out, it is similar to operations research that does not question how or why particular ends comes to be pursued but simply takes things as they are and assumes the problem to be solved is the manipulation of means and ends already brought into relationship (1972, 254).

As discussed above, the problem with utility is that it can be anything--

material to non-material, laudable to perverse--and, therefore, the instrumental version can be applied to any human behavior as long as the utility is known. The determination of utility, however, is not a simple task as Amartya Sen pointed out long ago in his excellent critique of behavioralism based on assumptions of uni-dimensional egoistic rationality (1977). Furthermore, what it cannot explain, and this is the inherent weakness of the instrumental version, are the differences between individuals, groups and societies.

Unfortunately, positive and most of neo-classical economics only considers material and pecuniary ends as utility. For example, Becker just as easily and theoretically justifiably could have analyzed racial discrimination in terms of white supremacy as the utility maximized. Non-bigoted behavior and enhanced material well-being of blacks and whites can be seen as constraints to maximizing racial supremacy rather than racism as a constraint to maximizing the material well-being of both whites and minority groups (Becker 1976, 15-30). This is Heap's point about consequentialist prescription based on instrumental rationality. In its broadest application--utility can be anything--it is limited, at best, to delineating the probable consequences of a course of action, not its desirability, undesirability or why one course of action among the many has been chosen.[17]

Ultimately we can identify instrumentally rational aspects in *all* behavior but then all behavior becomes just as rational as Schultz's Iowa farmer.[18] However, one wonders what utilities the idealized Iowa farmer is pursuing given Schultz's earlier works on U.S. agriculture. As Heap points out, sole reliance on instrumental rationality reduces us to a Hobbesian world of chaos and a form of relativism where everything can be demonstrated as just as rational as anything else (1989, 16).

This problem of relativity appears to be unrecognized by the formalists in anthropology. In the rush to demonstrate the instrumental rationality of economic--or other--behavior in a variety of institutional settings, from hunters and gatherers to industrial societies, the demonstration of self-seeking maximizing behavior is taken as sufficient evidence that formal principles are universally applicable (e.g. Schneider 1974).

True, one can find self-seeking and maximizing behavior everywhere. However, they can neither explain differences in utilities maximized cross-culturally nor the material outcomes for individuals (or society) that occur, e.g. self-seeking New Guinea Big Men who accumulate wealth in order to give it away to build a political following (Pospisil 1963) *vs.* pursuit of material income for personal consumption ascribed to American yuppies. If instrumental rationality explains everything, then it ultimately explains nothing because it cannot explain differences in the substantive behavior across individuals, groups, and whole systems.

At such a juncture, Heap finds procedural and expressive (or normative) senses of rationality important for explanation and prediction. Procedural rationality provides the historical and social location for individuals by defining organization and rules--i.e. Pesaran's information, or in anthropological terms social structure and culture--which make social life consistant, predictable and through which people go about living and doing things. This is something instrumental rationality based on individuals' endogenous preferences and intentions cannot do. These dimensions exist prior to and contemporaneously with individuals, and do not exist or come into being solely as the consequence of human intentions (1989, 116-146).

However, procedural rationality has its limitations in that alone it reduces people to social/cultural "dopes" or programmed robots and presents us with the problem of freedom. This point figures strongly in positive economics' individualist message, and as a base from which to discredit social conceptions of human existence and institutional bases of behavior. It has also been a conundrum for many functionalist approaches in the social sciences, i.e. self-regulating and self-equilibriating systems with participants mindlessly performing their assigned roles. What is often overlooked, however, is that orthodox instrumental rationality does exactly the same thing. If people are only egoistic and uni-dimensionally predisposed to maximize material gain, then they are just as programmed, have no freedom of choice and in Amartya Sen's words (1977) are "rational fools."

Heap's expressive (normative) rationality, or true interest, resolves this problem (1989, 148-176). Expressive rationality is that dimension of human existence in which people, both individually and socially, are self-conscious, try to make 'sense' of the world, weigh and evaluate courses of action and what they want to accomplish and be. It is concerned with ends, values and states of being, things that are worth doing and being in their own right. Expressive rationality is informed, follows or reacts against, but is not determined by procedural rationality (1989, 172-176). According to Heap, expressive rationality relates to the evolutionary formation and change in choices about who we are to be as individuals (1989, 175), and through collective choice (policy) who we are to be as a society (1989, 224). The implications are, of course, that an economy (or a society) does not arise spontaneously from disembodied individual preferences, nor can it be seen as an automatic mechanism specified and regulated by universal principles or human nature. Rather it is an artifact of human action and therefore is amenable to change through decision making and action.

In contrast to consequentialist prescription in instrumental rationality, Heap's notion of 'rights based' prescription for procedural and expressive (normative) rationality rests on concepts of justice derived from Berlin's (1958) positive freedom and Rawls (1972) arguments for equality. Berlin's positive freedom means actively controlling and regulating socio-politico institutions (the procedures) in contrast to his counter notion of negative freedom which is the absence of restraint as argued by the American New Right. Rawls' notion of justice centers on equality for primary social goods of liberty, opportunity, income, wealth and self respect. Most importantly, these rights are not the same as and cannot be reduced to sets of individual preferences in instrumental rationality. "From the point of view of individual preference satisfaction, no action ... is free from the arbitrariness of which the non-reducible procedural element imparts to every decision. (However) to make freedom only count with respect to a given set of procedures is also to make us a slave to a history (culture and social structure) which (is also) unavoidably arbitrary" (Heap 1988, 205). According to Heap, expressive rationality is necessary to complete the set because humans have doubts about what they do, reflect on their aims and purposes and are able to take corrective action which implies being able to make changes in procedures--which includes government and public policy.

Heap's arguments and concern, of course, are oriented to policy making in industrial commercial economies. Left unexamined are questions that intrigue an economic anthropologist, such as why economies and societies are so substantively different. For instance, are hunters and gatherers, horticulturalists, pastoralists, peasants, etc. the way they are simply because of differences in procedural and expressive rationality, even though they can all be demonstrated as being instrumentally rational? This puts us back into the conundrum of relativity, or different strokes for different folks, that bedevils functionalism and, along with vulgar materialist approaches, is also subject to the problem of the automaton.

Interestingly, Godelier in his book, *The Mental and the Material* (1986), addresses many of these issues with arguments similar to Heap's about procedural and expressive rationality. What is different about Godelier, of course, is his avowedly materialist argument: self-conscious human action in transforming nature and the material world to produce (through processes of production) socio-cultural existence, an interaction that has both willed and unwilled properties. Godelier provides the ontology that accounts for substantive differences in instrumental, procedural and expressive rationality that Heap does not consider.[19]

Conclusions And Implications For Anthropology

Several things are clear from the above discussion. First, the positive economics paradigm is undergoing close scrutiny; its limitations and liabilities are becoming recognized from within. Whether or not this is a significant crack in the edifice that will lead to its rejection or substantial modification is difficult to ascertain. With the demise of the ideological pressures of the cold war, however, it is interesting to speculate about what realizations might dawn on orthodox economists involved in restructuring the economies of erstwhile Soviet bloc states. Euphoria from having 'won' the cold war struggle is on the wane. With the emergence of social and cultural dimensions to this restructuring problem, encouraging doubts are being entertained about whether technology, training, capital, free markets and representative democracy are the sole answers. One would hope that much needed institutional and social considerations will once again come to the fore within mainstream U.S. economics and not just as derivatives of imperfect individuals who otherwise would not need them.

Should this happen, we should consider the implications for economic anthropology. First, as with this paper, examination of what is going on in a sister discipline is of value for new ideas and different ways of looking at things. Second, with the incorporation of institutional dimensions within mainstream economics a door would be reopened for economics to interact with other social sciences that can lead, in Schumpeter's terms, to a true cross-fertilization rather than the current cross-sterilization that has anthropologists talking primarily to themselves. Third, U.S. economic anthropology should be in a position to rise to the occasion and make its voice heard in theoretical and applied debate.

References

Adams, John. 1986. Peasant Rationality: Individuals, Groups, Cultures. *World Development* 14: 273-282.

Becker, Gary. 1976. *The Economic Approach to Human Behavior*. Chicago: University of Chicago Press.

Berlin, I. 1958 (1969) Two Concepts of Liberty. Reprinted in *Four Essays on Liberty.* London: Oxford University Press.

Bloch, B.J. 1990. The Economics of Dating--An Empirical Investigation. *South African Journal of Sociology* 21: 12-20.

Boeke, J.H. 1953. *Economics and Economic Policy of Dual Societies*. New York: Institute of Pacific Relations.

Boulding, Kenneth. 1956. *The Image: Knowledge in Life and Society*. Ann Arbor: University of Michigan Press.

Burling, Robbins. 1962. Maximization Theories and the Study of Economic Anthropology. *American Anthropologist* 64: 802-821.

Cancian, Frank. 1972. *Change and Uncertainty in a Peasant Economy*. Stanford: Stanford University Press.

Chang, Yunshik. 1989. Peasants Go to Town: The Rise of Commercial Farming in Korea. *Human Organization* 48(3): 236-251.

Coase, Ronald H. 1937. The Nature of the Firm. *Economica* 4: 386-405.

———.1960. The Problem of Social Costs. *Journal of Law and Economics* 3:1-44.

Cook, Scott. 1974. Economic Anthropology: Problems in Theory, Method, and Analysis. In John J. Honigmann, ed., *Handbook of Social and Cultural Anthropology*. Chicago: Rand McNally Publishing Co.

———.1973. Production, Ecology and Economic Anthropology: Notes Toward an Integrated Frame of Reference. *Social Science Information* 12: 25-52.

Commons, John R. 1934. *Institutional Economics*. New York: MacMillan.

Dahl, Robert. 1956. *A Preface to Democratic Theory*. Chicago: University of Chicago Press.

———.1982. *Dilemmas of Pluralist Democracy*. New Haven: Yale University Press.

Friedman, Milton. 1953. *Essays in Positive Economics.* Chicago: University of Chicago Press.

———.1962. *Capitalism and Freedom.* Chicago: University of Chicago Press.

Godelier, Maurice. 1972. *Rationality and Irrationality in Economics.* New York: Monthly Review Press.

———.1986. *The Mental and the Material.* London: Verso.

Green, F. 1979. The Consumption Function: A Study of a Failure in Positive Economics. In F. Green and P. Nore, eds., *Issues in Political Economy: A Critical Approach.* London: MacMillan.

———.1984. A Critique of the Neo-Fisherian Consumption Function. *Review of Radical Political Economics* 16(2/3): 95-114.

Greenberg, Edward S. 1989. *The American Political System: A Radical Approach*, 5th edition. Glenview, Ill.: Scott, Foresman & Co.

Heap, Shaun Hargreaves. 1989. *Rationality in Economics.* London: Basil Blackwell Ltd.

Higgins, Benjamin. 1959 (revised 2nd edition in 1968). *Economic Development.* New York: W.W. Norton.

Hodgson, Geoffrey M. 1988. *Economics and Institutions.* Cambridge: Polity Press.

Hollis, Martin and Edward J. Nell. 1975. *Rational Economic Man: A Philosophical Critique of Neo-Classical Economics.* Cambridge: University of Cambridge Press.

Hopper, W. David. 1957. The Economic Organization of a Village in North Central India. (Unpublished Ph.D. dissertation in anthropology and agricultural economics presented at Cornell University).

Knight, Franbk H. 1921. *Risk, Uncertainty, and Profit.* Boston: Houghton Mifflin Co.

Krishna, Raj. 1961. Farm Supply Response in the Punjab (India-Pakistan): A Case Study of Cotton. (Unpublished Ph.D. dissertation presented at University of Chicago).

Kuhn, Thomas. 1962. *The Structure of Scientific Revolutions.* Chicago: Chicago University Press.

LeClair, Edward E. 1962. Economic Theory and Economic Anthropology. *American Anthropologist* 64: 1179-1203.

Leibenstein, Harvey. 1976. *Beyond Economic Man: A New Foundation for Microeconomics.* Cambridge: Harvard University Press.

———.1979. A Branch of Economics is Missing: Micro-Micro Theory. *Journal of Economic Literature* 17: 477-502.

Levins, Richard A. 1989. On Farmers Who Solve Equations. *Choices* 4th Quarter: 8-10.

Lowi, Theodore. 1969. *The End of Liberalism.* New York: W.W. Norton & Company.

Menger, Carl. 1963. *Problems of Economics and Sociology.* Louis Schneider, ed., Francis J. Nock (trans. of 1883 work). Urbana: University of Illinois Press.

Montgomery, John D., Rufus B. Hughes and Raymond H. Davis. 1966. *Rural Improvement and Political Development: The JCRR Model.* Washington D.C.: American Society for Public Administration.

Muth, J.F. 1961. Rational Expectations and the Theory of Price Movements. *Econometrica* 29: 315-335.

Nair, Kusum. 1969. *The Lonely Furrow: Farming in the United States, Japan and India.* Ann Arbor: University of Michigan Press.

———.1979. *In Defense of the Irrational Peasant: Indian Agriculture After the Green Revolution.* Chicago: University of Chicago Press.

Nell, Edward J. 1988. Part I: Theory. In Edward J. Nell, ed., *Free Market Conservatism.* London: George Allen & Unwin.

North, Douglass C. 1990. *Institutions, Institutional Change and Economic Performance.* Cambridge: Cambridge University Press.

Ortiz, Sutti. 1973. *Uncertainties in Peasant Farming.* London: The Athalone Press.

Pesaran, M. Hashem. 1987. *The Limits to Rational Expectations.* London: Basil Blackwell, Ltd.

Pospisil, Leopold. *The Kapauku Papuans of West New Guinea.* New York: Holt, Rinehart & Winston.

Rawls, J. 1972. *A Theory of Justice.* Oxford: Oxford University Press.

Robbins, Lord Lionel. 1932. *An Essay on the Nature and Significance of Economic Science.* London: Macmillan.

Ruttan, Vernon W. 1975. Technology Transfer, Institutional Transfer, and Induced Technical and Institutional Change in Agricultural Development. In Lloyd G. Reynolds, ed., *Agriculture in Economic Development.* New Haven: Yale University Press.

Samuelson, Paul. 1938. A Note on the Pure Theory of Consumer's Behaviour. *Economics* 5: 3-16.

Schneider, Harold K. 1974. *Economic Man: The Anthropology of Economics.* New York: The Free Press.

Schultz, Theodore. 1945. *Agriculture in an Unstable Economy.* New York: McGraw-Hill Book Company.

———.1950. *Production and Welfare of Agriculture.* New York: Macmillan Company.

———.1964. *Transforming Traditional Agriculture*. New Haven: Yale University Press.

Schumpeter, J. 1986 (first published in 1954) *History of Economic Analysis*. New York: Oxford University Press.

Sen, Amartya K. 1977. Rational Fools: A Critique of the Behavioral Foundations of Economic Theory. *Philosophy and Public Affairs* 6: 317-344.

Simon, Herbert A. 1957. *Models of Man*. New York: John Wiley & Sons.

———.1967. Theories of Decision-Making in Economics and Behavioral Science. *Surveys of Economic Theory: Resource Allocation*. New York: St. Martin's Press.

Smith, Adam. *An Enquiry into the Nature of the Wealth of Nations*. Edwin Cannan, ed. Chicago: University of Chicago Press.

Tax, Sol. 1963. *Penny Capitalism*. Chicago: University of Chicago Press. (Originally published by the Institute of Social Anthropology, Smithsonian Institute Publication 16, Washington, D.C.: US Government Printing Office, 1953).

Walinsky, Louis J., ed. 1977. *The Selected Papers of Wolf Ladejinsky: Agrarian Reform as Unfinished Business*. New York: World Bank--Oxford University Press.

Wharton, Clifton R. 1971. Risk, Uncertainty and the Subsistence Farmer. In George Dalton, ed., *Economic Development and Social Change*. Garden City: The Natural History Press.

Williamson, Oliver. 1975. *Markets and Hierarchies: Analysis and Antitrust Implications*. New York: the Free Press.

Notes

1. For an excellent introduction to, update and discussion of the formalist-substantivist debate written by an economist for economists, see Adams 1986.

2. My use of these terms differs markedly from Max Weber's. In his formulation formal refers to "the extent of quantitative calculation or accounting which is technically possible .. and actually applied" in an economic system which finds it apex in monetized, capitalist economy; the former refers to "the degree in which a given group of persons ... is or could be adquately provided with goods by means of an economically oriented course of social action" (Weber 1947, 184-5).

3. One cannot discount the role of stupidity, ignorance, incompetence, imperfectability and passion in behavior (Commons 1934, 244-250, 682, 702).

4. The main references used on rationality and economy-society articulation used are by UK economists--Heap, Hodgson and Pesaran. Similarly, main philosophical critiques have come from UK philosophers, e.g. Hollis and Nell. Furthermore, the main anthropological writings about the subject since the 1970's come from French structural anthropologists, eg. Godelier. The only major exception to this is the US economist, Harvey Leibenstein, who denies that all economic actors maximize in his X-inefficiency argument (1972, 1979). Why the comparative silence in the US since the early 1970's is an intriguing question beyond the scope of this paper. A cogent argument for the hegemony of liberal-utilitarian thought--proceeding from Smith, Ricardo and Locke--setting the agenda and issues to be debated in the U.S. (parenthetically reflected in US folk ideology) stems from social, historical and ecological reasons presented by Edward S. Greenberg (1989, Ch. 2).

5. For an overview of institutional reform and effects in East, Southeast and South Asia see Walinsky's (1977) edited papers of Wolf Ladejinsky. For Taiwan see Montgomery, et. al. (1966), on the Joint Commission for Rural Reconstruction. For the effect of land reform in Korea, see Chang (1989).

6. Also represented in pluralist political thought, e.g. Robert Dahl (1956) before his recantation (1982).

7. I gratefully acknowledge Kusum Nair for bringing this to my attention. She and Schultz have been long protagonists on the rationality issue, the institutional base of economic behavior and international agricultural development (e.g. see Nair 1969, 1979). When she personally queried him about this *volte-face* in 1990, his only defense was that he understands U.S. farmers much better than farmers in developing nations (personal communication).

8. In its most vulgar form, this notion becomes extremely ethnocentric and an exercise in self-flattery and self-deception. Other people and systems are viewed as if looking into a mirror where one expects to find what one believes about oneself. An excellent pedagogical device demonstrating this is the comic character of Colonel Purdy in charge

of post World War II Okinawan rural reconstruction in *Tea House of the August Moon* (available on video).

9. An example is Douglas Ensminger, a rural sociologist, who beginning in the early 1950s spent about twenty years as Representative of Ford Foundation's India program. He had substantial input and influence on formulating agricultural development programs and policy during India's Green Revolution. He firmly held that the role of anthropology and sociology in economic development is the removal of social/cultural constraints to the introduction of improved technology (personal communication 1977).

10. Curiously, this is not believed for a minute by the advertising industry (Hodgson 1988, 107) or managers of election campaigns.

11. Other passages from Adam Smith considerably alter this authoritative reference. In his discussion of the three "orders", or classes, found in any "civilized society", Smith examines the interests and behavior of the landed, labor and those in business or commerce and their relation to the interests of society (1976, 275-278). The interests of the first two are consonant with the interests of society as the promotion of the former promotes the interests of the latter. However he finds the gentry indolent and not disposed to working their estates efficiently. Labor he finds ignorant and of such degraded habits that they are neither able to comprehend nor act on their best interests. Significantly, those who live by profit (businessmen and merchants) clearly comprehend and act on their interests. However their interests are not the same and at times opposite to the public interest and they should be viewed with great suspicion. They are "an order of men, whose interest is never exactly the same with that of the public, who have generally an interest to deceive and even oppress the public, and who accordingly have, upon many occasions, both deceived and oppressed it" (1976, 278). This is why Smith's notion of the ideal society abhors concentration of wealth and power whereby no individual actor or group can affect the market. Apart from these insights into human nature, the above passage alters the assumption that social utility automatically flows from unrestrained freedom to maximize individual utility and can be read as a justification for an active interventionist state.

12. See Levins' article, "On Farmers Who Solve Equations," for a satirical yet insightful critique of Friedman, econometrics and mathematical modeling (1989).

13. It is not clear from my limited reading whether or not a consistency is assumed between expectations and what actors actually do, the old problem of what people think or say and what they actually do.

14. Pesaran unfortunately does not examine or discuss the "degenerate" anomalies which might have led to some rethinking of the formulation.

15. What impact chaos theory, which explores the applications of non-linear equations, will have on positive economics is an interesting question.

16. One is struck by the similarity between this and an emphasis in current development thought in the U.S. that attaches great efficacy to improving the availability of information technology, computers and software, to farmers and businessmen in both the U.S. and the Third World.

17. As a confused undergraduate, I remember well the example my introductory economics professor used to demonstrate this: the production of guns and butter. I could easily grasp the scarcity of finite resources constraining the quantity that could be produced of either alone or in a mix and that the consequences of producing more guns meant less butter and vice-versa. As a metaphor, what perplexed me was why guns and butter--and by extension specifically anything--comes to be and is produced in an economy. The notion that it all depends on what people want and choose to do was inadequate. Different strokes for different folks did not cut it.

18. Leaving aside the problem of getting inside each individual's head to determine whether or not he or she is acting according to endogenously derived preferences. The short cut, assuming that behavior reveals preferences (Samuelson 1938), ultimately ends in tautology--behavior is explained in terms of preferences, preferences are explained in terms behavior.

19. And in the course of his argument neatly reconciles functionalist with materialist theory and explanation.

Contributors Section

James M. Acheson (Ph.D. Rochester, Anthropology) is Professor of Anthropology and Marine Studies at the University of Maine. He has done extensive fieldwork in fishing communities in New England, and in the Purepeche area of Mexico. He is the author of *The Lobster Gangs of Maine* and co-editor of *The Question of the Commons* (with Bonnie McCay).

Robert Bates (Ph.D. M.I.T., Political Science) is Professor of Political Science in the Department of Government at Harvard University. Although currently working in Columbia and Brazil, he specializes in the political economy of rural Africa. He has published a number of books including: *Beyond the Miracle of the Market: The Political Economy of Agrarian Development in Kenya; Essays on the Political Economy of Rural Africa*; and *Markets and States in Tropical Africa: The Political Basis of Agricultural Policies.*

Laurel Bossen (Ph.D. SUNY Albany, Anthropology) is Associate Professor of Anthropology at McGill University. She has conducted extensive fieldwork in Guatemala examining women's economic opportunities and constraints and has published *The Redivision of Labor: Women and Economic Choice in Four Guatemalan Communities (1984).* In recent years, her field research has concentrated on gender and development in rural China and examines the effect of economic reform and state family planning policies on rural households.

Jean-Philippe Colin (Ph.D. Montpellier, Economics) is an agricultural economist working with OSTROM. He has done fieldwork in Ivory Coast and Mexico. He is author of one book entitled *La Mutation d'un Économie de Plantation en Basse Côte d'Ivoire*. He is co-editor of two other books *Agro-economica de la Papa en México* and *Sistemas de Producción e Desarrollo Agricola.*

Jean Ensminger (Ph.D. Northwestern, Anthropology) is Associate Professor of Anthropology and a fellow in the Center in Political Economy at Washington, University in St. Louis. Her book, *Making a Market: The Institutional Transformation of an African Society* was published by the Cambridge University Press in 1992. This book and recent articles in the *American Anthropologist* and *American Ethnologist* attempt to apply a "new" institutional economic approach to an understanding of the economic and political transformations occurring in Africa.

Christina Gladwin (Ph.D. Stanford, Economics) is a Professor of Food and Resource Economics at the University of Florida in Gainesville, Florida. She has done substantial fieldwork in both West Africa and the United States.

Bruno Losch (M.A. Montpellier, Economics) is an economist with CIRAD. He has done fieldwork in Ivory Coast and Cameroons. He is the co-author of *Stratégies des Producteurs en Zone Caféière et Cacaoyère du Cameroun. Quelles Adaptations à la Crise? Montpellier: CIRAD.*

Judith E. Marti (Ph.D. UCLA, Anthropology) is Assistant Professor in the Department of Anthropology, California State University, Northridge. She co-edited *The Other Fifty Percent: Multicultural Perspectives on Gender Relations* and is currently at work on a book on 19th century Mexican public market and street vendors.

Paul V. McDowell (Ph.D. UBC, Anthropology) is documentation editor for Sage Publications and teaches anthropology for the Ventura Community College District, Ventura California. He is currently working on a manuscript that traces the integration of the Guatemalan indigenous economy into the national and global systems.

J. Allister McGregor (Ph.D. Bath, Development Economics) is lecturer in Development Studies in the School of Social Sciences at the University of

Bath. He has carried out research on credit and development in Bangladesh and currently is embarking on research into the social and economic organization of a lake fishing community in Southern Thailand. His essay in this volume came from a larger regional research project, with studies in Indonesia and Bangladesh, which he is coordinating.

Barry H. Michie (Ph.D. Michigan State, Anthropology) teaches anthropology and is a program officer in the Office of International Programs at Kansas State University. He has conducted research in India and has published articles on agrarian patron-client relations, money lenders and indigenous technology. His research interests are the logic and articulation of production systems with their environment, natural resource management and agroforestry.

Mark Moberg (Ph.D. UCLA, Anthropology) teaches anthropology at the University of South Alabama. He is the author of *Citrus, Strategy and Class: the Politics of Development in Southern Belize* and is currently conducting research on ethnicity and labor recruitment in the Belizean banana industry.

Melissa Rehfus (Ph.D Northwestern, Anthropology) is a manager for program research and development in one of the major insurance providers in the Southeast. Much of this paper is drawn from her 1991 Ph.D. dissertation, "The New Organization of Health Care in the United States: Decision Making of Physicians and Managed Care Plans."

Susan Russell (Ph.D. Illinois, Anthropology) is Associate Professor of Anthropology at Northern Illinois University, and conducts fieldwork in the Philippines. She has done extensive research with upland commercial vegetable producers and is currently working on labor contracts in maritime fishing communities.

Parker Shipton (Ph.D. Cambridge, Anthropology) is Research Associate, Harvard Institute for International Development, and Lecturer, Department of Anthropology, Harvard University. His research has focussed mainly on western Kenya and on the Sene-gambian region. Among his publications are a monograph entitled *Bitter Money: Cultural Economy and Some African Meanings of Forbidden Commodities* and his forthcoming book, *The Golden Pendulum: Culture, Credit, and Debt in Western Kenya.*

Richard Wilk (Ph.D. Arizona, Anthropology) is an Associate Professor of Anthropology at Indiana University. He has published a number of books and articles on household organization and economic anthropology including a monograph entitled *Household Ecology: Economic Change and Domestic Life Among the Kekchi Maya in Belize* and several edited and co-edited volumes *(e.g. The Household Economy; and Households: Comparative and Historical Studies of the Domestic Group).*